BIBLE
ANSWERS
for LIFE'S
QUESTIONS

BIBLE ANSWERS for LIFE'S QUESTIONS

What the Bible Says about God's Will, Emotions, Grieving, Marriage, Money, Divorce, Praying, and Worship

BARBOUR
PUBLISHING

Published by Barbour Publishing, Inc., P.O. Box 719, Uhrichsville, Ohio 44683, www.barbourbooks.com

Our mission is to publish and distribute inspirational products offering exceptional value and biblical encouragement to the masses.

ecpa Member of the
Evangelical Christian
Publishers Association

Printed in the United States of America.

CONTENTS

Introduction 9

Section 1: God's Will

Introduction: Finding God's Will 11
1. God's Will and His Promises to You 12
2. God's Will and How He's Created You to Fulfill It 15
3. God's Will Can Be Found 20
4. God's Will Regarding Your Spiritual Life 28
5. God's Will Regarding Your Money and Work 35
6. God's Will Regarding Sex, Marriage, and Family. 39
7. God's Will Regarding Dealing with Others 44
8. God's Will Regarding Your Character 48
9. God's Will May Be Painful. 51
10. God's Will May Involve Risk 56

Section 2: Emotions

Introduction: The Color of Life 59
1. Emotions of Love. 60
2. Emotions of Joy 65
3. Emotions of Peace 72
4. Emotions of Passion 76
5. Emotions of Anger. 82
6. Emotions of Sadness. 87
7. Emotions of Fear 97

Section 3: Grieving

Introduction: Uninvited Grief 102
1. You're Not Alone 103
2. Life-Changing Events 108
3. Assaulted by Anger. 114

4. Wrestling with Guilt. 117
5. Depression 120
6. The Recovery Process 124
7. Helping Your Children Grieve 128
8. Ministering to Others. 131
9. Spiritual Journey. 134
10. Knowing God during This Time 138
11. Lingering Hurts 143

Section 4: Marriage
Introduction: "And They Lived Happily Ever After" 146
1. Defining Marriage 147
2. True Love 151
3. You and Your Spouse 154
4. Divorce and Remarriage. 161
5. Communication 164
6. Anger and Abuse 167
7. Sex and Intimacy 174
8. You and Your Family. 180
9. Traits of a Strong Marriage. 185

Section 5: Money
Introduction: In God We Trust?. 191
1. Stewardship: It's All from Him 192
2. Income: Blessing and Responsibility. 199
3. Warning: Dangers Await 205
4. Poor and Needy: Receiving God's Extra Care 211
5. Giving: Hearing the Call 216
6. Obligations: Business, Debts, and Taxes. 223
7. Budgeting: Getting Ahead 226
8. True Riches: More Valuable Than Money. 230

Section 6: Divorce

Introduction: Why Is This Happening to Me?. 235
1. Can These Hurts Be Healed? 236
2. What Does God Think of Me Now? 241
3. Am I Wrong to Feel This Way? 246
4. Am I Alone?. 252
5. Where Will the Money Come From? 257
6. How Will This Affect My Kids?. 261
7. Will I Always Be This Exhausted? 264
8. What about Sex?. 267
9. Do I Have to Forgive? 271
10. Is Reconciliation Possible? 274
11. Can I Rebuild My Life? 277

Section 7: Praying

Introduction: Drawing Near. 281
1. The Value of Prayer. 282
2. Meeting the God of Our Prayer. 285
3. The Prayer of Adoration 290
4. The Prayer of Confession 296
5. The Prayer of Thanksgiving. 301
6. The Prayer of Supplication 305
7. Prayers of the Heart 311
8. Prayers for Others. 318
9. Qualities of Effective Prayer. 322
10. Hindrances to Prayer 327
Conclusion 330

Section 8: Worship

Introduction: Getting Everything Straight. 332
1. Why We Worship. 333
2. The Focus of Our Worship 338
3. Who Should Worship God 346
4. How We Should Worship 351
5. Worshipping God with Our Actions 355
6. Forms of Worship. 359
7. Personal Reasons to Worship God 365
8. Examples of Worship 375

INTRODUCTION

Life presents plenty of questions. Happily for us, the Bible offers answers.

Whether we're dealing with finances, our marriage, emotions, or our relationship with God, the Bible has answers for the questions we ask. You might be surprised at the detail scripture offers to the soul who truly seeks God's wisdom.

Bible Answers for Life's Questions provides scriptural insight for eight of the most important aspects of human existence: God's will, emotions, grieving, marriage, money, divorce, praying, and worship. You'll find more than 2,700 Bible passages, categorized under some 70 main headings and 400 subheadings. This organization should help you quickly pinpoint verses that directly address the life challenges you face.

Though scripture is the only true authority for life, *Bible Answers for Life's Questions* also provides helpful supporting materials. Personal stories, from real people who've "been there," provide encouragement that the questions you have about life are questions that others have faced and continue to deal with. The "One Moment at a Time" sections of this book provide practical advice on dealing with the vitally important topics that *Bible Answers for Life's Questions* covers.

With scriptures drawn from several easy-to-read Bible translations, this book is an ideal resource for personal reading or ministry use.

When you have questions about life, know that the Bible has answers. May this book point out God's personal wisdom for you.

WHAT THE BIBLE SAYS ABOUT GOD'S WILL

INTRODUCTION
FINDING GOD'S WILL

The Bible has more to say about finding God's will than you may realize.

To begin with, the Bible reveals God's universal will for His people. What that means is that God clearly outlines the steps He wants us to take in regard to our spiritual lives and character. In many places, the Bible plainly speaks of God's will for us on a variety of subjects such as money, honesty, and sex.

While God's will in these universal areas is unmistakable, many people seek God's specific guidance on other unique questions that may not seem to have the same clear answers: Which job should I take? Who should I marry? Where should I live?

Even when it comes to these individualized questions, the Bible does not disappoint. In its pages you will find practical wisdom to guide you in making decisions and finding God's unique plan for your life.

CHAPTER 1

GOD'S WILL AND HIS PROMISES TO YOU

God has never left me in the dark. There have been times I've changed jobs—even moved clear across the country—but I've always sensed His presence and peace while making each decision. Through the years I've learned that God is real, He cares for me, and that He really does have a plan for my life. There's never been a day that I've doubted that He's leading me along that path in His perfect timing.

■ *James, age 57, North Carolina* ■

CREATING YOU WITH A PURPOSE

"For I know the plans I have for you," declares the LORD, "plans to prosper you and not to harm you, plans to give you hope and a future."

JEREMIAH 29:11 NIV

"They are my people—I created each of them to bring honor to me."

ISAIAH 43:7 CEV

However, as it is written: "No eye has seen, no ear has heard, no mind has conceived what God has prepared for those who love him."

1 CORINTHIANS 2:9 NIV

It's in Christ that we find out who we are and what we are living for. Long before we first heard of Christ and got our hopes up, he had his eye on us, had designs on us for glorious living, part of the overall purpose he is working out in everything and everyone.

EPHESIANS 1:11–12 MSG

REVEALING HIS WILL

Therefore do not be foolish, but understand what the Lord's will is.

EPHESIANS 5:17 NIV

And he said, "The God of our fathers appointed you to know his will, to see the Righteous One and to hear a voice from his mouth."

ACTS 22:14 ESV

And so, from the day we heard, we have not ceased to pray for you, asking that you may be filled with the knowledge of his will in all

spiritual wisdom and understanding.
COLOSSIANS 1:9 ESV

"You explain deep mysteries, because even the dark is light to you."
DANIEL 2:22 CEV

And he made known to us the mystery of his will according to his good pleasure, which he purposed in Christ.
EPHESIANS 1:9 NIV

"The secret things belong to the LORD our God, but the things that are revealed belong to us and to our children forever, that we may do all the words of this law."
DEUTERONOMY 29:29 ESV

DIRECTING YOUR LIFE

Trust in the LORD with all your heart and lean not on your own understanding; in all your ways acknowledge him, and he will make your paths straight.
PROVERBS 3:5–6 NIV

If any of you lacks wisdom, he should ask God, who gives generously to all without finding fault, and it will be given to him.
JAMES 1:5 NIV

"Call to me and I will answer you and tell you great and unsearchable things you do not know."
JEREMIAH 33:3 NIV

Guide me in your truth and teach me, for you are God my Savior, and

my hope is in you all day long.
PSALM 25:5 NIV

For this God is our God for ever and ever; he will be our guide even to the end.
PSALM 48:14 NIV

And we know that in all things God works for the good of those who love him, who have been called according to his purpose.
ROMANS 8:28 NIV

"And if God cares so wonderfully for flowers that are here today and thrown into the fire tomorrow, he will certainly care for you. Why do you have so little faith?"
LUKE 12:28 NLT

REMAINING FAITHFUL TO YOU

"Praise be to the LORD, the God of my master Abraham, who has not abandoned his kindness and faithfulness to my master. As for me, the LORD has led me on the journey to the house of my master's relatives."
GENESIS 24:27 NIV

"I am with you and will watch over you wherever you go, and I will bring you back to this land. I will not leave you until I have done what I have promised you."
GENESIS 28:15 NIV

"Even to your old age and gray hairs I am he, I am he who will sustain you. I have made you and I will carry you; I will sustain you and I will rescue you."

ISAIAH 46:4 NIV

He said: "In my distress I called to the LORD, and he answered me. From the depths of the grave I called for help, and you listened to my cry."

JONAH 2:2 NIV

Being confident of this, that he who began a good work in you will carry it on to completion until the day of Christ Jesus.

PHILIPPIANS 1:6 NIV

ONE MOMENT AT A TIME
FIRST THINGS FIRST

1. **Get to know God.** If you want to hear His voice and sense His direction, you'll need to improve your relationship with God. Don't let the stress of making a decision squeeze out regular prayer and time with Him.

2. **Establish God's priorities in your life.** God is concerned about spreading the gospel message and growing the members of His church into Christlikeness. While your decisions may involve jobs, money, and life partners, those decisions should not be divorced from what God is doing in the world around you.

3. **Know your ultimate purpose.** While you search for His will, don't forget that your most significant calling is to be a child of God and a member of His kingdom. That truth should stay at the top of your list while you seek guidance on less significant issues.

CHAPTER 2

GOD'S WILL AND HOW HE'S CREATED YOU TO FULFILL IT

A number of years ago I met an employment counselor who was a Christian. She taught me many things about finding God's plan and direction that have changed the way I make decisions. Through her, I learned that God is an infinite God and created a world of people with infinite possibilities. My talents and passions are as unique as yours. Together our job is to discover how He has made us and to find our roles and places in this world and in His kingdom.

■ *Elizabeth, age 46, Ohio* ■

LIVING SUBJECT TO YOUR CREATOR

But now, O Jacob, listen to the LORD who created you. O Israel, the one who formed you says, "Do not be afraid, for I have ransomed you. I have called you by name; you are mine."

ISAIAH 43:1 NLT

So God created man in his own image, in the image of God he created him; male and female he created them.

GENESIS 1:27 NIV

Know that the LORD is God. It is he who made us, and we are his; we are his people, the sheep of his pasture.

PSALM 100:3 NIV

For the LORD, the Most High, is to be feared, a great king over all the earth.

PSALM 47:2 ESV

For you created my inmost being; you knit me together in my mother's womb. I praise you because I am fearfully and wonderfully made; your works are wonderful, I know that full well. My frame was not hidden from you when I was made in the secret place. When I was woven together in the depths of the earth, your eyes saw my unformed body. All the days ordained for me were written in your book before one of them came to be.

PSALM 139:13–16 NIV

When I consider your heavens, the work of your fingers, the moon and the stars, which you have set in place, what is man that you are mindful of him, the son of man that you care for him? You made him a little lower than the heavenly beings and crowned him with glory and honor.

PSALM 8:3–5 NIV

UNDERSTANDING YOUR GOD-GIVEN IDENTITY

You were bought at a price. Therefore honor God with your body.

1 CORINTHIANS 6:20 NIV

See how very much our Father loves us, for he calls us his children, and that is what we are!

1 JOHN 3:1 NLT

For all who are led by the Spirit of God are children of God. So you have not received a spirit that makes you fearful slaves. Instead, you received God's Spirit when he adopted you as his own children. Now we call him, "Abba, Father."

ROMANS 8:14–15 NLT

"I no longer call you servants, because a servant does not know his master's business. Instead, I have called you friends, for everything that I learned from my Father I have made known to you."

JOHN 15:15 NIV

Praise the God and Father of our Lord Jesus Christ for the spiritual blessings that Christ has brought us from heaven! Before the world was created, God had Christ choose us to live with him and to be his holy and innocent and loving people. God was kind and decided that Christ would choose us to be God's own adopted children. God was very kind to us because of the Son he dearly loves, and so we should praise God.

EPHESIANS 1:3–6 CEV

But to all who did receive him, who believed in his name, he gave the right to become children of God.

JOHN 1:12 ESV

You belong to God, so keep away from all these evil things. Try your best to please God and to be like him. Be faithful, loving, dependable, and gentle.

1 TIMOTHY 6:11 CEV

If someone claims, "I know God," but doesn't obey God's commandments, that person is a liar and is not living in the truth.

1 JOHN 2:4 NLT

DISCOVERING YOUR GIFTS AND TALENTS

These are the gifts Christ gave to the church: the apostles, the prophets, the evangelists, and the pastors and teachers. Their responsibility is to equip God's people to do his work and build up the church, the body of Christ.

EPHESIANS 4:11–12 NLT

There are different kinds of gifts, but the same Spirit. There are different kinds of service, but the same Lord. There are different kinds of working, but the same God works all of them in all men.

Now to each one the manifestation of the Spirit is given for the common good.

1 CORINTHIANS 12:4–7 NIV

Just as our bodies have many parts and each part has a special function, so it is with Christ's body. We are many parts of one body, and we all belong to each other.

In his grace, God has given us different gifts for doing certain things well. So if God has given you the ability to prophesy, speak out with as much faith as God has given you. If your gift is serving others, serve them well. If you are a teacher, teach well. If your gift is to encourage others, be encouraging. If it is giving, give generously. If God has given you leadership ability, take the responsibility seriously. And if you have a gift for showing kindness to others, do it gladly.

ROMANS 12:4–8 NLT

"This is to my Father's glory, that you bear much fruit, showing yourselves to be my disciples."

JOHN 15:8 NIV

All these gifts have a common origin, but are handed out one by one by the one Spirit of God. He decides who gets what, and when.

1 CORINTHIANS 12:11 MSG

BEING GOOD STEWARDS

Moreover, it is required of stewards that they be found trustworthy.

1 CORINTHIANS 4:2 ESV

Each one should use whatever gift he has received to serve others, faithfully administering God's grace in its various forms.

1 PETER 4:10 NIV

You put us in charge of your handcrafted world, repeated to us your Genesis-charge, made us lords of sheep and cattle, even animals out in the wild, birds flying and fish swimming, whales singing in the ocean deeps. GOD, brilliant Lord, your name echoes around the world.

PSALM 8:6–9 MSG

And the Lord said, "Who then is the faithful and wise manager, whom his master will set over his household, to give them their portion of food at the proper time? Blessed is that servant whom his master will find so doing when he comes."

LUKE 12:42–43 ESV

"Again, the Kingdom of Heaven can be illustrated by the story of a man going on a long trip. He called together his servants and entrusted his money to them while he was gone. He gave five bags of silver to one, two bags of silver to another, and one bag of silver to the last—dividing it in proportion to their abilities. He then left on his trip.

17

"The servant who received the five bags of silver began to invest the money and earned five more. The servant with two bags of silver also went to work and earned two more. But the servant who received the one bag of silver dug a hole in the ground and hid the master's money.

"After a long time their master returned from his trip and called them to give an account of how they had used his money. The servant to whom he had entrusted the five bags of silver came forward with five more and said, 'Master, you gave me five bags of silver to invest, and I have earned five more.'

"The master was full of praise. 'Well done, my good and faithful servant. You have been faithful in handling this small amount, so now I will give you many more responsibilities. Let's celebrate together!'

"The servant who had received the two bags of silver came forward and said, 'Master, you gave me two bags of silver to invest, and I have earned two more.'

"The master said, 'Well done, my good and faithful servant. You have been faithful in handling this small amount, so now I will give you many more responsibilities. Let's celebrate together!'

"Then the servant with the one bag of silver came and said, 'Master, I knew you were a harsh man, harvesting crops you didn't plant and gathering crops you didn't cultivate. I was afraid I would lose your money, so I hid it in the earth. Look, here is your money back.'

"But the master replied, 'You wicked and lazy servant! If you knew I harvested crops I didn't plant and gathered crops I didn't cultivate, why didn't you deposit my money in the bank? At least I could have gotten some interest on it.'

"Then he ordered, 'Take the money from this servant, and give it to the one with the ten bags of silver. To those who use well what they are given, even more will be given, and they will have an abundance. But from those who do nothing, even what little they have will be taken away.' "

MATTHEW 25:14–29 NLT

SUBMITTING TO GOD'S WILL

"Submit to God and be at peace with him; in this way prosperity will come to you."

JOB 22:21 NIV

And they did not do as we expected, but they gave themselves first to the Lord and then to us in keeping with God's will.

2 CORINTHIANS 8:5 NIV

"For whoever does the will of my Father in heaven is my brother and sister and mother."

MATTHEW 12:50 NIV

"Now make confession to the LORD, the God of your fathers, and do his will."

EZRA 10:11 NIV

"Not everyone who says to Me, 'Lord, Lord,' will enter the kingdom of heaven, but he who does the will of My Father who is in heaven will enter."

MATTHEW 7:21 NASB

You are free to use whatever is left over from the silver and gold for what you and your brothers decide is in keeping with the will of your God.

EZRA 7:18 MSG

The world and its desires pass away, but the man who does the will of God lives forever.

1 JOHN 2:17 NIV

IDENTIFYING YOUR GOD-GIVEN PASSIONS

The LORD gave me this message: "I knew you before I formed you in your mother's womb. Before you were born I set you apart and appointed you as my prophet to the nations."

JEREMIAH 1:4–5 NLT

For we are God's workmanship, created in Christ Jesus to do good works, which God prepared in advance for us to do.

EPHESIANS 2:10 NIV

ONE MOMENT AT A TIME
KNOWING HIM

1. **Learn more about God's character.** As you get to know Him, you'll discover that God's plan for your life will never contradict His character. For example, He'll never lead you to a job that requires you to avoid taxes, because God is a God of integrity. He'll never lead you to leave your spouse and run off with a coworker, because God is a God of commitment and purity. Get to know Him better and His plan will become clearer.

2. **Discover who you are.** Make a list of your gifts, your talents, and the things you are passionate about. Once you have your list, invite a close friend or family member to make their list about you as well. Their outside opinion may help you formulate a more objective assessment of your best strengths.

3. **Be a good steward.** We often think of stewardship in terms of money, but our responsibility goes well beyond dollars and cents. Are you getting good returns on the gifts and talents God has given you?

CHAPTER 3

GOD'S WILL CAN BE FOUND

In hindsight, I should not have been surprised that my fiancé and I broke up. The truth is, we should never have been engaged to begin with. My friends, my parents, and my sister tried to tell me, but I stubbornly refused to listen. I was too busy struggling to hold the relationship together in any way I could—including sex. Blinded by my emotions, it took me a long time to see that this relationship would never work.

■ *Amber, age 28, California* ■

SURRENDERING TO GOD'S PLAN

Look here, you who say, "Today or tomorrow we are going to a certain town and will stay there a year. We will do business there and make a profit." How do you know what your life will be like tomorrow? Your life is like the morning fog—it's here a little while, then it's gone. What you ought to say is, "If the Lord wants us to, we will live and do this or that." Otherwise you are boasting about your own plans, and all such boasting is evil.
JAMES 4:13–16 NLT

"I desire to do your will, O my God; your law is within my heart."
PSALM 40:8 NIV

"May your will be done on earth, as it is in heaven."
MATTHEW 6:10 NLT

But as he left, he promised, "I will come back if it is God's will." Then he set sail from Ephesus.
ACTS 18:21 NIV

But I will come to you very soon, if the Lord is willing, and then I will find out not only how these arrogant people are talking, but what power they have.
1 CORINTHIANS 4:19 NIV

"I didn't come from heaven to do what I want! I came to do what the Father wants me to do. He sent me."
JOHN 6:38 CEV

[Jesus prayed,] "Father, remove this cup from me. But please, not what I want. What do you want?"
LUKE 22:42 MSG

ACKNOWLEDGING THE SUPREMACY OF GOD'S PLAN

"Jesus must become more important, while I become less important."

JOHN 3:30 CEV

"I make known the end from the beginning, from ancient times, what is still to come. I say: My purpose will stand, and I will do all that I please."

ISAIAH 46:10 NIV

Whatever the LORD pleases, he does, in heaven and on earth, in the seas and all deeps.

PSALM 135:6 ESV

"But he stands alone, and who can oppose him? He does whatever he pleases."

JOB 23:13 NIV

God always does what he plans, and that's why he appointed Christ to choose us.

EPHESIANS 1:11 CEV

For God is working in you, giving you the desire and the power to do what pleases him.

PHILIPPIANS 2:13 NLT

All the peoples of the earth are regarded as nothing. He does as he pleases with the powers of heaven and the peoples of the earth. No one can hold back his hand or say to him: "What have you done?"

DANIEL 4:35 NIV

But Joseph said to them, "Don't be afraid. Am I in the place of God? You intended to harm me, but God intended it for good to accomplish what is now being done, the saving of many lives."

GENESIS 50:19–20 NIV

"So will the words that come out of my mouth not come back empty-handed. They'll do the work I sent them to do, they'll complete the assignment I gave them."

ISAIAH 55:11 MSG

In his heart a man plans his course, but the LORD determines his steps.

PROVERBS 16:9 NIV

Many are the plans in a man's heart, but it is the LORD's purpose that prevails.

PROVERBS 19:21 NIV

SEEKING DIRECTION THROUGH PRAYER

Lead me in the right path, O LORD, or my enemies will conquer me. Make your way plain for me to follow.

PSALM 5:8 NLT

Please, LORD, please save us. Please, LORD, please give us success.

PSALM 118:25 NLT

Since you are my rock and my fortress, for the sake of your name lead and guide me.

PSALM 31:3 NIV

Send forth your light and your truth, let them guide me; let them bring me to your holy mountain, to the place where you dwell.

PSALM 43:3 NIV

God, listen to me shout, bend an ear to my prayer. When I'm far from anywhere, down to my last gasp, I call out, "Guide me up High Rock Mountain!"

PSALM 61:1–2 MSG

PRAYING YOUR DREAMS LINE UP WITH HIS WILL

"This, then, is how you should pray: 'Our Father in heaven, hallowed be your name, your kingdom come, your will be done on earth as it is in heaven.'"

MATTHEW 6:9–10 NIV

And how bold and free we then become in his presence, freely asking according to his will, sure that he's listening.

1 JOHN 5:14 MSG

For God is my witness, whom I serve with my spirit in the gospel of his Son, that without ceasing I mention you always in my prayers, asking that somehow by God's will I may now at last succeed in coming to you.

ROMANS 1:9–10 ESV

LORD, we show our trust in you by obeying your laws; our heart's desire is to glorify your name.

ISAIAH 26:8 NLT

I appeal to you, brothers, by our Lord Jesus Christ and by the love of the Spirit, to strive together with me in your prayers to God on my behalf, that I may be delivered from the unbelievers in Judea, and that my service for Jerusalem may be acceptable to the saints, so that by God's will I may come to you with joy and be refreshed in your company.

ROMANS 15:30–32 ESV

Likewise the Spirit helps us in our weakness. For we do not know what to pray for as we ought, but the Spirit himself intercedes for us with groanings too deep for words. And he who searches hearts knows what is the mind of the Spirit, because the Spirit intercedes for the saints according to the will of God.

ROMANS 8:26–27 ESV

CONFESSING THE SIN THAT OBSCURES YOUR VIEW

If I had cherished sin in my heart, the Lord would not have listened.

PSALM 66:18 NIV

"We know that God does not hear sinners; but if anyone is God-fearing and does His will, He hears him."

JOHN 9:31 NASB

There's nothing wrong with God; the wrong is in you. Your wrong-headed lives caused the split between you and God. Your sins got between you so that he doesn't hear.

ISAIAH 59:2 MSG

Who may ascend into the hill of the LORD? And who may stand in His holy place? He who has clean hands and a pure heart, who has not lifted up his soul to falsehood and has not sworn deceitfully. He shall receive a blessing from the LORD and righteousness from the God of his salvation.

PSALM 24:3–5 NASB

The LORD detests the sacrifice of the wicked, but he delights in the prayers of the upright.

PROVERBS 15:8 NLT

The Lord watches over everyone who obeys him, and he listens to their prayers. But he opposes everyone who does evil.

1 PETER 3:12 CEV

GOING TO THE BIBLE TO FIND HIS WILL

Your word is a lamp to my feet and a light for my path.

PSALM 119:105 NIV

Direct my footsteps according to your word; let no sin rule over me.

PSALM 119:133 NIV

I believe in your commands; now teach me good judgment and knowledge. I used to wander off until you disciplined me; but now I closely follow your word. You are

good and do only good; teach me your decrees.

PSALM 119:66–68 NLT

All Scripture is inspired by God and is useful to teach us what is true and to make us realize what is wrong in our lives. It corrects us when we are wrong and teaches us to do what is right. God uses it to prepare and equip his people to do every good work.

2 TIMOTHY 3:16–17 NLT

"If you abide in me, and my words abide in you, ask whatever you wish, and it will be done for you."

JOHN 15:7 ESV

I have hidden your word in my heart that I might not sin against you. Praise be to you, O LORD; teach me your decrees.

PSALM 119:11–12 NIV

God's word is alive and working and is sharper than a double-edged sword. It cuts all the way into us, where the soul and the spirit are joined, to the center of our joints and bones. And it judges the thoughts and feelings in our hearts.

HEBREWS 4:12 NCV

Happy are those who don't listen to the wicked, who don't go where sinners go, who don't do what evil people do. They love the LORD's teachings, and they think about those teachings day and night.

PSALM 1:1–2 NCV

TRUSTING GOD AND HIS PLAN

Why am I restless? I trust you! And I will praise you again because you help me.

PSALM 42:5 CEV

Whether you turn to the right or to the left, your ears will hear a voice behind you, saying, "This is the way; walk in it."

ISAIAH 30:21 NIV

Some trust in chariots, and some in horses, but we trust in the name of the LORD our God.

PSALM 20:7 ESV

LORD, every morning you hear my voice. Every morning, I tell you what I need, and I wait for your answer.

PSALM 5:3 NCV

The LORD is my light and my salvation; whom shall I fear? The LORD is the stronghold of my life; of whom shall I be afraid?

PSALM 27:1 ESV

"Yet when you relied on the LORD, he delivered them into your hand."

2 CHRONICLES 16:8 NIV

Simon Peter answered, "Lord, there is no one else that we can go to!"

JOHN 6:68 CEV

That is why I am suffering here in prison. But I am not ashamed of it, for I know the one in whom I trust, and I am sure that he is able to guard what I have entrusted to him until the day of his return.

2 TIMOTHY 1:12 NLT

"Do not let your hearts be troubled. Trust in God; trust also in me."

JOHN 14:1 NIV

LISTENING TO GOOD ADVICE

Pay attention to advice and accept correction, so you can live sensibly.

PROVERBS 19:20 CEV

Timely advice is lovely, like golden apples in a silver basket. To one who listens, valid criticism is like a gold earring or other gold jewelry.

PROVERBS 25:11–12 NLT

Fools are headstrong and do what they like; wise people take advice.

PROVERBS 12:15 MSG

Without good advice everything goes wrong—it takes careful planning for things to go right.

PROVERBS 15:22 CEV

For lack of guidance a nation falls, but many advisers make victory sure.

PROVERBS 11:14 NIV

ACQUIRING WISDOM

But the wisdom from above is first of all pure. It is also peace loving, gentle at all times, and willing to yield to others. It is full of mercy

and good deeds. It shows no favoritism and is always sincere.

JAMES 3:17 NLT

God's kingdom isn't about eating
and drinking. It is about pleasing
God, about living in peace, and
about true happiness. All this comes
from the Holy Spirit.

ROMANS 14:17 CEV

Fear of the LORD is the foundation
of wisdom. Knowledge of the Holy
One results in good judgment.

PROVERBS 9:10 NLT

To the Jews who had believed him,
Jesus said, "If you hold to my teaching, you are really my disciples.
Then you will know the truth, and
the truth will set you free."

JOHN 8:31–32 NIV

The fear of the LORD is the beginning of wisdom; all those who
practice it have a good understanding. His praise endures forever!

PSALM 111:10 ESV

Buy the truth and do not sell it;
get wisdom, discipline and
understanding.

PROVERBS 23:23 NIV

BEING FAITHFUL IN ALL THINGS

"Whoever can be trusted with very
little can also be trusted with much,
and whoever is dishonest with very
little will also be dishonest with
much."

LUKE 16:10 NIV

"If you have raced with men on
foot and they have worn you out,
how can you compete with horses?
If you stumble in safe country, how
will you manage in the thickets by
the Jordan?"

JEREMIAH 12:5 NIV

If you fall to pieces in a crisis, there
wasn't much to you in the first place.

PROVERBS 24:10 MSG

"Yes," the king replied, "and to those
who use well what they are given,
even more will be given. But from
those who do nothing, even what
little they have will be taken away."

LUKE 19:26 NLT

Yes, each of us will give a personal
account to God.

ROMANS 14:12 NLT

Barnabas wanted to take John
along, the John nicknamed Mark.
But Paul wouldn't have him; he
wasn't about to take along a quit-
ter who, as soon as the going got
tough, had jumped ship on them in
Pamphylia.

ACTS 15:37–38 MSG

"Then the King will say to those
on his right, 'Come, you who are
blessed by my Father; take your
inheritance, the kingdom prepared
for you since the creation of the
world. For I was hungry and you
gave me something to eat, I was
thirsty and you gave me something
to drink, I was a stranger and you
invited me in, I needed clothes and
you clothed me, I was sick and you

looked after me, I was in prison and you came to visit me.' . . . "The King will reply, 'I tell you the truth, whatever you did for one of the least of these brothers of mine, you did for me.' "

MATTHEW 25:34–40 NIV

FINDING PEACE WHILE YOU WAIT

You will keep in perfect peace him whose mind is steadfast, because he trusts in you.

ISAIAH 26:3 NIV

"Peace I leave with you; My peace I give to you; not as the world gives do I give to you. Do not let your heart be troubled, nor let it be fearful."

JOHN 14:27 NASB

"I have told you all this so that you may have peace in me. Here on earth you will have many trials and sorrows. But take heart, because I have overcome the world."

JOHN 16:33 NLT

Don't worry about anything; instead, pray about everything. Tell God what you need, and thank him for all he has done. Then you will experience God's peace, which exceeds anything we can understand. His peace will guard your hearts and minds as you live in Christ Jesus.

PHILIPPIANS 4:6–7 NLT

I pray that God will be kind to you and will let you live in perfect peace! May you keep learning more and more about God and our Lord Jesus.

2 PETER 1:2 CEV

The LORD bless you and keep you; the LORD make his face to shine upon you and be gracious to you; the LORD lift up his countenance upon you and give you peace.

NUMBERS 6:24–26 ESV

ONE MOMENT AT A TIME
EXPLORING ALL ANGLES

1. **Ask God first.** The Bible reminds us to bring our requests to God. But when you do this, you also need to remember that you may receive an answer that you don't like. And while that may be difficult to swallow at first, remember that God has your entire life in His view, and He really does know what's best for you.

2. **Get good advice.** Our emotions can hinder us from making good choices. While you may feel excited about an opportunity or flattered by someone who wants you to take an assignment, get objective advice from levelheaded people you can trust.

3. **Be patient.** An old proverb, "Fools jump in where angels fear to tread," is often true. An opportunity that seems too good to pass up at the moment could turn out to be a mistake that you'll regret for years to come. Take your time, pray about it, and get advice before making a big decision.

CHAPTER 4

GOD'S WILL REGARDING YOUR SPIRITUAL LIFE

I've been consumed with trying to find God's plan for my life in the last few years. I've felt overwhelmed with trying to answer the big, life-changing questions on the forefront of my mind: Who am I supposed to marry? Should I go to grad school? Which job should I take? Recently, I realized that I've neglected my most important calling–developing my relationship with my heavenly Father. What's God's ultimate will for my life? To put it simply, it's to love God and know Him better.

■ *Justin, age 23, Massachusetts* ■

LOVING GOD

Love the LORD your God with all your heart and with all your soul and with all your strength.
DEUTERONOMY 6:5 NIV

"Now, vigilantly guard your souls: Love God, your God."
JOSHUA 23:11 MSG

What does the LORD your God want from you? The LORD wants you to respect and follow him, to love and serve him with all your heart and soul.
DEUTERONOMY 10:12 CEV

Know therefore that the LORD your God is God; he is the faithful God, keeping his covenant of love to a thousand generations of those who love him and keep his commands.
DEUTERONOMY 7:9 NIV

Love the LORD your God and keep his requirements, his decrees, his laws and his commands always.
DEUTERONOMY 11:1 NIV

"No one can serve two masters. For you will hate one and love the other; you will be devoted to one and despise the other. You cannot serve both God and money."
LUKE 16:13 NLT

That's right. If you diligently keep all this commandment that I command you to obey—love God, your God, do what he tells you, stick close to him—God on his part will drive out all these nations that stand in your way. Yes, he'll drive out nations much bigger and stronger than you.
DEUTERONOMY 11:22–23 MSG

OBEYING GOD'S COMMANDS

"The LORD commanded us to obey all these decrees and to fear the LORD our God, so that we might always prosper and be kept alive, as is the case today."

DEUTERONOMY 6:24 NIV

Teach me your decrees, O LORD; I will keep them to the end. Give me understanding and I will obey your instructions; I will put them into practice with all my heart.

PSALM 119:33–34 NLT

It is the LORD your God you must follow, and him you must revere. Keep his commands and obey him; serve him and hold fast to him.

DEUTERONOMY 13:4 NIV

How can a young person stay pure? By obeying your word. I have tried hard to find you—don't let me wander from your commands. I have hidden your word in my heart, that I might not sin against you.

PSALM 119:9–11 NLT

God's readiness to give and forgive is now public. Salvation's available for everyone! We're being shown how to turn our backs on a godless, indulgent life, and how to take on a God-filled, God-honoring life. This new life is starting right now, and is whetting our appetites for the glorious day when our great God and Savior, Jesus Christ, appears. He offered himself as a sacrifice to free us from a dark, rebellious life into this good, pure life, making us a people he can be proud of, energetic in goodness.

TITUS 2:11–14 MSG

When God is angry, money won't help you. Obeying God is the only way to be saved from death.

PROVERBS 11:4 CEV

MAINTAINING INTIMACY WITH GOD

He has showed you, O man, what is good. And what does the LORD require of you? To act justly and to love mercy and to walk humbly with your God.

MICAH 6:8 NIV

The LORD is near to all who call on him, to all who call on him in truth.

PSALM 145:18 NIV

"What good will it be for a man if he gains the whole world, yet forfeits his soul? Or what can a man give in exchange for his soul?"

MATTHEW 16:26 NIV

Come near to God, and God will come near to you. You sinners, clean sin out of your lives. You who are trying to follow God and the world at the same time, make your thinking pure.

JAMES 4:8 NCV

Seek the LORD while He may be found; call upon Him while He is near.

ISAIAH 55:6 NASB

Better is one day in your courts than a thousand elsewhere; I would rather be a doorkeeper in the house of my God than dwell in the tents of the wicked.

PSALM 84:10 NIV

"Yes, I am the vine; you are the branches. Those who remain in me, and I in them, will produce much fruit. For apart from me you can do nothing."

JOHN 15:5 NLT

You know me inside and out, you hold me together, you never fail to stand me tall in your presence so I can look you in the eye.

PSALM 41:12 MSG

CONTINUING TO GROW

It is God's will that you should be sanctified.

1 THESSALONIANS 4:3 NIV

But you, dear friends, carefully build yourselves up in this most holy faith by praying in the Holy Spirit.

JUDE 20 MSG

Like newborn babies, you must crave pure spiritual milk so that you will grow into a full experience of salvation. Cry out for this nourishment, now that you have had a taste of the Lord's kindness.

1 PETER 2:2–3 NLT

Teach me to do Your will, for You are my God; Your Spirit is good. Lead me in the land of uprightness.

PSALM 143:10 NKJV

Show me your ways, O LORD, teach me your paths.

PSALM 25:4 NIV

Do your best to improve your faith. You can do this by adding goodness, understanding, self-control, patience, devotion to God, concern for others, and love. If you keep growing in this way, it will show that what you know about our Lord Jesus Christ has made your lives useful and meaningful. But if you don't grow, you are like someone who is near-sighted or blind, and you have forgotten that your past sins are forgiven.

2 PETER 1:5–9 CEV

Therefore, my dear friends, as you have always obeyed—not only in my presence, but now much more in my absence—continue to work out your salvation with fear and trembling.

PHILIPPIANS 2:12 NIV

For I know that nothing good dwells in me, that is, in my flesh. For I have the desire to do what is right, but not the ability to carry it out. For I do not do the good I want, but the evil I do not want is what I keep on doing. Now if I do what I do not want, it is no longer I who do it, but sin that dwells within me. So I find it to be a law that when I want to do right, evil lies close at hand. For I delight in the law of God, in my inner being, but I see in my members another law waging war against the law of my mind and making me captive to the law of sin that dwells in my members. Wretched man that I am! Who will deliver me from this body of death? Thanks be to God through Jesus Christ our Lord!

ROMANS 7:18–25 ESV

But now that you have been set free from sin and have become slaves to God, the benefit you reap leads to holiness, and the result is eternal life.

ROMANS 6:22 NIV

And God is able to make all grace abound to you, so that in all things at all times, having all that you need, you will abound in every good work.

2 CORINTHIANS 9:8 NIV

PRAISING GOD

Give to the LORD the glory he deserves! Bring your offering and come into his courts.

PSALM 96:8 NLT

Tell everyone of every nation, "Praise the glorious power of the LORD. He is wonderful! Praise him and bring an offering into his temple. Worship the LORD, majestic and holy."

1 CHRONICLES 16:28–29 CEV

Oh, magnify the LORD with me, and let us exalt his name together!

PSALM 34:3 ESV

So whether you eat or drink or whatever you do, do it all for the glory of God.

1 CORINTHIANS 10:31 NIV

Let me shout God's name with a praising song, let me tell his greatness in a prayer of thanks.

PSALM 69:30 MSG

Great is the LORD and most worthy of praise; his greatness no one can fathom.

PSALM 145:3 NIV

Sing to the LORD, you saints of his; praise his holy name.

PSALM 30:4 NIV

Sing to God, O kingdoms of the earth, sing praises to the Lord.

PSALM 68:32 NASB

Then a voice came from the throne, saying: "Praise our God, all you his servants, you who fear him, both small and great!"

REVELATION 19:5 NIV

LORD All-Powerful, you are greater than all others. No one is like you, and you alone are God. Everything we have heard about you is true.

2 SAMUEL 7:22 CEV

For great is the LORD and most worthy of praise; he is to be feared above all gods. For all the gods of the nations are idols, but the LORD made the heavens. Splendor and majesty are before him; strength and glory are in his sanctuary. Ascribe to the LORD, O families of nations, ascribe to the LORD glory and strength. Ascribe to the LORD the glory due his name; bring an offering and come into his courts. Worship the LORD in the splendor of his holiness; tremble before him, all the earth.

PSALM 96:4–9 NIV

Join with me in praising the wonderful name of the LORD our God.

DEUTERONOMY 32:3 CEV

O LORD, our Lord, how majestic is Your name in all the earth, who have displayed Your splendor above the heavens!

PSALM 8:1 NASB

Oh, the depth of the riches of the wisdom and knowledge of God! How unsearchable his judgments, and his paths beyond tracing out! "Who has known the mind of the Lord? Or who has been his counselor?" "Who has ever given to God, that God should repay him?" For from him and through him and to him are all things. To him be the glory forever! Amen.

ROMANS 11:33–36 NIV

David praised the LORD in the presence of the whole assembly, saying, "Praise be to you, O LORD, God of our father Israel, from everlasting to everlasting. Yours, O LORD, is the greatness and the power and the glory and the majesty and the splendor, for everything in heaven and earth is yours. Yours, O LORD, is the kingdom; you are exalted as head over all. Wealth and honor come from you; you are the ruler of all things. In your hands are strength and power to exalt and give strength to all."

1 CHRONICLES 29:10–12 NIV

Lord, you have been our dwelling place in all generations. Before the mountains were brought forth, or ever you had formed the earth and the world, from everlasting to everlasting you are God.

PSALM 90:1–2 ESV

O LORD, you have examined my heart and know everything about me. You know when I sit down or stand up. You know my thoughts even when I'm far away. You see me when I travel and when I rest at home. You know everything I do. You know what I am going to say even before I say it, LORD. You go before me and follow me. You place your hand of blessing on my head. Such knowledge is too wonderful for me, too great for me to understand!

PSALM 139:1–6 NLT

"There is no one like you, O LORD, and there is no God but you, as we have heard with our own ears."

1 CHRONICLES 17:20 NIV

TELLING OTHERS ABOUT JESUS

Then Jesus came to them and said, "All authority in heaven and on earth has been given to me. Therefore go and make disciples of all nations, baptizing them in the name of the Father and of the Son and of the Holy Spirit, and teaching them to obey everything I have commanded you. And surely I am with you always, to the very end of the age."

MATTHEW 28:18–20 NIV

He said to his disciples, "The harvest is great, but the workers are few. So pray to the Lord who is in charge of the harvest; ask him to send more workers into his fields."

MATTHEW 9:37–38 NLT

For God was in Christ, reconciling the world to himself, no longer counting people's sins against them. And he gave us this wonderful message of reconciliation.

2 CORINTHIANS 5:19 NLT

"And you must also testify about me because you have been with me from the beginning of my ministry."

JOHN 15:27 NLT

Has the LORD redeemed you? Then speak out! Tell others he has redeemed you from your enemies.

PSALM 107:2 NLT

Pray also for me, that whenever I open my mouth, words may be given me so that I will fearlessly make known the mystery of the gospel, for which I am an ambassador in chains. Pray that I may declare it fearlessly, as I should.

EPHESIANS 6:19–20 NIV

So never be ashamed to tell others about our Lord.

2 TIMOTHY 1:8 NLT

But you are a chosen people, a royal priesthood, a holy nation, a people belonging to God, that you may declare the praises of him who called you out of darkness into his wonderful light.

1 PETER 2:9 NIV

BEING THANKFUL

Give thanks to the LORD, call on his name; make known among the nations what he has done.

PSALM 105:1 NIV

I pray that you will be grateful to God for letting you have part in what he has promised his people in the kingdom of light.

COLOSSIANS 1:12 CEV

So thank God for his marvelous love, for his miracle mercy to the children he loves.

PSALM 107:31 MSG

Devote yourselves to prayer with an alert mind and a thankful heart.

COLOSSIANS 4:2 NLT

O give thanks to the LORD, for He is good; for His lovingkindness is everlasting.

1 CHRONICLES 16:34 NASB

Now, our God, we give you thanks, and praise your glorious name.

1 CHRONICLES 29:13 NIV

LORD, I thank you for answering me. You have saved me.

PSALM 118:21 NCV

And whatever you do, whether in word or deed, do it all in the name of the Lord Jesus, giving thanks to God the Father through him.

COLOSSIANS 3:17 NIV

PRIORITIZING THE CHURCH

"I will build my church, and the gates of Hades will not overcome it."
MATTHEW 16:18 NIV

His intent was that now, through the church, the manifold wisdom of God should be made known to the rulers and authorities in the heavenly realms.
EPHESIANS 3:10 NIV

Christ is also the head of the church, which is his body. He is the beginning, supreme over all who rise from the dead. So he is first in everything.
COLOSSIANS 1:18 NLT

Let us not give up meeting together, as some are in the habit of doing, but let us encourage one another—and all the more as you see the Day approaching.
HEBREWS 10:25 NIV

Look after yourselves and everyone the Holy Spirit has placed in your care. Be like shepherds to God's church. It is the flock that he bought with the blood of his own Son.
ACTS 20:28 CEV

Christ did this, so that he would have a glorious and holy church, without faults or spots or wrinkles or any other flaws. . . . None of us hate our own bodies. We provide for them and take good care of them, just as Christ does for the church.
EPHESIANS 5:27, 29 CEV

ONE MOMENT AT A TIME
YOUR MOST IMPORTANT CALLING

1. **Don't forget.** Don't get so distracted trying to find God's will for your life in other areas that you neglect the most important area of all: knowing Him.

2. **Build the church.** Jesus clearly stated that His mission was to build His church. Consider how your job, activities, and relationships can play a role in advancing God's kingdom.

3. **Spread the word.** Others who see you turn down a big raise in order to spend more time with your family or buy an older car so that you can give the extra money to a needy person will wonder why you did so. Take every opportunity to show how God's love and calling are more important than your own personal ambition, and be prepared to explain the reason for your actions to the people who are watching.

CHAPTER 5

GOD'S WILL REGARDING YOUR MONEY AND WORK

Dollar signs do not always equal God's will. About a year ago, I took a six-figure job that promised me the world. Finally, I thought, the grass would be greener on my side of the fence. The irony is that my life has gotten worse instead of better. My eyes have become more focused on sales bonuses than on my relationship with God, and I spend more time thinking about ways to grow my portfolio rather than considering ways to mentor my kids. Honestly, I think I was more content before I took this job and I'm starting to wonder if I've made a terrible mistake.

■ *Tim, age 37, New Jersey* ■

STEERING CLEAR OF THE LOVE OF MONEY

Keep your lives free from the love of money.

HEBREWS 13:5 NIV

For the love of money is a root of all kinds of evil. Some people, eager for money, have wandered from the faith and pierced themselves with many griefs.

1 TIMOTHY 6:10 NIV

But people who long to be rich fall into temptation and are trapped by many foolish and harmful desires that plunge them into ruin and destruction.

1 TIMOTHY 6:9 NLT

Teach those who are rich in this world not to be proud and not to trust in their money, which is so unreliable. Their trust should be in God, who richly gives us all we need for our enjoyment.

1 TIMOTHY 6:17 NLT

Whoever trusts in his riches will fall, but the righteous will flourish like a green leaf.

PROVERBS 11:28 ESV

"Watch out! Be on your guard against all kinds of greed; a man's life does not consist in the abundance of his possessions."

LUKE 12:15 NIV

And if your wealth increases, don't make it the center of your life.

PSALM 62:10 NLT

Whoever loves money never has money enough; whoever loves wealth is never satisfied with his income. This too is meaningless.
ECCLESIASTES 5:10 NIV

HONORING YOUR DEBTS AND TAXES

Pay all that you owe, whether it is taxes and fees or respect and honor.
ROMANS 13:7 CEV

The wicked borrow and do not repay, but the righteous give generously.
PSALM 37:21 NIV

Let no debt remain outstanding, except the continuing debt to love one another, for he who loves his fellowman has fulfilled the law.
ROMANS 13:8 NIV

Then the Pharisees met together to plot how to trap Jesus into saying something for which he could be arrested. They sent some of their disciples, along with the supporters of Herod, to meet with him. "Teacher," they said, "we know how honest you are. You teach the way of God truthfully. You are impartial and don't play favorites. Now tell us what you think about this: Is it right to pay taxes to Caesar or not?" But Jesus knew their evil motives. "You hypocrites!" he said. "Why are you trying to trap me? Here, show me the coin used for the tax." When they handed him a Roman coin, he asked, "Whose picture and title

are stamped on it?" "Caesar's," they replied. "Well, then," he said, "give to Caesar what belongs to Caesar, and give to God what belongs to God." His reply amazed them, and they went away.
MATTHEW 22:15–22 NLT

REMEMBERING THE POOR

Religion that God our Father accepts as pure and faultless is this: to look after orphans and widows in their distress and to keep oneself from being polluted by the world.
JAMES 1:27 NIV

Tell them. . .to be rich in helping others, to be extravagantly generous.
1 TIMOTHY 6:18 MSG

"When you give a feast, invite the poor, the crippled, the lame, and the blind. They cannot pay you back. But God will bless you and reward you when his people rise from death."
LUKE 14:13–14 CEV

He who is kind to the poor lends to the LORD, and he will reward him for what he has done.
PROVERBS 19:17 NIV

A person who gets ahead by oppressing the poor or by showering gifts on the rich will end in poverty.
PROVERBS 22:16 NLT

"When you are harvesting your crops and forget to bring in a bundle of grain from your field, don't go back to get it. Leave it for the foreigners, orphans, and widows. Then the LORD your God will bless you in all you do. When you beat the olives from your olive trees, don't go over the boughs twice. Leave the remaining olives for the foreigners, orphans, and widows. When you gather the grapes in your vineyard, don't glean the vines after they are picked. Leave the remaining grapes for the foreigners, orphans, and widows."

DEUTERONOMY 24:19–21 NLT

"Cursed is anyone who denies justice to foreigners, orphans, or widows."

DEUTERONOMY 27:19 NLT

Do not mistreat widows or orphans. If you do, they will beg for my help, and I will come to their rescue. In fact, I will get so angry that I will kill your men and make widows of their wives and orphans of their children.

EXODUS 22:22–24 CEV

WORKING WITH INTEGRITY

Whatever you do, work at it with all your heart, as working for the Lord, not for men.

COLOSSIANS 3:23 NIV

Whatever your hand finds to do, do it with all your might, for in the grave, where you are going, there is neither working nor planning nor knowledge nor wisdom.

ECCLESIASTES 9:10 NIV

Make it your ambition to lead a quiet life, to mind your own business and to work with your hands, just as we told you, so that your daily life may win the respect of outsiders and so that you will not be dependent on anybody.

1 THESSALONIANS 4:11–12 NIV

Do not steal. Do not deceive or cheat one another.

LEVITICUS 19:11 NLT

Go to work in the morning and stick to it until evening without watching the clock. You never know from moment to moment how your work will turn out in the end.

ECCLESIASTES 11:6 MSG

In the name of the Lord Jesus Christ, we command you, brothers, to keep away from every brother who is idle and does not live according to the teaching you received from us.

2 THESSALONIANS 3:6 NIV

Now we learn that some of you just loaf around and won't do any work, except the work of a busybody. So, for the sake of our Lord Jesus Christ, we ask and beg these people to settle down and start working for a living.

2 THESSALONIANS 3:11–12 CEV

PRAYING FOR SUCCESS

Jabez cried out to the God of Israel, "Oh, that you would bless me and enlarge my territory! Let your hand be with me, and keep me from harm so that I will be free from

pain." And God granted his request.
1 CHRONICLES 4:10 NIV

"O Lord, let your ear be attentive to the prayer of this your servant and to the prayer of your servants who delight in revering your name. Give your servant success today by granting him favor in the presence of this man."
NEHEMIAH 1:11 NIV

"O LORD, God of my master, Abraham," he prayed. "Please give me success today, and show unfailing love to my master, Abraham."
GENESIS 24:12 NLT

Thus says the LORD, your Redeemer, the Holy One of Israel: "I am the LORD your God, who teaches you to profit, who leads you in the way you should go."
ISAIAH 48:17 ESV

ONE MOMENT AT A TIME
KEEPING MONEY IN ITS PLACE

1. **Provide, don't obsess.** Money is good and helpful, but the love of money can kill your spiritual life and your relationships. While you need to work hard and earn money, always keep the dollars in their place.

2. **Take money out of it.** When possible, evaluate decisions without thinking about money. That's not to say that you should make decisions that cause you to jump deeply into debt, but you should be keenly aware of the ways money can cloud your ability to make the best decision.

3. **Be a good steward.** While it's good to enjoy the gifts God has given you, He has not given them to you for the sole purpose of feeding your pleasures. You have a responsibility to look for ways to serve others with what you've been given.

CHAPTER 6

GOD'S WILL REGARDING SEX, MARRIAGE, AND FAMILY

When my friend told me she was having an affair with a married man, I couldn't believe it. And when she justified it by saying she knew that God wanted them to be together, my heart broke for her. I tried to tell her that nothing could be further from the truth, but she wouldn't hear it. Although her emotions were clouding her vision, I knew that the Bible is clear. God never leads us in ways that contradict His character or His Word. Sex outside of marriage is always wrong and can never be justified as part of God's plan.

■ *Janet, age 50, Indiana* ■

REMAINING DEVOTED TO YOUR SPOUSE

And this is why a man leaves father and mother and cherishes his wife. No longer two, they become "one flesh." This is a huge mystery, and I don't pretend to understand it all.
EPHESIANS 5:31–32 MSG

And further, submit to one another out of reverence for Christ. For wives, this means submit to your husbands as to the Lord. For a husband is the head of his wife as Christ is the head of the church. He is the Savior of his body, the church. As the church submits to Christ, so you wives should submit to your husbands in everything. For husbands, this means love your wives, just as Christ loved the church. He gave up his life for her.
EPHESIANS 5:21–25 NLT

Wives, understand and support your husbands by submitting to them in ways that honor the Master.
COLOSSIANS 3:18 MSG

Husbands, in the same way be considerate as you live with your wives, and treat them with respect as the weaker partner and as heirs with you of the gracious gift of life, so that nothing will hinder your prayers.
1 PETER 3:7 NIV

Be devoted to one another in brotherly love. Honor one another above yourselves.
ROMANS 12:10 NIV

If one part of our body hurts, we hurt all over. If one part of our body is honored, the whole body will be happy.

1 CORINTHIANS 12:26 CEV

Let's see how inventive we can be in encouraging love and helping out.

HEBREWS 10:24 MSG

HOLDING MARRIAGE IN HIGH REGARD

Do not be unequally yoked with unbelievers. For what partnership has righteousness with lawlessness? Or what fellowship has light with darkness?

2 CORINTHIANS 6:14 ESV

"Haven't you read the Scriptures?" Jesus replied. "They record that from the beginning 'God made them male and female.' And he said, 'This explains why a man leaves his father and mother and is joined to his wife, and the two are united into one.' Since they are no longer two but one, let no one split apart what God has joined together."

MATTHEW 19:4–6 NLT

Now, I will speak to the rest of you, though I do not have a direct command from the Lord. If a Christian man has a wife who is not a believer and she is willing to continue living with him, he must not leave her. And if a Christian woman has a husband who is not a believer and he is willing to continue living with her, she must not leave him. For the Christian wife brings holiness to her marriage, and the Christian husband brings holiness to his marriage. Otherwise, your children would not be holy, but now they are holy. (But if the husband or wife who isn't a believer insists on leaving, let them go. In such cases the Christian husband or wife is no longer bound to the other, for God has called you to live in peace.) Don't you wives realize that your husbands might be saved because of you? And don't you husbands realize that your wives might be saved because of you?

1 CORINTHIANS 7:12–16 NLT

"I hate divorce," says the LORD God of Israel.

MALACHI 2:16 NIV

Finishing is better than starting. Patience is better than pride.

ECCLESIASTES 7:8 NLT

GUARDING YOUR SEXUAL BEHAVIOR

Honor marriage, and guard the sacredness of sexual intimacy between wife and husband. God draws a firm line against casual and illicit sex.

HEBREWS 13:4 MSG

God's will is for you to be holy, so stay away from all sexual sin.

1 THESSALONIANS 4:3 NLT

"But I tell you that anyone who looks at a woman lustfully has already committed adultery with her in his heart."

MATTHEW 5:28 NIV

Instead, clothe yourself with the presence of the Lord Jesus Christ. And don't let yourself think about ways to indulge your evil desires.

ROMANS 13:14 NLT

Run from anything that stimulates youthful lusts. Instead, pursue righteous living, faithfulness, love, and peace. Enjoy the companionship of those who call on the Lord with pure hearts.

2 TIMOTHY 2:22 NLT

Flee from sexual immorality. Every other sin a person commits is outside the body, but the sexually immoral person sins against his own body.

1 CORINTHIANS 6:18 ESV

Let there be no sexual immorality, impurity, or greed among you. Such sins have no place among God's people.

EPHESIANS 5:3 NLT

The acts of the sinful nature are obvious: sexual immorality, impurity and debauchery.

GALATIANS 5:19 NIV

Put to death, therefore, whatever belongs to your earthly nature: sexual immorality, impurity, lust, evil desires and greed, which is idolatry.

COLOSSIANS 3:5 NIV

Because we belong to the day, we must live decent lives for all to see. Don't participate in the darkness of wild parties and drunkenness, or in sexual promiscuity and immoral living, or in quarreling and jealousy.

ROMANS 13:13 NLT

Do you not know that your body is a temple of the Holy Spirit, who is in you, whom you have received from God? You are not your own; you were bought at a price. Therefore honor God with your body.

1 CORINTHIANS 6:19-20 NIV

God has called us to live holy lives, not impure lives.

1 THESSALONIANS 4:7 NLT

RAISING YOUR CHILDREN

Train up a child in the way he should go; even when he is old he will not depart from it.

PROVERBS 22:6 ESV

Young people are prone to foolishness and fads; the cure comes through tough-minded discipline.

PROVERBS 22:15 MSG

Correct your children before it's too late; if you don't punish them, you are destroying them.

PROVERBS 19:18 CEV

To discipline a child produces wisdom, but a mother is disgraced by an undisciplined child.

PROVERBS 29:15 NLT

But watch out! Be careful never to forget what you yourself have seen. Do not let these memories escape from your mind as long as you live! And be sure to pass them on to your children and grandchildren. Never forget the day when you stood before the LORD your God at Mount Sinai, where he told me, "Summon the people before me, and I will personally instruct them. Then they will learn to fear me as long as they live, and they will teach their children to fear me also."

DEUTERONOMY 4:9–10 NLT

Fathers, do not provoke your children to anger, but bring them up in the discipline and instruction of the Lord.

EPHESIANS 6:4 ESV

Love GOD, your God, with your whole heart: love him with all that's in you, love him with all you've got! Write these commandments that I've given you today on your hearts. Get them inside of you and then get them inside your children. Talk about them wherever you are, sitting at home or walking in the street; talk about them from the time you get up in the morning to when you fall into bed at night. Tie them on your hands and foreheads as a reminder; inscribe them on the doorposts of your homes and on your city gates.

DEUTERONOMY 6:5–9 MSG

HONORING YOUR PARENTS

"Honor your father and your mother, so that you may live long in the land the LORD your God is giving you."

EXODUS 20:12 NIV

Grandchildren are the crowning glory of the aged; parents are the pride of their children.

PROVERBS 17:6 NLT

A wise child brings joy to a father; a foolish child brings grief to a mother.

PROVERBS 10:1 NLT

If anyone does not provide for his relatives, and especially for his immediate family, he has denied the faith and is worse than an unbeliever.

1 TIMOTHY 5:8 NIV

Anyone who steals from his father and mother and says, "What's wrong with that?" is no better than a murderer.

PROVERBS 28:24 NLT

ONE MOMENT AT A TIME
BE COMMITTED

1. **Get to know God's purity.** God will never lead you into justifying the use of pornography or enjoying sex outside of marriage. It's simply outside His character to do so.

2. **Put family first.** Focus on the needs of your family and children before focusing on the needs of your boss or employer.

3. **Build your marriage.** God's will is for you to have a healthy marriage and family. This requires an ongoing investment of your time and energy. Continually look for ways to deepen your relationship with your spouse. Find ways to grow together and protect your time as a couple.

CHAPTER 7

GOD'S WILL REGARDING DEALING WITH OTHERS

Forgiving my sister for the abuse she's heaped upon me has been difficult, but God keeps making it clear to me that I need to let go of my anger. While I've felt justified in holding on to my bitterness, I've come to realize that it's contrary to God's character. If He can forgive me for the multitude of sins I've committed against Him, surely I can forgive my sister for the comparatively few sins she's committed against me.

■ *Natasha, age 40, England* ■

LOVING OTHERS

" 'Love your neighbor as yourself.' There is no commandment greater than these."

MARK 12:31 NIV

No one has ever seen God; but if we love one another, God lives in us and his love is made complete in us.

1 JOHN 4:12 NIV

Dear children, let's not merely say that we love each other; let us show the truth by our actions.

1 JOHN 3:18 NLT

If I speak in the tongues of men and of angels, but have not love, I am only a resounding gong or a clanging cymbal. If I have the gift of prophecy and can fathom all mysteries and all knowledge, and if I have a faith that can move mountains, but have not love, I am nothing. If I give all I possess to the poor and surrender my body to the flames, but have not love, I gain nothing. Love is patient, love is kind. It does not envy, it does not boast, it is not proud. It is not rude, it is not self-seeking, it is not easily angered, it keeps no record of wrongs. Love does not delight in evil but rejoices with the truth. It always protects, always trusts, always hopes, always perseveres. Love never fails.

1 CORINTHIANS 13:1–8 NIV

Above all, clothe yourselves with love, which binds us all together in perfect harmony. And let the peace that comes from Christ rule in your hearts. For as members of one body you are called to live in peace. And always be thankful.

COLOSSIANS 3:14–15 NLT

My dear friends, we must love each other. Love comes from God, and when we love each other, it shows that we have been given new life. We are now God's children, and we know him.

1 JOHN 4:7 CEV

LIVING PEACEFULLY

Therefore let us pursue the things which make for peace and the things by which one may edify another.

ROMANS 14:19 NKJV

Work at living in peace with everyone, and work at living a holy life, for those who are not holy will not see the Lord.

HEBREWS 12:14 NLT

Blessed are the peacemakers, for they will be called sons of God.

MATTHEW 5:9 NIV

Anyone who loves to quarrel loves sin; anyone who trusts in high walls invites disaster.

PROVERBS 17:19 NLT

BEING FREE FROM ANGER

Let all bitterness and wrath and anger and clamor and slander be put away from you, along with all malice.

EPHESIANS 4:31 ESV

In your anger do not sin: Do not let the sun go down while you are still angry.

EPHESIANS 4:26 NIV

Human anger does not produce the righteousness God desires.

JAMES 1:20 NLT

Better to be patient than powerful; better to have self-control than to conquer a city.

PROVERBS 16:32 NLT

But now also put these things out of your life: anger, bad temper, doing or saying things to hurt others, and using evil words when you talk.

COLOSSIANS 3:8 NCV

"I'm telling you that anyone who is so much as angry with a brother or sister is guilty of murder. Carelessly call a brother 'idiot!' and you just might find yourself hauled into court. Thoughtlessly yell 'stupid!' at a sister and you are on the brink of hellfire. The simple moral fact is that words kill."

MATTHEW 5:22 MSG

FORGIVING OTHERS

"If you forgive those who sin against you, your heavenly Father will forgive you."

MATTHEW 6:14 NLT

"Pay attention to yourselves! If your brother sins, rebuke him, and if he repents, forgive him, and if he sins against you seven times in the day, and turns to you seven times, saying, 'I repent,' you must forgive him."

LUKE 17:3–4 ESV

45

Be kind and compassionate to one another, forgiving each other, just as in Christ God forgave you.

EPHESIANS 4:32 NIV

Then Peter came to Jesus and asked, "Lord, how many times shall I forgive my brother when he sins against me? Up to seven times?" Jesus answered, "I tell you, not seven times, but seventy-seven times."

MATTHEW 18:21–22 NIV

"But when you are praying, first forgive anyone you are holding a grudge against, so that your Father in heaven will forgive your sins, too."

MARK 11:25 NLT

God has chosen you and made you his holy people. He loves you. So you should always clothe yourselves with mercy, kindness, humility, gentleness, and patience. Bear with each other, and forgive each other. If someone does wrong to you, forgive that person because the Lord forgave you.

COLOSSIANS 3:12–13 NCV

"But love your enemies, do good to them, and lend to them without expecting to get anything back. Then your reward will be great, and you will be sons of the Most High, because he is kind to the ungrateful and wicked. Be merciful, just as your Father is merciful. "Do not judge, and you will not be judged. Do not condemn, and you will not be condemned. Forgive, and you will be forgiven. Give, and it will be given to you. A good measure, pressed down, shaken together and running over, will be poured into your lap. For with the measure you use, it will be measured to you."

LUKE 6:35–38 NIV

DISCIPLING EACH OTHER

As iron sharpens iron, so a friend sharpens a friend.

PROVERBS 27:17 NLT

Guide older men into lives of temperance, dignity, and wisdom, into healthy faith, love, and endurance. Guide older women into lives of reverence so they end up as neither gossips nor drunks, but models of goodness. By looking at them, the younger women will know how to love their husbands and children, be virtuous and pure, keep a good house, be good wives. We don't want anyone looking down on God's Message because of their behavior. Also, guide the young men to live disciplined lives.

TITUS 2:2–6 MSG

Bear one another's burdens, and so fulfill the law of Christ.

GALATIANS 6:2 ESV

Therefore encourage one another and build one another up, just as you are doing.

1 THESSALONIANS 5:11 ESV

It's better to have a partner than go it alone. Share the work, share the wealth. And if one falls down, the other helps, but if there's no one to help, tough!

ECCLESIASTES 4:9–10 MSG

My friends, we beg you to warn anyone who isn't living right. Encourage anyone who feels left out, help all who are weak, and be patient with everyone.

1 THESSALONIANS 5:14 CEV

You then, Timothy, my child, be strong in the grace we have in Christ Jesus. You should teach people whom you can trust the things you and many others have heard me say. Then they will be able to teach others.

2 TIMOTHY 2:1–2 NCV

ONE MOMENT AT A TIME
LIVING AT PEACE

1. **Live peacefully.** Hebrews 12:14 (NLT) reads, "Work at living in peace with everyone." While some people may be difficult to like or get along with, our call as Christians is to model peace to everyone.

2. **Look out for others.** Just as Christ came to serve and tell others about God's love and forgiveness, so we are called to represent Christ and carry that message to the world around us. Be on the lookout for ways to serve others.

3. **Forgive.** No matter how badly you've been hurt or how justified you feel in holding on to your bitterness, ask for God's help in extending forgiveness and moving on. If you choose not to forgive, bitterness will creep like a cancer into every area of your life.

CHAPTER 8

GOD'S WILL REGARDING YOUR CHARACTER

As a high school teacher at a Christian school, I enjoy working with kids who are concerned about finding God's will for their lives. Where should they go to college? Should they join the military? What career paths should they pursue? Many of them are consumed with God's plan for their futures. When they get fully worked up with these questions, I often tell them, "I can tell you with 100 percent certainty what God's plan for your life is." When they challenge me, I tell them the answer is simple: character. You want to know what God's will is for your life? It's to be a person with good character.

■ *Mitch, age 43, New York* ■

BEING FILLED WITH INTEGRITY

The integrity of the honest keeps them on track; the deviousness of crooks brings them to ruin.
PROVERBS 11:3 MSG

"I know, my God, that you test the heart and are pleased with integrity. All these things have I given willingly and with honest intent. And now I have seen with joy how willingly your people who are here have given to you."
1 CHRONICLES 29:17 NIV

"To the faithful you show yourself faithful; to those with integrity you show integrity."
2 SAMUEL 22:26 NLT

A good name is to be chosen rather than great riches, and favor is better than silver or gold.
PROVERBS 22:1 ESV

The man of integrity walks securely, but he who takes crooked paths will be found out.
PROVERBS 10:9 NIV

Better is a poor person who walks in his integrity than one who is crooked in speech and is a fool.
PROVERBS 19:1 ESV

RESISTING PRIDE

Pride goes before destruction, a haughty spirit before a fall.

PROVERBS 16:18 NIV

Too much pride can put you to shame. It's wiser to be humble.

PROVERBS 11:2 CEV

Too much pride causes trouble. Be sensible and take advice.

PROVERBS 13:10 CEV

To fear the LORD is to hate evil; I hate pride and arrogance, evil behavior and perverse speech.

PROVERBS 8:13 NIV

Always be humble and gentle. Be patient with each other, making allowance for each other's faults because of your love.

EPHESIANS 4:2 NLT

For by the grace given me I say to every one of you: Do not think of yourself more highly than you ought, but rather think of yourself with sober judgment, in accordance with the measure of faith God has given you.

ROMANS 12:3 NIV

One of Satan's angels was sent to make me suffer terribly, so that I would not feel too proud. Three times I begged the Lord to make this suffering go away. But he replied, "My kindness is all you need. My power is strongest when you are weak." So if Christ keeps giving me his power, I will gladly brag about how weak I am. Yes, I am glad to be weak or insulted or mistreated or to have troubles and sufferings, if it is for Christ. Because when I am weak, I am strong.

2 CORINTHIANS 12:7–10 CEV

Yes, all of you be submissive to one another, and be clothed with humility, for "God resists the proud, but gives grace to the humble." Therefore humble yourselves under the mighty hand of God, that He may exalt you in due time.

1 PETER 5:5–6 NKJV

This is what the LORD says: "The wise must not brag about their wisdom. The strong must not brag about their strength. The rich must not brag about their money. But if people want to brag, let them brag that they understand and know me. Let them brag that I am the LORD, and that I am kind and fair, and that I do things that are right on earth. This kind of bragging pleases me," says the LORD.

JEREMIAH 9:23–24 NCV

OVERCOMING TEMPTATION

The temptations in your life are no different from what others experience. And God is faithful. He will not allow the temptation to be more than you can stand. When you are tempted, he will show you a way out so that you can endure.

1 CORINTHIANS 10:13 NLT

Blessed is the man who perseveres under trial, because when he has stood the test, he will receive the crown of life that God has promised to those who love him. When tempted, no one should say, "God is tempting me." For God cannot be tempted by evil, nor does he tempt anyone.

JAMES 1:12–13 NIV

Dear brothers and sisters, when troubles come your way, consider it an opportunity for great joy. For you know that when your faith is tested, your endurance has a chance to grow.

JAMES 1:2–3 NLT

Finally, brothers, whatever is true, whatever is noble, whatever is right, whatever is pure, whatever is lovely, whatever is admirable—if anything is excellent or praiseworthy—think about such things.

PHILIPPIANS 4:8 NIV

Those who live according to the sinful nature have their minds set on what that nature desires; but those who live in accordance with the Spirit have their minds set on what the Spirit desires.

ROMANS 8:5 NIV

As obedient children, do not conform to the evil desires you had when you lived in ignorance.

1 PETER 1:14 NIV

For the grace of God that brings salvation has appeared to all men. It teaches us to say "No" to ungodliness and worldly passions, and to live self-controlled, upright and godly lives in this present age.

TITUS 2:11–12 NIV

ONE MOMENT AT A TIME
CHARACTER FIRST

1. **Have the proper focus.** Your life is not about what you do, but it's about who you are. Develop your character first and foremost.

2. **You are not the ultimate end.** God did not create the universe for you, but for Him. Work on developing your character so that you honor Him and worship Him with your life.

3. **Evaluate yourself.** Take an hour on a Sunday afternoon and ask God to help you evaluate areas of your character that need refinement. Choose one specifically and explore what the Bible says about it. Ask God to help you grow in this area.

CHAPTER 9

GOD'S WILL MAY BE PAINFUL

For a long time, I wanted to be doctor. I played with the toy medical kits as a kid and went off to college as a premed student. While I did pretty well, my MCAT scores were below average. And while I've sent many applications off to med schools, each has come back with a standard rejection letter. It's becoming fairly clear that God's plan for me is not what I had hoped it would be. Saying good-bye to my dream has been difficult, but I'm slowly working through it. While it still hurts, I realize that God has other plans for me, and because they're His plans, they're better.

■ *Lauren, age 26, Illinois* ■

TRUSTING THROUGH THE DISAPPOINTMENT

"Though he slay me, yet will I hope in him."

JOB 13:15 NIV

Listen to my cry for help, my King and my God, for I pray to no one but you.

PSALM 5:2 NLT

I'll never forget the trouble, the utter lostness, the taste of ashes, the poison I've swallowed. I remember it all—oh, how well I remember—the feeling of hitting the bottom. But there's one other thing I remember, and remembering, I keep a grip on hope: God's loyal love couldn't have run out, his merciful love couldn't have dried up.

LAMENTATIONS 3:19–22 MSG

Remember, it is better to suffer for doing good, if that is what God wants, than to suffer for doing wrong!

1 PETER 3:17 NLT

"You're blessed when you feel you've lost what is most dear to you. Only then can you be embraced by the One most dear to you."

MATTHEW 5:4 MSG

Taste and see that the LORD is good; blessed is the man who takes refuge in him.

PSALM 34:8 NIV

I learned God-worship when my pride was shattered. Heart-shattered lives ready for love don't for a moment escape God's notice.

PSALM 51:17 MSG

51

Do you not know? Have you not heard? The LORD is the everlasting God, the Creator of the ends of the earth. He will not grow tired or weary, and his understanding no one can fathom. He gives strength to the weary and increases the power of the weak. Even youths grow tired and weary, and young men stumble and fall; but those who hope in the LORD will renew their strength. They will soar on wings like eagles; they will run and not grow weary, they will walk and not be faint.

ISAIAH 40:28–31 NIV

Fig trees may no longer bloom, or vineyards produce grapes; olive trees may be fruitless, and harvest time a failure; sheep pens may be empty, and cattle stalls vacant—but I will still celebrate because the LORD God saves me. The LORD gives me strength. He makes my feet as sure as those of a deer, and he helps me stand on the mountains.

HABAKKUK 3:17–19 CEV

REFUSING TO ENVY OTHERS

Then I observed that most people are motivated to success because they envy their neighbors. But this, too, is meaningless—like chasing the wind.

ECCLESIASTES 4:4 NLT

You want what you don't have, so you scheme and kill to get it. You are jealous of what others have, but you can't get it, so you fight and wage war to take it away from them. Yet you don't have what you want because you don't ask God for it. And even when you ask, you don't get it because your motives are all wrong—you want only what will give you pleasure.

JAMES 4:2–3 NLT

"Resentment kills a fool, and envy slays the simple."

JOB 5:2 NIV

So put away all malice and all deceit and hypocrisy and envy and all slander.

1 PETER 2:1 ESV

It's healthy to be content, but envy can eat you up.

PROVERBS 14:30 CEV

SENSING GOD'S CARE WHEN DREAMS DISAPPEAR

The LORD is good to everyone. He showers compassion on all his creation. All of your works will thank you, LORD, and your faithful followers will praise you.

PSALM 145:9–10 NLT

Praise be to the God and Father of our Lord Jesus Christ, the Father of compassion and the God of all comfort, who comforts us in all our troubles, so that we can comfort those in any trouble with the comfort we ourselves have received from God. For just as the sufferings of Christ flow over into our lives, so also through Christ our comfort overflows.

2 CORINTHIANS 1:3–5 NIV

For the LORD your God is living among you. He is a mighty savior. He will take delight in you with gladness. With his love, he will calm all your fears. He will rejoice over you with joyful songs.

ZEPHANIAH 3:17 NLT

But Zion said, "I don't get it. God has left me. My Master has forgotten I even exist." [And God replied,] "Can a mother forget the infant at her breast, walk away from the baby she bore? But even if mothers forget, I'd never forget you—never. Look, I've written your names on the backs of my hands. The walls you're rebuilding are never out of my sight. Your builders are faster than your wreckers. The demolition crews are gone for good. Look up, look around, look well! See them all gathering, coming to you? As sure as I am the living God."

ISAIAH 49:14–18 MSG

"My covenant of blessing will never be broken," says the LORD, who has mercy on you.

ISAIAH 54:10 NLT

But you, O God, do see trouble and grief; you consider it to take it in hand. The victim commits himself to you; you are the helper of the fatherless.

PSALM 10:14 NIV

The LORD is like a father to his children, tender and compassionate to those who fear him.

PSALM 103:13 NLT

Pray that our LORD will make us strong and give us peace.

PSALM 29:11 CEV

God, high above, sees far below; no matter the distance, he knows everything about us.

PSALM 138:6 MSG

"And Solomon, my son, learn to know the God of your ancestors intimately. Worship and serve him with your whole heart and a willing mind. For the LORD sees every heart and knows every plan and thought. If you seek him, you will find him. But if you forsake him, he will reject you forever."

1 CHRONICLES 28:9 NLT

"Give ear and come to me; hear me, that your soul may live. I will make an everlasting covenant with you, my faithful love promised to David."

ISAIAH 55:3 NIV

"The God who made the world and everything in it is the Lord of heaven and earth and does not live in temples built by hands. And he is not served by human hands, as if he needed anything, because he himself gives all men life and breath and everything else. From one man he made every nation of men, that they should inhabit the whole earth; and he determined the times set for them and the exact places where they should live. God did this so that men would seek him and perhaps reach out for him and find him, though he is not far from each one of us."

ACTS 17:24–27 NIV

REMAINING CONTENT

Keep a sharp eye out for weeds of bitter discontent. A thistle or two gone to seed can ruin a whole garden in no time.

HEBREWS 12:15 MSG

"So do not worry, saying, 'What shall we eat?' or 'What shall we drink?' or 'What shall we wear?' For the pagans run after all these things, and your heavenly Father knows that you need them. But seek first his kingdom and his righteousness, and all these things will be given to you as well. Therefore do not worry about tomorrow, for tomorrow will worry about itself. Each day has enough trouble of its own."

MATTHEW 6:31–34 NIV

But if we have food and clothing, we will be content with that.

1 TIMOTHY 6:8 NIV

Unless the LORD builds the house, its builders labor in vain. . . . In vain you rise early and stay up late, toiling for food to eat—for he grants sleep to those he loves.

PSALM 127:1–2 NIV

I know what it is to be in need, and I know what it is to have plenty. I have learned the secret of being content in any and every situation, whether well fed or hungry, whether living in plenty or in want. I can do everything through him who gives me strength.

PHILIPPIANS 4:12–13 NIV

Yes, we should make the most of what God gives, both the bounty and the capacity to enjoy it, accepting what's given and delighting in the work. It's God's gift!

ECCLESIASTES 5:19 MSG

ONE MOMENT AT A TIME
FACING THE PAIN

1. **Admit the loss.** God is a caring Father who shows great compassion when the dreams of His children don't work out. You can pour out your pain to Him and know that He's listening.

2. **Find contentment.** While your plans may not line up with God's plans, you are still blessed. He has given you other gifts and opportunities that are yours to enjoy. Be sure to count those blessings and thank Him for them.

3. **Embrace God's plan.** When life takes an unexpected turn, you can embrace the change or get bogged down in disappointment. Don't let God-given opportunities pass by because you're too busy holding on to the wrong things.

CHAPTER 10

GOD'S WILL MAY INVOLVE RISK

Steps of faith can be scary, but I suppose that's why they require faith. When I felt led to change jobs, I was terrified. But as I read the Bible, I realized I was in good company. People like Abraham, Moses, and David all had great callings that began with scary steps of faith. God asked each one to leave a comfortable existence and follow His direction into a life filled with challenge and risk. But each also had the satisfaction of God's approval and reward. While I don't know how my next steps will turn out, I know that God's bigger than I can imagine and He'll protect me along the way.

■ *Nadia, age 42, Connecticut* ■

BEING BOLD

If any of you lacks wisdom, he should ask God, who gives generously to all without finding fault, and it will be given to him. But when he asks, he must believe and not doubt, because he who doubts is like a wave of the sea, blown and tossed by the wind.

JAMES 1:5–6 NIV

Don't worry about anything; instead, pray about everything. Tell God what you need, and thank him for all he has done.

PHILIPPIANS 4:6 NLT

So whenever we are in need, we should come bravely before the throne of our merciful God. There we will be treated with undeserved kindness, and we will find help.

HEBREWS 4:16 CEV

Be brave and strong! Don't be afraid. . . . The LORD your God will always be at your side, and he will never abandon you.

DEUTERONOMY 31:6 CEV

"Have I not commanded you? Be strong and courageous. Do not be terrified; do not be discouraged, for the LORD your God will be with you wherever you go."

JOSHUA 1:9 NIV

STEPPING OUT IN FAITH

Now unto him that is able to do exceeding abundantly above all that we ask or think, according to the power that worketh in us, unto him be glory in the church by Christ Jesus throughout all ages, world without end. Amen.

EPHESIANS 3:20–21 KJV

May the God of peace, who through the blood of the eternal covenant brought back from the dead our Lord Jesus, that great Shepherd of the sheep, equip you with everything good for doing his will, and may he work in us what is pleasing to him, through Jesus Christ, to whom be glory for ever and ever. Amen.

HEBREWS 13:20–21 NIV

But grow in the grace and knowledge of our Lord and Savior Jesus Christ. To him be glory both now and forever! Amen.

2 PETER 3:18 NIV

By faith Abraham, when called to go to a place he would later receive as his inheritance, obeyed and went, even though he did not know where he was going.

HEBREWS 11:8 NIV

It's impossible to please God apart from faith. And why? Because anyone who wants to approach God must believe both that he exists and that he cares enough to respond to those who seek him.

HEBREWS 11:6 MSG

PERSEVERING TO THE END

But you need to stick it out, staying with God's plan so you'll be there for the promised completion.

HEBREWS 10:36 MSG

Be careful about the way you live and about what you teach. Keep on doing this, and you will save not only yourself, but the people who hear you.

1 TIMOTHY 4:16 CEV

But I don't care what happens to me, as long as I finish the work that the Lord Jesus gave me to do.

ACTS 20:24 CEV

"To him who overcomes and does my will to the end, I will give authority over the nations."

REVELATION 2:26 NIV

Do you not know that in a race all the runners run, but only one gets the prize? Run in such a way as to get the prize.

1 CORINTHIANS 9:24 NIV

Epaphras, who is one of you and a servant of Christ Jesus, sends greetings. He is always wrestling in prayer for you, that you may stand firm in all the will of God, mature and fully assured.

COLOSSIANS 4:12 NIV

Those who live only to satisfy their own sinful nature will harvest decay and death from that sinful nature. But those who live to please the Spirit will harvest everlasting life from the Spirit. So let's not get tired of doing what is good. At just the right time we will reap a harvest of blessing if we don't give up.

GALATIANS 6:8–9 NLT

ONE MOMENT AT A TIME
TAKING A RISK

1. **Seek the greatest return.** It may always feel safer to stay put, but are there greater eternal returns for your gifts if you take the next step?

2. **You are called for God.** He has called you to serve Him. It is your job to go where He leads you and to love Him with all your heart, soul, mind, and strength.

3. **He never said it would be easy.** Faith requires stepping out in trust when you may not be able to orchestrate the outcome. The Bible is filled with stories of men and women who took difficult steps of faith that led them down a long and challenging road. But because they believed in the eternal rewards at the end of their journey, they stepped out anyway. They knew it was worth it.

WHAT THE BIBLE SAYS ABOUT EMOTIONS

INTRODUCTION

THE COLOR OF LIFE

Emotions give color to living. Everyday events become lasting memories based on the feelings they evoke in our hearts. Activities in themselves are just busyness—but the thrill and the pain of life drive us either to praise or to cry out to God. Through the highs and the lows—and the vast shades of emotion found in between—God draws us into a deeper appreciation of the life He's given us. Joys are sweeter when we have known pain; anguish hurts more if we have known true happiness. Taken together, this spectrum of emotion allows us to better understand ourselves, others, and God.

CHAPTER 1

EMOTIONS OF LOVE

My most precious memories and deepest joys revolve around the times
when I've given or received love. Of course, that includes romantic love—
but I'm also talking about the genuine affection and tender concern that
I've known in many of my relationships. Each time I find myself in the
middle of one of these love-filled moments, I feel so full of life—as though
I'm experiencing the true reason for living. I feel so connected to God
and to His love when I can see a glimpse of it reflected in His world.
I'm amazed when I stop to think that God could have created us with-
out emotions at all, yet He gave us something as precious as the ability
to love the way He's loved us.

■ *Samantha, age 46, Alabama* ■

AFFECTION

Don't just pretend to love others.
Really love them. Hate what is
wrong. Hold tightly to what is good.
Love each other with genuine affection, and take delight in honoring
each other.

ROMANS 12:9–10 NLT

Husbands, love your wives and do
not be harsh with them.

COLOSSIANS 3:19 NIV

For I have derived much joy and
comfort from your love, my brother,
because the hearts of the saints have
been refreshed through you.

PHILEMON 1:7 ESV

We loved you so much that we were
delighted to share with you not only
the gospel of God but our lives as
well, because you had become so
dear to us.

1 THESSALONIANS 2:8 NIV

CARING

Let's see how inventive we can be in
encouraging love and helping out.

HEBREWS 10:24 MSG

Be devoted to one another in brotherly love. Honor one another above
yourselves.

ROMANS 12:10 NIV

If anyone considers himself religious
and yet does not keep a tight rein

on his tongue, he deceives himself and his religion is worthless. Religion that God our Father accepts as pure and faultless is this: to look after orphans and widows in their distress and to keep oneself from being polluted by the world.

JAMES 1:26–27 NIV

Jesus replied: " 'Love the Lord your God with all your heart and with all your soul and with all your mind.' This is the first and greatest commandment. And the second is like it: 'Love your neighbor as yourself.' All the Law and the Prophets hang on these two commandments."

MATTHEW 22:37–40 NIV

It's better to have a partner than go it alone. Share the work, share the wealth. And if one falls down, the other helps, but if there's no one to help, tough! Two in a bed warm each other. Alone, you shiver all night. By yourself you're unprotected. With a friend you can face the worst. Can you round up a third? A three-stranded rope isn't easily snapped.

ECCLESIASTES 4:9–12 MSG

COMPASSION

Be kind and compassionate to one another, forgiving each other, just as in Christ God forgave you.

EPHESIANS 4:32 NIV

"Then the King will say to those on his right, 'Come, you who are blessed by my Father; take your inheritance, the kingdom prepared for you since the creation of the world. For I was hungry and you gave me something to eat, I was thirsty and you gave me something to drink, I was a stranger and you invited me in, I needed clothes and you clothed me, I was sick and you looked after me, I was in prison and you came to visit me.' . . . The King will reply, 'I tell you the truth, whatever you did for one of the least of these brothers of mine, you did for me.' "

MATTHEW 25:34–40 NIV

Bear with each other and forgive whatever grievances you may have against one another. Forgive as the Lord forgave you. And over all these virtues put on love, which binds them all together in perfect unity.

COLOSSIANS 3:13–14 NIV

But you, O God, do see trouble and grief; you consider it to take it in hand. The victim commits himself to you; you are the helper of the fatherless.

PSALM 10:14 NIV

A father to the fatherless, a defender of widows, is God in his holy dwelling.

PSALM 68:5 NIV

CONCERN

If there is a poor man among your brothers in any of the towns of the land that the LORD your God is giving you, do not be hardhearted or tightfisted toward your poor

61

brother. Rather be openhanded and freely lend him whatever he needs.

DEUTERONOMY 15:7–8 NIV

I'm glad in God, far happier than you would ever guess—happy that you're again showing such strong concern for me.

PHILIPPIANS 4:10 MSG

Share each other's burdens, and in this way obey the law of Christ.

GALATIANS 6:2 NLT

If one part of our body hurts, we hurt all over. If one part of our body is honored, the whole body will be happy.

1 CORINTHIANS 12:26 CEV

"Take my yoke upon you and learn from me, for I am gentle and humble in heart, and you will find rest for your souls. For my yoke is easy and my burden is light."

MATTHEW 11:29–30 NIV

LONGING

A cheerful look brings joy to the heart, and good news gives health to the bones.

PROVERBS 15:30 NIV

O LORD, be gracious to us; we long for you. Be our strength every morning, our salvation in time of distress.

ISAIAH 33:2 NIV

So it is right that I should feel as I do about all of you, for you have a special place in my heart. You share with me the special favor of God, both in my imprisonment and in defending and confirming the truth of the Good News.

PHILIPPIANS 1:7 NLT

Dear friends, I love you and long to see you. Please keep on being faithful to the Lord. You are my pride and joy.

PHILIPPIANS 4:1 CEV

LOVE

If I speak in the tongues of men and of angels, but have not love, I am only a resounding gong or a clanging cymbal. If I have the gift of prophecy and can fathom all mysteries and all knowledge, and if I have a faith that can move mountains, but have not love, I am nothing. If I give all I possess to the poor and surrender my body to the flames, but have not love, I gain nothing. Love is patient, love is kind. It does not envy, it does not boast, it is not proud. It is not rude, it is not self-seeking, it is not easily angered, it keeps no record of wrongs. Love does not delight in evil but rejoices with the truth. It always protects, always trusts, always hopes, always perseveres. Love never fails.

1 CORINTHIANS 13:1–8 NIV

One of the religion scholars came up. Hearing the lively exchanges of question and answer and seeing how sharp Jesus was in his answers, he put in his question: "Which is most important of all the commandments?" Jesus said, "The first in importance is, 'Listen, Israel: The Lord your God is one; so love the Lord God with all your passion and prayer and intelligence and energy.' And here is the second: 'Love others as well as you love yourself.' There is no other commandment that ranks with these."

MARK 12:28–31 MSG

Such love has no fear, because perfect love expels all fear. If we are afraid, it is for fear of punishment, and this shows that we have not fully experienced his perfect love.

1 JOHN 4:18 NLT

"Greater love has no one than this, that he lay down his life for his friends."

JOHN 15:13 NIV

Above all, clothe yourselves with love, which binds us all together in perfect harmony. And let the peace that comes from Christ rule in your hearts. For as members of one body you are called to live in peace. And always be thankful.

COLOSSIANS 3:14–15 NLT

TENDERNESS

Is there any encouragement from belonging to Christ? Any comfort from his love? Any fellowship together in the Spirit? Are your hearts tender and compassionate? Then

make me truly happy by agreeing wholeheartedly with each other, loving one another, and working together with one mind and purpose. Don't be selfish; don't try to impress others. Be humble, thinking of others as better than yourselves. Don't look out only for your own interests, but take an interest in others, too. You must have the same attitude that Christ Jesus had.

PHILIPPIANS 2:1–5 NLT

Finally, all of you should be of one mind. Sympathize with each other. Love each other as brothers and sisters. Be tenderhearted, and keep a humble attitude.

1 PETER 3:8 NLT

"Then the King will say, 'I'm telling the solemn truth: Whenever you did one of these things to someone overlooked or ignored, that was me—you did it to me.' "

MATTHEW 25:40 MSG

Since God chose you to be the holy people he loves, you must clothe yourselves with tenderhearted mercy, kindness, humility, gentleness, and patience.

COLOSSIANS 3:12 NLT

But the fruit of the Spirit is love, joy, peace, longsuffering, gentleness, goodness, faith, meekness, temperance: against such there is no law.

GALATIANS 5:22–23 KJV

ONE MOMENT AT A TIME
ENJOYING LOVE

1. **Celebrate friendship.** Genuine love is a hallmark of true friendships. Take time to savor this precious gift. Invite a friend to go to dinner or enjoy a weekend getaway. Let them know how much you value and appreciate the relationship that you share.

2. **Praise God.** God could have created people to be stoic and free of emotion. Instead, He's given us love partly so that we could better understand the love He has for us. Praise God for the love that He has shown you.

3. **Be an agent of care.** Almost everyone has something in their life that breaks their heart. For some, those moments are more regular and more present than for others. Look for someone who is in need of some love and concern and find a way to encourage that person today.

CHAPTER 2

EMOTIONS OF JOY

I feel bad for people who don't take time to enjoy life. So many of my friends are too busy with work and the other stresses of life that they don't stop to enjoy the great things that happen each day. I have a couple of friends, in fact, whom I haven't seen smile in a long time. It seems like when we get busy, the first thing to go is our joy. Somehow, I can't imagine that God intended for us to be so wrapped up in ourselves or our schedules that we can't take time to enjoy the life and world He's given us.

■ *Ji Sun, age 31, Oregon* ■

CHEERFULNESS

A happy heart makes the face cheerful, but heartache crushes the spirit.
PROVERBS 15:13 NIV

A cheerful disposition is good for your health; gloom and doom leave you bone-tired.
PROVERBS 17:22 MSG

O come, let us sing for joy to the LORD; let us shout joyfully to the rock of our salvation.
PSALM 95:1 NASB

Make a joyful noise to the LORD, all the earth; break forth into joyous song and sing praises!
PSALM 98:4 ESV

For the despondent, every day brings trouble; for the happy heart, life is a continual feast.
PROVERBS 15:15 NLT

So I commend the enjoyment of life, because nothing is better for a man under the sun than to eat and drink and be glad. Then joy will accompany him in his work all the days of the life God has given him under the sun.
ECCLESIASTES 8:15 NIV

And is there a man here who has planted a vineyard but hasn't yet enjoyed the grapes? Let him go home right now lest he die in battle and another man enjoy the grapes.
DEUTERONOMY 20:6 MSG

Nehemiah said, "Go and enjoy choice food and sweet drinks, and send some to those who have nothing prepared. This day is sacred to our Lord. Do not grieve, for the joy of the LORD is your strength."
NEHEMIAH 8:10 NIV

65

And it is a good thing to receive wealth from God and the good health to enjoy it. To enjoy your work and accept your lot in life—this is indeed a gift from God.

ECCLESIASTES 5:19 NLT

Even if you live a long time, don't take a single day for granted. Take delight in each light-filled hour, remembering that there will also be many dark days. And that most of what comes your way is smoke.

ECCLESIASTES 11:8 MSG

[God] richly gives us all we need for our enjoyment.

1 TIMOTHY 6:17 NLT

ENTHUSIASM

Never be lacking in zeal, but keep your spiritual fervor, serving the Lord.

ROMANS 12:11 NIV

Whatever your hand finds to do, do it with all your might; for there is no activity or planning or knowledge or wisdom in Sheol where you are going.

ECCLESIASTES 9:10 NASB

It is not good to have zeal without knowledge, nor to be hasty and miss the way.

PROVERBS 19:2 NIV

And whatever you do, whether in word or deed, do it all in the name of the Lord Jesus, giving thanks to God the Father through him.

COLOSSIANS 3:17 NIV

GRATITUDE

Give thanks in all circumstances, for this is God's will for you in Christ Jesus.

1 THESSALONIANS 5:18 NIV

Praise the LORD! Oh give thanks to the LORD, for he is good, for his steadfast love endures forever!

PSALM 106:1 ESV

Make thankfulness your sacrifice to God, and keep the vows you made to the Most High.

PSALM 50:14 NLT

What a beautiful thing, GOD, to give thanks, to sing an anthem to you, the High God!

PSALM 92:1 MSG

Let us come into his presence with thanksgiving; let us make a joyful noise to him with songs of praise! For the LORD is a great God, and a great King above all gods.

PSALM 95:2–3 ESV

Devote yourselves to prayer with an alert mind and a thankful heart.

COLOSSIANS 4:2 NLT

Sing to the LORD! Praise the LORD! For though I was poor and needy, he rescued me from my oppressors.

JEREMIAH 20:13 NLT

HAPPINESS

Let God All-Powerful be your silver
and gold, and you will find happiness by worshiping him.

JOB 22:25–26 CEV

May the LORD bless his people with
peace and happiness and let them
celebrate.

PSALM 64:10 CEV

Wisdom makes life pleasant and
leads us safely along. Wisdom is a
life-giving tree, the source of happiness for all who hold on to her.

PROVERBS 3:17–18 CEV

Is any one of you in trouble? He
should pray. Is anyone happy? Let
him sing songs of praise.

JAMES 5:13 NIV

You will come to know God
even better. His glorious power
will make you patient and strong
enough to endure anything, and
you will be truly happy.

COLOSSIANS 1:10–11 CEV

God's kingdom isn't about eating
and drinking. It is about pleasing
God, about living in peace, and
about true happiness. All this comes
from the Holy Spirit.

ROMANS 14:17 CEV

Happy are those who respect the
Lord, who want what he commands. Their descendants will be
powerful in the land; the children
of honest people will be blessed.

PSALM 112:1–2 NCV

I create light and darkness, happiness and sorrow. I, the LORD, do all
of this.

ISAIAH 45:7 CEV

Happy are those who don't listen
to the wicked, who don't go where
sinners go, who don't do what evil
people do. They love the LORD's
teachings, and they think about
those teachings day and night.

PSALM 1:1–2 NCV

HOPE

Happy is he who has the God of
Jacob for his help, whose hope is in
the LORD his God.

PSALM 146:5 NKJV

May your unfailing love rest upon
us, O LORD, even as we put our
hope in you.

PSALM 33:22 NIV

Why am I discouraged? Why is my
heart so sad? I will put my hope in
God! I will praise him again—my
Savior and my God!

PSALM 42:11 NLT

I wait for the LORD, my soul waits,
and in His word I do hope.

PSALM 130:5 NKJV

Praise be to the God and Father of
our Lord Jesus Christ! In his great
mercy he has given us new birth
into a living hope through the
resurrection of Jesus Christ from
the dead.

1 PETER 1:3 NIV

And this same God who takes care of me will supply all your needs from his glorious riches, which have been given to us in Christ Jesus.

PHILIPPIANS 4:19 NLT

For we know that when this earthly tent we live in is taken down (that is, when we die and leave this earthly body), we will have a house in heaven, an eternal body made for us by God himself and not by human hands.

2 CORINTHIANS 5:1 NLT

"For I know the plans I have for you," declares the LORD, "plans to prosper you and not to harm you, plans to give you hope and a future."

JEREMIAH 29:11 NIV

JOY

Be joyful in hope, patient in affliction, faithful in prayer.

ROMANS 12:12 NIV

You have put gladness in my heart, more than in the season that their grain and wine increased.

PSALM 4:7 NKJV

But the fruit of the Spirit is love, joy, peace, patience, kindness, goodness, faithfulness.

GALATIANS 5:22 NIV

Consider it pure joy, my brothers, whenever you face trials of many kinds, because you know that the testing of your faith develops perseverance. Perseverance must finish its work so that you may be mature and complete, not lacking anything.

JAMES 1:2–4 NIV

"Therefore you too have grief now; but I will see you again, and your heart will rejoice, and no one will take your joy away from you."

JOHN 16:22 NASB

Be full of joy in the Lord always. I will say again, be full of joy.

PHILIPPIANS 4:4 NCV

Though the fig tree does not bud and there are no grapes on the vines, though the olive crop fails and the fields produce no food, though there are no sheep in the pen and no cattle in the stalls, yet I will rejoice in the LORD, I will be joyful in God my Savior. The Sovereign LORD is my strength; he makes my feet like the feet of a deer, he enables me to go on the heights.

HABAKKUK 3:17–19 NIV

PLEASURE

A fool finds pleasure in evil conduct, but a man of understanding delights in wisdom.

PROVERBS 10:23 NIV

I will take pleasure in your laws and remember your words.

PSALM 119:16 CEV

Do not love this world nor the things it offers you, for when you love the world, you do not have the love of the Father in you. For the world offers only a craving for physical pleasure, a craving for everything we see, and pride in our achievements and possessions. These are not from the Father, but are from this world. And this world is fading away, along with everything that people crave. But anyone who does what pleases God will live forever.

1 JOHN 2:15–17 NLT

Seize life! . . . Oh yes—God takes pleasure in your pleasure! Dress festively every morning. Don't skimp on colors and scarves. . . . Each day is God's gift.

ECCLESIASTES 9:7–9 MSG

TRIUMPH

With God's help we will do mighty things, for he will trample down our foes.

PSALM 108:13 NLT

For the LORD your God is the one who goes with you to fight for you against your enemies to give you victory.

DEUTERONOMY 20:4 NIV

"O Lord, let your ear be attentive to the prayer of this your servant and to the prayer of your servants who delight in revering your name. Give your servant success today by granting him favor in the presence of this man."

NEHEMIAH 1:11 NIV

"You give me your shield of victory; you stoop down to make me great."

2 SAMUEL 22:36 NIV

With the LORD on my side, I will defeat all of my hateful enemies.

PSALM 118:7 CEV

I am grateful that God always makes it possible for Christ to lead us to victory. God also helps us spread the knowledge about Christ everywhere, and this knowledge is like the smell of perfume.

2 CORINTHIANS 2:14 CEV

Count on this: The wicked won't get off scot-free, and God's loyal people will triumph.

PROVERBS 11:21 MSG

The horse is made ready for the day of battle, but victory rests with the LORD.

PROVERBS 21:31 NIV

WONDER

Let all that I am praise the LORD. O LORD my God, how great you are! You are robed with honor and majesty. You are dressed in a robe of light. You stretch out the starry curtain of the heavens; you lay out the rafters of your home in the rain clouds. You make the clouds your chariot; you ride upon the wings of the wind. The winds are your messengers; flames of fire are your servants. . . .O LORD, what a variety of things you have made! In wisdom you have made them all. The earth is full of your creatures. Here is the ocean, vast and wide, teeming with life of every kind, both large and small.

PSALM 104:1–4, 24–25 NLT

O LORD, what is man that you care for him, the son of man that you think of him?

PSALM 144:3 NIV

"Who is like you, O LORD, among the gods? Who is like you, majestic in holiness, awesome in glorious deeds, doing wonders?"

EXODUS 15:11 ESV

LORD, I have heard of your fame; I stand in awe of your deeds, O LORD. Renew them in our day, in our time make them known; in wrath remember mercy.

HABAKKUK 3:2 NIV

Our LORD and Ruler, your name is wonderful everywhere on earth! You let your glory be seen in the heavens above. . . . I often think of the heavens your hands have made, and of the moon and stars you put in place. Then I ask, "Why do you care about us humans? Why are you concerned for us weaklings?" You made us a little lower than you yourself, and you have crowned us with glory and honor. You let us rule everything your hands have made. And you put all of it under our power—the sheep and the cattle, and every wild animal, the birds in the sky, the fish in the sea, and all ocean creatures. Our LORD and Ruler, your name is wonderful everywhere on earth!

PSALM 8:1–9 CEV

ONE MOMENT AT A TIME
SHARE THE JOY

1. **Volunteer.** There are plenty of places filled with hurting people that could use a warm smile. Volunteer at a nursing home or soup kitchen. Help out at a children's hospital. Connect with a prison chaplain and ask if there's an inmate who could use a visitor or letter.

2. **Be positive.** Many people live in a constant state of complaining. The weather is always wrong, the traffic too heavy, and the stores too crowded. Choose to look for the good in every situation, and allow your positive outlook to brighten up the world around you.

3. **Write your blessings down.** God's blessings can be seen in both the good and the hard times of life. Create a journal where you write down what you're thankful for each day. Some days this may be easier to do than others, but if you're looking for it, you'll see God's goodness no matter your circumstances. When you find yourself growing discouraged, look back through your journal and remember all the reasons you have to rejoice.

CHAPTER 3

EMOTIONS OF PEACE

I love rock climbing. It's hard work and can be dangerous. There's not a day of climbing that goes by where my muscles don't ache and my skin doesn't get scraped. But while there's some pain associated with the sport, there's nothing like the feeling you have when you stand on top of the rock you've conquered. You look down and think to yourself, I made it! The thrill of the relief and satisfaction make the temporary pain worthwhile.

■ *Ryan, age 27, Wyoming* ■

COMFORT

Praise be to the God and Father of our Lord Jesus Christ, the Father of compassion and the God of all comfort, who comforts us in all our troubles, so that we can comfort those in any trouble with the comfort we ourselves have received from God. For just as the sufferings of Christ flow over into our lives, so also through Christ our comfort overflows.

2 CORINTHIANS 1:3–5 NIV

For this is what the LORD says: . . . "As a mother comforts her child, so will I comfort you. . . ." When you see this, your heart will rejoice and you will flourish like grass; the hand of the LORD will be made known to his servants, but his fury will be shown to his foes.

ISAIAH 66:12–14 NIV

Even though I walk through the valley of the shadow of death, I will fear no evil, for you are with me; your rod and your staff, they comfort me.

PSALM 23:4 NIV

He comforts us in all our troubles so that we can comfort others. When they are troubled, we will be able to give them the same comfort God has given us.

2 CORINTHIANS 1:4 NLT

CONTENTMENT

Be still in the presence of the LORD, and wait patiently for him to act. Don't worry about evil people who prosper or fret about their wicked schemes. . . . It is better to be godly and have little than to be evil and rich.

PSALM 37:7, 16 NLT

"So do not worry, saying, 'What shall we eat?' or 'What shall we drink?' or 'What shall we wear?' For the pagans run after all these things, and your heavenly Father knows that you need them. But seek first his kingdom and his righteousness, and all these things will be given to you as well. Therefore do not worry about tomorrow, for tomorrow will worry about itself. Each day has enough trouble of its own."

MATTHEW 6:31–34 NIV

O God, I beg two favors from you; let me have them before I die. First, help me never to tell a lie. Second, give me neither poverty nor riches! Give me just enough to satisfy my needs. For if I grow rich, I may deny you and say, "Who is the LORD?" And if I am too poor, I may steal and thus insult God's holy name.

PROVERBS 30:7–9 NLT

I know what it is to be in need, and I know what it is to have plenty. I have learned the secret of being content in any and every situation, whether well fed or hungry, whether living in plenty or in want. I can do everything through him who gives me strength.

PHILIPPIANS 4:12–13 NIV

But if we have food and clothing, we will be content with that.

1 TIMOTHY 6:8 NIV

Yet true godliness with contentment is itself great wealth. After all, we brought nothing with us when we came into the world, and we can't take anything with us when we leave it.

1 TIMOTHY 6:6–7 NLT

PEACE

"I will heal my people and will let them enjoy abundant peace and security."

JEREMIAH 33:6 NIV

"I have told you these things, so that in me you may have peace. In this world you will have trouble. But take heart! I have overcome the world."

JOHN 16:33 NIV

Let the peace of Christ rule in your hearts, since as members of one body you were called to peace. And be thankful.

COLOSSIANS 3:15 NIV

"Peace I leave with you; my peace I give to you. Not as the world gives do I give to you. Let not your hearts be troubled, neither let them be afraid."

JOHN 14:27 ESV

You keep him in perfect peace whose mind is stayed on you, because he trusts in you. Trust in the LORD forever, for the LORD GOD is an everlasting rock.

ISAIAH 26:3–4 ESV

Pursue righteous living, faithfulness, love, and peace. Enjoy the companionship of those who call on the Lord with pure hearts.

2 TIMOTHY 2:22 NLT

"Though the mountains be shaken and the hills be removed, yet my unfailing love for you will not be shaken nor my covenant of peace be removed," says the LORD, who has compassion on you.

ISAIAH 54:10 NIV

"Be still, and know that I am God; I will be exalted among the nations, I will be exalted in the earth."

PSALM 46:10 NIV

Since everything around us is going to be destroyed like this, what holy and godly lives you should live, looking forward to the day of God and hurrying it along. On that day, he will set the heavens on fire, and the elements will melt away in the flames. But we are looking forward to the new heavens and new earth he has promised, a world filled with God's righteousness. And so, dear friends, while you are waiting for these things to happen, make every effort to be found living peaceful lives that are pure and blameless in his sight.

2 PETER 3:11–14 NLT

RELIEF

In my anguish I cried to the LORD, and he answered by setting me free.

PSALM 118:5 NIV

The LORD replied, "My Presence will go with you, and I will give you rest."

EXODUS 33:14 NIV

When I felt my feet slipping, you came with your love and kept me steady. And when I was burdened with worries, you comforted me and made me feel secure.

PSALM 94:18–19 CEV

Hear my prayer, O LORD; let my cry come to you! Do not hide your face from me in the day of my distress! Incline your ear to me; answer me speedily in the day when I call!

PSALM 102:1–2 ESV

I sought the LORD, and he answered me; he delivered me from all my fears.

PSALM 34:4 NIV

Blessed is the man you discipline, O LORD, the man you teach from your law; you grant him relief from days of trouble, till a pit is dug for the wicked.

PSALM 94:12–13 NIV

SATISFACTION

A man can do nothing better than to eat and drink and find satisfaction in his work. This too, I see, is from the hand of God.

ECCLESIASTES 2:24 NIV

Yes, we should make the most of what God gives, both the bounty and the capacity to enjoy it, accepting what's given and delighting in the work. It's God's gift!

ECCLESIASTES 5:19 MSG

Rejoice in the Lord always. I will say it again: Rejoice! Let your gentleness be evident to all. The Lord is near. Do not be anxious about anything, but in everything, by prayer and petition, with thanksgiving, present your requests to God. And the peace of God, which transcends all understanding, will guard your hearts and your minds in Christ Jesus.

PHILIPPIANS 4:4–7 NIV

Make it your ambition to lead a quiet life, to mind your own business and to work with your hands, just as we told you, so that your daily life may win the respect of outsiders and so that you will not be dependent on anybody.

1 THESSALONIANS 4:11–12 NIV

ONE MOMENT AT A TIME
BE SATISFIED

1. **Take time.** Sometimes we're so busy crossing tasks off our list that we don't take time to enjoy life along the way. If that's the case with you, slow down enough to appreciate the good things God's given you today.

2. **Savor the happy times.** Take your family or friends to dinner or enjoy a trip together. Like a runner who takes a victory lap at the end of a race, savor the moments together. Write a prayer of thanks to God for these special times.

3. **Create better habits.** While stress is a useful tool and strong motivator, you should not live a life filled with 24/7 stress. Before long, you'll find yourself burning out. Carve out intervals for rest. Set aside time to relax with the people you love. Building in breaks along the way will help you live with a healthier balance.

CHAPTER 4

EMOTIONS OF PASSION

Our passions are gifts that exist on a razor's edge. On one side is a healthy desire to get out of bed, conquer the world, and improve our lives. On the other side is a selfish ambition that consumes and can lead you to a path of sinful decisions. Passion unchecked can lead to unhealthy traits like greed, envy, or lust. Being able to distinguish between healthy motivation and sinful obsession is key to living a life that honors God.

■ *Trent, age 57, Tennessee* ■

AMBITION

In his heart a man plans his course, but the LORD determines his steps.
PROVERBS 16:9 NIV

Everything comes from the Lord. All things were made because of him and will return to him. Praise the Lord forever! Amen.
ROMANS 11:36 CEV

"I own the silver, I own the gold," decrees [God].
HAGGAI 2:8 MSG

The blessing of the LORD makes a person rich, and he adds no sorrow with it.
PROVERBS 10:22 NLT

The desires of good people lead straight to the best, but wicked ambition ends in angry frustration.
PROVERBS 11:23 MSG

"Submit to God and be at peace with him; in this way prosperity will come to you."
JOB 22:21 NIV

COURAGE

So whenever we are in need, we should come bravely before the throne of our merciful God. There we will be treated with undeserved kindness, and we will find help.
HEBREWS 4:16 CEV

Be brave and strong! Don't be afraid. . . . The LORD your God will always be at your side, and he will never abandon you.
DEUTERONOMY 31:6 CEV

The high and lofty one who lives in eternity, the Holy One, says this: "I live in the high and holy place with those whose spirits are contrite and humble. I restore the crushed spirit of the humble and revive the courage of those with repentant hearts."

ISAIAH 57:15 NLT

"Have I not commanded you? Be strong and courageous. Do not be terrified; do not be discouraged, for the LORD your God will be with you wherever you go."

JOSHUA 1:9 NIV

DESIRE

Instead, clothe yourself with the presence of the Lord Jesus Christ. And don't let yourself think about ways to indulge your evil desires.

ROMANS 13:14 NLT

Put to death, therefore, whatever belongs to your earthly nature: sexual immorality, impurity, lust, evil desires and greed, which is idolatry.

COLOSSIANS 3:5 NIV

For everything in the world—the cravings of sinful man, the lust of his eyes and the boasting of what he has and does—comes not from the Father but from the world.

1 JOHN 2:16 NIV

Think about the things of heaven, not the things of earth. For you died to this life, and your real life is hidden with Christ in God. And when Christ, who is your life, is revealed to the whole world, you will share in all his glory.

COLOSSIANS 3:2–4 NLT

The righteousness of the upright delivers them, but the unfaithful are trapped by evil desires.

PROVERBS 11:6 NIV

DETERMINATION

To this end we always pray for you, that our God may make you worthy of his calling and may fulfill every resolve for good and every work of faith by his power, so that the name of our Lord Jesus may be glorified in you, and you in him, according to the grace of our God and the Lord Jesus Christ.

2 THESSALONIANS 1:11–12 ESV

Therefore, I urge you, brothers, in view of God's mercy, to offer your bodies as living sacrifices, holy and pleasing to God—this is your spiritual act of worship. Do not conform any longer to the pattern of this world, but be transformed by the renewing of your mind. Then you will be able to test and approve what God's will is—his good, pleasing and perfect will.

ROMANS 12:1–2 NIV

"Suppose one of you wants to build a tower. Will he not first sit down and estimate the cost to see if he has enough money to complete it? For if he lays the foundation and is not able to finish it, everyone who sees it will ridicule him, saying, 'This fellow began to build and was not able to finish.' "

LUKE 14:28–30 NIV

Finishing is better than starting. Patience is better than pride.

ECCLESIASTES 7:8 NLT

God blesses those who patiently endure testing and temptation. Afterward they will receive the crown of life that God has promised to those who love him. And remember, when you are being tempted, do not say, "God is tempting me." God is never tempted to do wrong, and he never tempts anyone else.

JAMES 1:12–13 NLT

Because the Sovereign LORD helps me, I will not be disgraced. Therefore, I have set my face like a stone, determined to do his will. And I know that I will not be put to shame. He who gives me justice is near. Who will dare to bring charges against me now? Where are my accusers? Let them appear! See, the Sovereign LORD is on my side! Who will declare me guilty? All my enemies will be destroyed like old clothes that have been eaten by moths!

ISAIAH 50:7–9 NLT

ENVY

Then I observed that most people are motivated to success because they envy their neighbors. But this, too, is meaningless—like chasing the wind.

ECCLESIASTES 4:4 NLT

Whenever people are jealous or selfish, they cause trouble and do all sorts of cruel things.

JAMES 3:16 CEV

You want what you don't have, so you scheme and kill to get it. You are jealous of what others have, but you can't get it, so you fight and wage war to take it away from them. Yet you don't have what you want because you don't ask God for it. And even when you ask, you don't get it because your motives are all wrong—you want only what will give you pleasure.

JAMES 4:2–3 NLT

It's healthy to be content, but envy can eat you up.

PROVERBS 14:30 CEV

Let us not become conceited, provoking and envying each other.

GALATIANS 5:26 NIV

GREED

Greed causes fighting; trusting the LORD leads to prosperity.

PROVERBS 28:25 NLT

Whoever loves money never has money enough; whoever loves wealth is never satisfied with his income. This too is meaningless.

ECCLESIASTES 5:10 NIV

"Watch out! Be on your guard against all kinds of greed; a man's life does not consist in the abundance of his possessions."

LUKE 12:15 NIV

The trustworthy person will get a rich reward, but a person who wants quick riches will get into trouble.

PROVERBS 28:20 NLT

But people who long to be rich fall into temptation and are trapped by many foolish and harmful desires that plunge them into ruin and destruction.

1 TIMOTHY 6:9 NLT

INFATUATION

Above all else, guard your heart, for it is the wellspring of life.

PROVERBS 4:23 NIV

Do not lust in your heart after her beauty or let her captivate you with her eyes, for the prostitute reduces you to a loaf of bread, and the adulteress preys upon your very life. Can a man scoop fire into his lap without his clothes being burned? Can a man walk on hot coals without his feet being scorched? So is he who sleeps with another man's wife; no one who touches her will go unpunished.

PROVERBS 6:25–29 NIV

I saw some naive young men, and one in particular who lacked common sense. He was crossing the street near the house of an immoral woman, strolling down the path by her house. . . . She threw her arms around him and kissed him, and with a brazen look she said, ". . .Come, let's drink our fill of love until morning. Let's enjoy each other's caresses, for my husband is not home. He's away on a long trip. . . ." So she seduced him with her pretty speech and enticed him with her flattery. . . . He was like a bird flying into a snare, little knowing it would cost him his life. So listen to me, my sons, and pay attention to my words. Don't let your hearts stray away toward her. Don't wander down her wayward path. For she has been the ruin of many; many men have been her victims.

PROVERBS 7:7–8, 13, 18–19,21, 23–26 NLT

LUST

God has called us to live holy lives, not impure lives.

1 THESSALONIANS 4:7 NLT

"But I tell you that anyone who looks at a woman lustfully has already committed adultery with her in his heart."

MATTHEW 5:28 NIV

Let us behave decently, as in the daytime, not in orgies and drunkenness, not in sexual immorality and debauchery, not in dissension and jealousy.

ROMANS 13:13 NIV

Run from anything that stimulates youthful lusts. Instead, pursue righteous living, faithfulness, love, and peace.

2 TIMOTHY 2:22 NLT

Flee from sexual immorality. Every other sin a person commits is outside the body, but the sexually immoral person sins against his own body.

1 CORINTHIANS 6:18 ESV

Let there be no sexual immorality, impurity, or greed among you. Such sins have no place among God's people.

EPHESIANS 5:3 NLT

"I made a covenant with my eyes not to look lustfully at a girl."

JOB 31:1 NIV

PASSION

Don't you realize that your body is the temple of the Holy Spirit, who lives in you and was given to you by God? You do not belong to yourself, for God bought you with a high price. So you must honor God with your body.

1 CORINTHIANS 6:19–20 NLT

So whether you eat or drink or whatever you do, do it all for the glory of God.

1 CORINTHIANS 10:31 NIV

For the grace of God that brings salvation has appeared to all men. It teaches us to say "No" to ungodliness and worldly passions, and to live self-controlled, upright and godly lives in this present age.

TITUS 2:11–12 NIV

Delight yourself in the LORD and he will give you the desires of your heart.

PSALM 37:4 NIV

Place me like a seal over your heart, like a seal on your arm; for love is as strong as death, its jealousy unyielding as the grave. It burns like blazing fire, like a mighty flame. Many waters cannot quench love; rivers cannot wash it away. If one were to give all the wealth of his house for love, it would be utterly scorned.

SONG OF SOLOMON 8:6–7 NIV

PLAYFULNESS

There is a time for everything, and a season for every activity under heaven: a time to be born and a time to die, a time to plant and a time to uproot, a time to kill and a time to heal, a time to tear down and a time to build, a time to weep and a time to laugh, a time to mourn and a time to dance.

ECCLESIASTES 3:1–4 NIV

Relish life with the spouse you love each and every day of your precarious life. Each day is God's gift. It's all you get in exchange for the hard work of staying alive. Make the most of each one!

ECCLESIASTES 9:9 MSG

You who are young, make the most of your youth. Relish your youthful vigor. Follow the impulses of your heart. If something looks good to you, pursue it. But know also that not just anything goes; you have to

answer to God for every last bit of it.
ECCLESIASTES 11:9 MSG

On your feet now—applaud GOD!
Bring a gift of laughter, sing your-
selves into his presence.
PSALM 100:1 MSG

PRIDE

Too much pride causes trouble. Be
sensible and take advice.
PROVERBS 13:10 CEV

To fear the LORD is to hate evil;
I hate pride and arrogance, evil
behavior and perverse speech.
PROVERBS 8:13 NIV

Pride goes before destruction, a
haughty spirit before a fall.
PROVERBS 16:18 NIV

Too much pride can put you to
shame. It's wiser to be humble.
PROVERBS 11:2 CEV

ONE MOMENT AT A TIME
LIVING PASSIONATELY

1. **Separate the good from the bad.** Examine the desires you have and
evaluate where healthy desires may be crossing into destructive be-
haviors. Ask God to help you refocus your passions into channels that
honor Him.

2. **Enlist help.** Just sharing your struggles with someone who cares
will help you keep them in perspective. Share with a family member or
friend and ask them to hold you accountable so that you don't let areas
of weakness get the best of you.

3. **Memorize Romans 12:1–2.** Commit this verse to memory and then
determine to live it out. Every day you have the opportunity to choose
to offer your passions to God as an act of worship.

CHAPTER 5

EMOTIONS OF ANGER

*No one makes me as angry as my extended family! They set up unrea-
sonable expectations and hold me to standards that I have no way of
meeting. And sure enough, I feel the sting of their criticism when I don't
live up to what they have in mind. Hardly a week goes by when I'm not
given a guilt trip or a lecture letting me in on yet another way I've let
them down. Sometimes I just want to move out of state and get away
from this craziness—at least then the anger wouldn't come bubbling up
so quickly. But as soon as I start fantasizing about running away,
I realize that there must be a better way.*

■ *Shandrice, age 34, Connecticut* ■

ANGER

A gentle answer turns away wrath,
but a harsh word stirs up anger.
PROVERBS 15:1 NASB

"In your anger do not sin": Do not
let the sun go down while you are
still angry.
EPHESIANS 4:26 NIV

Human anger does not produce the
righteousness God desires.
JAMES 1:20 NLT

Don't befriend angry people or associate with hot-tempered people,
or you will learn to be like them
and endanger your soul.
PROVERBS 22:24–25 NLT

Better to be patient than powerful;

better to have self-control than to
conquer a city.
PROVERBS 16:32 NLT

Using good sense can put out the
flames of anger.
PROVERBS 29:8 CEV

BITTERNESS

Keep a sharp eye out for weeds of
bitter discontent. A thistle or two
gone to seed can ruin a whole garden in no time.
HEBREWS 12:15 MSG

Let all bitterness and wrath and
anger and clamor and slander be
put away from you, along with all
malice.
EPHESIANS 4:31 ESV

Above all else, guard your heart, for it is the wellspring of life.

PROVERBS 4:23 NIV

"But when you are praying, first forgive anyone you are holding a grudge against, so that your Father in heaven will forgive your sins, too."

MARK 11:25 NLT

Dear friends, let us continue to love one another, for love comes from God. Anyone who loves is a child of God and knows God. But anyone who does not love does not know God, for God is love.

1 JOHN 4:7–8 NLT

Be patient and trust the LORD. Don't let it bother you when all goes well for those who do sinful things. Don't be angry or furious. Anger can lead to sin.

PSALM 37:7–8 CEV

Then Peter came to Jesus and asked, "Lord, how many times shall I forgive my brother when he sins against me? Up to seven times?" Jesus answered, "I tell you, not seven times, but seventy-seven times."

MATTHEW 18:21–22 NIV

CONTEMPT

When wickedness arrives, shame's not far behind; contempt for life is contemptible.

PROVERBS 18:3 MSG

"But love your enemies, do good to them, and lend to them without

expecting to get anything back. Then your reward will be great, and you will be sons of the Most High, because he is kind to the ungrateful and wicked. Be merciful, just as your Father is merciful. Do not judge, and you will not be judged. Do not condemn, and you will not be condemned. Forgive, and you will be forgiven. Give, and it will be given to you. A good measure, pressed down, shaken together and running over, will be poured into your lap. For with the measure you use, it will be measured to you."

LUKE 6:35–38 NIV

"I'm telling you that anyone who is so much as angry with a brother or sister is guilty of murder. Carelessly call a brother 'idiot!' and you just might find yourself hauled into court. Thoughtlessly yell 'stupid!' at a sister and you are on the brink of hellfire. The simple moral fact is that words kill."

MATTHEW 5:22 MSG

FRUSTRATION

And he passed in front of Moses, proclaiming, "The LORD, the LORD, the compassionate and gracious God, slow to anger, abounding in love and faithfulness."

EXODUS 34:6 NIV

We grow weary in our present bodies, and we long to put on our heavenly bodies like new clothing . . . . While we live in these earthly bodies, we groan and sigh, but it's not that we want to die and get rid of these bodies that clothe us. Rather, we want to put on our new bodies so that these dying bodies will be swallowed up by life.

2 CORINTHIANS 5:2, 4 NLT

For the creation was subjected to frustration, not by its own choice, but by the will of the one who subjected it, in hope that the creation itself will be liberated from its bondage to decay and brought into the glorious freedom of the children of God. We know that the whole creation has been groaning as in the pains of childbirth right up to the present time. . . . In the same way, the Spirit helps us in our weakness. We do not know what we ought to pray for, but the Spirit himself intercedes for us with groans that words cannot express.

ROMANS 8:20–26 NIV

God, you're my last chance of the day. I spend the night on my knees before you. Put me on your salvation agenda; take notes on the trouble I'm in. I've had my fill of trouble; I'm camped on the edge of hell. I'm written off as a lost cause, one more statistic, a hopeless case. Abandoned as already dead, one more body in a stack of corpses, and not so much as a gravestone— I'm a black hole in oblivion. You've dropped me into a bottomless pit, sunk me in a pitch-black abyss. I'm battered senseless by your rage, relentlessly pounded by your waves of anger. You turned my friends against me, made me horrible to

them. I'm caught in a maze and can't find my way out, blinded by tears of pain and frustration.

PSALM 88:1–9 MSG

HATE

Only fools get angry quickly and hold a grudge.

ECCLESIASTES 7:9 CEV

But now you must stop doing such things. You must quit being angry, hateful, and evil. You must no longer say insulting or cruel things about others.

COLOSSIANS 3:8 CEV

Anyone who claims to be in the light but hates his brother is still in the darkness. Whoever loves his brother lives in the light, and there is nothing in him to make him stumble. But whoever hates his brother is in the darkness and walks around in the darkness; he does not know where he is going, because the darkness has blinded him.

1 JOHN 2:9–11 NIV

People may cover their hatred with pleasant words, but they're deceiving you. They pretend to be kind, but don't believe them. Their hearts are full of many evils. While their hatred may be concealed by trickery, their wrongdoing will be exposed in public.

PROVERBS 26:24–26 NLT

"Do not hate your brother in your heart. Rebuke your neighbor frankly

so you will not share in his guilt."
LEVITICUS 19:17 NIV

Bear with each other and forgive
whatever grievances you may have
against one another. Forgive as the
Lord forgave you.
COLOSSIANS 3:13 NIV

HOSTILITY

"Blessed are those who are persecuted because of righteousness, for
theirs is the kingdom of heaven.
Blessed are you when people insult
you, persecute you and falsely say
all kinds of evil against you because
of me. Rejoice and be glad, because
great is your reward in heaven, for
in the same way they persecuted the
prophets who were before you."
MATTHEW 5:10–12 NIV

Don't be angry or furious. Anger
can lead to sin.
PSALM 37:8 CEV

"But I tell you: Love your enemies
and pray for those who persecute
you."
MATTHEW 5:44 NIV

If you see your enemy hungry, go
buy him lunch; if he's thirsty, bring
him a drink. Your generosity will
surprise him with goodness, and
GOD will look after you.
PROVERBS 25:21–22 MSG

IRRITATION

Don't be quick to fly off the handle.
Anger boomerangs. You can spot a
fool by the lumps on his head.
ECCLESIASTES 7:9 MSG

Don't grumble against each other,
brothers, or you will be judged. The
Judge is standing at the door!
JAMES 5:9 NIV

Fools have short fuses and explode
all too quickly; the prudent quietly
shrug off insults.
PROVERBS 12:16 MSG

My dear brothers, take note of this:
Everyone should be quick to listen,
slow to speak and slow to become
angry.
JAMES 1:19 NIV

A hot-tempered person starts fights;
a cool-tempered person stops them.
PROVERBS 15:18 NLT

It makes a lot of sense to be a person of few words and to stay calm.
PROVERBS 17:27 CEV

VENGEFULNESS

Beloved, never avenge yourselves,
but leave it to the wrath of God, for
it is written, "Vengeance is mine,
I will repay, says the Lord." To the
contrary, "if your enemy is hungry,
feed him; if he is thirsty, give him
something to drink; for by so doing
you will heap burning coals on his
head." Do not be overcome by evil,

but overcome evil with good.

ROMANS 12:19–21 ESV

People insulted Christ, but he did not insult them in return. Christ suffered, but he did not threaten. He let God, the One who judges rightly, take care of him.

1 PETER 2:23 NCV

"You shall not take vengeance or bear a grudge against the sons of your own people, but you shall love your neighbor as yourself: I am the LORD."

LEVITICUS 19:18 ESV

Don't say, "I'll get even; I'll do to him what he did to me."

PROVERBS 24:29 NCV

Make sure that nobody pays back wrong for wrong, but always try to be kind to each other and to everyone else.

1 THESSALONIANS 5:15 NIV

It is a righteous thing with God to repay with tribulation those who trouble you.

2 THESSALONIANS 1:6 NKJV

For we know him that hath said, Vengeance belongeth unto me, I will recompense, saith the Lord.

HEBREWS 10:30 KJV

O LORD, the God of vengeance, O God of vengeance, let your glorious justice shine forth!

PSALM 94:1 NLT

ONE MOMENT AT A TIME
DEALING WITH ANGER

1. **Prepare to be provoked.** If certain people or situations set you off, then learn to anticipate those times. Prepare yourself in advance so that you don't find yourself giving in to anger so quickly.

2. **Don't assume the worst.** Once tensions are high, it's easy to read harsh motivations into every action or word. Try to take a step back and believe the best intentions of others.

3. **Don't be a casualty.** Living with chronic anger or bitterness creates an unexpected victim: you.

CHAPTER 6

EMOTIONS OF SADNESS

*I was unprepared for the flood of emotions that swept over me when
I lost my job. Before it happened, I thought my job was just a means
for income. But since I've been laid off, I've suffered from feelings of
rejection, discouragement, defeat, and shame. I don't even want to get
out of bed and look for a new job. Being crippled by my emotions is a
completely new experience for me. I feel like I'm drowning, and I'm not
sure how much longer I can keep my nose above water.*

■ *Quincy, age 41, Delaware* ■

BOREDOM

Go to work in the morning and
stick to it until evening without
watching the clock. You never know
from moment to moment how your
work will turn out in the end.

ECCLESIASTES 11:6 MSG

Lazy hands make a man poor, but
diligent hands bring wealth.

PROVERBS 10:4 NIV

In the name of the Lord Jesus
Christ, we command you, brothers, to keep away from every
brother who is idle and does not
live according to the teaching you
received from us.

2 THESSALONIANS 3:6 NIV

A shiftless man lives in a tumble-
down shack; a lazy woman ends up
with a leaky roof.

ECCLESIASTES 10:18 MSG

We urge you, brothers, warn those
who are idle, encourage the timid,
help the weak, be patient with
everyone.

1 THESSALONIANS 5:14 NIV

CONFUSION

"And you will know the truth, and
the truth will set you free."

JOHN 8:32 NLT

Direct my footsteps according to
your word; let no sin rule over me.

PSALM 119:133 NIV

Whether you turn to the right or to
the left, your ears will hear a voice
behind you, saying, "This is the
way; walk in it."

ISAIAH 30:21 NIV

Lead me in the right path, O LORD,
or my enemies will conquer me.

Make your way plain for me to
follow.

PSALM 5:8 NLT

For this God is our God for ever
and ever; he will be our guide even
to the end.

PSALM 48:14 NIV

Lady Wisdom goes to town, stands
in a prominent place, and invites
everyone within sound of her voice:
"Are you confused about life, don't
know what's going on? Come with
me, oh come, have dinner with me!
I've prepared a wonderful spread—
fresh-baked bread, roast lamb, carefully selected wines. Leave your im-
poverished confusion and live! Walk
up the street to a life with meaning."

PROVERBS 9:3–6 MSG

DEFEAT

Now to him who is able to keep
you from stumbling and to present
you blameless before the presence
of his glory with great joy, to the
only God, our Savior, through Jesus
Christ our Lord, be glory, majesty,
dominion, and authority, before all
time and now and forever. Amen.

JUDE 24–25 ESV

"The LORD himself will fight for
you. Just stay calm."

EXODUS 14:14 NLT

Trust in him at all times, O people;
pour out your hearts to him, for
God is our refuge.

PSALM 62:8 NIV

What, then, shall we say in response
to this? If God is for us, who can be
against us? He who did not spare
his own Son, but gave him up for
us all—how will he not also, along
with him, graciously give us all
things? Who will bring any charge
against those whom God has chosen? It is God who justifies. Who
is he that condemns? Christ Jesus,
who died—more than that, who
was raised to life—is at the right
hand of God and is also interceding
for us. Who shall separate us from
the love of Christ? Shall trouble or
hardship or persecution or famine
or nakedness or danger or sword? As
it is written: "For your sake we face
death all day long; we are considered as sheep to be slaughtered."
No, in all these things we are more
than conquerors through him who
loved us.

ROMANS 8:31–37 NIV

[God] redeems your life from the
pit and crowns you with love and
compassion.

PSALM 103:4 NIV

"For I know the plans I have for
you," declares the LORD, "plans
to prosper you and not to harm
you, plans to give you hope and a
future."

JEREMIAH 29:11 NIV

DEPRESSION

The LORD your God is with you, he
is mighty to save. He will take great
delight in you, he will quiet you

with his love, he will rejoice over you with singing.

ZEPHANIAH 3:17 NIV

I waited patiently for the LORD to help me, and he turned to me and heard my cry. He lifted me out of the pit of despair, out of the mud and the mire. He set my feet on solid ground and steadied me as I walked along.

PSALM 40:1–2 NLT

The LORD is close to the broken-hearted; he rescues those whose spirits are crushed.

PSALM 34:18 NLT

I lift my hands to you in prayer. I thirst for you as parched land thirsts for rain. Come quickly, LORD, and answer me, for my depression deepens. Don't turn away from me, or I will die. Let me hear of your unfailing love each morning, for I am trusting you. Show me where to walk, for I give myself to you.

PSALM 143:6–8 NLT

I have received such wonderful revelations from God. So to keep me from becoming proud, I was given a thorn in my flesh, a messenger from Satan to torment me and keep me from becoming proud. Three different times I begged the Lord to take it away. Each time he said, "My grace is all you need. My power works best in weakness." So now I am glad to boast about my weaknesses, so that the power of Christ can work through me.

2 CORINTHIANS 12:7–9 NLT

DISCOURAGEMENT

Why am I discouraged? Why am I restless? I trust you! And I will praise you again because you help me.

PSALM 42:5 CEV

"The LORD himself goes before you and will be with you; he will never leave you nor forsake you. Do not be afraid; do not be discouraged."

DEUTERONOMY 31:8 NIV

"Do not be afraid or discouraged because of this vast army. For the battle is not yours, but God's."

2 CHRONICLES 20:15 NIV

"You will not have to fight this battle. Take up your positions; stand firm and see the deliverance the LORD will give you, O Judah and Jerusalem. Do not be afraid; do not be discouraged. Go out to face them tomorrow, and the LORD will be with you."

2 CHRONICLES 20:17 NIV

He heals the brokenhearted and binds up their wounds.

PSALM 147:3 NIV

May our Lord Jesus Christ himself and God our Father, who loved us and by his grace gave us eternal encouragement and good hope, encourage your hearts and strengthen you in every good deed and word.

2 THESSALONIANS 2:16–17 NIV

EMBARRASSMENT

In you, O Lord, do I take refuge;
let me never be put to shame!

PSALM 71:1 ESV

He has never let you down, never
looked the other way when you
were being kicked around. He has
never wandered off to do his own
thing; he has been right there,
listening.

PSALM 22:24 MSG

For God gave us a spirit not of fear
but of power and love and self-
control.

2 TIMOTHY 1:7 ESV

Great is his faithfulness; his mercies begin afresh each morning.
I say to myself, "The Lord is my
inheritance; therefore, I will hope
in him!"

LAMENTATIONS 3:23–24 NLT

The Lord is good, a refuge in times
of trouble. He cares for those who
trust in him.

NAHUM 1:7 NIV

Let us fix our eyes on Jesus, the author and perfecter of our faith, who
for the joy set before him endured
the cross, scorning its shame, and
sat down at the right hand of the
throne of God. Consider him who
endured such opposition from sinful men, so that you will not grow
weary and lose heart.

HEBREWS 12:2–3 NIV

EMPTINESS

How great is the love the Father has
lavished on us, that we should be
called children of God! And that is
what we are! The reason the world
does not know us is that it did not
know him.

1 JOHN 3:1 NIV

How precious are your thoughts
about me, O God. They cannot be
numbered! I can't even count them;
they outnumber the grains of sand!
And when I wake up, you are still
with me!

PSALM 139:17–18 NLT

"What is the price of five sparrows—two copper coins? Yet God
does not forget a single one of them.
And the very hairs on your head are
all numbered. So don't be afraid;
you are more valuable to God than
a whole flock of sparrows."

LUKE 12:6–7 NLT

"The thief comes only to steal and
kill and destroy; I have come that
they may have life, and have it to
the full."

JOHN 10:10 NIV

For he will command his angels
concerning you to guard you in all
your ways.

PSALM 91:11 NIV

"Your Father knows exactly what
you need even before you ask him!"

MATTHEW 6:8 NLT

GRIEF

People are born for trouble as readily as sparks fly up from a fire.

JOB 5:7 NLT

I'm still in your presence, but you've taken my hand. You wisely and tenderly lead me, and then you bless me.

PSALM 73:23–24 MSG

"Naked I came from my mother's womb, and naked I will depart. The LORD gave and the LORD has taken away; may the name of the LORD be praised."

JOB 1:21 NIV

What I am saying, dear brothers and sisters, is that our physical bodies cannot inherit the Kingdom of God. These dying bodies cannot inherit what will last forever. But let me reveal to you a wonderful secret. We will not all die, but we will all be transformed! It will happen in a moment, in the blink of an eye, when the last trumpet is blown. For when the trumpet sounds, those who have died will be raised to live forever. And we who are living will also be transformed. For our dying bodies must be transformed into bodies that will never die; our mortal bodies must be transformed into immortal bodies. Then, when our dying bodies have been transformed into bodies that will never die, this Scripture will be fulfilled: "Death is swallowed up in victory. O death, where is your victory? O death, where is your sting?"

1 CORINTHIANS 15:50–55 NLT

My friends, we want you to understand how it will be for those followers who have already died. Then you won't grieve over them and be like people who don't have any hope. We believe that Jesus died and was raised to life. We also believe that when God brings Jesus back again, he will bring with him all who had faith in Jesus before they died.

1 THESSALONIANS 4:13–14 CEV

I saw a new heaven and a new earth. . . . I heard a loud voice shout from the throne: God's home is now with his people. He will live with them, and they will be his own. Yes, God will make his home among his people. He will wipe all tears from their eyes, and there will be no more death, suffering, crying, or pain. These things of the past are gone forever.

REVELATION 21:1–4 CEV

You don't need to cry anymore. The Lord is kind, and as soon as he hears your cries for help, he will come.

ISAIAH 30:19 CEV

GUILT

If we confess our sins, he is faithful and just and will forgive us our sins and purify us from all unrighteousness.

1 JOHN 1:9 NIV

"I—yes, I alone—will blot out your sins for my own sake and will never think of them again."

ISAIAH 43:25 NLT

91

Don't stay far away, LORD! My strength comes from you, so hurry and help. Rescue me from enemy swords and save me from those dogs. Don't let lions eat me. You rescued me from the horns of wild bulls.

PSALM 22:19–21 CEV

Anyone who belongs to Christ has become a new person. The old life is gone; a new life has begun! And all of this is a gift from God, who brought us back to himself through Christ. And God has given us this task of reconciling people to him. For God was in Christ, reconciling the world to himself, no longer counting people's sins against them. And he gave us this wonderful message of reconciliation. So we are Christ's ambassadors; God is making his appeal through us. We speak for Christ when we plead, "Come back to God!" For God made Christ, who never sinned, to be the offering for our sin, so that we could be made right with God through Christ.

2 CORINTHIANS 5:17–21 NLT

As far as the east is from the west, so far does he remove our transgressions from us.

PSALM 103:12 ESV

Therefore, there is now no condemnation for those who are in Christ Jesus, because through Christ Jesus the law of the Spirit of life set me free from the law of sin and death.

ROMANS 8:1–2 NIV

HOPELESSNESS

Being confident of this, that he who began a good work in you will carry it on to completion until the day of Christ Jesus.

PHILIPPIANS 1:6 NIV

LORD, you know the hopes of the helpless. Surely you will hear their cries and comfort them.

PSALM 10:17 NLT

"But I will restore you to health and heal your wounds," declares the LORD, "because you are called an outcast, Zion for whom no one cares."

JEREMIAH 30:17 NIV

Do you not know? Have you not heard? The LORD is the everlasting God, the Creator of the ends of the earth. He will not grow tired or weary, and his understanding no one can fathom. He gives strength to the weary and increases the power of the weak. Even youths grow tired and weary, and young men stumble and fall; but those who hope in the LORD will renew their strength. They will soar on wings like eagles; they will run and not grow weary, they will walk and not be faint.

ISAIAH 40:28–31 NIV

For our citizenship is in heaven, from which also we eagerly wait for a Savior, the Lord Jesus Christ.

PHILIPPIANS 3:20 NASB

For you have been my hope, O Sovereign LORD, my confidence since my youth.

PSALM 71:5 NIV

LONELINESS

The LORD your God will always be at your side, and he will never abandon you.

DEUTERONOMY 31:6 CEV

Turn to me and be gracious to me, for I am lonely and afflicted.

PSALM 25:16 NIV

Do you have any idea how very homesick we became for you, dear friends? Even though it hadn't been that long and it was only our bodies that were separated from you, not our hearts, we tried our very best to get back to see you.

1 THESSALONIANS 2:17 MSG

"Don't be afraid, I've redeemed you. I've called your name. You're mine. When you're in over your head, I'll be there with you. When you're in rough waters, you will not go down. When you're between a rock and a hard place, it won't be a dead end—because I am GOD, your personal God, the Holy of Israel, your Savior. I paid a huge price for you: all of Egypt, with rich Cush and Seba thrown in! That's how much you mean to me! That's how much I love you! I'd sell off the whole world to get you back, trade the creation just for you."

ISAIAH 43:1–4 MSG

God sets the lonely in families, he leads forth the prisoners with singing; but the rebellious live in a sun-scorched land.

PSALM 68:6 NIV

PAIN

I'll never forget the trouble, the utter lostness, the taste of ashes, the poison I've swallowed. I remember it all—oh, how well I remember—the feeling of hitting the bottom. But there's one other thing I remember, and remembering, I keep a grip on hope: God's loyal love couldn't have run out, his merciful love couldn't have dried up.

LAMENTATIONS 3:19–22 MSG

I learned God-worship when my pride was shattered. Heart-shattered lives ready for love don't for a moment escape God's notice.

PSALM 51:17 MSG

Because God's children are human beings—made of flesh and blood—the Son also became flesh and blood. For only as a human being could he die, and only by dying could he break the power of the devil, who had the power of death. Only in this way could he set free all who have lived their lives as slaves to the fear of dying. We also know that the Son did not come to help angels; he came to help the descendants of Abraham. Therefore, it was necessary for him to be made in every respect like us, his brothers and sisters, so that he could be our merciful and faithful High Priest before God. Then he could offer a sacrifice that would take away the sins of the people. Since he himself has gone through suffering and testing, he is able to help us when we are being tested.

HEBREWS 2:14–18 NLT

As a father has compassion on his children, so the LORD has compassion on those who fear him.

PSALM 103:13 NIV

Be merciful to me, LORD, for I am faint; O LORD, heal me, for my bones are in agony.

PSALM 6:2 NIV

"Though he slay me, yet will I hope in him."

JOB 13:15 NIV

For he has not ignored or belittled the suffering of the needy. He has not turned his back on them, but has listened to their cries for help.

PSALM 22:24 NLT

Pray that our LORD will make us strong and give us peace.

PSALM 29:11 CEV

You've kept track of my every toss and turn through the sleepless nights, each tear entered in your ledger, each ache written in your book.

PSALM 56:8 MSG

REJECTION

But Zion said, "I don't get it. God has left me. My Master has forgotten I even exist." [And God replied,] "Can a mother forget the infant at her breast, walk away from the baby she bore? But even if mothers forget, I'd never forget you—never. Look, I've written your names on the backs of my hands. The walls you're rebuilding are never out of my sight. Your builders are faster than your wreckers. The demolition crews are gone for good. Look up, look around, look well! See them all gathering, coming to you? As sure as I am the living God."

ISAIAH 49:14–16 MSG

God assured us, "I'll never let you down, never walk off and leave you."

HEBREWS 13:5 MSG

There are "friends" who destroy each other, but a real friend sticks closer than a brother.

PROVERBS 18:24 NLT

REMORSE

Godly sorrow brings repentance that leads to salvation and leaves no regret, but worldly sorrow brings death.

2 CORINTHIANS 7:10 NIV

Be strong and take heart, all you who hope in the LORD.

PSALM 31:24 NIV

He personally carried our sins in his body on the cross so that we can be dead to sin and live for what is right. By his wounds you are healed.

1 PETER 2:24 NLT

In him we have redemption through his blood, the forgiveness of sins, in accordance with the riches of God's grace that he lavished on us with all wisdom and understanding.

EPHESIANS 1:7–8 NIV

"Come now, let's settle this," says the LORD. "Though your sins are like scarlet, I will make them as white as snow. Though they are red like crimson, I will make them as white as wool."

ISAIAH 1:18 NLT

SADNESS

Praise be to the God and Father of our Lord Jesus Christ, the Father of compassion and the God of all comfort.

2 CORINTHIANS 1:3 NIV

For you, O LORD, have delivered my soul from death, my eyes from tears, my feet from stumbling.

PSALM 116:8 NIV

But you, O Sovereign LORD, deal well with me for your name's sake; out of the goodness of your love, deliver me. For I am poor and needy, and my heart is wounded within me.

PSALM 109:21–22 NIV

And now, God, do it again—bring rains to our drought-stricken lives. So those who planted their crops in despair will shout hurrahs at the harvest, so those who went off with heavy hearts will come home laughing, with armloads of blessing.

PSALM 126:4–6 MSG

The Sovereign LORD will wipe away the tears from all faces; he will remove the disgrace of his people from all the earth. The LORD has spoken.

ISAIAH 25:8 NIV

Bring joy to your servant, for to you, O Lord, I lift up my soul.

PSALM 86:4 NIV

SHAME

"You're blessed when you feel you've lost what is most dear to you. Only then can you be embraced by the One most dear to you."

MATTHEW 5:4 MSG

On that day you will be glad, even if you have to go through many hard trials for a while. Your faith will be like gold that has been tested in a fire. And these trials will prove that your faith is worth much more than gold that can be destroyed. They will show that you will be given praise and honor and glory when Jesus Christ returns. You have never seen Jesus, and you don't see him now. But still you love him and have faith in him, and no words can tell how glad and happy you are to be saved. That's why you have faith.

1 PETER 1:6–9 CEV

"Do not be afraid; you will not suffer shame. Do not fear disgrace; you will not be humiliated. You will forget the shame of your youth and remember no more the reproach of your widowhood."

ISAIAH 54:4 NIV

I call as my heart grows faint; lead me to the rock that is higher than I. For you have been my refuge, a strong tower against the foe.

PSALM 61:2–3 NIV

I have stuck unto thy testimonies: O LORD, put me not to shame.

PSALM 119:31 KJV

Yea, let none that wait on thee be ashamed: let them be ashamed which transgress without cause.

PSALM 25:3 KJV

ONE MOMENT AT A TIME
KNOWING PAIN

1. **Get support.** Pain is an emotion that shouldn't be held privately. Find a friend or a family member who can share your burden and help you through the difficult days. If you can't find the help you need or feel like you're in too deep to get out, meet with a counselor who can help you work through what you're feeling.

2. **Recognize the loss.** When you've experienced a loss, the swirl of complicating emotions can surprise you. Get on top of them again by recognizing what you're feeling. Write down each emotion and identify the different facets of this situation that make you feel so bad.

3. **Don't be crippled.** Times of grief are normal and expected, but once you've grieved appropriately it's important that you take steps to move on with the life God has given you.

CHAPTER 7

EMOTIONS OF FEAR

I know that most karaoke singing sounds bad. And believe me, I'm not so deaf as to think that my own is any better than anyone else's. But a few years ago when the karaoke craze was taking off, I forced myself to do it. It wasn't because I dreamt of being a rock star or fantasized about making my own music video; the truth is that crowds terrified me, and I've always been terribly self-conscious of my voice. I did it because I was tired of my fears conquering me. Though it seemed like a small thing at the time, it proved to be a turning point for me. It showed me that I don't have to be ruled by my fear, and it's given me the courage to step out of its grip.

■ *Julie, age 47, Wisconsin* ■

ANXIETY

Do not be anxious about anything, but in everything, by prayer and petition, with thanksgiving, present your requests to God. And the peace of God, which transcends all understanding, will guard your hearts and your minds in Christ Jesus.

PHILIPPIANS 4:6–7 NIV

God cares for you, so turn all your worries over to him.

1 PETER 5:7 CEV

"Can all your worries add a single moment to your life? And if worry can't accomplish a little thing like that, what's the use of worrying over bigger things?"

LUKE 12:25–26 NLT

"Come to me, all you who are weary and burdened, and I will give you rest."

MATTHEW 11:28 NIV

Let the LORD lead you and trust him to help.

PSALM 37:5 CEV

DENIAL

"Should God then reward you on your terms, when you refuse to repent? You must decide, not I; so tell me what you know."

JOB 34:33 NIV

Your Majesty, please be willing to do what I say. Turn from your sins and start living right; have mercy on those who are mistreated. Then all will go well with you for a long time.

DANIEL 4:27 CEV

Do not be hardhearted or tight-fisted toward your poor brother.

DEUTERONOMY 15:7 NIV

Don't be stubborn! Don't rebel like those people who were tested in the desert.

HEBREWS 3:8 CEV

Do not think of yourself more highly than you ought, but rather think of yourself with sober judgment, in accordance with the measure of faith God has given you.

ROMANS 12:3 NIV

DISTRESS

I was in terrible trouble when I called out to you, but from your temple you heard me and answered my prayer.

2 SAMUEL 22:7 CEV

I am in pain and distress; may your salvation, O God, protect me.

PSALM 69:29 NIV

Consider my affliction and my trouble, and forgive all my sins.

PSALM 25:18 ESV

I call on the LORD in my distress, and he answers me.

PSALM 120:1 NIV

Be kind to me, God—I'm in deep, deep trouble again. I've cried my

eyes out; I feel hollow inside.

PSALM 31:9 MSG

FEAR

Say to those with anxious heart, "Take courage, fear not. Behold, your God will come with vengeance; the recompense of God will come, but He will save you."

ISAIAH 35:4 NASB

There is no fear in love. But perfect love drives out fear, because fear has to do with punishment. The one who fears is not made perfect in love.

1 JOHN 4:18 NIV

"My Spirit remains among you. Do not fear."

HAGGAI 2:5 NIV

But now, this is what the LORD says—he who created you, O Jacob, he who formed you, O Israel: "Fear not, for I have redeemed you; I have summoned you by name; you are mine."

ISAIAH 43:1 NIV

INSECURITY

I praise you because I am fearfully and wonderfully made; your works are wonderful, I know that full well.

PSALM 139:14 NIV

Therefore, if anyone is in Christ, he is a new creation; the old has gone, the new has come!

2 CORINTHIANS 5:17 NIV

He gave his life to free us from every kind of sin, to cleanse us, and to make us his very own people, totally committed to doing good deeds.

TITUS 2:14 NLT

Before I shaped you in the womb, I knew all about you. Before you saw the light of day, I had holy plans for you: A prophet to the nations— that's what I had in mind for you.

JEREMIAH 1:5 MSG

The Spirit has given each of us a special way of serving others.

1 CORINTHIANS 12:7 CEV

LAZINESS

If a man is lazy, the rafters sag; if his hands are idle, the house leaks.

ECCLESIASTES 10:18 NIV

Sloth makes you poor; diligence brings wealth.

PROVERBS 10:4 MSG

The lazy man does not roast his game, but the diligent man prizes his possessions.

PROVERBS 12:27 NIV

The sluggard buries his hand in the dish; it wears him out to bring it back to his mouth.

PROVERBS 26:15 ESV

We do not want you to become lazy, but to imitate those who through faith and patience inherit what has been promised.

HEBREWS 6:12 NIV

All hard work brings a profit, but mere talk leads only to poverty.

PROVERBS 14:23 NIV

NERVOUSNESS

Trust in the LORD with all your heart and lean not on your own understanding; in all your ways acknowledge him, and he will make your paths straight.

PROVERBS 3:5–6 NIV

Even strong young lions sometimes go hungry, but those who trust in the LORD will lack no good thing.

PSALM 34:10 NLT

The fear of human opinion disables; trusting in God protects you from that.

PROVERBS 29:25 MSG

For God did not give us a spirit of timidity, but a spirit of power, of love and of self-discipline.

2 TIMOTHY 1:7 NIV

PANIC

"And if God cares so wonderfully for flowers that are here today and thrown into the fire tomorrow, he will certainly care for you. Why do you have so little faith?"

LUKE 12:28 NLT

I, your God, have a firm grip on you and I'm not letting go. I'm telling you, "Don't panic. I'm right here to help you."

ISAIAH 41:13 MSG

The angel of the LORD encamps around those who fear him, and delivers them.

PSALM 34:7 ESV

"I am with you and will watch over you wherever you go, and I will bring you back to this land. I will not leave you until I have done what I have promised you."

GENESIS 28:15 NIV

You, LORD, are the light that keeps me safe. I am not afraid of anyone. You protect me, and I have no fears.

PSALM 27:1 CEV

Only God can save me, and I calmly wait for him. God alone is the mighty rock that keeps me safe and the fortress where I am secure.

PSALM 62:1-2 CEV

God is there, ready to help; I'm fearless no matter what. Who or what can get to me?

HEBREWS 13:6 MSG

My flesh and my heart fail; but God is the strength of my heart and my portion forever.

PSALM 73:26 NKJV

Fear and trembling have beset me; horror has overwhelmed me. . . . But I call to God, and the LORD saves me.

PSALM 55:5, 16 NIV

The LORD is my shepherd, I shall not be in want. He makes me lie down in green pastures, he leads me beside quiet waters, he restores my soul. He guides me in paths of righteousness for his name's sake.

PSALM 23:1-3 NIV

SHOCK

Pile your troubles on GOD's shoulders—he'll carry your load, he'll help you out. He'll never let good people topple into ruin.

PSALM 55:22 MSG

God is our refuge and strength, an ever-present help in trouble. Therefore we will not fear, though the earth give way and the mountains fall into the heart of the sea, though its waters roar and foam and the mountains quake with their surging.

PSALM 46:1-3 NIV

ONE MOMENT AT A TIME
OVERCOMING FEAR

1. **Don't obsess.** Refuse to let fear rule over you. If something is bothering you, either meet it head-on or move on to something else. Don't let fear paralyze you.

2. **Surround yourself with good friends.** Some fears are good and will help you steer clear of situations you should avoid. But some fears are irrational, and good friends can give you a loving push to conquer them.

3. **Try something new.** What would be a healthy fear for you to learn to overcome? Try something new that might be difficult for you. Are you afraid of being in front of a crowd? Find an occasion to give a short speech. Was there a falling out with an old friend? Find a way to reconnect and reconcile. Start with finding small ways to overcome some of the fears you may have.

WHAT THE BIBLE SAYS ABOUT GRIEVING

INTRODUCTION

UNINVITED GRIEF

The heartache of grief can come from many places: a death, a divorce, or even the loss of a dream. These losses can cause tremendous disappointment and pain. And while these dark valleys change our lives forever, we are not meant to wallow in a state of endless depression. Instead, the process of grieving can keep us from becoming permanently crippled by loss, helping us to continue to walk through it.

Counselors have identified five stages of grief: (1) denial, (2) anger, (3) guilt, (4) depression, and (5) acceptance. Each stage represents a natural response to loss. People who are grieving will work through these stages in their own order and on their own timetable. While this book is not a road map through these stages, it does contain verses that can strengthen your spirit as you experience this difficult time. Turn the pages of this book and begin to find ways God's Word can be a salve to your wounded spirit.

CHAPTER 1

YOU'RE NOT ALONE

I sat numbly at my husband's graveside and wished for the pain to go away. I wanted so badly to share the heartache with my best friend. But that friend now lay lifeless, unable to listen or respond to the pain his death had caused me. He had left this life without a final good-bye, and I just wasn't ready to part ways. I had much more to tell him, and we had much more life to share. In the days to come, it meant so much to have other people around. And while they couldn't take away the pain, it was nice to have people nearby even if they were only able to listen, hug, and cry along with me.

■ *Stacey, age 42, Minnesota* ■

BELIEVING IN A GOD WHO CARES

You don't need to cry anymore. The LORD is kind, and as soon as he hears your cries for help, he will come.

ISAIAH 30:19 CEV

For this is what the high and lofty One says—he who lives forever, whose name is holy: "I live in a high and holy place, but also with him who is contrite and lowly in spirit, to revive the spirit of the lowly and to revive the heart of the contrite."

ISAIAH 57:15 NIV

You notice everything I do and everywhere I go.

PSALM 139:3 CEV

GOD keeps an eye on his friends, his ears pick up every moan and groan.

PSALM 34:15 MSG

He reached down from on high and took hold of me; he drew me out of deep waters.

PSALM 18:16 NIV

I'm still in your presence, but you've taken my hand. You wisely and tenderly lead me, and then you bless me.

PSALM 73:23–24 MSG

Come near to God and he will come near to you.

JAMES 4:8 NIV

The beloved of the LORD rests in safety—the High God surrounds him all day long—the beloved rests

103

between his shoulders.

DEUTERONOMY 33:12 NRSV

"The young women will dance for joy, and the men—old and young—will join in the celebration. I will turn their mourning into joy. I will comfort them and exchange their sorrow for rejoicing."

JEREMIAH 31:13 NLT

Whom have I in heaven but you? And earth has nothing I desire besides you.

PSALM 73:25 NIV

FOLLOWING A GOD WHO KNOWS YOUR PAIN

"Though he slay me, yet will I hope in him."

JOB 13:15 NIV

Praise be to the God and Father of our Lord Jesus Christ, the Father of compassion and the God of all comfort, who comforts us in all our troubles, so that we can comfort those in any trouble with the comfort we ourselves have received from God. For just as the sufferings of Christ flow over into our lives, so also through Christ our comfort overflows.

2 CORINTHIANS 1:3–5 NIV

Because God's children are human beings—made of flesh and blood—the Son also became flesh and blood. For only as a human being could he die, and only by

dying could he break the power of the devil, who had the power of death. Only in this way could he set free all who have lived their lives as slaves to the fear of dying. We also know that the Son did not come to help angels; he came to help the descendants of Abraham. Therefore, it was necessary for him to be made in every respect like us, his brothers and sisters, so that he could be our merciful and faithful High Priest before God. Then he could offer a sacrifice that would take away the sins of the people. Since he himself has gone through suffering and testing, he is able to help us when we are being tested.

HEBREWS 2:14–18 NLT

Therefore he is able to save completely those who come to God through him, because he always lives to intercede for them.

HEBREWS 7:25 NIV

He was despised and rejected by men, a man of sorrows, and familiar with suffering. Like one from whom men hide their faces he was despised, and we esteemed him not.

ISAIAH 53:3 NIV

CRYING OUT TO GOD

"Until now you have not asked for anything in my name. Ask and you will receive, and your joy will be complete."

JOHN 16:24 NIV

"Which of you, if his son asks for bread, will give him a stone? Or if he asks for a fish, will give him a snake? If you, then, though you are evil, know how to give good gifts to your children, how much more will your Father in heaven give good gifts to those who ask him!"

MATTHEW 7:9–11 NIV

"And if God cares so wonderfully for flowers that are here today and thrown into the fire tomorrow, he will certainly care for you. Why do you have so little faith?"

LUKE 12:28 NLT

And we are confident that he hears us whenever we ask for anything that pleases him. And since we know he hears us when we make our requests, we also know that he will give us what we ask for.

1 JOHN 5:14–15 NLT

God. . .richly gives us all we need for our enjoyment.

1 TIMOTHY 6:17 NLT

You want something you don't have, and you will do anything to get it. You will even kill! But you still cannot get what you want, and you won't get it by fighting and arguing. You should pray for it. Yet even when you do pray, your prayers are not answered, because you pray just for selfish reasons.

JAMES 4:2–3 CEV

Every good and perfect gift is from above, coming down from the Father of the heavenly lights, who does not change like shifting shadows.

JAMES 1:17 NIV

"I know what I'm doing. I have it all planned out—plans to take care of you, not abandon you, plans to give you the future you hope for."

JEREMIAH 29:11 MSG

Praise be to the Lord, to God our Savior, who daily bears our burdens.

PSALM 68:19 NIV

Pile your troubles on GOD's shoulders—he'll carry your load, he'll help you out. He'll never let good people topple into ruin.

PSALM 55:22 MSG

FINDING SAFETY WITH HIM

"I, your GOD, have a firm grip on you and I'm not letting go. I'm telling you, 'Don't panic. I'm right here to help you.' "

ISAIAH 41:13 MSG

"Don't be afraid, for I am with you. Don't be discouraged, for I am your God. I will strengthen you and help you. I will hold you up with my victorious right hand."

ISAIAH 41:10 NLT

You hear, O LORD, the desire of the afflicted; you encourage them, and you listen to their cry.

PSALM 10:17 NIV

The angel of the LORD encamps around those who fear him, and delivers them.

PSALM 34:7 ESV

105

"Have I not commanded you? Be strong and courageous. Do not be terrified; do not be discouraged, for the LORD your God will be with you wherever you go."

JOSHUA 1:9 NIV

You have allowed me to suffer much hardship, but you will restore me to life again and lift me up from the depths of the earth.

PSALM 71:20 NLT

God is our refuge and strength, an ever-present help in trouble. Therefore we will not fear, though the earth give way and the mountains fall into the heart of the sea, though its waters roar and foam and the mountains quake with their surging.

PSALM 46:1–3 NIV

ALLOWING FRIENDS TO CARE

Bear one another's burdens, and so fulfill the law of Christ.

GALATIANS 6:2 ESV

It's better to have a partner than go it alone. Share the work, share the wealth. And if one falls down, the other helps, but if there's no one to help, tough! Two in a bed warm each other. Alone, you shiver all night. By yourself you're unprotected. With a friend you can face the worst. Can you round up a third? A three-stranded rope isn't easily snapped.

ECCLESIASTES 4:9–12 MSG

Jesus answered: Love the Lord your God with all your heart, soul, and mind. This is the first and most important commandment. The second most important commandment is like this one. And it is, "Love others as much as you love yourself." All the Law of Moses and the Books of the Prophets are based on these two commandments.

MATTHEW 22:37–40 CEV

God put our bodies together in such a way that even the parts that seem the least important are valuable. He did this to make all parts of the body work together smoothly, with each part caring about the others. If one part of our body hurts, we hurt all over. If one part of our body is honored, the whole body will be happy.

1 CORINTHIANS 12:24–26 CEV

JOINING THE UNIVERSAL EXPERIENCE

"People are born for trouble as readily as sparks fly up from a fire."

JOB 5:7 NLT

"How frail is humanity! How short is life, how full of trouble!"

JOB 14:1 NLT

So what do people get in this life for all their hard work and anxiety?

ECCLESIASTES 2:22 NLT

We all come to the end of our lives as naked and empty-handed as on the day we were born. We can't take our riches with us. And this, too, is a very serious problem. People leave this world no better off than when they came. All their hard work is for nothing—like working for the wind. Throughout their lives, they live under a cloud—frustrated, discouraged, and angry.

ECCLESIASTES 5:15–17 NLT

"Naked I came from my mother's womb, and naked I will depart. The LORD gave and the LORD has taken away; may the name of the LORD be praised."

JOB 1:21 NIV

Yet you brought me out of the womb; you made me trust in you even at my mother's breast. From birth I was cast upon you; from my mother's womb you have been my God. Do not be far from me, for trouble is near and there is no one to help.

PSALM 22:9–11 NIV

ONE MOMENT AT A TIME
DON'T FLY SOLO

1. **Grief is inevitable.** We all are touched by significant losses at some point in our lives. Don't try to walk through the dark periods alone but seek out a friend who can sit and listen. Talking about your grief is vital.

2. **Don't disconnect.** Talking with others can help you keep perspective and find the support you need. Resist the temptation to retreat into your own private world.

3. **God knows your pain.** God knew that when death entered the world (Genesis 3), our lives would have seasons of difficulty. He experienced pain Himself through the sufferings of Christ. God can empathize with you. Share your pain with Him.

CHAPTER 2

LIFE-CHANGING EVENTS

Within a year's time, my family experienced a lot of changes. My parents died early in the year. And while their health had been poor for a long time, the end was still very difficult for all of us. Soon after their deaths, my nephew was killed in an accident and my sister filed for divorce. In the course of this difficult year, I learned how painful life is and how healthy grieving can be.

■ *Norm, age 39, Oregon* ■

FEELING THE STING OF DEATH

Jesus told her, "I am the resurrection and the life. Anyone who believes in me will live, even after dying. Everyone who lives in me and believes in me will never ever die."

JOHN 11:25–26 NLT

Christ died and rose again for this very purpose—to be Lord both of the living and of the dead.

ROMANS 14:9 NLT

Precious in the sight of the LORD is the death of his saints.

PSALM 116:15 ESV

[This grace] has now been revealed through the appearing of our Savior, Christ Jesus, who has destroyed death and has brought life and immortality to light through the gospel.

2 TIMOTHY 1:10 NIV

"Because of God's tender mercy, the morning light from heaven is about to break upon us, to give light to those who sit in darkness and in the shadow of death, and to guide us to the path of peace."

LUKE 1:78–79 NLT

Behold, the eye of the LORD is on those who fear him, on those who hope in his steadfast love, that he may deliver their soul from death and keep them alive in famine.

PSALM 33:18–19 ESV

And I heard a voice from heaven saying, "Write this down: Blessed are those who die in the Lord from now on. Yes, says the Spirit, they are blessed indeed, for they will rest from their hard work; for their good deeds follow them!"

REVELATION 14:13 NLT

For to me, living means living for Christ, and dying is even better.

PHILIPPIANS 1:21 NLT

We are confident, I say, and would prefer to be away from the body and at home with the Lord.

2 CORINTHIANS 5:8 NIV

Brothers, we do not want you to be ignorant about those who fall asleep, or to grieve like the rest of men, who have no hope.

1 THESSALONIANS 4:13 NIV

For what I received I passed on to you as of first importance: that Christ died for our sins according to the Scriptures, that he was buried, that he was raised on the third day according to the Scriptures. . . . But if it is preached that Christ has been raised from the dead, how can some of you say that there is no resurrection of the dead? If there is no resurrection of the dead, then not even Christ has been raised. And if Christ has not been raised, our preaching is useless and so is your faith.

1 CORINTHIANS 15:3–4, 12–14 NIV

I declare to you, brothers, that flesh and blood cannot inherit the kingdom of God, nor does the perishable inherit the imperishable. Listen, I tell you a mystery: We will not all sleep, but we will all be changed—in a flash, in the twinkling of an eye, at the last trumpet. For the trumpet will sound, the dead will be raised imperishable, and we will be changed. For the perishable must clothe itself with the imperishable, and the mortal with immortality. When the perishable has been clothed with the imperishable, and the mortal with immortality, then the saying that is written will come true: "Death has been swallowed up in victory." "Where, O death, is your victory? Where, O death, is your sting?"

1 CORINTHIANS 15:50–55 NIV

Someone may ask, "How are the dead raised? With what kind of body will they come?" . . . The body that is sown is perishable, it is raised imperishable; it is sown in dishonor, it is raised in glory; it is sown in weakness, it is raised in power; it is sown a natural body, it is raised a spiritual body.

1 CORINTHIANS 15:35, 42–44 NIV

LOSING A DREAM

"So do not worry, saying, 'What shall we eat?' or 'What shall we drink?' or 'What shall we wear?' For the pagans run after all these things, and your heavenly Father knows that you need them. But seek first his kingdom and his righteousness, and all these things will be given to you as well. Therefore do not worry about tomorrow, for tomorrow will worry about itself. Each day has enough trouble of its own."

MATTHEW 6:31–34 NIV

Yes, we should make the most of what God gives, both the bounty and the capacity to enjoy it, accepting what's given and delighting in the work. It's God's gift!

ECCLESIASTES 5:19 MSG

109

God, I beg two favors from you; let me have them before I die. First, help me never to tell a lie. Second, give me neither poverty nor riches! Give me just enough to satisfy my needs. For if I grow rich, I may deny you and say, "Who is the LORD?" And if I am too poor, I may steal and thus insult God's holy name.

PROVERBS 30:7–9 NLT

God is there, ready to help; I'm fearless no matter what. Who or what can get to me?

HEBREWS 13:6 MSG

For this is what the LORD says. . . "As a mother comforts her child, so will I comfort you. . . ." When you see this, your heart will rejoice and you will flourish like grass; the hand of the LORD will be made known to his servants, but his fury will be shown to his foes.

ISAIAH 66:12–14 NIV

The LORD is my shepherd, I shall not be in want. He makes me lie down in green pastures, he leads me beside quiet waters, he restores my soul. He guides me in paths of righteousness for his name's sake.

PSALM 23:1–3 NIV

But Zion said, "I don't get it. GOD has left me. My Master has forgotten I even exist." [And God replied,] "Can a mother forget the infant at her breast, walk away from the baby she bore? But even if mothers forget, I'd never forget you—never. Look, I've written your names on the backs of my hands.

The walls you're rebuilding are never out of my sight. Your builders are faster than your wreckers. The demolition crews are gone for good. Look up, look around, look well! See them all gathering, coming to you? As sure as I am the living God"—GOD's Decree—"you're going to put them on like so much jewelry, you're going to use them to dress up like a bride."

ISAIAH 49:14–18 MSG

FACING ILLNESS

Be humble in the presence of God's mighty power, and he will honor you when the time comes. God cares for you, so turn all your worries over to him.

1 PETER 5:6–7 CEV

For his Spirit joins with our spirit to affirm that we are God's children. And since we are his children, we are his heirs. In fact, together with Christ we are heirs of God's glory. But if we are to share his glory, we must also share his suffering. Yet what we suffer now is nothing compared to the glory he will reveal to us later.

ROMANS 8:16–18 NLT

The LORD hears his people when they call to him for help. He rescues them from all their troubles. The LORD is close to the brokenhearted; he rescues those whose spirits are crushed.

PSALM 34:17–18 NLT

We wait in hope for the LORD; he is our help and our shield. In him our hearts rejoice, for we trust in his holy name. May your unfailing love rest upon us, O LORD, even as we put our hope in you.

PSALM 33:20–22 NIV

As he went along, he saw a man blind from birth. His disciples asked him, "Rabbi, who sinned, this man or his parents, that he was born blind?" "Neither this man nor his parents sinned," said Jesus, "but this happened so that the work of God might be displayed in his life."

JOHN 9:1–3 NIV

Each time he said, "My grace is all you need. My power works best in weakness." So now I am glad to boast about my weaknesses, so that the power of Christ can work through me. That's why I take pleasure in my weaknesses, and in the insults, hardships, persecutions, and troubles that I suffer for Christ. For when I am weak, then I am strong.

2 CORINTHIANS 12:9–10 NLT

"LORD, remind me how brief my time on earth will be. Remind me that my days are numbered—how fleeting my life is. You have made my life no longer than the width of my hand. My entire lifetime is just a moment to you; at best, each of us is but a breath." We are merely moving shadows, and all our busy rushing ends in nothing. We heap up wealth, not knowing who will spend it. And so, Lord, where do I put my hope? My only hope is in you.

PSALM 39:4–7 NLT

You, LORD, are the one I praise. So heal me and rescue me! Then I will be completely well and perfectly safe.

JEREMIAH 17:14 CEV

DEALING WITH DIVORCE

My flesh and my heart fail; but God is the strength of my heart and my portion forever.

PSALM 73:26 NKJV

If we are faithless, he will remain faithful, for he cannot disown himself.

2 TIMOTHY 2:13 NIV

He has never let you down, never looked the other way when you were being kicked around. He has never wandered off to do his own thing; he has been right there, listening.

PSALM 22:24 MSG

Now to him who is able to keep you from stumbling and to present you blameless before the presence of his glory with great joy, to the only God, our Savior, through Jesus Christ our Lord, be glory, majesty, dominion, and authority, before all time and now and forever. Amen.

JUDE 24–25 ESV

"The LORD will fight for you; you need only to be still."

EXODUS 14:14 NIV

That is why I am suffering as I am. Yet I am not ashamed, because I know whom I have believed, and am convinced that he is able to guard what I have entrusted to him for that day.

2 TIMOTHY 1:12 NIV

As the Scripture says, "Anyone who trusts in him will never be put to shame."

ROMANS 10:11 NIV

"Do not be afraid; you will not suffer shame. Do not fear disgrace; you will not be humiliated. You will forget the shame of your youth and remember no more the reproach of your widowhood."

ISAIAH 54:4 NIV

So now there is no condemnation for those who belong to Christ Jesus.

ROMANS 8:1 NLT

Let us fix our eyes on Jesus, the author and perfecter of our faith, who for the joy set before him endured the cross, scorning its shame, and sat down at the right hand of the throne of God. Consider him who endured such opposition from sinful men, so that you will not grow weary and lose heart.

HEBREWS 12:2–3 NIV

EXPERIENCING THE LOSS OF A CHILD

Then little children were brought to Jesus for him to place his hands on them and pray for them. But the disciples rebuked those who brought them. Jesus said, "Let the little children come to me, and do

not hinder them, for the kingdom of heaven belongs to such as these."

MATTHEW 19:13–14 NIV

Jesus called them back. "Let these children alone. Don't get between them and me. These children are the kingdom's pride and joy."

LUKE 18:16 MSG

For you created my inmost being; you knit me together in my mother's womb. I praise you because I am fearfully and wonderfully made; your works are wonderful, I know that full well. . . . Your eyes saw my unformed body. All the days ordained for me were written in your book before one of them came to be.

PSALM 139:13–14, 16 NIV

"But now, Lord, what do I look for? My hope is in you."

PSALM 39:7 NIV

Let your steadfast love comfort me according to your promise to your servant.

PSALM 119:76 ESV

SAYING GOOD-BYE TO A PARENT

Even if my father and mother abandon me, the LORD will hold me close.

PSALM 27:10 NLT

God sets the lonely in families, he leads forth the prisoners with singing; but the rebellious live in a sun-scorched land.

PSALM 68:6 NIV

"I will be a Father to you, and you will be my sons and daughters, says the Lord Almighty."

2 CORINTHIANS 6:18 NIV

God assured us, "I'll never let you down, never walk off and leave you."

HEBREWS 13:5 MSG

"No, I will not abandon you as orphans—I will come to you."

JOHN 14:18 NLT

ONE MOMENT AT A TIME
MAKING A LIFE CHANGE

1. **Grieve the loss.** Losing a job or having a marriage fall apart can seem minor compared to the death of a family member. And while your situation may not seem as severe as someone else's, grieving is still productive. It is important to work through each emotion and understand what you are feeling so that you can find the closure you need.

2. **Don't venture alone.** If you are facing an illness, divorce, or the loss of a family member, help may be available. Consider attending a grief support group, and talk to others who are going through—or have gone through—similar situations.

3. **Consider becoming a volunteer.** Nursing homes and children's hospitals are filled with hurting people. Your experience and ability to empathize may be what other families need.

CHAPTER 3

ASSAULTED BY ANGER

Before my daughter's death, I wasn't an angry person. But losing her changed everything, and overnight I was filled with anger as I have never experienced it before. I'm angry at her for sneaking out the night she died. I'm angry at the drunk driver who caused the accident. I'm angry at God who let all this happen during His watch. It isn't fair! I can't understand why all this would happen. Why, God? Why?

■ Yolanda, age 44, West Virginia ■

DEALING WITH ANGER

Be patient and trust the LORD. Don't let it bother you when all goes well for those who do sinful things. Don't be angry or furious. Anger can lead to sin.

PSALM 37:7–8 CEV

Don't befriend angry people or associate with hot-tempered people, or you will learn to be like them and endanger your soul.

PROVERBS 22:24–25 NLT

Beloved, never avenge yourselves, but leave it to the wrath of God, for it is written, "Vengeance is mine, I will repay, says the Lord." To the contrary, "if your enemy is hungry, feed him; if he is thirsty, give him something to drink; for by so doing you will heap burning coals on his head." Do not be overcome by evil, but overcome evil with good.

ROMANS 12:19–21 ESV

Let all bitterness and wrath and anger and clamor and slander be put away from you, along with all malice.

EPHESIANS 4:31 ESV

Better to be patient than powerful; better to have self-control than to conquer a city.

PROVERBS 16:32 NLT

Fools have short fuses and explode all too quickly; the prudent quietly shrug off insults.

PROVERBS 12:16 MSG

My dear brothers, take note of this: Everyone should be quick to listen, slow to speak and slow to become angry.

JAMES 1:19 NIV

EXTENDING FORGIVENESS TO OTHERS

Dear friends, let us continue to love one another, for love comes from God. Anyone who loves is a child of God and knows God. But anyone who does not love does not know God, for God is love.

1 JOHN 4:7–8 NLT

Be gentle with one another, sensitive. Forgive one another as quickly and thoroughly as God in Christ forgave you.

EPHESIANS 4:32 MSG

Then Peter came to Jesus and asked, "Lord, how many times shall I forgive my brother when he sins against me? Up to seven times?" Jesus answered, "I tell you, not seven times, but seventy-seven times."

MATTHEW 18:21–22 NIV

"And when you stand praying, if you hold anything against anyone, forgive him, so that your Father in heaven may forgive you your sins."

MARK 11:25 NIV

COMBATING BITTERNESS

Don't grumble against each other, brothers, or you will be judged. The Judge is standing at the door!

JAMES 5:9 NIV

Above all else, guard your heart, for it is the wellspring of life.

PROVERBS 4:23 NIV

See to it that no one misses the grace of God and that no bitter root grows up to cause trouble and defile many.

HEBREWS 12:15 NIV

Anyone who claims to be in the light but hates his brother is still in the darkness. Whoever loves his brother lives in the light, and there is nothing in him to make him stumble. But whoever hates his brother is in the darkness and walks around in the darkness; he does not know where he is going, because the darkness has blinded him.

1 JOHN 2:9–11 NIV

People may cover their hatred with pleasant words, but they're deceiving you. They pretend to be kind, but don't believe them. Their hearts are full of many evils. While their hatred may be concealed by trickery, their wrongdoing will be exposed in public.

PROVERBS 26:24–26 NLT

ONE MOMENT AT A TIME
UNDERSTANDING ANGER

1. **Don't apologize for how you feel.** Anger during a time of grieving is normal. Give yourself permission, if needed, to feel angry.

2. **Let it out.** Keeping anger pent up inside you can turn you into a time bomb just waiting to explode at the most inappropriate moments. Find productive ways to release your emotions.

3. **Be honest with God.** While it can be unnerving to find yourself angry with God, you can be honest with Him about how you feel. Reading the psalms will help you find many places David vented to God honestly yet reverently. See Psalm 22, for example.

4. **Consider joining a support group.** Meeting with others who can empathize can help you. And being able to help others will aid you, too.

CHAPTER 4

WRESTLING WITH GUILT

*I should have tried to make things right. I should have let him know
how I really felt. I should have been a better friend. I shouldn't have
held back so much. I spent entire days beating myself up with
thoughts like these. I finally had to come to terms with myself:
I'm human, and yes, I've failed. . .but God forgives.*

■ *Wayne, age 69, Illinois* ■

EMBRACING FORGIVENESS

If we confess our sins, he is faithful and just and will forgive us our sins and purify us from all unrighteousness.

1 JOHN 1:9 NIV

In him we have redemption through his blood, the forgiveness of sins, in accordance with the riches of God's grace that he lavished on us with all wisdom and understanding.

EPHESIANS 1:7–8 NIV

Therefore, if anyone is in Christ, he is a new creation; the old has gone, the new has come! All this is from God, who reconciled us to himself through Christ and gave us the ministry of reconciliation: that God was reconciling the world to himself in Christ, not counting men's sins against them. And he has committed to us the message of recon-

ciliation. We are therefore Christ's ambassadors, as though God were making his appeal through us. We implore you on Christ's behalf: Be reconciled to God. God made him who had no sin to be sin for us, so that in him we might become the righteousness of God.

2 CORINTHIANS 5:17–21 NIV

He personally carried our sins in his body on the cross so that we can be dead to sin and live for what is right. By his wounds you are healed.

1 PETER 2:24 NLT

God rescued us from dead-end alleys and dark dungeons. He's set us up in the kingdom of the Son he loves so much, the Son who got us out of the pit we were in, got rid of the sins we were doomed to keep repeating.

COLOSSIANS 1:13–14 MSG

My little children, I am writing these things to you so that you may not sin. But if anyone does sin, we

117

have an advocate with the Father, Jesus Christ the righteous.

1 JOHN 2:1 NRSV

Help us, O God of our salvation! Help us for the glory of your name. Save us and forgive our sins for the honor of your name.

PSALM 79:9 NLT

But you, O Lord, are a compassionate and gracious God, slow to anger, abounding in love and faithfulness.

PSALM 86:15 NIV

Praise the LORD, O my soul; all my inmost being, praise his holy name. Praise the LORD, O my soul, and forget not all his benefits—who forgives all your sins and heals all your diseases, who redeems your life from the pit and crowns you with love and compassion.

PSALM 103:1–4 NIV

LETTING GO OF YOUR GUILT

As far as the east is from the west, so far does he remove our transgressions from us.

PSALM 103:12 ESV

"Come now, let's settle this," says the LORD. "Though your sins are like scarlet, I will make them as white as snow. Though they are red like crimson, I will make them as white as wool."

ISAIAH 1:18 NLT

"I—yes, I alone—will blot out your sins for my own sake and will never think of them again."

ISAIAH 43:25 NLT

Don't stay far away, LORD! My strength comes from you, so hurry and help. Rescue me from enemy swords and save me from those dogs. Don't let lions eat me. You rescued me from the horns of wild bulls.

PSALM 22:19–21 CEV

Not that I have already obtained all this, or have already been made perfect, but I press on to take hold of that for which Christ Jesus took hold of me.

PHILIPPIANS 3:12 NIV

"Be still, and know that I am God; I will be exalted among the nations, I will be exalted in the earth."

PSALM 46:10 NIV

ONE MOMENT AT A TIME
GUILT BUSTERS

1. **Free yourself from false guilt.** False guilt can hinder your recovery if you unreasonably blame yourself for things you did or didn't do.

2. **Say you're sorry.** Because you are human, you may have legitimate guilt about things you have said, done, or not done. And while you can no longer address that person directly, it can be healthy to release what you are feeling. Write your loved one a letter. Visit the graveside to say you're sorry. And while you may wish to go backward in time and do something differently, that choice isn't an option. In the end, the only thing you may be able to do is choose to let go of the guilt or resentment.

3. **Allow yourself to live.** Many people feel guilty for laughing or finding enjoyment during their time of grief. It's okay to take a break from the pain. Eventually you will want to find a way to resume enjoying life while treasuring the memories you hold dear.

CHAPTER 5

DEPRESSION

*Grief is debilitating. After the funeral was over and everyone went home,
I found myself exhausted. I didn't answer the phone, and on most days,
I didn't even go outside to get the mail. And while my boss expected me
back at work a few days later, I couldn't bring myself to go back so quickly.
I ended up losing the job but found that I didn't care anymore. I'm doing
better now, though. And through all this, I have been able to survive because I remember that God cares and that this pain will eventually pass.*

◼ *Reginald, age 26, North Carolina* ◼

FEELING DEPRESSION

I waited patiently for the LORD to
help me, and he turned to me and
heard my cry. He lifted me out of
the pit of despair, out of the mud
and the mire. He set my feet on
solid ground and steadied me as I
walked along.

PSALM 40:1–2 NLT

Yet you are enthroned as the Holy
One; you are the praise of Israel. In
you our fathers put their trust; they
trusted and you delivered them.
They cried to you and were saved;
in you they trusted and were not
disappointed.

PSALM 22:3–5 NIV

See how very much our Father loves
us, for he calls us his children, and
that is what we are!

1 JOHN 3:1 NLT

"The LORD your God is with you,
he is mighty to save. He will take
great delight in you, he will quiet
you with his love, he will rejoice
over you with singing."

ZEPHANIAH 3:17 NIV

"He cuts off every branch in me
that bears no fruit, while every
branch that does bear fruit he
prunes so that it will be even more
fruitful."

JOHN 15:2 NIV

"I have told you these things, so
that in me you may have peace. In
this world you will have trouble.
But take heart! I have overcome the
world."

JOHN 16:33 NIV

"Ask and it will be given to you;
seek and you will find; knock and
the door will be opened to you. For
everyone who asks receives; he who

seeks finds; and to him who knocks, the door will be opened."

MATTHEW 7:7–8 NIV

For his anger lasts only a moment, but his favor lasts a lifetime; weeping may remain for a night, but rejoicing comes in the morning.

PSALM 30:5 NIV

BEING ALONE

"And lo, I am with you always, even to the end of the age."

MATTHEW 28:20 NKJV

"It is the LORD who goes before you. He will be with you; he will not leave you or forsake you. Do not fear or be dismayed."

DEUTERONOMY 31:8 ESV

Turn to me and be gracious to me, for I am lonely and afflicted. The troubles of my heart have multiplied; free me from my anguish.

PSALM 25:16–17 NIV

"For the sake of his great name the LORD will not reject his people, because the LORD was pleased to make you his own."

1 SAMUEL 12:22 NIV

Even though I walk through the valley of the shadow of death, I will fear no evil, for you are with me; your rod and your staff, they comfort me.

PSALM 23:4 NIV

I will be glad and rejoice in your

love, for you saw my affliction and knew the anguish of my soul.

PSALM 31:7 NIV

But I trust in you, O LORD; I say, "You are my God." My times are in your hands; deliver me from my enemies and from those who pursue me.

PSALM 31:14–15 NIV

For the LORD your God is a merciful God; he will not abandon or destroy you or forget the covenant with your forefathers, which he confirmed to them by oath.

DEUTERONOMY 4:31 NIV

"I am not alone, for my Father is with me."

JOHN 16:32 NIV

CRYING WITH A BROKEN HEART

We are hard pressed on every side, but not crushed; perplexed, but not in despair; persecuted, but not abandoned; struck down, but not destroyed. We always carry around in our body the death of Jesus, so that the life of Jesus may also be revealed in our body.

2 CORINTHIANS 4:8–10 NIV

Trust in him at all times, O people; pour out your hearts to him, for God is our refuge.

PSALM 62:8 NIV

"Don't be afraid, I've redeemed you. I've called your name. You're mine.

121

When you're in over your head, I'll be there with you. When you're in rough waters, you will not go down. When you're between a rock and a hard place, it won't be a dead end—because I am GOD, your personal God, the Holy of Israel, your Savior. I paid a huge price for you: all of Egypt, with rich Cush and Seba thrown in! That's how much you mean to me! That's how much I love you! I'd sell off the whole world to get you back, trade the creation just for you."

ISAIAH 43:1–4 MSG

What, then, shall we say in response to this? If God is for us, who can be against us? He who did not spare his own Son, but gave him up for us all—how will he not also, along with him, graciously give us all things? Who will bring any charge against those whom God has chosen? It is God who justifies. Who is he that condemns? Christ Jesus, who died—more than that, who was raised to life—is at the right hand of God and is also interceding for us. Who shall separate us from the love of Christ? Shall trouble or hardship or persecution or famine or nakedness or danger or sword? As it is written: "For your sake we face death all day long; we are considered as sheep to be slaughtered." No, in all these things we are more than conquerors through him who loved us.

ROMANS 8:31–37 NIV

The LORD God is waiting to show how kind he is and to have pity on you. The LORD always does right; he blesses those who trust him.

ISAIAH 30:18 CEV

LIVING WITH ANXIETY

God cares for you, so turn all your worries over to him.

1 PETER 5:7 CEV

Trust in the LORD with all your heart and lean not on your own understanding; in all your ways acknowledge him, and he will make your paths straight.

PROVERBS 3:5–6 NIV

"Your Father knows exactly what you need even before you ask him!"

MATTHEW 6:8 NLT

"What is the price of five sparrows—two copper coins? Yet God does not forget a single one of them. And the very hairs on your head are all numbered. So don't be afraid; you are more valuable to God than a whole flock of sparrows."

LUKE 12:6–7 NLT

"Can all your worries add a single moment to your life? And if worry can't accomplish a little thing like that, what's the use of worrying over bigger things?"

LUKE 12:25–26 NLT

Trust in the LORD and do good; dwell in the land and enjoy safe pasture. Delight yourself in the LORD and he will give you the desires of your heart.

PSALM 37:3–4 NIV

Even strong young lions sometimes go hungry, but those who trust in the LORD will lack no good thing.

PSALM 34:10 NLT

ONE MOMENT AT A TIME
KEEPING THE MEMORY ALIVE

1. **Keep moving.** Don't allow yourself to spiral endlessly downward. Create a short list of things to do and make sure you complete at least one productive task each day.

2. **Add walking to your schedule.** The chemical changes that happen in your body as you exercise can be a healthy way to clear your mind and reinvigorate your heart.

3. **Journal.** Write about episodes that make you laugh or cry, or simply capture the character and personality of the person you remember.

CHAPTER 6

THE RECOVERY PROCESS

*I think that someone who hasn't really encountered grief can't under-
stand what people call "recovery." The truth is I will never fully recover.
I work hard, and every day is easier than the last one, but I'll never be
the person I was before this happened. Honestly, I don't know if I'd
want to be. While the pain has been difficult, I'm a better person for
having gone through this experience.*

■ *Ryan, age 61, Oklahoma* ■

FINDING HEALING

Beloved, do not be surprised at
the fiery ordeal that is taking place
among you to test you, as though
something strange were happening
to you. But rejoice insofar as you
are sharing Christ's sufferings, so
that you may also be glad and shout
for joy when his glory is revealed.

1 PETER 4:12–13 NRSV

O LORD my God, I cried to you for
help, and you have healed me.

PSALM 30:2 NRSV

Heal me, O LORD, and I shall be
healed; save me, and I shall be
saved, for You are my praise.

JEREMIAH 17:14 NKJV

"Blessed are you who are poor,
for yours is the kingdom of God.
Blessed are you who are hungry
now, for you shall be satisfied.
Blessed are you who weep now, for
you shall laugh."

LUKE 6:20–21 ESV

Therefore we do not lose heart.
Though outwardly we are wasting
away, yet inwardly we are being
renewed day by day.

2 CORINTHIANS 4:16 NIV

"I will heal my people and will let
them enjoy abundant peace and
security."

JEREMIAH 33:6 NIV

We can say with confidence, "The
LORD is my helper, so I will have
no fear. What can mere people do
to me?"

HEBREWS 13:6 NLT

Though you have made me see troubles, many and bitter, you will restore
my life again; from the depths of the
earth you will again bring me up.

PSALM 71:20 NIV

These hard times are small potatoes compared to the coming
good times, the lavish celebration
prepared for us.

2 CORINTHIANS 4:17 MSG

BECOMING A SURVIVOR

On that day you will be glad, even if you have to go through many hard trials for a while. Your faith will be like gold that has been tested in a fire. And these trials will prove that your faith is worth much more than gold that can be destroyed. They will show that you will be given praise and honor and glory when Jesus Christ returns. You have never seen Jesus, and you don't see him now. But still you love him and have faith in him, and no words can tell how glad and happy you are to be saved. That's why you have faith.

1 PETER 1:6–9 CEV

Be strong and take heart, all you who hope in the LORD.

PSALM 31:24 NIV

May our Lord Jesus Christ himself and God our Father, who loved us and by his grace gave us eternal encouragement and good hope, encourage your hearts and strengthen you in every good deed and word.

2 THESSALONIANS 2:16–17 NIV

And if the Spirit of him who raised Jesus from the dead is living in you, he who raised Christ from the dead will also give life to your mortal bodies through his Spirit, who lives in you.

ROMANS 8:11 NIV

"The thief comes only to steal and kill and destroy; I have come that they may have life, and have it to the full."

JOHN 10:10 NIV

Guide me by your truth and instruct me. You keep me safe, and I always trust you.

PSALM 25:5 CEV

MENDING YOUR SOUL

Nevertheless, God's solid foundation stands firm, sealed with this inscription: "The Lord knows those who are his."

2 TIMOTHY 2:19 NIV

Jesus answered by quoting Deuteronomy: "It takes more than bread to stay alive. It takes a steady stream of words from God's mouth."

MATTHEW 4:4 MSG

Oh yes, he's our God, and we're the people he pastures, the flock he feeds. Drop everything and listen, listen as he speaks.

PSALM 95:7 MSG

It is no longer I who live, but Christ lives in me. So I live in this earthly body by trusting in the Son of God, who loved me and gave himself for me.

GALATIANS 2:20 NLT

And this is the secret: Christ lives in you. This gives you assurance of sharing his glory.

COLOSSIANS 1:27 NLT

You will come to know God even better. His glorious power will make you patient and strong enough to endure anything, and you will be truly happy.

COLOSSIANS 1:10–11 CEV

"For in him we live and move and have our being."

ACTS 17:28 NIV

He heals the brokenhearted and binds up their wounds.

PSALM 147:3 NIV

COMING TO TERMS WITH GRIEF

Be still in the presence of the LORD, and wait patiently for him to act. Don't worry about evil people who prosper or fret about their wicked schemes. . . . It is better to be godly and have little than to be evil and rich.

PSALM 37:7, 16 NLT

You keep him in perfect peace whose mind is stayed on you, because he trusts in you. Trust in the LORD forever, for the LORD GOD is an everlasting rock.

ISAIAH 26:3–4 ESV

Rejoice in the Lord always. I will say it again: Rejoice! Let your gentleness be evident to all. The Lord is near. Do not be anxious about anything, but in everything, by prayer and petition, with thanksgiving, present your requests to God. And the peace of God, which transcends all understanding, will guard your hearts and your minds in Christ Jesus.

PHILIPPIANS 4:4–7 NIV

So if Christ keeps giving me his power, I will gladly brag about how weak I am. Yes, I am glad to be weak or insulted or mistreated or to have troubles and sufferings, if it is for Christ. Because when I am weak, I am strong.

2 CORINTHIANS 12:9–10 CEV

I'm glad in God, far happier than you would ever guess—happy that you're again showing such strong concern for me. Not that you ever quit praying and thinking about me. You just had no chance to show it. Actually, I don't have a sense of needing anything personally. I've learned by now to be quite content whatever my circumstances. I'm just as happy with little as with much, with much as with little. I've found the recipe for being happy whether full or hungry, hands full or hands empty. Whatever I have, wherever I am, I can make it through anything in the One who makes me who I am. . . . You can be sure that God will take care of everything you need, his generosity exceeding even yours in the glory that pours from Jesus. Our God and Father abounds in glory that just pours out into eternity. Yes.

PHILIPPIANS 4:10–13, 19–20 MSG

DISCOVERING RELIEF

Though an army besiege me, my heart will not fear; though war break out against me, even then will I be confident.

PSALM 27:3 NIV

When I felt my feet slipping, you came with your love and kept me steady. And when I was burdened with worries, you comforted me and made me feel secure.

PSALM 94:18–19 CEV

The LORD replied, "My Presence will go with you, and I will give you rest."

EXODUS 33:14 NIV

Showing respect to the LORD brings true life—if you do it, you can relax without fear of danger.

PROVERBS 19:23 CEV

I sought the LORD, and he answered me; he delivered me from all my fears.

PSALM 34:4 NIV

Think about the things of heaven, not the things of earth. For you died to this life, and your real life is hidden with Christ in God. And when Christ, who is your life, is revealed to the whole world, you will share in all his glory.

COLOSSIANS 3:2–4 NLT

ONE MOMENT AT A TIME
GETTING GOING AGAIN

1. **Tell their story.** Share the story of your loved ones with friends and family. Sharing pictures and favorite memories is a healthy way to celebrate their memory and your connection with them.

2. **Create a memory book.** Assemble pictures, memories, poems, news clippings, and even a copy of your loved one's funeral service.

3. **Do something your loved one would enjoy.** Did your loved one have a favorite food or enjoy a favorite vacation destination? Bring a friend and enjoy an event that your loved one would have enjoyed, as a way to honor his or her memory.

CHAPTER 7

HELPING YOUR CHILDREN GRIEVE

Having to tell my kids about their friend's death was one of the most gut-wrenching experiences of my life. Not only did they suffer through the sharp sting of loss, but their innocence was ripped away as they passed along the word of their friend's death. They have no framework yet for understanding death and its consequences. They have played so many video games I think they expect their friend to come back as easily as characters do when the letters flash "Game Over" on the screen. I wonder how many weeks it will be before they fully understand their friend is never coming back.

■ *Anna, age 36, Maine* ■

REDUCING THEIR LOAD

But Jesus said, "Let the little children come to me and do not hinder them, for to such belongs the kingdom of heaven."
MATTHEW 19:14 ESV

[God] comforts us in all our troubles, so that we can comfort those in any trouble with the comfort we ourselves have received from God.
2 CORINTHIANS 1:4 NIV

God is our refuge and strength, always ready to help in times of trouble.
PSALM 46:1 NLT

Have mercy on me, O God, have mercy on me, for in you my soul takes refuge. I will take refuge in the shadow of your wings until the disaster has passed.
PSALM 57:1 NIV

I am surrounded by trouble, but you protect me against my angry enemies. With your own powerful arm you keep me safe.
PSALM 138:7 CEV

HELPING THEM HEAL

Stoop down and reach out to those who are oppressed. Share their burdens, and so complete Christ's law.
GALATIANS 6:2 MSG

Be brave and strong! Don't be afraid. . . . The LORD your God will always be at your side, and he will never abandon you.

DEUTERONOMY 31:6 CEV

"Do not be terrified; do not be discouraged, for the LORD your God will be with you wherever you go."

JOSHUA 1:9 NIV

"Peace I leave with you; my peace I give to you. Not as the world gives do I give to you. Let not your hearts be troubled, neither let them be afraid."

JOHN 14:27 ESV

If your heart is broken, you'll find GOD right there; if you're kicked in the gut, he'll help you catch your breath.

PSALM 34:18 MSG

Our LORD, we belong to you. We tell you what worries us, and you won't let us fall.

PSALM 55:22 CEV

The people of Zion said, "The LORD has turned away and forgotten us." The LORD answered, "Could a mother forget a child who nurses at her breast? Could she fail to love an infant who came from her own body? Even if a mother could forget, I will never forget you. A picture of your city is drawn on my hand. You are always in my thoughts!"

ISAIAH 49:14–16 CEV

"You're blessed when you feel you've lost what is most dear to you. Only then can you be embraced by the One most dear to you."

MATTHEW 5:4 MSG

"Do not let your hearts be troubled. Trust in God; trust also in me. In my Father's house are many rooms; if it were not so, I would have told you. I am going there to prepare a place for you. And if I go and prepare a place for you, I will come back and take you to be with me that you also may be where I am. You know the way to the place where I am going."

JOHN 14:1–4 NIV

ONE MOMENT AT A TIME
HELPING CHILDREN COPE

1. **Teach your kids that death is part of life.** Our own fear of death as well as our desire to protect children keeps us from teaching kids that death is natural. It is important that they learn about death as well as how to grieve in a healthy way. These moments can also become appropriate moments to share the gospel with your children.

2. **Let them see you grieve.** Kids learn a lot from parents and other adults. If they see you remain stoic, they may learn to grieve that way, too. But if they see you go through a full range of emotions, they may become more comfortable with their own feelings.

3. **Answer their questions.** Death raises a lot of questions for children. Answer them honestly and to the best of your ability. If you don't know an answer, it is okay to tell them that, too.

4. **Let them talk.** Talking about their loss is crucial. Let them tell stories or share things they find significant. Because children may not have the same breadth of stories, they may tell the same ones over and over again. If that's the case, let them talk freely without cutting them off.

CHAPTER 8

MINISTERING TO OTHERS

*When my husband died of cancer, I wanted to die, too. I never thought
I'd make it through the dark days that followed. I'm grateful for the
people who stuck with me and helped me through my pain. They helped
me find joy again and encouraged me to find things to be grateful for.
Once I did, I found that God began using me to provide comfort and
encouragement to others who needed it. I know what it's like to be broken, and I have learned that while you can't take away another person's
pain, you can listen, love, hug, pray, and encourage them with the hope
that God does heal and will make them whole again.*

■ *Frances, age 63, Colorado* ■

FINDING YOUR JOY AGAIN

Though the fig tree does not bud
and there are no grapes on the vines,
though the olive crop fails and the
fields produce no food, though
there are no sheep in the pen and no
cattle in the stalls, yet I will rejoice
in the LORD, I will be joyful in God
my Savior. The Sovereign LORD is
my strength; he makes my feet like
the feet of a deer, he enables me to
go on the heights.

HABAKKUK 3:17–19 NIV

"Now is your time of grief, but
I will see you again and you will
rejoice, and no one will take away
your joy."

JOHN 16:22 NIV

Those who sow in tears will reap
with songs of joy. He who goes out
weeping, carrying seed to sow, will
return with songs of joy, carrying
sheaves with him.

PSALM 126:5–6 NIV

Now those you have rescued will return to Jerusalem, singing on their
way. They will be crowned with
great happiness, never again to be
burdened with sadness and sorrow.

ISAIAH 51:11 CEV

You have put gladness in my heart,
more than in the season that their
grain and wine increased.

PSALM 4:7 NKJV

Be joyful in hope, patient in affliction, faithful in prayer.

ROMANS 12:12 NIV

Then my soul will rejoice in the
LORD, exulting in his salvation.

PSALM 35:9 ESV

But I trust in your unfailing love;
my heart rejoices in your salvation.

PSALM 13:5 NIV

"These things I have spoken to you,
that my joy may be in you, and that
your joy may be full."

JOHN 15:11 ESV

BEING GRATEFUL FOR LIFE

Always be joyful. Never stop praying. Be thankful in all circumstances,
for this is God's will for you who
belong to Christ Jesus.

1 THESSALONIANS 5:16–18 NLT

Thanks be to God for his indescribable gift!

2 CORINTHIANS 9:15 NIV

"Sacrifice thank offerings to God,
fulfill your vows to the Most High."

PSALM 50:14 NIV

Shout with joy to the LORD, all
the earth! Worship the LORD with
gladness. Come before him, singing
with joy. Acknowledge that the
LORD is God! He made us, and we
are his. We are his people, the sheep
of his pasture. Enter his gates with
thanksgiving; go into his courts
with praise. Give thanks to him and
praise his name.

PSALM 100:1–4 NLT

HELPING OTHERS

Praise be to the God and Father of
our Lord Jesus Christ, the Father
of compassion and the God of all
comfort, who comforts us in all our
troubles, so that we can comfort
those in any trouble with the
comfort we ourselves have received
from God. For just as the sufferings
of Christ flow over into our lives,
so also through Christ our comfort
overflows.

2 CORINTHIANS 1:3–5 NIV

If one part of our body hurts, we
hurt all over. If one part of our
body is honored, the whole body
will be happy.

1 CORINTHIANS 12:26 CEV

Be devoted to one another in brotherly love. Honor one another above
yourselves.

ROMANS 12:10 NIV

Let's see how inventive we can be in
encouraging love and helping out.

HEBREWS 10:24 MSG

Rejoice with those who rejoice;
mourn with those who mourn.

ROMANS 12:15 NIV

Religion that God our Father accepts as pure and faultless is this:
to look after orphans and widows
in their distress and to keep oneself
from being polluted by the world.

JAMES 1:27 NIV

"When you are harvesting your
crops and forget to bring in a

bundle of grain from your field, don't go back to get it. Leave it for the foreigners, orphans, and widows. Then the LORD your God will bless you in all you do. When you beat the olives from your olive trees, don't go over the boughs twice. Leave the remaining olives for the foreigners, orphans, and widows. When you gather the grapes in your vineyard, don't glean the vines after they are picked. Leave the remaining grapes for the foreigners, orphans, and widows."

DEUTERONOMY 24:19–21 NLT

Be rich in helping others. . .be extravagantly generous.

1 TIMOTHY 6:18 MSG

Cheerfully share your home with those who need a meal or a place to stay.

1 PETER 4:9 NLT

Each of you has been blessed with one of God's many wonderful gifts to be used in the service of others. So use your gift well.

1 PETER 4:10 CEV

ONE MOMENT AT A TIME
JUST BE THERE

1. **Don't try to fill the silence.** Sometimes it is enough to sit with the person who is grieving. Don't feel the need to come up with something profound to say. Rather, a loving smile and a tender touch are all that are needed.

2. **Learn to empathize.** Sympathy can come across in a condescending manner. Instead, make an effort to show empathy—which means putting yourself in the other person's shoes. Do more than simply tell someone you're sorry. Work hard at trying to enter into his or her world.

3. **Pray.** In the end, only God can salve a hurting heart. Sometimes the best way you can be a friend is to pray for the hurting person.

CHAPTER 9

SPIRITUAL JOURNEY

Even though I have been a pastor for a number of years, I don't always have ready answers for grieving families. Recently, as I stood at the graveside of a dear friend, I was struck with the fact that we can't answer most of our questions because we don't know enough. Really, I don't think we know enough to even ask the right questions. Death is a mystery to us. Only God sees the full picture. He alone knows what happens on the other side of eternal life and just how these events play a role in His perfect plan.

■ *Jack, age 53, New York* ■

QUESTIONING GOD

For my thoughts are not your thoughts, nor are your ways my ways, says the LORD.

ISAIAH 55:8 NRSV

The suffering won't last forever. It won't be long before this generous God who has great plans for us in Christ—eternal and glorious plans they are!—will have you put together and on your feet for good.

1 PETER 5:10 MSG

"You intended to harm me, but God intended it for good to accomplish what is now being done, the saving of many lives."

GENESIS 50:20 NIV

"You're blessed when you're at the end of your rope. With less of you there is more of God and his rule.

"You're blessed when you feel you've lost what is most dear to you. Only then can you be embraced by the One most dear to you. You're blessed when you're content with just who you are—no more, no less. That's the moment you find yourselves proud owners of everything that can't be bought. You're blessed when you've worked up a good appetite for God. He's food and drink in the best meal you'll ever eat. You're blessed when you care. At the moment of being 'care-full,' you find yourselves cared for. You're blessed when you get your inside world—your mind and heart—put right. Then you can see God in the outside world. You're blessed when you can show people how to cooperate instead of compete or fight. That's when you discover who you really are, and your place in God's family. You're blessed when your commitment to God provokes persecution. The persecution drives you even deeper into God's kingdom."

MATTHEW 5:3–10 MSG

TRUSTING GOD'S PLAN

"I am with you and will watch over you wherever you go, and I will bring you back to this land. I will not leave you until I have done what I have promised you."

GENESIS 28:15 NIV

Those who know your name will trust in you, for you, LORD, have never forsaken those who seek you.

PSALM 9:10 NIV

You, LORD, are the light that keeps me safe. I am not afraid of anyone. You protect me, and I have no fears.

PSALM 27:1 CEV

Yet I am poor and needy; may the Lord think of me. You are my help and my deliverer; O my God, do not delay.

PSALM 40:17 NIV

Where can I go from your Spirit? Where can I flee from your presence? If I go up to the heavens, you are there; if I make my bed in the depths, you are there. If I rise on the wings of the dawn, if I settle on the far side of the sea, even there your hand will guide me, your right hand will hold me fast.

PSALM 139:7–10 NIV

The LORD directs the steps of the godly. He delights in every detail of their lives.

PSALM 37:23 NLT

One thing I ask of the LORD, this is what I seek: that I may dwell in the house of the LORD all the days of my life, to gaze upon the beauty of the LORD and to seek him in his temple. For in the day of trouble he will keep me safe in his dwelling; he will hide me in the shelter of his tabernacle and set me high upon a rock.

PSALM 27:4–5 NIV

BELIEVING IN A FUTURE HOPE

Now we know that if the earthly tent we live in is destroyed, we have a building from God, an eternal house in heaven, not built by human hands.

2 CORINTHIANS 5:1 NIV

"In my Father's house are many rooms; if it were not so, I would have told you. I am going there to prepare a place for you."

JOHN 14:2 NIV

Our citizenship is in heaven. And we eagerly await a Savior from there, the Lord Jesus Christ.

PHILIPPIANS 3:20 NIV

For this we declare to you by a word from the Lord, that we who are alive, who are left until the coming of the Lord, will not precede those who have fallen asleep. For the Lord himself will descend from heaven with a cry of command, with the voice of an archangel, and with the sound of the trumpet of God. And the dead in Christ will rise first. Then we who are alive, who are left, will be caught up together with them in the clouds to meet the Lord in the air, and so we will always be with the Lord. Therefore encourage one another with these words.

1 THESSALONIANS 4:15–18 ESV

"He will wipe every tear from their eyes. There will be no more death or mourning or crying or pain, for the old order of things has passed away."

REVELATION 21:4 NIV

Then I heard what seemed to be the voice of a great multitude, like the roar of many waters and like the sound of mighty peals of thunder, crying out, "Hallelujah! For the Lord our God the Almighty reigns."

REVELATION 19:6 ESV

"For the Lamb at the center of the throne will be their shepherd; he will lead them to springs of living water. And God will wipe away every tear from their eyes."

REVELATION 7:17 NIV

The LORD All-Powerful will destroy the power of death and wipe away all tears. No longer will his people be insulted everywhere. The LORD has spoken!

ISAIAH 25:8 CEV

REFRESHING YOUR HEART

The Holy Spirit helps us in our weakness. For example, we don't know what God wants us to pray for. But the Holy Spirit prays for us with groanings that cannot be expressed in words.

ROMANS 8:26 NLT

The LORD is near to all who call on him, to all who call on him in truth. He fulfills the desires of those who fear him; he hears their cry and saves them.

PSALM 145:18–19 NIV

On the day I called, you answered me, you increased my strength of soul.

PSALM 138:3 NRSV

Let me abide in your tent forever, find refuge under the shelter of your wings.

PSALM 61:4 NRSV

Search me, O God, and know my heart; test me and know my anxious thoughts.

PSALM 139:23 NLT

Let all bitterness and wrath and anger and clamor and slander be put away from you, along with all malice.

EPHESIANS 4:31 ESV

I am still confident of this: I will see the goodness of the LORD in the land of the living. Wait for the LORD; be strong and take heart and wait for the LORD.

PSALM 27:13–14 NIV

In peace I will lie down and sleep, for you alone, O LORD, will keep me safe.

PSALM 4:8 NLT

ONE MOMENT AT A TIME
CLINGING TO FAITH

1. **Consider this:** C. S. Lewis wrote in *A Grief Observed*: "Can a mortal ask questions which God finds unanswerable? Quite easily, I should think. All nonsense questions are unanswerable. How many hours are there in a mile? Is yellow square or round? Probably half the questions we ask—half of our great theological and metaphysical problems—are like that. . . . When I lay these questions before God I get no answer, but a rather special sort of 'no answer.' It is not the locked door. It is more like a silent, certainly not uncompassionate gaze. As though He shook his head not in refusal but waiving the question. Like, 'Peace, child; you don't understand.' "

2. **Look for growth.** God can use pain to help you grow. Many Bible characters grew closest to God through their darkest hours.

3. **Hold on to what you know.** When you are in pain, your emotions are screaming—sometimes drowning out the truths of God that you discovered when life wasn't so hard. Hold on to the truths of God's character—those haven't changed even though your circumstances have. Though you may have trouble seeing it, God is still good, still wise, still loving, and still with you.

CHAPTER 10

KNOWING GOD DURING THIS TIME

There were times in the months following my mom's death that I was angry at God. I worked through it, though, and realize now that God is truly my best Friend. While I have family and friends, they will all fail me—and eventually die. And one day I will, too. The thought used to scare me, but the closer I grow to God, the less it does. God is my ultimate source of comfort and strength, and without Him I would truly have no hope.

■ *Capri, age 19, Nevada* ■

KNOWING GOD'S LOVE

I am convinced that neither death nor life, neither angels nor demons, neither the present nor the future, nor any powers, neither height nor depth, nor anything else in all creation, will be able to separate us from the love of God that is in Christ Jesus our Lord.

ROMANS 8:38–39 NIV

The LORD is good, a refuge in times of trouble. He cares for those who trust in him.

NAHUM 1:7 NIV

We know what real love is because Jesus gave up his life for us.

1 JOHN 3:16 NLT

God put his love on the line for us by offering his Son in sacrificial death while we were of no use whatever to him.

ROMANS 5:8 MSG

Great is his faithfulness; his mercies begin afresh each morning. I say to myself, "The LORD is my inheritance; therefore, I will hope in him!"

LAMENTATIONS 3:23–24 NLT

In a desert land he found him, in a barren and howling waste. He shielded him and cared for him; he guarded him as the apple of his eye.

DEUTERONOMY 32:10 NIV

Know therefore that the LORD your God is God; he is the faithful God, keeping his covenant of love to a thousand generations of those who love him and keep his commands.

DEUTERONOMY 7:9 NIV

"For God so loved the world, that he gave his only Son, that whoever believes in him should not perish but have eternal life."

JOHN 3:16 ESV

I pray that you, being rooted and established in love, may have power, together with all the saints, to grasp how wide and long and high and deep is the love of Christ, and to know this love that surpasses knowledge—that you may be filled to the measure of all the fullness of God.

EPHESIANS 3:17–19 NIV

GRIPPING GOD'S GRACE

You surely don't think much of God's wonderful goodness or of his patience and willingness to put up with you. Don't you know that the reason God is good to you is because he wants you to turn to him?

ROMANS 2:4 CEV

"But in your great mercy you did not put an end to them or abandon them, for you are a gracious and merciful God."

NEHEMIAH 9:31 NIV

"You have granted me life and steadfast love, and your care has preserved my spirit."

JOB 10:12 ESV

I always thank God for you because of his grace given you in Christ Jesus. For in him you have been enriched in every way—in all your speaking and in all your knowledge—because our testimony about Christ was confirmed in you. Therefore you do not lack any spiritual gift as you eagerly wait for our Lord Jesus Christ to be revealed. He will keep you strong to the end, so that you will be blameless on the day of our Lord Jesus Christ.

1 CORINTHIANS 1:4–8 NIV

For you are a people holy to the LORD your God. The LORD your God has chosen you out of all the peoples on the face of the earth to be his people, his treasured possession.

DEUTERONOMY 7:6 NIV

For it is by grace you have been saved, through faith—and this not from yourselves, it is the gift of God—not by works, so that no one can boast.

EPHESIANS 2:8–9 NIV

"Repent, then, and turn to God, so that your sins may be wiped out, that times of refreshing may come from the Lord."

ACTS 3:19 NIV

God is able to make all grace abound to you, so that in all things at all times, having all that you need, you will abound in every good work.

2 CORINTHIANS 9:8 NIV

Whenever we are in need, we should come bravely before the throne of our merciful God. There we will be treated with undeserved kindness, and we will find help.

HEBREWS 4:16 CEV

EXPERIENCING GOD'S CONCERN

How precious are your thoughts about me, O God. They cannot be numbered! I can't even count them; they outnumber the grains of sand! And when I wake up, you are still with me!

PSALM 139:17–18 NLT

"Before I shaped you in the womb, I knew all about you. Before you saw the light of day, I had holy plans for you: A prophet to the nations—that's what I had in mind for you."

JEREMIAH 1:5 MSG

He gave his life to free us from every kind of sin, to cleanse us, and to make us his very own people, totally committed to doing good deeds.

TITUS 2:14 NLT

Praise the God and Father of our Lord Jesus Christ for the spiritual blessings that Christ has brought us from heaven! Before the world was created, God had Christ choose us to live with him and to be his holy and innocent and loving people. God was kind and decided that Christ would choose us to be God's own adopted children. God was very kind to us because of the Son he dearly loves, and so we should praise God.

EPHESIANS 1:3–6 CEV

"I no longer call you servants, because a servant does not know his master's business. Instead, I have called you friends, for everything that I learned from my Father I have made known to you."

JOHN 15:15 NIV

For you are all children of God through faith in Christ Jesus.

GALATIANS 3:26 NLT

But to all who did receive him, who believed in his name, he gave the right to become children of God.

JOHN 1:12 ESV

For all who are led by the Spirit of God are children of God. So you have not received a spirit that makes you fearful slaves. Instead, you received God's Spirit when he adopted you as his own children. Now we call him, "Abba, Father."

ROMANS 8:14–15 NLT

You keep track of all my sorrows. You have collected all my tears in your bottle. You have recorded each one in your book.

PSALM 56:8 NLT

HOLDING ON TO GOD'S STRENGTH

Do you not know? Have you not heard? The Lord is the everlasting God, the Creator of the ends of the earth. He will not grow tired or weary, and his understanding no one can fathom. He gives strength to the weary and increases the power of the weak. Even youths grow tired and weary, and young men stumble and fall; but those who hope in the LORD will renew their strength. They will soar on wings like eagles; they will run and not grow weary, they will walk and not be faint.

ISAIAH 40:28–31 NIV

You are my hiding place; you will protect me from trouble and surround me with songs of deliverance.

PSALM 32:7 NIV

Then Jesus said, "Come to me, all of you who are weary and carry heavy burdens, and I will give you rest. Take my yoke upon you. Let me teach you, because I am humble and gentle at heart, and you will find rest for your souls. For my yoke is easy to bear, and the burden I give you is light."

MATTHEW 11:28–30 NLT

But the Lord stood by me and gave me strength.

2 TIMOTHY 4:17 NRSV

For he will command his angels concerning you to guard you in all your ways.

PSALM 91:11 NIV

I look up to the mountains; does my strength come from mountains? No, my strength comes from GOD, who made heaven, and earth, and mountains.

PSALM 121:1–2 MSG

Be gracious to me, O LORD, for I am languishing; heal me, O LORD,

for my bones are troubled. My soul also is greatly troubled. But you, O LORD—how long? Turn, O LORD, deliver my life; save me for the sake of your steadfast love.

PSALM 6:2–4 ESV

STRENGTHENING YOUR FAITH

I rise before dawn and cry for help; I hope in your words.

PSALM 119:147 ESV

My comfort in my suffering is this: Your promise preserves my life.

PSALM 119:50 NIV

I acknowledged my sin to you, and I did not cover my iniquity; I said, "I will confess my transgressions to the LORD," and you forgave the iniquity of my sin.

PSALM 32:5 ESV

Your word is a lamp to my feet and a light to my path.

PSALM 119:105 ESV

This is a trustworthy saying that deserves full acceptance (and for this we labor and strive), that we have put our hope in the living God, who is the Savior of all men, and especially of those who believe.

1 TIMOTHY 4:9–10 NIV

ONE MOMENT AT A TIME
DEEPENING YOUR FAITH

1. **Read a book.** Christian bookstores offer many titles that can help you grow in intimacy with God through your time of grief.

2. **Become better acquainted with Job.** Few people experience the extreme loss and pain the biblical character Job faced. While Job's friends and family were unable to comfort him, his faith in God was ultimately strengthened. Toward the end of the account, he says to God: "My ears had heard of you but now my eyes have seen you" (Job 42:5 NIV). Read Job and identify with what he learned.

3. **Consider creating a blog or journal.** Your emotional highs and lows can yield tremendous growth. Regular writing can help you organize your thoughts and process the lessons God may be teaching you.

CHAPTER 11

LINGERING HURTS

Sometimes my pain haunts me. I'll be doing well for a number of days, and then a song, a news story, or even a smell will set me off. Without warning I'm lost to the renewed pain and tears that suddenly engulf me. I'm probably most surprised that the heartache is just as strong today as it was months ago. It seems like I should be getting over this by now. Is this normal?

◼ *Karla, age 31, Iowa* ◼

COPING WITH ENDURING PAIN

I'll never forget the trouble, the utter lostness, the taste of ashes, the poison I've swallowed. I remember it all—oh, how well I remember—the feeling of hitting the bottom. But there's one other thing I remember, and remembering, I keep a grip on hope: GOD's loyal love couldn't have run out, his merciful love couldn't have dried up.

LAMENTATIONS 3:19–22 MSG

Bring joy to your servant, for to you, O Lord, I lift up my soul.

PSALM 86:4 NIV

I learned God-worship when my pride was shattered. Heart-shattered lives ready for love don't for a moment escape God's notice.

PSALM 51:17 MSG

For he has not ignored or belittled the suffering of the needy. He has not turned his back on them, but has listened to their cries for help.

PSALM 22:24 NLT

Pray that our LORD will make us strong and give us peace.

PSALM 29:11 CEV

Praise be to the God and Father of our Lord Jesus Christ, the Father of compassion and the God of all comfort.

2 CORINTHIANS 1:3 NIV

REMINDING YOURSELF OF GOD'S CONSTANT CARE

So let's do it—full of belief, confident that we're presentable inside and out. Let's keep a firm grip on the promises that keep us going. He always keeps his word.

HEBREWS 10:22–23 MSG

The LORD your God will always be at your side, and he will never abandon you.

DEUTERONOMY 31:6 CEV

The LORD is my rock, my fortress and my deliverer; my God is my rock, in whom I take refuge. He is my shield and the horn of my salvation, my stronghold.

PSALM 18:2 NIV

"The eternal God is your refuge, and underneath are the everlasting arms. He will drive out your enemy before you, saying, 'Destroy him!' "

DEUTERONOMY 33:27 NIV

"Though the mountains be shaken and the hills be removed, yet my unfailing love for you will not be shaken nor my covenant of peace be removed," says the LORD, who has compassion on you.

ISAIAH 54:10 NIV

Give thanks to the LORD, for he is good! His faithful love endures forever.

PSALM 107:1 NLT

EXPERIENCING NEW HOPE

For you have been my hope, O Sovereign LORD, my confidence since my youth.

PSALM 71:5 NIV

Being confident of this, that he who began a good work in you will carry it on to completion until the day of Christ Jesus.

PHILIPPIANS 1:6 NIV

But you, O Sovereign LORD, deal well with me for your name's sake; out of the goodness of your love, deliver me. For I am poor and needy, and my heart is wounded within me.

PSALM 109:21–22 NIV

To all who mourn in Israel, he will give a crown of beauty for ashes, a joyous blessing instead of mourning, festive praise instead of despair. In their righteousness, they will be like great oaks that the LORD has planted for his own glory.

ISAIAH 61:3 NLT

Why am I discouraged? Why am I restless? I trust you! And I will praise you again because you help me.

PSALM 42:5 CEV

And this same God who takes care of me will supply all your needs from his glorious riches, which have been given to us in Christ Jesus.

PHILIPPIANS 4:19 NLT

Trust in the LORD and do good. Then you will live safely in the land and prosper.

PSALM 37:3 NLT

Praise the LORD! Oh give thanks to the LORD, for he is good, for his steadfast love endures forever!

PSALM 106:1 ESV

Consider it pure joy, my brothers, whenever you face trials of many kinds, because you know that the testing of your faith develops perseverance. Perseverance must finish its work so that you may be mature and complete, not lacking anything.

JAMES 1:2–4 NIV

ONE MOMENT AT A TIME
SCARS HEAL SLOWLY

1. **Be patient with others.** Friends and family may not understand why you are still grieving. Sometimes they may be insensitive, and other times they may be afraid to bring up your loss for fear of upsetting you. Either way, remember that they love you and probably mean well.

2. **Believe life is still worth living.** Work through the difficult feelings, but don't dwell on them without purpose. Embrace the life God has given you.

3. **Celebrate with a memorial a year after your loss.** Grief does not follow a calendar or have an ending date. Planning a private or public memorial after some time has passed can help you celebrate this person's life a little further removed from the sting of the initial loss.

4. **Monitor your media.** Music lyrics, movies, and TV shows can conjure up difficult emotions. Choose your entertainment carefully.

WHAT THE BIBLE SAYS ABOUT MARRIAGE

INTRODUCTION

"AND THEY LIVED HAPPILY EVER AFTER"

That romantic line concludes many make-believe stories in which a man and woman enjoy endless warm emotions and a trouble-free life. The problem is that real-life marriages don't unfold between the covers of a fairy-tale book. While many couples hold on to this unrealistic ideal, most marriages in the world cannot be classified as "happy."

Contrary to Hollywood's presentations, successful marriages are maintained by choices—not by feelings. The decision to remain faithful is deliberate. The choice to put your spouse's interests ahead of your own is often a conscious one. Whether you're a newlywed or have been married for decades, you can learn much from the Bible about marriage and successful human relationships. Read through the following collection of Bible verses and begin finding God's wisdom for improving your marriage.

CHAPTER 1

DEFINING MARRIAGE

"One flesh." That phrase grabbed me during a recent wedding I attended. Imagine what it would be like to actually attain "oneness" with someone physically, emotionally, and spiritually. While my husband and I share some values and some general dreams, there are a number of areas where I simply live my life and he lives his. I suppose that's natural to some extent. But that wedding has got me thinking: Should our lives overlap more? Are there additional core values we should be sharing?

■ *Ashley, age 48, Montana* ■

ACHIEVING ONENESS

And this is why a man leaves father and mother and cherishes his wife. No longer two, they become "one flesh." This is a huge mystery, and I don't pretend to understand it all.

EPHESIANS 5:31–32 MSG

So God created man in his own image, in the image of God he created him; male and female he created them.God blessed them and said to them, "Be fruitful and increase in number; fill the earth and subdue it. Rule over the fish of the sea and the birds of the air and over every living creature that moves on the ground."

GENESIS 1:27–28 NIV

Life is short, and you love your wife, so enjoy being with her. This is what you are supposed to do as you struggle through life on this earth.

ECCLESIASTES 9:9 CEV

I want them to be encouraged and knit together by strong ties of love. I want them to have complete confidence that they understand God's mysterious plan, which is Christ himself.

COLOSSIANS 2:2 NLT

"For where two or three are gathered in my name, I am there among them."

MATTHEW 18:20 NRSV

You do well when you complete the Royal Rule of the Scriptures: "Love others as you love yourself."

JAMES 2:8 MSG

No one has ever seen God; if we love one another, God lives in us, and his love is perfected in us.

1 JOHN 4:12 NRSV

How wonderful and pleasant it is when brothers live together in harmony!

PSALM 133:1 NLT

You were all called to travel on the same road and in the same direction, so stay together, both outwardly and inwardly. You have one Master, one faith, one baptism, one God and Father of all, who rules over all, works through all, and is present in all. Everything you are and think and do is permeated with Oneness.

EPHESIANS 4:4–6 MSG

SUBMITTING TO EACH OTHER

And further, submit to one another out of reverence for Christ. For wives, this means submit to your husbands as to the Lord. For a husband is the head of his wife as Christ is the head of the church. He is the Savior of his body, the church. As the church submits to Christ, so you wives should submit to your husbands in everything. For husbands, this means love your wives, just as Christ loved the church. He gave up his life for her.

EPHESIANS 5:21–25 NLT

Let us then pursue what makes for peace and for mutual upbuilding.

ROMANS 14:19 NRSV

Is there any encouragement from belonging to Christ? Any comfort from his love? Any fellowship together in the Spirit? Are your hearts tender and compassionate? Then make me truly happy by agreeing wholeheartedly with each other, loving one another, and working together with one mind and purpose. Don't be selfish; don't try to impress others. Be humble, thinking of others as better than yourselves. Don't look out only for your own interests, but take an interest in others, too. You must have the same attitude that Christ Jesus had.

PHILIPPIANS 2:1–5 NLT

In the same way, husbands ought to love their wives as they love their own bodies. For a man who loves his wife actually shows love for himself. No one hates his own body but feeds and cares for it, just as Christ cares for the church. And we are members of his body. . . . So again I say, each man must love his wife as he loves himself, and the wife must respect her husband.

EPHESIANS 5:28–30, 33 NLT

"Here is a simple rule of thumb for behavior: Ask yourself what you want people to do for you; then grab the initiative and do it for them!"

LUKE 6:31 MSG

But Jesus called the disciples together and said: You know that foreign rulers like to order their people around. And their great leaders have full power over everyone they rule. But don't act like them. If you want to be great, you must be the servant of all the others. And if you want to be first, you must be the slave of the rest. The Son of Man did not come to be a slave master, but a slave who will give his life to rescue many people.

MATTHEW 20:25–28 CEV

However, each one of you also must love his wife as he loves himself, and the wife must respect her husband.

EPHESIANS 5:33 NIV

Wives, understand and support your husbands by submitting to them in ways that honor the Master.

COLOSSIANS 3:18 MSG

As God's chosen ones, holy and beloved, clothe yourselves with compassion, kindness, humility, meekness, and patience.

COLOSSIANS 3:12 NRSV

SHARING A VISION

It's better to have a partner than go it alone. Share the work, share the wealth. And if one falls down, the other helps, but if there's no one to help, tough!

ECCLESIASTES 4:9–10 MSG

Can two walk together, unless they are agreed?

AMOS 3:3 NKJV

By yourself you're unprotected. With a friend you can face the worst. Can you round up a third? A three-stranded rope isn't easily snapped.

ECCLESIASTES 4:12 MSG

As iron sharpens iron, so a friend sharpens a friend.

PROVERBS 27:17 NLT

But more than anything else, put God's work first and do what he wants. Then the other things will be yours as well. Don't worry about tomorrow. It will take care of itself. You have enough to worry about today.

MATTHEW 6:33–34 CEV

Commit your works to the LORD and your plans will be established.

PROVERBS 16:3 NASB

"For I know the plans I have for you," says the Lord. "They are plans for good and not for disaster, to give you a future and a hope. In those days when you pray, I will listen. If you look for me whole-heartedly, you will find me."

JEREMIAH 29:11–13 NLT

That is what the Scriptures mean when they say, "No eye has seen, no ear has heard, and no mind has imagined what God has prepared for those who love him."

1 CORINTHIANS 2:9 NLT

ONE MOMENT AT A TIME
BECOMING ONE

1. **Face the size of the task.** Succeeding at marriage is difficult and should not be taken lightly. Commit yourself to the active and ongoing task of making your relationship a success. If you let your marriage mature by chance, it is unlikely to succeed.

2. **Evaluate against the right standard.** If you compare yourself with friends, you probably have a better marriage than some of them. Compare yourself, however, with the standard God gave. In what ways does your marriage model Christ's relationship with the church? In what ways do you need to improve?

3. **Pursue oneness.** Because both you and your spouse are human, it's unlikely that you'll achieve perfect unity. Still, marriages where both partners are working toward similar goals tend to be healthier than those where each spouse is concerned only for one's own plans and dreams. Find an area or two where you and your spouse do well. Continue to improve that strength. Isolate an area where you could stand to improve. Go to dinner or take a weekend away to discuss ways you might grow together.

CHAPTER 2

TRUE LOVE

On any given day, the amount of affection I feel for my husband
can swing as wildly as my blood sugar levels. A fond memory
can make my stomach jump like a schoolgirl, but that can quickly
fade into annoyance as I pick up his dirty socks again.
Sometimes the swings concern me. Am I normal?

■ *Joanna, age 32, Utah* ■

DEFINING LOVE

Dear children, let's not merely say that we love each other; let us show the truth by our actions.

1 JOHN 3:18 NLT

Such love has no fear, because perfect love expels all fear. If we are afraid, it is for fear of punishment, and this shows that we have not fully experienced his perfect love.

1 JOHN 4:18 NLT

For husbands, this means love your wives, just as Christ loved the church. He gave up his life for her.

EPHESIANS 5:25 NLT

If I speak in the tongues of men and of angels, but have not love, I am only a resounding gong or a clanging cymbal. If I have the gift of prophecy and can fathom all mysteries and all knowledge, and if I have a faith that can move mountains, but have not love, I am nothing. If I give all I possess to the poor and surrender my body to the flames, but have not love, I gain nothing. Love is patient, love is kind. It does not envy, it does not boast, it is not proud. It is not rude, it is not self-seeking, it is not easily angered, it keeps no record of wrongs. Love does not delight in evil but rejoices with the truth. It always protects, always trusts, always hopes, always perseveres. Love never fails.

1 CORINTHIANS 13:1–8 NIV

Above all, clothe yourselves with love, which binds us all together in perfect harmony. And let the peace that comes from Christ rule in your hearts. For as members of one body you are called to live in peace. And always be thankful.

COLOSSIANS 3:14–15 NLT

" 'Love others as much as you love yourself.' No other commandment is more important than these."

MARK 12:31 CEV

"There is no greater love than to lay down one's life for one's friends."

JOHN 15:13 NLT

BEING STEADFAST

Now it is required that those who have been given a trust must prove faithful.

1 CORINTHIANS 4:2 NIV

Many will say they are loyal friends, but who can find one who is truly reliable?

PROVERBS 20:6 NLT

Love the LORD, all his saints! The LORD preserves the faithful, but the proud he pays back in full.

PSALM 31:23 NIV

God blesses his loyal people.

PROVERBS 28:20 CEV

"Whoever can be trusted with very little can also be trusted with much, and whoever is dishonest with very little will also be dishonest with much."

LUKE 16:10 NIV

Do you know the saying, "Drink from your own rain barrel, draw water from your own spring-fed well"? It's true. Otherwise, you may one day come home and find your barrel empty and your well polluted.

PROVERBS 5:15–16 MSG

"But at the beginning of creation God 'made them male and female.' 'For this reason a man will leave his father and mother and be united to his wife, and the two will become one flesh.' So they are no longer two, but one. Therefore what God has joined together, let man not separate."

MARK 10:6–9 NIV

Do not let loyalty and faithfulness forsake you; bind them around your neck, write them on the tablet of your heart. So you will find favor and good repute in the sight of God and of people.

PROVERBS 3:3–4 NRSV

For the LORD loves justice; he will not forsake his saints. They are preserved forever, but the children of the wicked shall be cut off.

PSALM 37:28 ESV

"To the faithful you show yourself faithful; to those with integrity you show integrity."

2 SAMUEL 22:26 NLT

For example, by law a married woman is bound to her husband as long as he is alive, but if her husband dies, she is released from the law of marriage.

ROMANS 7:2 NIV

SHOWING AFFECTION

Don't just pretend to love others. Really love them. Hate what is wrong. Hold tightly to what is good. Love each other with genuine affection, and take delight in honoring each other.

ROMANS 12:9–10 NLT

The light of the eyes rejoices the heart, and good news refreshes the body.

PROVERBS 15:30 NRSV

"And since I, your Lord and Teacher, have washed your feet, you ought to wash each other's feet. I have given you an example to follow. Do as I have done to you."

JOHN 13:14–15 NLT

So it is right that I should feel as I do about all of you, for you have a special place in my heart. You share with me the special favor of God, both in my imprisonment and in defending and confirming the truth of the Good News.

PHILIPPIANS 1:7 NLT

A glad heart makes a cheerful countenance, but by sorrow of heart the spirit is broken.

PROVERBS 15:13 NRSV

For I have derived much joy and comfort from your love, my brother, because the hearts of the saints have been refreshed through you.

PHILEMON 1:7 ESV

We loved you so much that we were delighted to share with you not only the gospel of God but our lives as well, because you had become so dear to us.

1 THESSALONIANS 2:8 NIV

ONE MOMENT AT A TIME
LEARNING TO LOVE

1. **Redefine love.** Love is not just a feeling but a purposeful decision to be kind and sacrificial to the other person. Love is something you can choose to show no matter what you are feeling toward your spouse.

2. **Allow affection to follow.** Once you've been married for a while, the degree of affection you feel toward your spouse can vary. Whether you feel giddy or lethargic, make it your goal to live so that your spouse doesn't sense a difference because of your actions. You'll find that as you act lovingly, the warm emotions may follow.

3. **Be committed.** There may be moments that you fantasize about being married to someone else, or you may look back at your courtship and wonder if you married the right person. While doubts are natural, don't let them get in the way of the commitment you've made. Unless you are in an abusive situation, recommit to stay in your marriage. Don't linger on the dangerous daydreams. Instead, focus on your spouse and on your life together.

CHAPTER 3

YOU AND YOUR SPOUSE

I got married late. Some of my friends said I had a fear of commitment. Others said I loved my job too much. The truth is, I got married late because I was holding out for Mr. Perfect. It wasn't until I was approaching forty that I finally realized that Mr. Perfect didn't exist. While I love my new husband and our life together, I often counsel perfectionistic young women to be less picky. Sometimes it's enough if the man is headed in the right direction, loves Jesus, and puts you first. I've come to realize that they don't get much more perfect than that.

■ *Krista, age 40, California* ■

DEFINING THE IDEAL MAN

Better a poor man whose walk is blameless than a rich man whose ways are perverse.
PROVERBS 28:6 NIV

The righteous man leads a blameless life; blessed are his children after him.
PROVERBS 20:7 NIV

The man of integrity walks securely, but he who takes crooked paths will be found out.
PROVERBS 10:9 NIV

But there are preconditions: A leader must be well-thought-of, committed to his wife, cool and collected, accessible, and hospitable. He must know what he's talking about, not be overfond of wine, not pushy but gentle, not thin-skinned, not money-hungry. He must handle his own affairs well, attentive to his own children and having their respect. For if someone is unable to handle his own affairs, how can he take care of God's church? He must not be a new believer, lest the position go to his head and the Devil trip him up. Outsiders must think well of him, or else the Devil will figure out a way to lure him into his trap.
1 TIMOTHY 3:2–7 MSG

Blessed is the man who finds wisdom, the man who gains understanding, for she is more profitable than silver and yields better returns than gold.
PROVERBS 3:13–14 NIV

A man's pride brings him low, but a man of lowly spirit gains honor.
PROVERBS 29:23 NIV

154

DEFINING THE IDEAL WOMAN

Charm is deceptive, and beauty does not last; but a woman who fears the LORD will be greatly praised.

PROVERBS 31:30 NLT

Similarly, teach the older women to live in a way that honors God. They must not slander others or be heavy drinkers. Instead, they should teach others what is good. These older women must train the younger women to love their husbands and their children, to live wisely and be pure, to work in their homes, to do good, and to be submissive to their husbands. Then they will not bring shame on the word of God.

TITUS 2:3–5 NLT

Who can find a virtuous and capable wife? She is more precious than rubies. Her husband can trust her, and she will greatly enrich his life. She brings him good, not harm, all the days of her life. She finds wool and flax and busily spins it. She is like a merchant's ship, bringing her food from afar. She gets up before dawn to prepare breakfast for her household and plan the day's work for her servant girls. She goes to inspect a field and buys it; with her earnings she plants a vineyard. She is energetic and strong, a hard worker. She makes sure her dealings are profitable; her lamp burns late into the night. Her hands are busy spinning thread, her fingers twisting fiber. She extends a helping hand to the poor and opens her arms to the needy. She has no fear of winter for her household, for everyone has warm clothes. She makes her own bedspreads. She dresses in fine linen and purple gowns. . . . She is clothed with strength and dignity, and she laughs without fear of the future. When she speaks, her words are wise, and she gives instructions with kindness. She carefully watches everything in her household and suffers nothing from laziness.

PROVERBS 31:10–22, 25–27 NLT

A kindhearted woman gains respect, but ruthless men gain only wealth.

PROVERBS 11:16 NIV

A helpful wife is a jewel for her husband, but a shameless wife will make his bones rot.

PROVERBS 12:4 CEV

A woman's family is held together by her wisdom, but it can be destroyed by her foolishness.

PROVERBS 14:1 CEV

ASPIRING TO BE A GODLY MATE

Rather train yourself for godliness.

1 TIMOTHY 4:7 ESV

Like newborn babies, crave pure spiritual milk, so that by it you may grow up in your salvation.

1 PETER 2:2 NIV

155

God blesses those people who want to obey him more than to eat or drink. They will be given what they want!

MATTHEW 5:6 CEV

Dear friends, I urge you, as aliens and strangers in the world, to abstain from sinful desires, which war against your soul.

1 PETER 2:11 NIV

So I say, let the Holy Spirit guide your lives. Then you won't be doing what your sinful nature craves.

GALATIANS 5:16 NLT

But the Holy Spirit produces this kind of fruit in our lives: love, joy, peace, patience, kindness, goodness, faithfulness, gentleness, and self-control. There is no law against these things!

GALATIANS 5:22–23 NLT

And we are instructed to turn from godless living and sinful pleasures. We should live in this evil world with wisdom, righteousness, and devotion to God.

TITUS 2:12 NLT

Dear friends, God is good. So I beg you to offer your bodies to him as a living sacrifice, pure and pleasing. That's the most sensible way to serve God. Don't be like the people of this world, but let God change the way you think. Then you will know how to do everything that is good and pleasing to him.

ROMANS 12:1–2 CEV

Avoid every kind of evil.

1 THESSALONIANS 5:22 NIV

In view of all this, make every effort to respond to God's promises. Supplement your faith with a generous provision of moral excellence, and moral excellence with knowledge, and knowledge with self-control, and self-control with patient endurance, and patient endurance with godliness, and godliness with brotherly affection, and brotherly affection with love for everyone. The more you grow like this, the more productive and useful you will be in your knowledge of our Lord Jesus Christ.

2 PETER 1:5–8 NLT

In this way, you may know the truth and take an accurate report to those who sent you.

PROVERBS 22:21 NLT

Let us cleanse ourselves from all filthiness of the flesh and spirit, perfecting holiness in the fear of God.

2 CORINTHIANS 7:1 NKJV

Since everything around us is going to be destroyed like this, what holy and godly lives you should live, looking forward to the day of God and hurrying it along. On that day, he will set the heavens on fire, and the elements will melt away in the flames. But we are looking forward to the new heavens and new earth he has promised, a world filled with God's righteousness. And so, dear friends, while you are waiting for these things to happen, make every effort to be found living peaceful lives that are pure and blameless in his sight.

2 PETER 3:11–14 NLT

Anyone who claims to be intimate with God ought to live the same kind of life Jesus lived.

1 JOHN 2:6 MSG

God is not unjust; he will not forget your work and the love you have shown him as you have helped his people and continue to help them. We want each of you to show this same diligence to the very end, in order to make your hope sure. We do not want you to become lazy, but to imitate those who through faith and patience inherit what has been promised.

HEBREWS 6:10–12 NIV

Now may the God of peace make you holy in every way, and may your whole spirit and soul and body be kept blameless until our Lord Jesus Christ comes again.

1 THESSALONIANS 5:23 NLT

LOOKING BEYOND YOUR SPOUSE'S FAULTS

Always be humble and gentle. Patiently put up with each other and love each other. Try your best to let God's Spirit keep your hearts united. Do this by living at peace.

EPHESIANS 4:2–3 CEV

"Pay attention to yourselves! If your brother sins, rebuke him, and if

he repents, forgive him, and if he sins against you seven times in the day, and turns to you seven times, saying, 'I repent,' you must forgive him."

LUKE 17:3–4 ESV

If you forgive others for the wrongs they do to you, your Father in heaven will forgive you.

MATTHEW 6:14 CEV

He who covers a transgression seeks love, but he who repeats a matter separates friends.

PROVERBS 17:9 NKJV

"If your brother sins against you, go and tell him his fault, between you and him alone. If he listens to you, you have gained your brother."

MATTHEW 18:15 ESV

Hatred stirs up strife, but love covers all offenses.

PROVERBS 10:12 NRSV

Be kind and compassionate to one another, forgiving each other, just as in Christ God forgave you.

EPHESIANS 4:32 NIV

"So now I am giving you a new commandment: Love each other. Just as I have loved you, you should love each other."

JOHN 13:34 NLT

"Be merciful, just as your Father is merciful."

LUKE 6:36 NIV

Your kindness will reward you, but your cruelty will destroy you.

PROVERBS 11:17 NLT

So if you are about to place your gift on the altar and remember that someone is angry with you, leave your gift there in front of the altar. Make peace with that person, then come back and offer your gift to God.

MATTHEW 5:23–24 CEV

SUPPORTING EACH OTHER

Share each other's burdens, and in this way obey the law of Christ.

GALATIANS 6:2 NLT

If one part of our body hurts, we hurt all over. If one part of our body is honored, the whole body will be happy.

1 CORINTHIANS 12:26 CEV

Be devoted to one another in brotherly love. Honor one another above yourselves.

ROMANS 12:10 NIV

Let's see how inventive we can be in encouraging love and helping out.

HEBREWS 10:24 MSG

It's better to have a partner than go it alone. Share the work, share the wealth. And if one falls down, the other helps, but if there's no one to help, tough! Two in a bed warm each other. Alone, you shiver all night. By yourself you're unprotected. With a friend you can face the worst. Can

you round up a third? A three-stranded rope isn't easily snapped.

ECCLESIASTES 4:9–12 MSG

Jesus replied: "'Love the Lord your God with all your heart and with all your soul and with all your mind.' This is the first and greatest commandment. And the second is like it: 'Love your neighbor as yourself.' All the Law and the Prophets hang on these two commandments."

MATTHEW 22:37–40 NIV

RESPECTING YOUR SPOUSE

These older women must train the younger women to love their husbands and their children, to live wisely and be pure, to work in their homes, to do good, and to be submissive to their husbands. Then they will not bring shame on the word of God.

TITUS 2:4–5 NLT

Husbands, in the same way be considerate as you live with your wives, and treat them with respect as the weaker partner and as heirs with you of the gracious gift of life, so that nothing will hinder your prayers.

1 PETER 3:7 NIV

LIVING WITH AN UNBELIEVING SPOUSE

Instead, you must worship Christ as Lord of your life. And if someone asks about your Christian hope, always be ready to explain it. But do this in a gentle and respectful way. Keep your conscience clear. Then if people speak against you, they will be ashamed when they see what a good life you live because you belong to Christ.

1 PETER 3:15–16 NLT

Wives, in the same way be submissive to your husbands so that, if any of them do not believe the word, they may be won over without words by the behavior of their wives, when they see the purity and reverence of your lives.

1 PETER 3:1–2 NIV

"Let me tell you why you are here. You're here to be salt-seasoning that brings out the God-flavors of this earth. If you lose your saltiness, how will people taste godliness? You've lost your usefulness and will end up in the garbage. Here's another way to put it: You're here to be light, bringing out the God-colors in the world. God is not a secret to be kept. We're going public with this, as public as a city on a hill."

MATTHEW 5:13–14 MSG

Let your light so shine before men, that they may see your good works and glorify your Father in heaven.

MATTHEW 5:16 NKJV

Now, I will speak to the rest of you, though I do not have a direct command from the Lord. If a Christian man has a wife who is not a believer and she is willing to continue living with him, he must not leave her. And if a Christian woman has a husband who is not a believer and he is willing to continue living with her, she must not leave him. For the Christian wife brings holiness to her marriage, and the Christian husband brings holiness to his marriage. Otherwise, your children would not be holy, but now they are holy. (But if the husband or wife who isn't a believer insists on leaving, let them go. In such cases the Christian husband or wife is no longer bound to the other, for God has called you to live in peace.) Don't you wives realize that your husbands might be saved because of you? And don't you husbands realize that your wives might be saved because of you?

1 CORINTHIANS 7:12–16 NLT

ONE MOMENT AT A TIME
LIVING TOGETHER

1. **Count your blessings first.** Rather than become obsessed with your spouse's weaknesses, devote some time in your daily prayer to thank God for some specific strengths that you value in your spouse.

2. **Remember that neither of you is perfect.** Sure, it's easy to point out the faults of your partner, but you have your own weaknesses, too. Focus on fixing yourself before you set out to improve your spouse.

3. **Evaluate yourself humbly.** Don't take an "I'll fix this about me if you fix that about you" attitude. Ask your spouse to help you identify and work on a specific weakness in your own life.

4. **Demonstrate Christ's love every day.** Whether or not your spouse is a Christian, work hard at showing him or her the love Christ has shown you.

CHAPTER 4

DIVORCE AND REMARRIAGE

I have no doubt that my first marriage was a mistake. She was the wrong girl and I was certainly the wrong guy. While I was a Christian at the time, I was pretty immature and self-absorbed. I was quick to blame my wife for every conflict we faced. The divorce came quickly and she remarried within a few months. As for me, I've thought about getting remarried but my guilt lingers. Has God forgiven me for the role I played in that failure? Would God be okay with my giving marriage another shot?

■ *Jeremy, age 26, New York* ■

AVOIDING DIVORCE

But for those who are married, I have a command that comes not from me, but from the Lord. A wife must not leave her husband. But if she does leave him, let her remain single or else be reconciled to him. And the husband must not leave his wife.

1 CORINTHIANS 7:10–11 NLT

"You have heard the law that says, 'A man can divorce his wife by merely giving her a written notice of divorce.' But I say that a man who divorces his wife, unless she has been unfaithful, causes her to commit adultery. And anyone who marries a divorced woman also commits adultery."

MATTHEW 5:31–32 NLT

"Haven't you read the Scriptures?" Jesus replied. "They record that from the beginning 'God made them male and female.' And he said, 'This explains why a man leaves his father and mother and is joined to his wife, and the two are united into one.' Since they are no longer two but one, let no one split apart what God has joined together."

MATTHEW 19:4–6 NLT

"I hate divorce," says the LORD God of Israel.

MALACHI 2:16 NIV

Above all, love each other deeply, because love covers over a multitude of sins.

1 PETER 4:8 NIV

Jesus replied, "Moses permitted divorce only as a concession to your hard hearts, but it was not what God had originally intended. And I tell you this, whoever divorces his wife and marries someone else commits

161

adultery—unless his wife has been unfaithful." Jesus' disciples then said to him, "If this is the case, it is better not to marry!" "Not everyone can accept this statement," Jesus said. "Only those whom God helps. Some are born as eunuchs, some have been made eunuchs by others, and some choose not to marry for the sake of the Kingdom of Heaven. Let anyone accept this who can."

MATTHEW 19:8–12 NLT

Finishing is better than starting. Patience is better than pride. Control your temper, for anger labels you a fool.

ECCLESIASTES 7:8–9 NLT

BECOMING REMARRIED

Here is my advice for people who have never been married and for widows. You should stay single, just as I am. But if you don't have enough self-control, then go ahead and get married. After all, it is better to marry than to burn with desire.

1 CORINTHIANS 7:8–9 CEV

A righteous man is cautious in friendship, but the way of the wicked leads them astray.

PROVERBS 12:26 NIV

Those who trust their own insight are foolish, but anyone who walks in wisdom is safe.

PROVERBS 28:26 NLT

Stay away from people who are not followers of the Lord! Can someone who is good get along with someone who is evil? Are light and darkness the same? Is Christ a friend of Satan? Can people who follow the Lord have anything in common with those who don't?

2 CORINTHIANS 6:14–15 CEV

He who finds a wife finds a good thing, and obtains favor from the Lord.

PROVERBS 18:22 NRSV

You may inherit all you own from your parents, but a sensible wife is a gift from the LORD.

PROVERBS 19:14 CEV

Trust in the LORD and do good; dwell in the land and enjoy safe pasture. Delight yourself in the LORD and he will give you the desires of your heart. Commit your way to the LORD; trust in him and he will do this.

PSALM 37:3–5 NIV

ONE MOMENT AT A TIME
CONSIDERING REMARRIAGE

1. **Divorce is not the unforgivable sin.** If you have been divorced, there were probably plenty of sinful actions, thoughts, and attitudes on both sides of the table. It is important to remember that God forgives His children more than they deserve. God's forgiveness is complete and final.

2. **Consider a time to move on.** Reconciliation with your ex can be a God-honoring goal. If that goal is in your heart and your ex-spouse is open to it, then keep the matter in prayer and take steps to see if it is reasonable. If your spouse has moved on, it is important that you don't hold on to an unrealistic dream so that it cripples your life. If your previous marriage is over, then you may need to accept the finality of that fact and move on with your life.

3. **Don't point fingers.** Most marriages end with each party thinking that the ex-spouse was primarily to blame for the collapse of the relationship. Sit with a pastor or a close friend and focus instead on yourself. What can your divorce experience teach you? How can you become a better friend (or perhaps even a better spouse) in the future?

CHAPTER 5

COMMUNICATION

How can my wife not know that her spending drives me crazy?
Sure, I understand that day trips and vacations build memories for the
kids, but does it really require so much? To be honest, though, I can't
even discuss it with her without my blood pressure going through the
roof. We've got to talk about it soon or we'll go broke.

■ *Miguel, age 53, Tennessee* ■

COMMUNICATING WELL

Don't use foul or abusive language.
Let everything you say be good and
helpful, so that your words will be
an encouragement to those who
hear them.

> EPHESIANS 4:29 NLT

Fools show their anger at once, but
the prudent ignore an insult.

> PROVERBS 12:16 NRSV

Therefore each of you must put off
falsehood and speak truthfully to
his neighbor, for we are all members
of one body.

> EPHESIANS 4:25 NIV

Obscene stories, foolish talk, and
coarse jokes—these are not for you.
Instead, let there be thankfulness to
God.

> EPHESIANS 5:4 NLT

Timely advice is lovely, like golden
apples in a silver basket. To one who
listens, valid criticism is like a gold
earring or other gold jewelry.

> PROVERBS 25:11–12 NLT

May the words of my mouth and
the meditation of my heart be
pleasing in your sight, O LORD, my
Rock and my Redeemer.

> PSALM 19:14 NIV

LISTENING WELL

A truly wise person uses few words;
a person with understanding is
even-tempered.

> PROVERBS 17:27 NLT

Do you see someone who is hasty
in speech? There is more hope for a
fool than for anyone like that.

> PROVERBS 29:20 NRSV

Answering before listening is both
stupid and rude.

> PROVERBS 18:13 MSG

A fool gives full vent to anger, but
the wise quietly holds it back.

> PROVERBS 29:11 NRSV

"Why do you look at the speck of sawdust in your brother's eye and pay no attention to the plank in your own eye?"

MATTHEW 7:3 NIV

Know this, my beloved brothers: let every person be quick to hear, slow to speak, slow to anger.

JAMES 1:19 ESV

When words are many, sin is not absent, but he who holds his tongue is wise.

PROVERBS 10:19 NIV

Watch your tongue and keep your mouth shut, and you will stay out of trouble.

PROVERBS 21:23 NLT

HANDLING CONFLICT

Husbands, love your wives and never treat them harshly.

COLOSSIANS 3:19 NLT

Whoever is slow to anger has great understanding, but he who has a hasty temper exalts folly.

PROVERBS 14:29 ESV

If you churn milk you get butter; if you pound on your nose, you get blood—and if you stay angry, you get in trouble.

PROVERBS 30:33 CEV

Don't hit back; discover beauty in everyone.

ROMANS 12:17 MSG

Do not gloat when your enemy falls; when he stumbles, do not let your heart rejoice, or the LORD will see and disapprove.

PROVERBS 24:17–18 NIV

Rash words are like sword thrusts, but the tongue of the wise brings healing.

PROVERBS 12:18 NRSV

Therefore encourage one another and build each other up, just as in fact you are doing.

1 THESSALONIANS 5:11 NIV

AVOIDING SQUABBLES

Work at living in peace with everyone, and work at living a holy life, for those who are not holy will not see the Lord.

HEBREWS 12:14 NLT

Greed causes fighting; trusting the LORD leads to prosperity.

PROVERBS 28:25 NLT

Sensible people control their temper; they earn respect by overlooking wrongs.

PROVERBS 19:11 NLT

A gentle answer turns away wrath, but a harsh word stirs up anger.

PROVERBS 15:1 NIV

Starting a quarrel is like breaching a dam; so drop the matter before a dispute breaks out.

PROVERBS 17:14 NIV

"Do not judge others, and you will not be judged. For you will be treated as you treat others. The standard you use in judging is the standard by which you will be judged. And why worry about a speck in your friend's eye when you have a log in your own? How can you think of saying to your friend, 'Let me help you get rid of that speck in your eye,' when you can't see past the log in your own eye? Hypocrite! First get rid of the log in your own eye; then you will see well enough to deal with the speck in your friend's eye."

MATTHEW 7:1–5 NLT

Blessed are the peacemakers, for they will be called sons of God.

MATTHEW 5:9 NIV

The hotheaded do things they'll later regret; the coldhearted get the cold shoulder.

PROVERBS 14:17 MSG

A quarrelsome person in a dispute is like kerosene thrown on a fire.

PROVERBS 26:21 MSG

Anyone who loves to quarrel loves sin; anyone who trusts in high walls invites disaster.

PROVERBS 17:19 NLT

Peacemakers who sow in peace raise a harvest of righteousness.

JAMES 3:18 NIV

Kind words are like honey—sweet to the soul and healthy for the body.

PROVERBS 16:24 NLT

Better a dry crust eaten in peace than a house filled with feasting— and conflict.

PROVERBS 17:1 NLT

ONE MOMENT AT A TIME
DEALING WITH CONFLICT

1. **Listen.** It takes humility and restraint to listen without justifying yourself or defending your actions. Become a great listener. Learn to lose an argument rather than winning at all costs.

2. **Don't expect mind reading.** Many conflicts occur because the expectations aren't clear. Does your spouse know the things that drive you crazy? Or do you get upset when he or she hasn't lived up to expectations you've never communicated?

3. **Get off-site.** Do you have a topic that needs to be discussed? Perhaps something regarding money? Or something else regarding the kids? Try going off-site rather than talking at home. Discussing your topic over coffee at a neutral location can help discharge the situation.

CHAPTER 6

ANGER AND ABUSE

When we were dating, I thought it was sweet that he got jealous. I liked that he paid such close attention to what I wear and who I spend time with. I couldn't believe that such an amazing, perfect guy would want to be with me. But now that we've been married awhile, I'm not so sure. He gets really upset when I talk too much to anyone else. He says nasty things about certain clothes I wear. It seems like I can't do anything right. Everything I do makes him angry. Maybe it is my fault. Maybe I have no reason to feel afraid—but I do.

■ Madeline, age 36, Arkansas ■

DEALING WITH ANGER

A hot-tempered person starts fights; a cool-tempered person stops them.
PROVERBS 15:18 NLT

Be patient and trust the LORD. Don't let it bother you when all goes well for those who do sinful things. Don't be angry or furious. Anger can lead to sin.
PSALM 37:7–8 CEV

Don't get so angry that you sin. Don't go to bed angry.
EPHESIANS 4:26 CEV

Only fools get angry quickly and hold a grudge.
ECCLESIASTES 7:9 CEV

"I'm telling you that anyone who is so much as angry with a brother or sister is guilty of murder. Carelessly call a brother 'idiot!' and you just might find yourself hauled into court. Thoughtlessly yell 'stupid!' at a sister and you are on the brink of hellfire. The simple moral fact is that words kill."
MATTHEW 5:22 MSG

But now you must stop doing such things. You must quit being angry, hateful, and evil. You must no longer say insulting or cruel things about others.
COLOSSIANS 3:8 CEV

Don't befriend angry people or associate with hot-tempered people, or you will learn to be like them and endanger your soul.
PROVERBS 22:24–25 NLT

Beloved, never avenge yourselves, but leave it to the wrath of God, for it is written, "Vengeance is mine,

I will repay, says the Lord." To the contrary, "if your enemy is hungry, feed him; if he is thirsty, give him something to drink; for by so doing you will heap burning coals on his head." Do not be overcome by evil, but overcome evil with good.

ROMANS 12:19–21 ESV

If you see your enemy hungry, go buy him lunch; if he's thirsty, bring him a drink. Your generosity will surprise him with goodness, and GOD will look after you.

PROVERBS 25:21–22 MSG

"Blessed are those who are persecuted because of righteousness, for theirs is the kingdom of heaven. Blessed are you when people insult you, persecute you and falsely say all kinds of evil against you because of me. Rejoice and be glad, because great is your reward in heaven, for in the same way they persecuted the prophets who were before you."

MATTHEW 5:10–12 NIV

Let all bitterness and wrath and anger and clamor and slander be put away from you, along with all malice.

EPHESIANS 4:31 ESV

Better to be patient than powerful; better to have self-control than to conquer a city.

PROVERBS 16:32 NLT

Fools have short fuses and explode all too quickly; the prudent quietly shrug off insults.

PROVERBS 12:16 MSG

RESISTING BITTERNESS

See to it that no one misses the grace of God and that no bitter root grows up to cause trouble and defile many.

HEBREWS 12:15 NIV

Above all else, guard your heart, for it is the wellspring of life.

PROVERBS 4:23 NIV

Anyone who claims to be in the light but hates his brother is still in the darkness. Whoever loves his brother lives in the light, and there is nothing in him to make him stumble. But whoever hates his brother is in the darkness and walks around in the darkness; he does not know where he is going, because the darkness has blinded him.

1 JOHN 2:9–11 NIV

Don't grumble against each other, brothers, or you will be judged. The Judge is standing at the door!

JAMES 5:9 NIV

People may cover their hatred with pleasant words, but they're deceiving you. They pretend to be kind, but don't believe them. Their hearts are full of many evils. While their hatred may be concealed by trickery, their wrongdoing will be exposed in public.

PROVERBS 26:24–26 NLT

KEEPING SHORT ACCOUNTS

Then Peter came to Jesus and asked, "Lord, how many times shall I forgive my brother when he sins against me? Up to seven times?" Jesus answered, "I tell you, not seven times, but seventy-seven times."

MATTHEW 18:21–22 NIV

"But I tell you: Love your enemies and pray for those who persecute you."

MATTHEW 5:44 NIV

Whenever you stand up to pray, you must forgive what others have done to you. Then your Father in heaven will forgive your sins.

MARK 11:25 CEV

Be kind and compassionate to one another, forgiving each other, just as in Christ God forgave you.

EPHESIANS 4:32 NIV

Bear with each other and forgive whatever grievances you may have against one another. Forgive as the Lord forgave you.

COLOSSIANS 3:13 NIV

Dear friends, let us continue to love one another, for love comes from God. Anyone who loves is a child of God and knows God. But anyone who does not love does not know God, for God is love.

1 JOHN 4:7–8 NLT

The Lord passed in front of Moses, calling out, "Yahweh! The LORD! The God of compassion and mercy! I am slow to anger and filled with unfailing love and faithfulness."

EXODUS 34:6 NLT

"But love your enemies, do good to them, and lend to them without expecting to get anything back. Then your reward will be great, and you will be sons of the Most High, because he is kind to the ungrateful and wicked. Be merciful, just as your Father is merciful. Do not judge, and you will not be judged. Do not condemn, and you will not be condemned. Forgive, and you will be forgiven. Give, and it will be given to you. A good measure, pressed down, shaken together and running over, will be poured into your lap. For with the measure you use, it will be measured to you."

LUKE 6:35–38 NIV

CONFRONTING ABUSE

"You're blessed when you feel you've lost what is most dear to you. Only then can you be embraced by the One most dear to you."

MATTHEW 5:4 MSG

A prudent person foresees danger and takes precautions. The simpleton goes blindly on and suffers the consequences.

PROVERBS 22:3 NLT

Yet what we suffer now is nothing compared to the glory he will reveal to us later.

ROMANS 8:18 NLT

"I have told you these things, so that in me you may have peace. In this world you will have trouble. But take heart! I have overcome the world."

JOHN 16:33 NIV

I can do everything through him who gives me strength.

PHILIPPIANS 4:13 NIV

God gave us a spirit not of fear but of power and love and self-control.

2 TIMOTHY 1:7 ESV

On that day you will be glad, even if you have to go through many hard trials for a while. Your faith will be like gold that has been tested in a fire. And these trials will prove that your faith is worth much more than gold that can be destroyed. They will show that you will be given praise and honor and glory when Jesus Christ returns. You have never seen Jesus, and you don't see him now. But still you love him and have faith in him, and no words can tell how glad and happy you are to be saved. That's why you have faith.

1 PETER 1:6–9 CEV

Be brave and strong! Don't be afraid of the nations on the other side of the Jordan. The LORD your God will always be at your side, and he will never abandon you.

DEUTERONOMY 31:6 CEV

Don't be afraid. I am with you. Don't tremble with fear. I am your God. I will make you strong, as I protect you with my arm and give you victories.

ISAIAH 41:10 CEV

Be fair to the poor and to orphans. Defend the helpless and everyone in need.

PSALM 82:3 CEV

The LORD will lead you into the land. He will always be with you and help you, so don't ever be afraid of your enemies.

DEUTERONOMY 31:8 CEV

"Peace I leave with you; my peace I give you. I do not give to you as the world gives. Do not let your hearts be troubled and do not be afraid."

JOHN 14:27 NIV

The angel of the LORD encamps around those who fear him, and delivers them.

PSALM 34:7 NRSV

GETTING HELP

But God has so composed the body, giving greater honor to the part that lacked it, that there may be no division in the body, but that the members may have the same care for one another. If one member suffers, all suffer together; if one member is honored, all rejoice together.

1 CORINTHIANS 12:24–26 ESV

"Have I not commanded you? Be strong and courageous. Do not be terrified; do not be discouraged, for the LORD your God will be with you wherever you go."

JOSHUA 1:9 NIV

"And if God cares so wonderfully for flowers that are here today and thrown into the fire tomorrow, he will certainly care for you. Why do you have so little faith?"

LUKE 12:28 NLT

I look up to the mountains; does my strength come from mountains? No, my strength comes from God, who made heaven, and earth, and mountains.

PSALM 121:1–2 MSG

I, your God, have a firm grip on you and I'm not letting go. I'm telling you, "Don't panic. I'm right here to help you."

ISAIAH 41:13 MSG

The Lord is my rock, my fortress and my deliverer; my God is my rock, in whom I take refuge. He is my shield and the horn of my salvation, my stronghold.

PSALM 18:2 NIV

People of Jerusalem, you don't need to cry anymore. The Lord is kind, and as soon as he hears your cries for help, he will come.

ISAIAH 30:19 CEV

For he will command his angels concerning you to guard you in all your ways.

PSALM 91:11 NIV

You are my hiding place; you will protect me from trouble and surround me with songs of deliverance.

PSALM 32:7 NIV

"When you pass through the waters, I will be with you; and when you pass through the rivers, they will not sweep over you. When you walk through the fire, you will not be burned; the flames will not set you ablaze."

ISAIAH 43:2 NIV

Though you have made me see troubles, many and bitter, you will restore my life again; from the depths of the earth you will again bring me up.

PSALM 71:20 NIV

Therefore we do not lose heart. Though outwardly we are wasting away, yet inwardly we are being renewed day by day.

2 CORINTHIANS 4:16 NIV

God is our refuge and strength, an ever-present help in trouble. Therefore we will not fear, though the earth give way and the mountains fall into the heart of the sea, though its waters roar and foam and the mountains quake with their surging.

PSALM 46:1–3 NIV

"For I know the plans I have for you," declares the LORD, "plans to prosper you and not to harm you, plans to give you hope and a future."

JEREMIAH 29:11 NIV

Pile your troubles on God's shoulders—he'll carry your load, he'll help you out. He'll never let good people topple into ruin.

PSALM 55:22 MSG

Praise be to the Lord, to God our Savior, who daily bears our burdens.

PSALM 68:19 NIV

"The LORD is my rock and my fortress and my deliverer."

2 SAMUEL 22:2 NKJV

You hear, O Lord, the desire of the afflicted; you encourage them, and you listen to their cry.

PSALM 10:17 NIV

RECOVERING FROM ABUSE

By his wounds you are healed.

1 PETER 2:24 NLT

"The thief comes only to steal and kill and destroy; I have come that they may have life, and have it to the full."

JOHN 10:10 NIV

May our Lord Jesus Christ himself and God our Father, who loved us and by his grace gave us eternal encouragement and good hope, encourage your hearts and strengthen you in every good deed and word.

2 THESSALONIANS 2:16–17 NIV

He heals the brokenhearted and binds up their wounds.

PSALM 147:3 NIV

Be strong and take heart, all you who hope in the Lord.

PSALM 31:24 NIV

The Spirit of God, who raised Jesus from the dead, lives in you. And just as God raised Christ Jesus from the dead, he will give life to your mortal bodies by this same Spirit living within you.

ROMANS 8:11 NLT

Yet what we suffer now is nothing compared to the glory he will reveal to us later.

ROMANS 8:18 NLT

On that day you will be glad, even if you have to go through many hard trials for a while. Your faith will be like gold that has been tested in a fire. And these trials will prove that your faith is worth much more than gold that can be destroyed. They will show that you will be given praise and honor and glory when Jesus Christ returns. You have never seen Jesus, and you don't see him now. But still you love him and have faith in him, and no words can tell how glad and happy you are to be saved. That's why you have faith.

1 PETER 1:6–9 CEV

ONE MOMENT AT A TIME
FINDING SAFETY

1. **If you're in an abusive relationship, reject the lies your spouse feeds you.** You did not bring the abuse on yourself. You don't deserve to take the brunt of anger. You do deserve to be treated with respect.

2. **Forgiveness doesn't mean living with abuse.** Forgiveness doesn't mean it's okay for someone else to treat you abusively. Love your spouse enough to confront the sin and refuse to live with it.

3. **Don't isolate yourself.** Reach out until you find someone who really listens, understands, and takes steps to help you.

4. **If you feel afraid for your physical safety, get out fast.** God has given you an internal warning system—listen to it. Take immediate measures to protect yourself and develop a safe plan for getting out. If you need help, call an agency such as the National Domestic Violence Hotline.

CHAPTER 7

SEX AND INTIMACY

I've learned that the words sex *and* intimacy *are not interchangeable. While many people describe sex as "being intimate," it's really only intimacy if it reflects what comes out of your heart. Sex can be a picture of the intimate closeness, vulnerability, tenderness, and concern that exist between partners. I've also learned, though, that it's possible to become intimate with someone when there's no sex involved. Recently I found myself letting my heart become intimate with a coworker. While we haven't done anything physically inappropriate, I realize I've crossed an emotional line I should have reserved for my wife.*

■ *Don, age 30, Illinois* ■

LIVING INTIMATELY

Place me like a seal over your heart, like a seal on your arm; for love is as strong as death, its jealousy unyielding as the grave. It burns like blazing fire, like a mighty flame.

SONG OF SOLOMON 8:6 NIV

Fulfill my joy by being like-minded, having the same love, being of one accord, of one mind.

PHILIPPIANS 2:2 NKJV

If a man has recently married, he must not be sent to war or have any other duty laid on him. For one year he is to be free to stay at home and bring happiness to the wife he has married.

DEUTERONOMY 24:5 NIV

The LORD God said, "It is not good for the man to be alone. I will make a helper suitable for him." . . .So the LORD God caused the man to fall into a deep sleep; and while he was sleeping, he took one of the man's ribs and closed up the place with flesh. Then the LORD God made a woman from the rib he had taken out of the man, and he brought her to the man. The man said, "This is now bone of my bones and flesh of my flesh; she shall be called 'woman,' for she was taken out of man." For this reason a man will leave his father and mother and be united to his wife, and they will become one flesh.

GENESIS 2:18, 21–24 NIV

ENJOYING SEX

My lover is mine, and I am his. Nightly he strolls in our garden, delighting in the flowers.
SONG OF SOLOMON 2:16 MSG

May your fountain be blessed, and may you rejoice in the wife of your youth. A loving doe, a graceful deer—may her breasts satisfy you always, may you ever be captivated by her love.
PROVERBS 5:18–19 NIV

Let him kiss me with the kisses of his mouth! For your love is better than wine.
SONG OF SOLOMON 1:2 ESV

But because there is so much sexual immorality, each man should have his own wife, and each woman should have her own husband. The husband should fulfill his wife's sexual needs, and the wife should fulfill her husband's needs. The wife gives authority over her body to her husband, and the husband gives authority over his body to his wife. Do not deprive each other of sexual relations, unless you both agree to refrain from sexual intimacy for a limited time so you can give yourselves more completely to prayer. Afterward, you should come together again so that Satan won't be able to tempt you because of your lack of self-control.
1 CORINTHIANS 7:2–5 NLT

I belong to my lover, and his desire is for me.
SONG OF SOLOMON 7:10 NIV

As an apricot tree stands out in the forest, my lover stands above the young men in town. All I want is to sit in his shade, to taste and savor his delicious love.
SONG OF SOLOMON 2:3 MSG

MAINTAINING PURITY

Honor marriage, and guard the sacredness of sexual intimacy between wife and husband. God draws a firm line against casual and illicit sex.
HEBREWS 13:4 MSG

The acts of the sinful nature are obvious: sexual immorality, impurity and debauchery.
GALATIANS 5:19 NIV

Put to death, therefore, whatever belongs to your earthly nature: sexual immorality, impurity, lust, evil desires and greed, which is idolatry.
COLOSSIANS 3:5 NIV

Instead, clothe yourself with the presence of the Lord Jesus Christ. And don't let yourself think about ways to indulge your evil desires.
ROMANS 13:14 NLT

Run from anything that stimulates youthful lusts. Instead, pursue righteous living, faithfulness, love, and peace. Enjoy the companionship of those who call on the Lord with pure hearts.
2 TIMOTHY 2:22 NLT

175

Flee from sexual immorality. Every other sin a person commits is outside the body, but the sexually immoral person sins against his own body.

1 CORINTHIANS 6:18 ESV

But immorality or any impurity or greed must not even be named among you, as is proper among saints.

EPHESIANS 5:3 NASB

So behave properly, as people do in the day. Don't go to wild parties or get drunk or be vulgar or indecent. Don't quarrel or be jealous.

ROMANS 13:13 CEV

Don't you realize that your body is the temple of the Holy Spirit, who lives in you and was given to you by God? You do not belong to yourself, for God bought you with a high price. So you must honor God with your body.

1 CORINTHIANS 6:19–20 NLT

But now you must be holy in everything you do, just as God who chose you is holy. For the Scriptures say, "You must be holy because I am holy."

1 PETER 1:15–16 NLT

God didn't choose you to be filthy, but to be pure.

1 THESSALONIANS 4:7 CEV

God's will is for you to be holy, so stay away from all sexual sin.

1 THESSALONIANS 4:3 NLT

But each person is tempted when he is lured and enticed by his own desire.

JAMES 1:14 ESV

"But I tell you that anyone who looks at a woman lustfully has already committed adultery with her in his heart."

MATTHEW 5:28 NIV

WARNINGS AGAINST UNFAITHFULNESS

For these commands are a lamp, this teaching is a light, and the corrections of discipline are the way to life, keeping you from the immoral woman, from the smooth tongue of the wayward wife. Do not lust in your heart after her beauty or let her captivate you with her eyes, for the prostitute reduces you to a loaf of bread, and the adulteress preys upon your very life. Can a man scoop fire into his lap without his clothes being burned? Can a man walk on hot coals without his feet being scorched? So is he who sleeps with another man's wife; no one who touches her will go unpunished.

PROVERBS 6:23–29 NIV

My son, pay close attention and don't forget what I tell you to do. . . .From the window of my house, I once happened to see some foolish young men. . . . One of these young men turned the corner and was walking by the house of an unfaithful wife. She was dressed fancy like a woman of the street with only one thing in mind. . . . She grabbed him and kissed him, and with no sense of shame, she said: ". . .Let's go there [on my bed] and make love all night. My husband is traveling, and he's far away. . . ." And so, she tricked him with all of her sweet talk and her flattery. Right away he followed her like an ox on the way to be slaughtered, or like a fool on the way to be punished and killed with arrows. He was no more than a bird rushing into a trap, without knowing it would cost him his life. My son, pay close attention to what I have said. Don't even think about that kind of woman or let yourself be misled by someone like her. Such a woman has caused the downfall and destruction of a lot of men. Her house is a one-way street leading straight down to the world of the dead.

PROVERBS 1, 6, 9–10, 13, 18–19, 21–27 CEV

The mouth of an immoral woman is a deep pit; he who is abhorred by the LORD will fall there.

PROVERBS 22:14 NKJV

Now then, my sons, listen to me; do not turn aside from what I say. Keep to a path far from her, do not go near the door of her house. . . . Drink water from your own cistern, running water from your own well. Should your springs overflow in the streets, your streams of water in the public squares? Let them be yours alone, never to be shared with strangers. May your fountain be blessed, and may you rejoice in the wife of your youth. A loving doe, a graceful deer—may her breasts satisfy you always, may you ever be captivated by her love. Why be captivated, my son, by an adulteress? Why embrace the bosom of another man's wife? For a man's ways are in full view of the LORD, and he examines all his paths. The evil deeds of a wicked man ensnare him; the cords of his sin hold him fast. He will die for lack of discipline, led astray by his own great folly.

PROVERBS 5:7–8, 15–23 NIV

GUARDING AGAINST IMMORALITY

Be self-controlled and alert. Your enemy the devil prowls around like a roaring lion looking for someone to devour. Resist him, standing firm in the faith, because you know that your brothers throughout the world are undergoing the same kind of sufferings. And the God of all grace, who called you to his eternal glory in Christ, after you have suffered a little while, will himself restore you and make you strong, firm and steadfast.

1 PETER 5:8–10 NIV

So humble yourselves before God. Resist the devil, and he will flee from you.

JAMES 4:7 NLT

No testing has overtaken you that is not common to everyone. God is faithful, and he will not let you be tested beyond your strength, but

177

with the testing he will also provide the way out so that you may be able to endure it.

1 CORINTHIANS 10:13 NRSV

Blessed is anyone who endures temptation. Such a one has stood the test and will receive the crown of life that the Lord has promised to those who love him. No one, when tempted, should say, "I am being tempted by God"; for God cannot be tempted by evil and he himself tempts no one.

JAMES 1:12–13 NRSV

My brothers and sisters, whenever you face trials of any kind, consider it nothing but joy, because you know that the testing of your faith produces endurance.

JAMES 1:2–3 NRSV

For we do not have a high priest who is unable to sympathize with our weaknesses, but we have one who has been tempted in every way, just as we are—yet was without sin. Let us then approach the throne of grace with confidence, so that we may receive mercy and find grace to help us in our time of need.

HEBREWS 4:15–16 NIV

How can a young man keep his way pure? By living according to your word. I seek you with all my heart; do not let me stray from your commands. I have hidden your word in my heart that I might not sin against you.

PSALM 119:9–11 NIV

Finally, brothers, whatever is true, whatever is noble, whatever is right, whatever is pure, whatever is lovely, whatever is admirable—if anything is excellent or praiseworthy—think about such things.

PHILIPPIANS 4:8 NIV

With all your heart you must trust the LORD and not your own judgment. Always let him lead you, and he will clear the road for you to follow.

PROVERBS 3:5–6 CEV

Let us not become weary in doing good, for at the proper time we will reap a harvest if we do not give up. Therefore, as we have opportunity, let us do good to all people, especially to those who belong to the family of believers.

GALATIANS 6:9–10 NIV

Those who live according to the sinful nature have their minds set on what that nature desires; but those who live in accordance with the Spirit have their minds set on what the Spirit desires.

ROMANS 8:5 NIV

Put on all the armor that God gives, so you can defend yourself against the devil's tricks.

EPHESIANS 6:11 CEV

As obedient children, do not conform to the evil desires you had when you lived in ignorance.

1 PETER 1:14 NIV

Train me in good common sense; I'm thoroughly committed to living your way.

PSALM 119:66 MSG

For the grace of God that brings salvation has appeared to all men. It teaches us to say "No" to ungodliness and worldly passions, and to live self-controlled, upright and godly lives in this present age.

TITUS 2:11–12 NIV

For sin shall not be master over you, for you are not under law but under grace.

ROMANS 6:14 NASB

For this reason, since the day we heard about you, we have not stopped praying for you and asking God to fill you with the knowledge of his will through all spiritual wisdom and understanding. And we pray this in order that you may live a life worthy of the Lord and may please him in every way: bearing fruit in every good work, growing in the knowledge of God, being strengthened with all power according to his glorious might so that you may have great endurance and patience, and joyfully giving thanks to the Father, who has qualified you to share in the inheritance of the saints in the kingdom of light.

COLOSSIANS 1:9–12 NIV

And now that Jesus has suffered and was tempted, he can help anyone else who is tempted.

HEBREWS 2:18 CEV

ONE MOMENT AT A TIME
KEEPING YOUR MARRIAGE PURE

1. **Broaden your definition of intimacy.** Being intimate with someone is much more than just the physical relationship. Save your body—and your heart—for the one to whom it belongs. Just as bodies become intertwined, work on letting your hearts and lives reflect that same closeness.

2. **Talk about it.** The subject of sex can be sensitive for many couples. Find a way to talk about it even if it is awkward at first. Define expectations, explain interests, and share your frustrations. If you're too embarrassed to talk about it, you will not solve the problems you need to discuss.

3. **Fight for purity.** Sin is often enjoyable at the moment, and lust is no exception. Giving in to it, however, leads to guilt, strained intimacy, and resentfulness when your spouse doesn't live up to unreasonable fantasies you've enjoyed. Steer clear of places, books, Internet sites, or people who lure you into this temptation.

CHAPTER 8

YOU AND YOUR FAMILY

My marriage has another woman in it. In fact, my wife encourages it. We frequently have her over and we leave our kids with her. Sound strange? The other woman is my mother-in-law. You'd think with how quickly we go along with her opinions that she is an equal partner in our marriage. I've tried to talk to my wife about it and she says she agrees with me, but she's just not willing to stand up to her mom or set appropriate boundaries.

■ *Carl, age 38, Connecticut* ■

SHARING GOD'S PERSPECTIVE ON CHILDREN

Children are a gift from the LORD; they are a reward from him. Children born to a young man are like arrows in a warrior's hands. How joyful is the man whose quiver is full of them! He will not be put to shame when he confronts his accusers at the city gates.

PSALM 127:3–5 NLT

For you created my inmost being; you knit me together in my mother's womb. I praise you because I am fearfully and wonderfully made; your works are wonderful, I know that full well. My frame was not hidden from you when I was made in the secret place. When I was woven together in the depths of the earth, your eyes saw my unformed body. All the days ordained for me were written in your book before one of them came to be.

PSALM 139:13–16 NIV

All you who fear GOD, how blessed you are! how happily you walk on his smooth straight road! You worked hard and deserve all you've got coming. Enjoy the blessing! Revel in the goodness! Your wife will bear children as a vine bears grapes, your household lush as a vineyard. The children around your table as fresh and promising as young olive shoots. Stand in awe of God's Yes. Oh, how he blesses the one who fears GOD!

PSALM 128:1–4 MSG

BEING INTENTIONAL ABOUT PARENTING

Train up a child in the way he should go; even when he is old he will not depart from it.

PROVERBS 22:6 ESV

"But watch out! Be careful never to forget what you yourself have seen.

Do not let these memories escape from your mind as long as you live! And be sure to pass them on to your children and grandchildren. Never forget the day when you stood before the LORD your God at Mount Sinai, where he told me, 'Summon the people before me, and I will personally instruct them. Then they will learn to fear me as long as they live, and they will teach their children to fear me also.' "

DEUTERONOMY 4:9–10 NLT

Memorize his laws and tell them to your children over and over again. Talk about them all the time, whether you're at home or walking along the road or going to bed at night, or getting up in the morning. Write down copies and tie them to your wrists and foreheads to help you obey them. Write these laws on the door frames of your homes and on your town gates.

DEUTERONOMY 6:6–9 CEV

"For I have chosen him, so that he will direct his children and his household after him to keep the way of the LORD by doing what is right and just, so that the LORD will bring about for Abraham what he has promised him."

GENESIS 18:19 NIV

"But if serving the LORD seems undesirable to you, then choose for yourselves this day whom you will serve, whether the gods your forefathers served beyond the River, or the gods of the Amorites, in whose land you are living. But as for me and my household, we will serve the LORD."

JOSHUA 24:15 NIV

From infancy you have known the holy Scriptures, which are able to make you wise for salvation through faith in Christ Jesus.

2 TIMOTHY 3:15 NIV

Fathers, do not provoke your children to anger, but bring them up in the discipline and instruction of the Lord.

EPHESIANS 6:4 ESV

SERVING TOGETHER

"You must present as the LORD's portion the best and holiest part of everything given to you."

NUMBERS 18:29 NIV

Jesus sat down near the collection box in the Temple and watched as the crowds dropped in their money. Many rich people put in large amounts. Then a poor widow came and dropped in two small coins. Jesus called his disciples to him and said, "I tell you the truth, this poor widow has given more than all the others who are making contributions. For they gave a tiny part of their surplus, but she, poor as she is, has given everything she had to live on."

MARK 12:41–44 NLT

Those who are generous are blessed,
for they share their bread with the
poor.

PROVERBS 22:9 NRSV

"For truly, I say to you, whoever
gives you a cup of water to drink
because you belong to Christ will
by no means lose his reward."

MARK 9:41 ESV

Give freely and spontaneously.
Don't have a stingy heart. The way
you handle matters like this triggers
GOD, your God's, blessing in everything you do, all your work and
ventures. There are always going to
be poor and needy people among
you. So I command you: Always be
generous, open purse and hands,
give to your neighbors in trouble,
your poor and hurting neighbors.

DEUTERONOMY 15:10–11 MSG

When God's people are in need, be
ready to help them. Always be eager
to practice hospitality.

ROMANS 12:13 NLT

ENFORCING DISCIPLINE

Young people are prone to foolishness and fads; the cure comes
through tough-minded discipline.

PROVERBS 22:15 MSG

Correct your children before it's too
late; if you don't punish them, you
are destroying them.

PROVERBS 19:18 CEV

He who spares the rod hates his
son, but he who loves him is careful
to discipline him.

PROVERBS 13:24 NIV

And you have forgotten that word
of encouragement that addresses
you as sons: "My son, do not make
light of the Lord's discipline, and
do not lose heart when he rebukes
you, because the Lord disciplines
those he loves, and he punishes
everyone he accepts as a son." Endure hardship as discipline; God is
treating you as sons. For what son is
not disciplined by his father? If you
are not disciplined (and everyone
undergoes discipline), then you are
illegitimate children and not true
sons. Moreover, we have all had
human fathers who disciplined us
and we respected them for it. How
much more should we submit to
the Father of our spirits and live!
Our fathers disciplined us for a
little while as they thought best; but
God disciplines us for our good,
that we may share in his holiness.
No discipline seems pleasant at
the time, but painful. Later on,
however, it produces a harvest of
righteousness and peace for those
who have been trained by it.

HEBREWS 12:5–11 NIV

Don't be afraid to correct your
young ones; a spanking won't kill
them. A good spanking, in fact,
might save them from something
worse than death.

PROVERBS 23:13–14 MSG

To discipline a child produces wisdom, but a mother is disgraced by an undisciplined child.

PROVERBS 29:15 NLT

HONORING PARENTS

"Honor your father and your mother, so that you may live long in the land the LORD your God is giving you."

EXODUS 20:12 NIV

But if a widow has children or grandchildren, these should learn first of all to put their religion into practice by caring for their own family and so repaying their parents and grandparents, for this is pleasing to God.

1 TIMOTHY 5:4 NIV

Grandchildren are the crown of the aged, and the glory of children is their parents.

PROVERBS 17:6 NRSV

A wise son makes a glad father, but a foolish son is the grief of his mother.

PROVERBS 10:1 NKJV

But standing by the cross of Jesus were his mother and his mother's sister, Mary the wife of Clopas, and Mary Magdalene. When Jesus saw his mother and the disciple whom he loved standing nearby, he said to his mother, "Woman, behold, your son!" Then he said to the disciple, "Behold, your mother!" And from that hour the disciple took her to his own home.

JOHN 19:25–27 ESV

If anyone does not provide for his relatives, and especially for his immediate family, he has denied the faith and is worse than an unbeliever.

1 TIMOTHY 5:8 NIV

Anyone who steals from his father and mother and says, "What's wrong with that?" is no better than a murderer.

PROVERBS 28:24 NLT

If any believing woman has relatives who are widows, let her care for them. Let the church not be burdened, so that it may care for those who are truly widows.

1 TIMOTHY 5:16 ESV

The women said to Naomi: "Praise be to the LORD, who this day has not left you. . . . For your daughter-in-law, who loves you and who is better to you than seven sons."

RUTH 4:14–15 NIV

My child, listen when your father corrects you. Don't neglect your mother's instruction.

PROVERBS 1:8 NLT

For God commanded, "Honor your father and your mother," and, "Whoever reviles father or mother must surely die." But you say, "If anyone tells his father or his mother, 'What you would have gained from me is given to God,' he need not honor his father." So for the sake of your tradition you have made void the word of God.

MATTHEW 15:4–6 ESV

183

ONE MOMENT AT A TIME
LOVING YOUR CHILDREN

1. **Don't leave it to chance.** Identify character traits you would like to see developed in your children. Create a specific plan to help make those changes a reality.

2. **Build a relationship.** If you own a dog, you can probably get the animal to toe the line with a combination of positive and negative reinforcements. Kids, however, need much, much more. Work hard at being more than the general who snaps orders and expects full compliance. Get to know your kids, listen to them, and create an atmosphere that is tailored to their success and that also encourages obedience.

3. **Build a support system.** One hundred years ago, a typical family might have had a few generations (and perhaps some extended family) living nearby or even under the same roof. In those days, finding support, getting advice, and soliciting help was easy. Today's families are very different. Make sure you have a network you can compare notes and exchange ideas with. Find a group that you can be honest with—without feeling the need to compete with them.

4. **Honor your own parents.** The Bible's command to honor our parents does not come with an age limit. No matter how you feel about them, the office of parent should be respected.

CHAPTER 9

TRAITS OF A STRONG MARRIAGE

It took awhile, but I finally found the secret to a good marriage. It's actually pretty simple: I had to realize that it's not about me. When I go through our routine by looking out for her (her needs, her choices, her preferences), I find we really start to click. Yes, I end up living a life of sacrifice, but I'd say we finally have a great marriage. And if you think I'm nothing but a doormat, then you haven't seen the whole picture. What I've found is that the more I give, the more she gives in return. Honestly, life has never been better.

■ *Robert, age 57, Texas* ■

CHOOSING A JOYFUL SPIRIT

Be joyful in hope, patient in affliction, faithful in prayer.
ROMANS 12:12 NIV

Be glad in the LORD and rejoice, you righteous ones; And shout for joy, all you who are upright in heart.
PSALM 32:11 NASB

In him our hearts rejoice, for we trust in his holy name.
PSALM 33:21 NLT

For the kingdom of God is not a matter of eating and drinking, but of righteousness, peace and joy in the Holy Spirit.
ROMANS 14:17 NIV

Then my soul will rejoice in the LORD, exulting in his salvation.
PSALM 35:9 ESV

Make a joyful noise to the LORD, all the earth!
PSALM 100:1 ESV

Rejoice in the Lord always. I will say it again: Rejoice!
PHILIPPIANS 4:4 NIV

Rejoice always.
1 THESSALONIANS 5:16 ESV

The precepts of the LORD are right, rejoicing the heart; the commandment of the LORD is pure, enlightening the eyes.
PSALM 19:8 NASB

But I trust in your unfailing love; my heart rejoices in your salvation.
PSALM 13:5 NIV

May the God of hope fill you with all joy and peace as you trust in him, so that you may overflow with

185

hope by the power of the Holy
Spirit.

ROMANS 15:13 NIV

I will be glad and exult in you; I
will sing praise to your name, O
Most High.

PSALM 9:2 NRSV

You have put gladness in my heart.

PSALM 4:7 NKJV

Worship God in adoring embrace,
celebrate in trembling awe.

PSALM 2:11 MSG

"These things I have spoken to you,
that my joy may be in you, and that
your joy may be full."

JOHN 15:11 ESV

FEELING SECURE IN YOUR IDENTITY IN CHRIST

For you are all children of God
through faith in Christ Jesus.

GALATIANS 3:26 NLT

All this is from God, who reconciled us to himself through Christ
and gave us the ministry of reconciliation: that God was reconciling
the world to himself in Christ, not
counting men's sins against them.
And he has committed to us the
message of reconciliation. We are
therefore Christ's ambassadors, as
though God were making his appeal through us. We implore you
on Christ's behalf: Be reconciled to

God. God made him who had no
sin to be sin for us, so that in him
we might become the righteousness
of God.

2 CORINTHIANS 5:18–21 NIV

But to all who did receive him, who
believed in his name, he gave the
right to become children of God.

JOHN 1:12 ESV

For all who are led by the Spirit
of God are children of God. So
you have not received a spirit that
makes you fearful slaves. Instead,
you received God's Spirit when he
adopted you as his own children.
Now we call him, "Abba, Father."

ROMANS 8:14–15 NLT

"I no longer call you servants,
because a servant does not know his
master's business. Instead, I have
called you friends, for everything
that I learned from my Father I
have made known to you."

JOHN 15:15 NIV

Praise the God and Father of our
Lord Jesus Christ for the spiritual
blessings that Christ has brought us
from heaven! Before the world was
created, God had Christ choose us
to live with him and to be his holy
and innocent and loving people.
God was kind and decided that
Christ would choose us to be God's
own adopted children. God was
very kind to us because of the Son
he dearly loves, and so we should
praise God.

EPHESIANS 1:3–6 CEV

KNOWING YOUR SELF-WORTH

How precious are your thoughts about me, O God. They cannot be numbered! I can't even count them; they outnumber the grains of sand! And when I wake up, you are still with me!

PSALM 139:17–18 NLT

"Before I shaped you in the womb, I knew all about you. Before you saw the light of day, I had holy plans for you: A prophet to the nations— that's what I had in mind for you."

JEREMIAH 1:5 MSG

He gave his life to free us from every kind of sin, to cleanse us, and to make us his very own people, totally committed to doing good deeds.

TITUS 2:14 NLT

"For the LORD your God is living among you. He is a mighty savior. He will take delight in you with gladness. With his love, he will calm all your fears. He will rejoice over you with joyful songs."

ZEPHANIAH 3:17 NLT

REMAINING HUMBLE

So, if you think you are standing firm, be careful that you don't fall!

1 CORINTHIANS 10:12 NIV

Humble yourselves, therefore, under the mighty hand of God so that at the proper time he may exalt you.

1 PETER 5:6 ESV

The LORD sustains the humble but casts the wicked to the ground.

PSALM 147:6 NIV

For the LORD delights in his people; he crowns the humble with victory.

PSALM 149:4 NLT

For my part, I am going to boast about nothing but the Cross of our Master, Jesus Christ. Because of that Cross, I have been crucified in relation to the world, set free from the stifling atmosphere of pleasing others and fitting into the little patterns that they dictate.

GALATIANS 6:14 MSG

Let another praise you, and not your own mouth; someone else, and not your own lips.

PROVERBS 27:2 NIV

"Blessed are the poor in spirit, for theirs is the kingdom of heaven."

MATTHEW 5:3 NKJV

He has showed you, O man, what is good. And what does the LORD require of you? To act justly and to love mercy and to walk humbly with your God.

MICAH 6:8 NIV

Because of the privilege and authority God has given me, I give each of you this warning: Don't think you are better than you really are. Be honest in your evaluation of yourselves, measuring yourselves by the faith God has given us.

ROMANS 12:3 NLT

DEALING WITH DIFFICULTIES

My flesh and my heart fail; but God is the strength of my heart and my portion forever.

PSALM 73:26 NKJV

Give all your worries and cares to God, for he cares about you.

1 PETER 5:7 NLT

"The LORD will fight for you; you need only to be still."

EXODUS 14:14 NIV

Trust in him at all times, O people; pour out your hearts to him, for God is our refuge.

PSALM 62:8 NIV

To him who is able to keep you from falling and to present you before his glorious presence without fault and with great joy—to the only God our Savior be glory, majesty, power and authority, through Jesus Christ our Lord, before all ages, now and forevermore!

JUDE 24–25 NIV

We are afflicted in every way, but not crushed; perplexed, but not driven to despair; persecuted, but not forsaken; struck down, but not destroyed; always carrying in the body the death of Jesus, so that the life of Jesus may also be manifested in our bodies.

2 CORINTHIANS 4:8–10 ESV

The LORD is close to the broken-hearted; he rescues those whose spirits are crushed.

PSALM 34:18 NLT

"Don't be afraid, I've redeemed you. I've called your name. You're mine. When you're in over your head, I'll be there with you. When you're in rough waters, you will not go down. When you're between a rock and a hard place, it won't be a dead end—because I am GOD, your personal God, the Holy of Israel, your Savior. I paid a huge price for you: all of Egypt, with rich Cush and Seba thrown in! That's how much you mean to me! That's how much I love you! I'd sell off the whole world to get you back, trade the creation just for you."

ISAIAH 43:1–4 MSG

FINDING STRENGTH IN CHRIST

Do you not know? Have you not heard? The LORD is the everlasting God, the Creator of the ends of the earth. He will not grow tired or weary, and his understanding no one can fathom. He gives strength to the weary and increases the power of the weak. Even youths grow tired and weary, and young men stumble and fall; but those who hope in the LORD will renew their strength. They will soar on wings like eagles; they will run and not grow weary, they will walk and not be faint.

ISAIAH 40:28–31 NIV

Then Jesus said, "Come to me, all of you who are weary and carry heavy burdens, and I will give you rest. Take my yoke upon you. Let me teach you, because I am humble and gentle at heart, and you will find rest for your souls. For my yoke is easy to bear, and the burden I give you is light."

MATTHEW 11:28–30 NLT

But he replied, "My kindness is all you need. My power is strongest when you are weak." So if Christ keeps giving me his power, I will gladly brag about how weak I am. Yes, I am glad to be weak or insulted or mistreated or to have troubles and sufferings, if it is for Christ. Because when I am weak, I am strong.

2 CORINTHIANS 12:9–10 CEV

The LORD is my light and my salvation—whom shall I fear? The LORD is the stronghold of my life—of whom shall I be afraid? . . . Though an army besiege me, my heart will not fear; though war break out against me, even then will I be confident.

PSALM 27:1, 3 NIV

The eternal God is your refuge, and underneath are the everlasting arms. He will drive out your enemy before you.

DEUTERONOMY 33:27 NIV

When I felt my feet slipping, you came with your love and kept me steady. And when I was burdened with worries, you comforted me and made me feel secure.

PSALM 94:18–19 CEV

BEING GRATEFUL FOR WHAT GOD GIVES YOU

Shout with joy to the LORD, all the earth! Worship the LORD with gladness. Come before him, singing with joy. Acknowledge that the LORD is God! He made us, and we are his. We are his people, the sheep of his pasture. Enter his gates with thanksgiving; go into his courts with praise. Give thanks to him and praise his name.

PSALM 100:1–4 NLT

Offer to God a sacrifice of thanksgiving. And pay your vows to the Most High.

PSALM 50:14 NASB

Give thanks to the LORD, for he is good! His faithful love endures forever.

PSALM 107:1 NLT

GLORIFYING GOD TOGETHER

Give to the LORD, O families of the peoples, give to the LORD glory and strength.

1 CHRONICLES 16:28 NKJV

Oh, magnify the LORD with me, and let us exalt his name together!

PSALM 34:3 ESV

Not to us, O Lord, not to us, but to your name give glory, for the sake of your steadfast love and your faithfulness!

PSALM 115:1 NRSV

So whether you eat or drink or whatever you do, do it all for the glory of God.

1 CORINTHIANS 10:31 NIV

You who fear the Lord, praise him! All you offspring of Jacob, glorify him, and stand in awe of him, all you offspring of Israel!

PSALM 22:23 ESV

Let me shout God's name with a praising song, let me tell his greatness in a prayer of thanks.

PSALM 69:30 MSG

I will praise you, O Lord my God, with all my heart; I will glorify your name forever.

PSALM 86:12 NIV

You are my God, and I will give you thanks; you are my God, and I will exalt you.

PSALM 118:28 NIV

ONE MOMENT AT A TIME
CHOOSING UNITY

1. **Be a giver.** Giving is hard work, and putting someone else's needs ahead of your own is a difficult, conscious choice. Start small. Set reasonable goals for initial changes you can make.

2. **Don't be petty.** It's easy to hold a grudge, bicker, and squabble over little things. Choose kindness instead and let offenses roll over you without hanging on to them.

3. **Do life together.** Many married couples live under the same roof and communicate through complaining about life or bickering with each other. Take a different approach. Tackle life together. Work to stay on the same team and go face challenges together.

WHAT THE BIBLE SAYS ABOUT MONEY

INTRODUCTION

IN GOD WE TRUST

Most people turn to the Bible for inspiration. They read well-known passages and find comfort in learning about God, who loves them. And while this is the primary reason the Bible was written, many readers don't realize that the Bible can also be a practical tool in approaching your monthly budget. The truth is, the Bible contains more than fifteen hundred passages on the topic of money and giving, which makes it one of the most frequented subjects in the Bible. Why did God devote so much time to this area? Probably because what Billy Graham once said is true: "If a person gets his attitude toward money straight, it will help straighten out almost every other area in his life." So what's God's perspective on money? Turn the next few pages and begin to find out.

CHAPTER 1

STEWARDSHIP: IT'S ALL FROM HIM

I used to think that my money was my business. I had worked hard at saving, had enjoyed watching my investments grow, and had patted myself on the back for being so frugal. Then as I've begun to read the Bible, I've had my attitudes on money turned upside down. The more I read, the more I realize that God is the owner of everything and that He has merely lent me some of His assets. And while I enjoy the money that passes through my wallet, I'm growing more and more convinced it isn't really mine—it's His.

■ *Josh, age 28, California* ■

RECOGNIZING GOD'S OWNERSHIP

The earth and everything on it belong to the LORD. The world and its people belong to him.

PSALM 24:1 CEV

The land cannot be sold permanently because the land is mine and you are foreigners—you're my tenants.

LEVITICUS 25:23 MSG

For all the animals of the forest are mine, and I own the cattle on a thousand hills. I know every bird on the mountains, and all the animals of the field are mine. If I were hungry, I would not tell you, for all the world is mine and everything in it.

PSALM 50:10–12 NLT

Everything comes from the Lord. All things were made because of him and will return to him. Praise the Lord forever! Amen.

ROMANS 11:36 CEV

"I own the silver, I own the gold." Decree of God-of-the-Angel-Armies.

HAGGAI 2:8 MSG

You care for the land and water it; you enrich it abundantly. The streams of God are filled with water to provide the people with grain, for so you have ordained it. You drench its furrows and level its ridges; you soften it with showers and bless its crops.

PSALM 65:9–10 NIV

"Yours, O LORD, is the greatness and the power and the glory and the majesty and the splendor, for everything in heaven and earth is yours. Yours, O LORD, is the kingdom; you are exalted as head over all. Wealth and honor come from you; you are the ruler of all things. In your hands are strength and power to exalt and give strength to all. Now, our God, we give you thanks, and praise your glorious name. But who am I, and who are my people, that we should be able to give as generously as this? Everything comes from you, and we have given you only what comes from your hand. We are aliens and strangers in your sight, as were all our forefathers. Our days on earth are like a shadow, without hope. O LORD our God, as for all this abundance that we have provided for building you a temple for your Holy Name, it comes from your hand, and all of it belongs to you. I know, my God, that you test the heart and are pleased with integrity. All these things have I given willingly and with honest intent. And now I have seen with joy how willingly your people who are here have given to you. O LORD, God of our fathers Abraham, Isaac and Israel, keep this desire in the hearts of your people forever, and keep their hearts loyal to you."

1 CHRONICLES 29:11–18 NIV

REMEMBERING THAT GOD IS RESPONSIBLE FOR YOUR WEALTH

God's blessing makes life rich; nothing we do can improve on God.

PROVERBS 10:22 MSG

"Submit to God and be at peace with him; in this way prosperity will come to you."

JOB 22:21 NIV

"And the LORD will guide you continually and satisfy your desire in scorched places and make your bones strong; and you shall be like a watered garden, like a spring of water, whose waters do not fail."

ISAIAH 58:11 ESV

Rejoice, you people of Jerusalem! Rejoice in the LORD your God! For the rain he sends demonstrates his faithfulness. Once more the autumn rains will come, as well as the rains of spring.

JOEL 2:23 NLT

"I will send you rain in its season, and the ground will yield its crops and the trees of the field their fruit. Your threshing will continue until grape harvest and the grape harvest will continue until planting, and you will eat all the food you want and live in safety in your land."

LEVITICUS 26:4–5 NIV

"Nevertheless He did not leave Himself without witness, in that He did good, gave us rain from heaven

193

and fruitful seasons, filling our hearts with food and gladness."

ACTS 14:17 NKJV

He gave food to those who fear him, he remembered to keep his ancient promise.

PSALM 111:5 MSG

The LORD is my shepherd; I have all that I need.

PSALM 23:1 NLT

Praise the LORD! Happy are those who fear the LORD, who greatly delight in his commandments. Their descendants will be mighty in the land; the generation of the upright will be blessed.

PSALM 112:1–2 NRSV

"If you carefully obey all the commands I am giving you today, and if you love the LORD your God and serve him with all your heart and soul, then he will send the rains in their proper seasons—the early and late rains—so you can bring in your harvests of grain, new wine, and olive oil. He will give you lush pastureland for your livestock, and you yourselves will have all you want to eat."

DEUTERONOMY 11:13–15 NLT

"Keep the charge of the LORD your God, walking in his ways and keeping his statutes, his commandments, his ordinances, and his testimonies, as it is written in the law of Moses, so that you may prosper in all that you do and wherever you turn."

1 KINGS 2:3 NRSV

The house of the righteous contains great treasure, but the income of the wicked brings them trouble.

PROVERBS 15:6 NIV

SEEING BIBLICAL EXAMPLES OF GOD'S BLESSING

The Lord was pleased that Solomon had asked for wisdom. So God replied, "Because you have asked for wisdom in governing my people with justice and have not asked for a long life or wealth or the death of your enemies—I will give you what you asked for! I will give you a wise and understanding heart such as no one else has had or ever will have! And I will also give you what you did not ask for—riches and fame! No other king in all the world will be compared to you for the rest of your life!"

1 KINGS 3:10–13 NLT

And Samuel said, "Though you are little in your own eyes, are you not the head of the tribes of Israel? The LORD anointed you king over Israel."

1 SAMUEL 15:17 ESV

Now therefore, thus shall you say to My servant David, "Thus says the LORD of hosts: 'I took you from the sheepfold, from following the sheep, to be ruler over My people, over Israel. And I have been with you wherever you have gone, and have cut off all your enemies from before you, and have made you a great name, like the name of the

great men who are on the earth.' "
2 SAMUEL 7:8–9 NKJV

After Job had prayed for his friends, the LORD made him prosperous again and gave him twice as much as he had before.

JOB 42:10 NIV

Happy are those who do not follow the advice of the wicked, or take the path that sinners tread, or sit in the seat of scoffers; but their delight is in the law of the LORD, and on his law they meditate day and night. They are like trees planted by streams of water, which yield their fruit in its season, and their leaves do not wither. In all that they do, they prosper.

PSALM 1:1–3 NRSV

REALIZING GOD ENTRUSTS YOU

But remember the LORD your God, for it is he who gives you the ability to produce wealth, and so confirms his covenant, which he swore to your forefathers, as it is today.

DEUTERONOMY 8:18 NIV

You put us in charge of your handcrafted world, repeated to us your Genesis-charge, made us lords of sheep and cattle, even animals out in the wild, birds flying and fish swimming, whales singing in the ocean deeps. GOD, brilliant Lord, your name echoes around the world.

PSALM 8:6–9 MSG

And the Lord said, "Who then is the faithful and wise manager, whom his master will set over his household, to give them their portion of food at the proper time? Blessed is that servant whom his master will find so doing when he comes."

LUKE 12:42–43 ESV

Moreover, it is required of stewards that they be found trustworthy.

1 CORINTHIANS 4:2 ESV

Each one should use whatever gift he has received to serve others, faithfully administering God's grace in its various forms.

1 PETER 4:10 NIV

Look here, you who say, "Today or tomorrow we are going to a certain town and will stay there a year. We will do business there and make a profit." How do you know what your life will be like tomorrow? Your life is like the morning fog— it's here a little while, then it's gone. What you ought to say is, "If the Lord wants us to, we will live and do this or that." Otherwise you are boasting about your own plans, and all such boasting is evil.

JAMES 4:13–16 NLT

"Again, the Kingdom of Heaven can be illustrated by the story of a man going on a long trip. He called together his servants and entrusted his money to them while he was gone. He gave five bags of silver to one, two bags of silver to another, and one bag of silver to the last— dividing it in proportion to their

195

abilities. He then left on his trip.

"The servant who received the five bags of silver began to invest the money and earned five more. The servant with two bags of silver also went to work and earned two more. But the servant who received the one bag of silver dug a hole in the ground and hid the master's money.

"After a long time their master returned from his trip and called them to give an account of how they had used his money. The servant to whom he had entrusted the five bags of silver came forward with five more and said, 'Master, you gave me five bags of silver to invest, and I have earned five more.'

"The master was full of praise. 'Well done, my good and faithful servant. You have been faithful in handling this small amount, so now I will give you many more responsibilities. Let's celebrate together!'

"The servant who had received the two bags of silver came forward and said, 'Master, you gave me two bags of silver to invest, and I have earned two more.'

"The master said, 'Well done, my good and faithful servant. You have been faithful in handling this small amount, so now I will give you many more responsibilities. Let's celebrate together!'

"Then the servant with the one bag of silver came and said, 'Master, I knew you were a harsh man, harvesting crops you didn't plant and gathering crops you didn't cultivate. I was afraid I would lose your money, so I hid it in the earth. Look, here is your money back.'

"But the master replied, 'You wicked and lazy servant! If you knew I harvested crops I didn't plant and gathered crops I didn't cultivate, why didn't you deposit my money in the bank? At least I could have gotten some interest on it.'

"Then he ordered, 'Take the money from this servant, and give it to the one with the ten bags of silver. To those who use well what they are given, even more will be given, and they will have an abundance. But from those who do nothing, even what little they have will be taken away.'"

MATTHEW 25:14–29 NLT

BEING ACCOUNTABLE TO GOD

Here now is my final conclusion: Fear God and obey his commands, for this is everyone's duty. God will judge us for everything we do, including every secret thing, whether good or bad.

ECCLESIASTES 12:13–14 NLT

"From everyone who has been given much, much will be demanded; and from the one who has been entrusted with much, much more will be asked."

LUKE 12:48 NIV

If you fully obey the LORD your God and carefully follow all his commands I give you today, the LORD your God will set you high above all the nations on earth. All these blessings will come upon you and accompany you if you obey the LORD your God.

DEUTERONOMY 28:1–2 NIV

God will make you the head, not the tail; you'll always be the top dog, never the bottom dog, as you obediently listen to and diligently keep the commands of GOD, your God, that I am commanding you today.

DEUTERONOMY 28:13 MSG

"Woe to him who builds his house by unrighteousness, and his upper rooms by injustice, who makes his neighbor serve him for nothing and does not give him his wages."

JEREMIAH 22:13 ESV

Nothing in all creation is hidden from God. Everything is naked and exposed before his eyes, and he is the one to whom we are accountable.

HEBREWS 4:13 NLT

It is better to live right and be poor than to be sinful and rich. The wicked will lose all of their power, but the LORD gives strength to everyone who is good.

PSALM 37:16–17 CEV

Yes, each of us will give a personal account to God.

ROMANS 14:12 NLT

LOOSENING YOUR GRIP

John replied, "If you have two shirts, give one to the poor. If you have food, share it with those who are hungry."

LUKE 3:11 NLT

"Give to anyone who asks; and when things are taken away from you, don't try to get them back."

LUKE 6:30 NLT

If there is a poor man among your brothers in any of the towns of the land that the LORD your God is giving you, do not be hardhearted or tightfisted toward your poor brother. Rather be openhanded and freely lend him whatever he needs.

DEUTERONOMY 15:7–8 NIV

Now the full number of those who believed were of one heart and soul, and no one said that any of the things that belonged to him was his own, but they had everything in common. . . . There was not a needy person among them, for as many as were owners of lands or houses sold them and brought the proceeds of what was sold and laid it at the apostles' feet, and it was distributed to each as any had need. . . . And all who believed were together and had all things in common. And they were selling their possessions and belongings and distributing the proceeds to all, as any had need.

ACTS 4:32, 34–35; 2:44–45 ESV

"So therefore, any one of you who does not renounce all that he has cannot be my disciple."

LUKE 14:33 ESV

People who boast of their wealth don't understand; they will die, just like animals.

PSALM 49:20 NLT

ONE MOMENT AT A TIME
LEARNING TO LET GO

1. **Reassess ownership.** Everything you own comes from God. How does that reality cause you to look differently at big items (such as your home or car)? How about some smaller items (consider your MP3 player, phone, or even the cash in your wallet)?

2. **What's your most valuable possession?** Create a mental list of your favorite things. Which of them would be the hardest for you to share with others? What can you do to loosen your grip on this item?

3. **Challenge yourself.** Give away a special possession that would benefit someone else more than it would benefit you. What truth about God could you experience by fulfilling this challenge?

4. **Let go.** What regular indulgence could you forgo this week? Rather than spend the money, collect it and donate it somewhere that will further God's work in the world.

CHAPTER 2

INCOME: BLESSING AND RESPONSIBILITY

Money itself is not bad. God gave us the responsibility to work and the luxury to enjoy the fruits of that labor. I've learned that both the work and the reward are treasures from Him. Sure, there are days that I can't stand my job, but even then I try to remind myself that work itself is a gift from God. The ability to earn a living and enjoy what I've fairly earned are two of the greatest blessings I've ever enjoyed.

■ *Richard, age 50, Illinois* ■

KEEPING A RIGHT PERSPECTIVE

Yet true godliness with contentment is itself great wealth. After all, we brought nothing with us when we came into the world, and we can't take anything with us when we leave it.

1 TIMOTHY 6:6–7 NLT

Do not be overawed when a man grows rich, when the splendor of his house increases; for he will take nothing with him when he dies, his splendor will not descend with him. Though while he lived he counted himself blessed—and men praise you when you prosper—he will join the generation of his fathers, who will never see the light of life.

PSALM 49:16–19 NIV

The more you have, the more people come to help you spend it. So what good is wealth—except perhaps to watch it slip through your fingers!

ECCLESIASTES 5:11 NLT

We all come to the end of our lives as naked and empty-handed as on the day we were born. We can't take our riches with us.

ECCLESIASTES 5:15 NLT

Do not wear yourself out to get rich; have the wisdom to show restraint.

PROVERBS 23:4 NIV

Whoever makes deals with strangers is sure to get burned; if you keep a cool head, you'll avoid rash bargains.

PROVERBS 11:15 MSG

"No servant can serve two masters. Either he will hate the one and love the other, or he will be devoted to the one and despise the other. You cannot serve both God and Money."

LUKE 16:13 NIV

Unless the LORD builds the house, its builders labor in vain. . . . In vain you rise early and stay up late, toiling for food to eat—for he grants sleep to those he loves.

PSALM 127:1–2 NIV

Cast but a glance at riches, and they are gone, for they will surely sprout wings and fly off to the sky like an eagle.

PROVERBS 23:5 NIV

A thick bankroll is no help when life falls apart, but a principled life can stand up to the worst.

PROVERBS 11:4 MSG

People who work hard sleep well, whether they eat little or much. But the rich seldom get a good night's sleep.

ECCLESIASTES 5:12 NLT

BENEFITING FROM HARD WORK

Work brings profit, but mere talk leads to poverty!

PROVERBS 14:23 NLT

Whatever you do, work at it with all your heart, as working for the Lord, not for men.

COLOSSIANS 3:23 NIV

Whatever your hand finds to do, do it with all your might, for in the grave, where you are going, there is neither working nor planning nor knowledge nor wisdom.

ECCLESIASTES 9:10 NIV

He who works his land will have abundant food, but he who chases fantasies lacks judgment.

PROVERBS 12:11 NIV

Work hard, and you will have a lot of food; waste time, and you will have a lot of trouble.

PROVERBS 28:19 CEV

Make it your ambition to lead a quiet life, to mind your own business and to work with your hands, just as we told you, so that your daily life may win the respect of outsiders and so that you will not be dependent on anybody.

1 THESSALONIANS 4:11–12 NIV

AVOIDING LAZINESS

Laziness leads to poverty; hard work makes you rich.

PROVERBS 10:4 CEV

Now we learn that some of you just loaf around and won't do any work, except the work of a busybody. So, for the sake of our Lord Jesus Christ, we ask and beg these people to settle down and start working for a living.

2 THESSALONIANS 3:11–12 CEV

Lazy people want much but get little, but those who work hard will prosper.

PROVERBS 13:4 NLT

In the name of the Lord Jesus Christ, we command you, brothers, to keep away from every brother who is idle and does not live according to the teaching you received from us. For you yourselves know how you ought to follow our example. We were not idle when we were with you, nor did we eat anyone's food without paying for it. On the contrary, we worked night and day, laboring and toiling so that we would not be a burden to any of you. We did this, not because we do not have the right to such help, but in order to make ourselves a model for you to follow.

2 THESSALONIANS 3:6–9 NIV

I passed by the field of a sluggard, by the vineyard of a man lacking sense, and behold, it was all overgrown with thorns; the ground was covered with nettles, and its stone wall was broken down. Then I saw and considered it; I looked and received instruction. A little sleep, a little slumber, a little folding of the hands to rest, and poverty will come upon you like a robber, and want like an armed man.

PROVERBS 24:30–34 ESV

Lazy people take food in their hand but don't even lift it to their mouth.

PROVERBS 19:24 NLT

The desire of the lazy man kills him, for his hands refuse to labor.

PROVERBS 21:25 NKJV

Lazy people sleep soundly, but idleness leaves them hungry.

PROVERBS 19:15 NLT

FINDING CONTENTMENT

"So do not worry, saying, 'What shall we eat?' or 'What shall we drink?' or 'What shall we wear?' For the pagans run after all these things, and your heavenly Father knows that you need them. But seek first his kingdom and his righteousness, and all these things will be given to you as well. Therefore do not worry about tomorrow, for tomorrow will worry about itself. Each day has enough trouble of its own."

MATTHEW 6:31–34 NIV

Yes, we should make the most of what God gives, both the bounty and the capacity to enjoy it, accepting what's given and delighting in the work. It's God's gift!

ECCLESIASTES 5:19 MSG

O God, I beg two favors from you; let me have them before I die. First, help me never to tell a lie. Second, give me neither poverty nor riches! Give me just enough to satisfy my needs. For if I grow rich, I may deny you and say, "Who is the LORD?" And if I am too poor, I may steal and thus insult God's holy name.

PROVERBS 30:7–9 NLT

Be still in the presence of the LORD, and wait patiently for him to act. Don't worry about evil people who prosper or fret about their wicked schemes. . . . It is better to be godly and have little than to be evil and rich.

PSALM 37:7, 16 NLT

A stingy man is eager to get rich and is unaware that poverty awaits him.

PROVERBS 28:22 NIV

Rejoice in the Lord always. I will say it again: Rejoice! Let your gentleness be evident to all. The Lord is near. Do not be anxious about anything, but in everything, by prayer and petition, with thanksgiving, present your requests to God. And the peace of God, which transcends all understanding, will guard your hearts and your minds in Christ Jesus.

PHILIPPIANS 4:4–7 NIV

But if we have food and clothing, we will be content with that.

I TIMOTHY 6:8 NIV

I'm glad in God, far happier than you would ever guess—happy that you're again showing such strong concern for me. Not that you ever quit praying and thinking about me. You just had no chance to show it. Actually, I don't have a sense of needing anything personally. I've learned by now to be quite content whatever my circumstances. I'm just as happy with little as with much, with much as with little. I've found the recipe for being happy whether full or hungry, hands full or hands empty. Whatever I have, wherever I am, I can make it through anything in the One who makes me who I am. . . . You can be sure that God will take care of everything you need, his generosity exceeding even yours in the glory that pours from Jesus. Our God and Father abounds in glory that just pours out into eternity. Yes.

PHILIPPIANS 4:10–13, 19–20 MSG

REJECTING DISHONEST GAINS

The LORD detests the use of dishonest scales, but he delights in accurate weights.

PROVERBS 11:1 NLT

Moses said to Israel: Don't try to cheat people by having two sets of weights or measures, one to get more when you are buying, and the other to give less when you are selling. If you weigh and measure things honestly, the LORD your God will let you enjoy a long life in the land he is giving you. But the LORD is disgusted with anyone who cheats or is dishonest.

DEUTERONOMY 25:13–16 CEV

"Do you expect me to overlook obscene wealth you've piled up by cheating and fraud? Do you think I'll tolerate shady deals and shifty scheming? I'm tired of the violent rich bullying their way with bluffs and lies. I'm fed up. Beginning now, you're finished. You'll pay for your sins down to your last cent. No matter how much you get, it will never be enough—hollow stomachs, empty hearts. No matter how hard you work, you'll have nothing to show for it—bankrupt lives, wasted souls."

MICAH 6:10–14 MSG

CULTIVATING A GRATEFUL HEART

Thanks be to God for his indescribable gift!

2 CORINTHIANS 9:15 NIV

Always be joyful. Never stop praying. Be thankful in all circumstances, for this is God's will for you who belong to Christ Jesus.

1 THESSALONIANS 5:16–18 NLT

Give thanks to the LORD, for he is good! His faithful love endures forever.

PSALM 107:1 NLT

Make thankfulness your sacrifice to God, and keep the vows you made to the Most High.

PSALM 50:14 NLT

Shout with joy to the LORD, all the earth! Worship the LORD with gladness. Come before him, singing with joy. Acknowledge that the LORD is God! He made us, and we are his. We are his people, the sheep of his pasture. Enter his gates with thanksgiving; go into his courts with praise. Give thanks to him and praise his name.

PSALM 100:1–4 NLT

ONE MOMENT AT A TIME
ENJOYING WORK

1. **Read Genesis 1–3.** Why is it significant that God gave people responsibility to work before the world (and work) was corrupted by sin?

2. **Count your blessings.** Take a sheet of notebook paper and make a list of many reasons that work is a blessing from God. Don't stop until you've filled the paper.

3. **Be diligent.** Even on days you don't enjoy your job, perform it with your best effort. Don't let laziness or discontentment rob you from enjoying the gift of work.

4. **Don't fall for the vanishing act.** Proverbs 23:5 (NIV) says, "Cast but a glance at riches, and they are gone." In what ways have you found that verse to be true?

5. **Put on blinders.** No matter how much you have, there will always be others who have more than you. Choose to be content rather than yearn for what you don't have.

CHAPTER 3

WARNING: DANGERS AWAIT

"I can't; I need to work." That phrase feels like the main mantra in my life. Be a team mom? I can't. Get involved in women's ministry? Sorry, I work that night. I know I'm quick to accept overtime hours at the expense of my family relationships, but we need the money. Sure, everyone says you can get by with less, but when I look at what we'd have to give up, I don't think that's very practical.

■ *Joan, age 43, Colorado* ■

GUARDING YOUR HEART

Teach those who are rich in this world not to be proud and not to trust in their money, which is so unreliable. Their trust should be in God, who richly gives us all we need for our enjoyment.
1 TIMOTHY 6:17 NLT

Above all else, guard your heart, for it is the wellspring of life.
PROVERBS 4:23 NIV

Whom have I in heaven but you? And earth has nothing I desire besides you.
PSALM 73:25 NIV

"Watch out! Be on your guard against all kinds of greed; a man's life does not consist in the abundance of his possessions."
LUKE 12:15 NIV

Keep your lives free from the love of money and be content with what you have, because God has said, "Never will I leave you; never will I forsake you."
HEBREWS 13:5 NIV

Selfish people cause trouble, but you will live a full life if you trust the LORD.
PROVERBS 28:25 CEV

For the love of money is a root of all kinds of evil. Some people, eager for money, have wandered from the faith and pierced themselves with many griefs.
1 TIMOTHY 6:10 NIV

And if your wealth increases, don't make it the center of your life.
PSALM 62:10 NLT

"Be careful that no one entices you by riches; do not let a large bribe turn you aside."
JOB 36:18 NIV

God's Message: "Don't let the wise brag of their wisdom. Don't let heroes brag of their exploits. Don't let the rich brag of their riches."

JEREMIAH 9:23 MSG

PROTECTING YOUR SPIRITUAL LIFE

"It's obvious, isn't it? The place where your treasure is, is the place you will most want to be, and end up being."

LUKE 12:34 MSG

Whoever trusts in his riches will fall, but the righteous will flourish like a green leaf.

PROVERBS 11:28 ESV

"No one can serve two masters. Either he will hate the one and love the other, or he will be devoted to the one and despise the other. You cannot serve both God and Money."

MATTHEW 6:24 NIV

So put to death the sinful, earthly things lurking within you. Have nothing to do with sexual immorality, impurity, lust, and evil desires. Don't be greedy, for a greedy person is an idolater, worshiping the things of this world.

COLOSSIANS 3:5 NLT

"If I have put my trust in gold or said to pure gold, 'You are my security,' if I have rejoiced over my great wealth, the fortune my hands had gained, . . .then these also would be sins to be judged, for I would have

been unfaithful to God on high."

JOB 31:24–25, 28 NIV

The idols of the nations are made of silver and gold.

PSALM 115:4 CEV

Jesus looked around and said to his disciples, "How hard it is for the rich to enter the kingdom of God!" The disciples were amazed at his words. But Jesus said again, "Children, how hard it is to enter the kingdom of God! It is easier for a camel to go through the eye of a needle than for a rich man to enter the kingdom of God." The disciples were even more amazed, and said to each other, "Who then can be saved?" Jesus looked at them and said, "With man this is impossible, but not with God; all things are possible with God."

MARK 10:23–27 NIV

And he told them this parable: "The ground of a certain rich man produced a good crop. He thought to himself, 'What shall I do? I have no place to store my crops.' Then he said, 'This is what I'll do. I will tear down my barns and build bigger ones, and there I will store all my grain and my goods. And I'll say to myself, "You have plenty of good things laid up for many years. Take life easy; eat, drink and be merry."'

"But God said to him, 'You fool! This very night your life will be demanded from you. Then who will get what you have prepared for yourself?'

"This is how it will be with anyone

who stores up things for himself but is not rich toward God."

LUKE 12:16–21 NIV

AVOIDING GREED

The trustworthy person will get a rich reward, but a person who wants quick riches will get into trouble.

PROVERBS 28:20 NLT

Greed causes fighting; trusting the LORD leads to prosperity.

PROVERBS 28:25 NLT

But people who long to be rich fall into temptation and are trapped by many foolish and harmful desires that plunge them into ruin and destruction.

1 TIMOTHY 6:9 NLT

Whoever loves money never has money enough; whoever loves wealth is never satisfied with his income. This too is meaningless.

ECCLESIASTES 5:10 NIV

Whoever is greedy for unjust gain troubles his own household, but he who hates bribes will live.

PROVERBS 15:27 ESV

You're addicted to thrills? What an empty life! The pursuit of pleasure is never satisfied.

PROVERBS 21:17 MSG

Speaking to the people, he went on, "Take care! Protect yourself against the least bit of greed. Life is not defined by what you have, even when you have a lot."

LUKE 12:15 MSG

Riches disappear in the blink of an eye; wealth sprouts wings and flies off into the wild blue yonder.

PROVERBS 23:5 MSG

A leech has twin daughters named "Gimme" and "Gimme more."

PROVERBS 30:15 MSG

If a man shuts his ears to the cry of the poor, he too will cry out and not be answered.

PROVERBS 21:13 NIV

SIDESTEPPING COVETING

"You must not covet your neighbor's house. You must not covet your neighbor's wife, male or female servant, ox or donkey, or anything else that belongs to your neighbor."

EXODUS 20:17 NLT

What causes fights and quarrels among you? Don't they come from your desires that battle within you? You want something but don't get it. You kill and covet, but you cannot have what you want. You quarrel and fight. You do not have, because you do not ask God.

JAMES 4:1–2 NIV

For the world offers only a craving for physical pleasure, a craving for everything we see, and pride in our achievements and possessions. These are not from the Father, but are from this world.

1 JOHN 2:16 NLT

The righteousness of the upright delivers them, but the unfaithful are trapped by evil desires.

PROVERBS 11:6 NIV

The wicked brag about their deepest desires. Those greedy people hate and curse you, LORD. The wicked are too proud to turn to you or even think about you.

PSALM 10:3–4 CEV

Then I observed that most people are motivated to success because they envy their neighbors. But this, too, is meaningless—like chasing the wind.

ECCLESIASTES 4:4 NLT

For riches don't last forever, and the crown might not be passed to the next generation.

PROVERBS 27:24 NLT

SPIRALING INTO CONFLICT

When one of you has a dispute with another believer, how dare you file a lawsuit and ask a secular court to decide the matter instead of taking it to other believers! Don't you realize that someday we believers will judge the world? And since you are going to judge the world, can't you decide even these little things among yourselves? Don't you realize that we will judge angels? So you should surely be able to resolve ordinary disputes in this life. If you have legal disputes about such matters, why go to out-side judges who are not respected by the church? I am saying this to shame you. Isn't there anyone in all the church who is wise enough to decide these issues? But instead, one believer sues another—right in front of unbelievers! Even to have such lawsuits with one another is a defeat for you. Why not just accept the injustice and leave it at that? Why not let yourselves be cheated? Instead, you yourselves are the ones who do wrong and cheat even your fellow believers.

1 CORINTHIANS 6:1–8 NLT

PASSING BY ANXIETY

Trust in the LORD with all your heart and lean not on your own understanding; in all your ways acknowledge him, and he will make your paths straight.

PROVERBS 3:5–6 NIV

"Your Father knows exactly what you need even before you ask him!"

MATTHEW 6:8 NLT

"Come to me, all you who are weary and burdened, and I will give you rest."

MATTHEW 11:28 NIV

"What is the price of five sparrows—two copper coins? Yet God does not forget a single one of them. And the very hairs on your head are all numbered. So don't be afraid; you are more valuable to God than a whole flock of sparrows."

LUKE 12:6–7 NLT

"Can all your worries add a single moment to your life? And if worry can't accomplish a little thing like that, what's the use of worrying over bigger things?"

LUKE 12:25–26 NLT

Trust in the LORD and do good; dwell in the land and enjoy safe pasture. Delight yourself in the LORD and he will give you the desires of your heart.

PSALM 37:3–4 NIV

And we know that all things work together for good to those who love God—to those who are the called according to His purpose.

ROMANS 8:28 NKJV

I know what it is to be in need, and I know what it is to have plenty. I have learned the secret of being content in any and every situation, whether well fed or hungry, whether living in plenty or in want. I can do everything through him who gives me strength.

PHILIPPIANS 4:12–13 NIV

God cares for you, so turn all your worries over to him.

1 PETER 5:7 CEV

But God shows undeserved kindness to everyone. That's why he appointed Christ Jesus to choose you to share in his eternal glory. You will suffer for a while, but God will make you complete, steady, strong, and firm.

1 PETER 5:10 CEV

Even strong young lions sometimes go hungry, but those who trust in the LORD will lack no good thing.

PSALM 34:10 NLT

"The seed that fell among thorns stands for those who hear, but as they go on their way they are choked by life's worries, riches and pleasures, and they do not mature."

LUKE 8:14 NIV

FEEDING SELF-INDULGENCE

What sorrow for you who buy up house after house and field after field, until everyone is evicted and you live alone in the land.

ISAIAH 5:8 NLT

Don't depend on things like fancy hairdos or gold jewelry or expensive clothes to make you look beautiful. Be beautiful in your heart by being gentle and quiet. This kind of beauty will last, and God considers it very special.

1 PETER 3:3–4 CEV

"The greatest among you will be your servant. All who exalt themselves will be humbled, and all who humble themselves will be exalted."

MATTHEW 23:11–12 NRSV

People curse the man who hoards grain, but blessing crowns him who is willing to sell.

PROVERBS 11:26 NIV

ONE MOMENT AT A TIME
REFOCUSING YOUR PERSPECTIVE

1. **Be careful.** The lure of money can pull your heart away from more important priorities. Be sure to guard what you value most.

2. **Enlist carefully.** Where do your allegiances lie? Serve Christ and build His kingdom rather than being focused on your own.

3. **Prune back greed.** For the next month, toss the catalogues that arrive in the mail. Delete the spam that encourages you to buy. Mute radio and TV commercials that cause you to crave for more. If you do this for a month, will your life really be worse off?

4. **Resist anxiety by refocusing.** Rather than dwell on your needs, shortfalls, and financial problems, focus instead on the solutions and the steps needed to accomplish them. Most of all, keep your eyes focused on Jesus, who promises to give you the relief you need (Matthew 11:28).

CHAPTER 4

POOR AND NEEDY: RECEIVING GOD'S EXTRA CARE

The poor are always with us. I've been in the ministry for thirty years, and I've always encouraged my congregations to reach out to those who are struggling financially. Yes, it has made a difference in our area. More importantly, though, it has made a difference in the lives of our people. Nothing helps get your heart realigned better than seeing the childlike faith of someone who has nothing.

■ *Jim, age 62, Louisiana* ■

RESPECTING THE POOR

Whoever mocks the poor insults his Maker; he who is glad at calamity will not go unpunished.

PROVERBS 17:5 ESV

The rich and the poor have this in common, the LORD is the maker of them all.

PROVERBS 22:2 NKJV

The poor man and the oppressor have this in common: The LORD gives sight to the eyes of both.

PROVERBS 29:13 NIV

Then this message came to Zechariah from the LORD: "This is what the LORD of Heaven's Armies says: Judge fairly, and show mercy and kindness to one another. Do not oppress widows, orphans, foreigners, and the poor. And do not scheme against each other."

ZECHARIAH 7:8–10 NLT

The people of the land have practiced extortion and committed robbery. They have oppressed the poor and needy, and have extorted from the sojourner without justice. . . . Therefore I have poured out my indignation upon them. I have consumed them with the fire of my wrath. I have returned their way upon their heads, declares the Lord GOD.

EZEKIEL 22:29, 31 ESV

"Then I will draw near to you for judgment. I will be a swift witness against the sorcerers, against the adulterers, against those who swear falsely, against those who oppress the hired worker in his wages, the widow and the fatherless, against those who thrust aside the sojourner, and do not fear me, says the LORD of hosts.

MALACHI 3:5 ESV

SHARING GOD'S CONCERN FOR THE POOR

When you give a feast, invite the poor, the crippled, the lame, and the blind. They cannot pay you back. But God will bless you and reward you when his people rise from death.

LUKE 14:13–14 CEV

Then the King will say, "I'm telling the solemn truth: Whenever you did one of these things to someone overlooked or ignored, that was me—you did it to me."

MATTHEW 25:40 MSG

He who has pity on the poor lends to the LORD, and He will pay back what he has given.

PROVERBS 19:17 NKJV

Whoever oppresses the poor to increase his own wealth, or gives to the rich, will only come to poverty.

PROVERBS 22:16 ESV

Do not move an ancient boundary stone or encroach on the fields of the fatherless, for their Defender is strong; he will take up their case against you.

PROVERBS 23:10–11 NIV

If a king judges the poor with fairness, his throne will always be secure.

PROVERBS 29:14 NIV

But you, O God, do see trouble and grief; you consider it to take it in hand. The victim commits himself to you; you are the helper of the fatherless.

PSALM 10:14 NIV

The LORD is on my side as my helper; I shall look in triumph on those who hate me.

PSALM 118:7 ESV

A father to the fatherless, a defender of widows, is God in his holy dwelling.

PSALM 68:5 NIV

The LORD destroys the homes of those who are proud, but he protects the property of widows.

PROVERBS 15:25 CEV

HEARING THEIR NEEDS

"The poor and needy seek water, but there is none, Their tongues fail for thirst. I, the LORD, will hear them; I, the God of Israel, will not forsake them."

ISAIAH 41:17 NKJV

I was a nobody, but I prayed, and the LORD saved me from all my troubles.

PSALM 34:6 CEV

Incline your ear, O LORD, and answer me, for I am poor and needy.

PSALM 86:1 ESV

The poor will see and be glad—you who seek God, may your hearts live! The LORD hears the needy and does not despise his captive people.

PSALM 69:32–33 NIV

WATCHING GOD WORK ON THEIR BEHALF

I know that the LORD secures justice for the poor and upholds the cause of the needy.

PSALM 140:12 NIV

But he lifted the needy out of their affliction and increased their families like flocks.

PSALM 107:41 NIV

But I will give repeated thanks to the LORD, praising him to everyone. For he stands beside the needy, ready to save them from those who condemn them.

PSALM 109:30–31 NLT

God lifts the poor and needy from dust and ashes.

PSALM 113:7 CEV

All my bones shall say, "LORD, who is like You, delivering the poor from him who is too strong for him, yes, the poor and the needy from him who plunders him?"

PSALM 35:10 NKJV

SENSING OUR DUTY TO HELP

When you are harvesting your crops and forget to bring in a bundle of grain from your field, don't go back to get it. Leave it for the foreigners, orphans, and widows. Then the LORD your God will bless you in all you do. When you beat the olives from your olive trees, don't go over the boughs twice. Leave the remaining olives for the foreigners, orphans, and widows. When you gather the grapes in your vineyard, don't glean the vines after they are picked. Leave the remaining grapes for the foreigners, orphans, and widows.

DEUTERONOMY 24:19–21 NLT

Religion that God our Father accepts as pure and faultless is this: to look after orphans and widows in their distress and to keep oneself from being polluted by the world.

JAMES 1:27 NIV

Cheerfully share your home with those who need a meal or a place to stay.

1 PETER 4:9 NLT

Tell them. . .to be rich in helping others, to be extravagantly generous.

1 TIMOTHY 6:18 MSG

I have never cheated widows or others in need, and I have always shared my food with orphans. Since the time I was young, I have cared for orphans and helped widows. I provided clothes for the poor. . . . If I have ever raised my arm to threaten an orphan when the power was mine, I hope that arm will fall from its socket. I could not have been abusive; I was terrified at the thought that God might punish me.

JOB 31:16–19, 21–23 CEV

Our people must learn to do good by meeting the urgent needs of others; then they will not be unproductive.

TITUS 3:14 NLT

NEGLECTING THE POOR

"Cursed is anyone who denies justice to foreigners, orphans, or widows."

DEUTERONOMY 27:19 NLT

Do not mistreat widows or orphans. If you do, they will beg for my help, and I will come to their rescue. In fact, I will get so angry that I will kill your men and make widows of their wives and orphans of their children.

EXODUS 22:22–24 CEV

Your rulers are rebels, companions of thieves; they all love bribes and chase after gifts. They do not defend the cause of the fatherless; the widow's case does not come before them. Therefore the Lord, the LORD Almighty, the Mighty One of Israel, declares: "Ah, I will get relief from my foes and avenge myself on my enemies. I will turn my hand against you; I will thoroughly purge away your dross and remove all your impurities."

ISAIAH 1:23–25 NIV

You rich people should cry and weep! Terrible things are going to happen to you. Your treasures have already rotted, and moths have eaten your clothes. Your money has rusted, and the rust will be evidence against you, as it burns your body like fire. Yet you keep on storing up wealth in these last days. You refused to pay the people who worked in your fields, and now their unpaid wages are shouting out against you.

The Lord All-Powerful has surely heard the cries of the workers who harvested your crops. While here on earth, you have thought only of filling your own stomachs and having a good time. But now you are like fat cattle on their way to be butchered. You have condemned and murdered innocent people, who couldn't even fight back.

JAMES 5:1–6 CEV

What sorrow awaits the unjust judges and those who issue unfair laws. They deprive the poor of justice and deny the rights of the needy among my people. They prey on widows and take advantage of orphans.

ISAIAH 10:1–2 NLT

RESISTING THE TEMPTATION TO SHOW FAVORITISM

"Do not pervert justice; do not show partiality to the poor or favoritism to the great, but judge your neighbor fairly."

LEVITICUS 19:15 NIV

Do not rob the poor because he is poor, nor oppress the afflicted at the gate; for the LORD will plead their cause, and plunder the soul of those who plunder them.

PROVERBS 22:22–23 NKJV

My brothers and sisters, do you with your acts of favoritism really believe in our glorious Lord Jesus

Christ? For if a person with gold rings and in fine clothes comes into your assembly, and if a poor person in dirty clothes also comes in, and if you take notice of the one wearing the fine clothes and say, "Have a seat here, please," while to the one who is poor you say, "Stand there," or, "Sit at my feet," have you not made distinctions among yourselves, and become judges with evil thoughts? Listen, my beloved brothers and sisters. Has not God chosen the poor in the world to be rich in faith and to be heirs of the kingdom that he has promised to those who love him? But you have dishonored the poor. Is it not the rich who oppress you? Is it not they who drag you into court? Is it not they who blaspheme the excellent name that was invoked over you? You do well if you really fulfill the royal law according to the scripture, "You shall love your neighbor as yourself." But if you show partiality, you commit sin and are convicted by the law as transgressors.

JAMES 2:1–9 NRSV

ONE MOMENT AT A TIME
SEEING NEW NEEDS

1. **Look for opportunities.** Needy people are not always standing on a street corner looking for handouts. Who are the young, the unemployed, or divorcées you know who may also be struggling?

2. **Consider it your problem, too.** Don't dismiss needy people because you believe they brought their situations on themselves. If you know of a need, consider that God may have appointed you the agent to help meet it.

3. **Facilitate a solution.** Some needs are greater than what you can fulfill. Can you help organize a group or create a plan to help do what you cannot do on your own?

CHAPTER 5

GIVING: HEARING THE CALL

The guilt arrives each week as I sit in church and pass the offering plate without dropping in more than a crumpled dollar. I always look at the pile of checks and wonder, How do other people do it? Am I the only one who thinks money is a little tight right now?

■ *Betsy, age 53, Arkansas* ■

HEARING THE CALL OF GENEROSITY

Three times a year all your men must appear before the LORD your God at the place he will choose: at the Feast of Unleavened Bread, the Feast of Weeks and the Feast of Tabernacles. No man should appear before the LORD empty-handed: Each of you must bring a gift in proportion to the way the LORD your God has blessed you.

DEUTERONOMY 16:16–17 NIV

On the first day of every week, each one of you should set aside a sum of money in keeping with his income, saving it up, so that when I come no collections will have to be made.

1 CORINTHIANS 16:2 NIV

In his grace, God has given us different gifts for doing certain things well. So if God has given you the ability to prophesy, speak out with as much faith as God has given you. If your gift is serving others, serve them well. If you are a teacher, teach well. If your gift is to encourage others, be encouraging. If it is giving, give generously. If God has given you leadership ability, take the responsibility seriously. And if you have a gift for showing kindness to others, do it gladly.

ROMANS 12:6–8 NLT

"Should people cheat God? Yet you have cheated me! But you ask, 'What do you mean? When did we ever cheat you?' You have cheated me of the tithes and offerings due to me."

MALACHI 3:8 NLT

If a Hebrew man or Hebrew woman was sold to you and has served you for six years, in the seventh year you must set him or her free, released into a free life. And when you set them free don't send them off empty-handed. Provide them with some animals, plenty of bread and wine and oil. Load them with provisions from all the blessings with which GOD, your God, has blessed you. Don't for a minute forget that you were once slaves

in Egypt and GOD, your God, redeemed you from that slave world.
DEUTERONOMY 15:12–15 MSG

If you are a thief, quit stealing. Instead, use your hands for good hard work, and then give generously to others in need.
EPHESIANS 4:28 NLT

"Give as freely as you have received!"
MATTHEW 10:8 NLT

"But love your enemies, do good, and lend, hoping for nothing in return; and your reward will be great, and you will be sons of the Most High. For He is kind to the unthankful and evil."
LUKE 6:35 NKJV

GIVING TO GOD AND THE CHURCH

"Tell the Israelites to bring me an offering. You are to receive the offering for me from each man whose heart prompts him to give."
EXODUS 25:2 NIV

"But who am I, and who are my people, that we should be able to give as generously as this? Everything comes from you, and we have given you only what comes from your hand."
1 CHRONICLES 29:14 NIV

"Bring the best of the firstfruits of your soil to the house of the LORD your God."
EXODUS 23:19 NIV

"You must present as the LORD's portion the best and holiest part of everything given to you."
NUMBERS 18:29 NIV

So then, as we have opportunity, let us do good to everyone, and especially to those who are of the household of faith.
GALATIANS 6:10 ESV

All the Lord's followers often met together, and they shared everything they had. They would sell their property and possessions and give the money to whoever needed it. Day after day they met together in the temple. They broke bread together in different homes and shared their food happily and freely.
ACTS 2:44–46 CEV

For God is not unjust. He will not forget how hard you have worked for him and how you have shown your love to him by caring for other believers, as you still do.
HEBREWS 6:10 NLT

What good is it, my brothers, if a man claims to have faith but has no deeds? Can such faith save him? Suppose a brother or sister is without clothes and daily food. If one of you says to him, "Go, I wish you well; keep warm and well fed," but does nothing about his physical needs, what good is it? In the same way, faith by itself, if it is not accompanied by action, is dead.
JAMES 2:14–17 NIV

217

This is how we know what love is: Jesus Christ laid down his life for us. And we ought to lay down our lives for our brothers. If anyone has material possessions and sees his brother in need but has no pity on him, how can the love of God be in him? Dear children, let us not love with words or tongue but with actions and in truth.

1 JOHN 3:16–18 NIV

If there is a poor man among your brothers in any of the towns of the land that the LORD your God is giving you, do not be hardhearted or tightfisted toward your poor brother.

DEUTERONOMY 15:7 NIV

When God's people are in need, be ready to help them. Always be eager to practice hospitality.

ROMANS 12:13 NLT

Let each of you look not only to his own interests, but also to the interests of others.

PHILIPPIANS 2:4 ESV

READING EXAMPLES FROM THE EARLY CHURCH

And now, brothers, we want you to know about the grace that God has given the Macedonian churches. Out of the most severe trial, their overflowing joy and their extreme poverty welled up in rich generosity. For I testify that they gave as much as they were able, and even beyond their ability. Entirely on their own, they urgently pleaded with us for the privilege of sharing in this service to the saints. And they did not do as we expected, but they gave themselves first to the Lord and then to us in keeping with God's will.

2 CORINTHIANS 8:1–5 NIV

So the believers in Antioch decided to send relief to the brothers and sisters in Judea, everyone giving as much as they could. This they did, entrusting their gifts to Barnabas and Saul to take to the elders of the church in Jerusalem.

ACTS 11:29–30 NLT

I am now on my way to Jerusalem to deliver the money that the Lord's followers in Macedonia and Achaia collected for God's needy people. This is something they really wanted to do. But sharing their money with the Jews was also like paying back a debt, because the Jews had already shared their spiritual blessings with the Gentiles. After I have safely delivered this money, I will visit you and then go on to Spain.

ROMANS 15:25–28 CEV

BEING GENEROUS WHEN YOU DON'T HAVE MUCH

Jesus sat down near the collection box in the Temple and watched as the crowds dropped in their money. Many rich people put in large amounts. Then a poor widow came and dropped in two small coins. Jesus called his disciples to him and said, "I tell you the truth, this poor widow has given more than all the others who are making contributions. For they gave a tiny part of their surplus, but she, poor as she is, has given everything she had to live on."

MARK 12:41–44 NLT

You insult your Maker when you exploit the powerless; when you're kind to the poor, you honor God.

PROVERBS 14:31 MSG

"Give, and you will receive. Your gift will return to you in full— pressed down, shaken together to make room for more, running over, and poured into your lap. The amount you give will determine the amount you get back."

LUKE 6:38 NLT

Do not neglect to show hospitality to strangers, for thereby some have entertained angels unawares.

HEBREWS 13:2 ESV

BLESSINGS OF GIVING

Yes, you will be enriched in every way so that you can always be generous. And when we take your gifts to those who need them, they will thank God. So two good things will result from this ministry of giving—the needs of the believers in Jerusalem will be met, and they will joyfully express their thanks to God. As a result of your ministry, they will give glory to God. For your generosity to them and to all believers will prove that you are obedient to the Good News of Christ.

2 CORINTHIANS 9:11–13 NLT

And I have been a constant example of how you can help those in need by working hard. You should remember the words of the Lord Jesus: "It is more blessed to give than to receive."

ACTS 20:35 NLT

Azariah, chief priest of the family of Zadok, answered, "From the moment of this huge outpouring of gifts to The Temple of GOD, there has been plenty to eat for everyone with food left over. GOD has blessed his people—just look at the evidence!"

2 CHRONICLES 31:10 MSG

God can bless you with everything you need, and you will always have more than enough to do all kinds of good things for others. . . . You will be blessed in every way, and you will be able to keep on being generous. Then many people will thank God when we deliver your gift.

2 CORINTHIANS 9:8, 11 CEV

Honor the LORD with your wealth, with the firstfruits of all your crops; then your barns will be filled to overflowing, and your vats will brim over with new wine.

PROVERBS 3:9–10 NIV

A generous man will himself be blessed, for he shares his food with the poor.

PROVERBS 22:9 NIV

219

Blessed is he who has regard for the weak; the LORD delivers him in times of trouble. The LORD will protect him and preserve his life; he will bless him in the land and not surrender him to the desire of his foes.

PSALM 41:1–2 NIV

He who gives to the poor will lack nothing, but he who closes his eyes to them receives many curses.

PROVERBS 28:27 NIV

"I the LORD search the heart and examine the mind, to reward a man according to his conduct, according to what his deeds deserve."

JEREMIAH 17:10 NIV

"Bring all the tithes into the store-house so there will be enough food in my Temple. If you do," says the LORD of Heaven's Armies, "I will open the windows of heaven for you. I will pour out a blessing so great you won't have enough room to take it in! Try it! Put me to the test!"

MALACHI 3:10 NLT

Good will come to him who is generous and lends freely, who conducts his affairs with justice.

PSALM 112:5 NIV

"For truly, I say to you, whoever gives you a cup of water to drink because you belong to Christ will by no means lose his reward."

MARK 9:41 ESV

HAVING THE RIGHT HEART ABOUT GIVING

"Be careful not to do your 'acts of righteousness' before men, to be seen by them. If you do, you will have no reward from your Father in heaven. So when you give to the needy, do not announce it with trumpets, as the hypocrites do in the synagogues and on the streets, to be honored by men. I tell you the truth, they have received their reward in full. But when you give to the needy, do not let your left hand know what your right hand is doing, so that your giving may be in secret. Then your Father, who sees what is done in secret, will reward you."

MATTHEW 6:1–4 NIV

So I thought it necessary to urge the brothers to visit you in advance and finish the arrangements for the generous gift you had promised. Then it will be ready as a generous gift, not as one grudgingly given.

2 CORINTHIANS 9:5 NIV

Remember this saying, "A few seeds make a small harvest, but a lot of seeds make a big harvest." Each of you must make up your own mind about how much to give. But don't feel sorry that you must give and don't feel that you are forced to give. God loves people who love to give.

2 CORINTHIANS 9:6–7 CEV

Give freely and spontaneously. Don't have a stingy heart. The way you handle matters like this triggers

GOD, your God's, blessing in everything you do, all your work and ventures. There are always going to be poor and needy people among you. So I command you: Always be generous, open purse and hands, give to your neighbors in trouble, your poor and hurting neighbors.

DEUTERONOMY 15:10–11 MSG

The LORD is disgusted by gifts from the wicked, but it makes him happy when his people pray.

PROVERBS 15:8 CEV

If your enemy is hungry, give him food to eat; if he is thirsty, give him water to drink.

PROVERBS 25:21 NIV

If I give all I possess to the poor and surrender my body to the flames, but have not love, I gain nothing.

1 CORINTHIANS 13:3 NIV

Do not withhold good from those who deserve it, when it is in your power to act. Do not say to your neighbor, "Come back later; I'll give it tomorrow"—when you now have it with you.

PROVERBS 3:27–28 NIV

GIVING AS AN ACT OF WORSHIP

I have received full payment and even more; I am amply supplied, now that I have received from Epaphroditus the gifts you sent. They are a fragrant offering, an acceptable sacrifice, pleasing to God.

PHILIPPIANS 4:18 NIV

Then the king will say to those on his right, "My father has blessed you! Come and receive the kingdom that was prepared for you before the world was created. When I was hungry, you gave me something to eat, and when I was thirsty, you gave me something to drink. When I was a stranger, you welcomed me."

MATTHEW 25:34–35 CEV

I'll tell you what it really means to worship the LORD. Remove the chains of prisoners who are chained unjustly. Free those who are abused! Share your food with everyone who is hungry; share your home with the poor and homeless. Give clothes to those in need; don't turn away your relatives. Then your light will shine like the dawning sun, and you will quickly be healed. Your honesty will protect you as you advance, and the glory of the LORD will defend you from behind.

ISAIAH 58:6–8 CEV

Do not neglect to do good and to share what you have, for such sacrifices are pleasing to God.

HEBREWS 13:16 ESV

ONE MOMENT AT A TIME
GIVING WHEN IT HURTS

1. **Give anyway.** Yes, it's tight. Yes, it hurts to part with what you've earned. But yes, it's worth it.

2. **Look for needs.** Put $10 or $25 in your pocket for the sole purpose of giving it away. You'll be surprised with the creative ways you'll be able to bless others.

3. **Check your attitude.** Make sure you're not giving with resentment or because you crave the positive attention you receive from being generous. Give cheerfully and without expecting (or hoping) for the positive affirmation of others.

CHAPTER 6

OBLIGATIONS: BUSINESS, DEBTS, AND TAXES

Believe me, writing the monthly credit card checks is as hard for me as for the next person. I keep trying to get out from under them, but the struggle gets the best of me sometimes. While the credit card checks can be frustrating, I rarely mind writing the quarterly tax checks. Being a small business owner, I often have to scrape by to make the payments. But while it's often painful, I never resent those checks to Uncle Sam. By paying taxes, I'm acknowledging that I've actually made money—and I'm thankful to God for that.

■ *Paul, age 37, Missouri* ■

REPAYING YOUR DEBT

Pay all that you owe, whether it is taxes and fees or respect and honor.
ROMANS 13:7 CEV

Let no debt remain outstanding, except the continuing debt to love one another, for he who loves his fellowman has fulfilled the law.
ROMANS 13:8 NIV

The wicked borrow and do not repay, but the righteous give generously.
PSALM 37:21 NIV

The rich rule over the poor, and the borrower is servant to the lender.
PROVERBS 22:7 NIV

Do not be a man who strikes hands in pledge or puts up security for debts; if you lack the means to pay, your very bed will be snatched from under you.
PROVERBS 22:26–27 NIV

PAYING CAESAR

After Jesus and his disciples arrived in Capernaum, the collectors of the two-drachma tax came to Peter and asked, "Doesn't your teacher pay the temple tax?" "Yes, he does," he replied. When Peter came into the house, Jesus was the first to speak. "What do you think, Simon?" he asked. "From whom do the kings of the earth collect duty and taxes—from their own sons or from others?" "From others," Peter answered. "Then the sons are exempt," Jesus said to him. "But so that we may not offend them, go to the lake and throw out your line. Take the first fish you catch; open its mouth and you will find a four-drachma coin. Take it and give it to them for my tax and yours."

MATTHEW 17:24–27 NIV

Then the Pharisees met together to plot how to trap Jesus into saying something for which he could be arrested. They sent some of their disciples, along with the supporters of Herod, to meet with him. "Teacher," they said, "we know how honest you are. You teach the way of God truthfully. You are impartial and don't play favorites. Now tell us what you think about this: Is it right to pay taxes to Caesar or not?" But Jesus knew their evil motives. "You hypocrites!" he said. "Why are you trying to trap me? Here, show me the coin used for the tax." When they handed him a Roman coin, he asked, "Whose picture and title are stamped on it?" "Caesar's," they replied. "Well, then," he said, "give to Caesar what belongs to Caesar, and give to God what belongs to God." His reply amazed them, and they went away.

MATTHEW 22:15–22 NLT

Obey the rulers who have authority over you. Only God can give authority to anyone, and he puts these rulers in their places of power. People who oppose the authorities are opposing what God has done, and they will be punished.

ROMANS 13:1–2 CEV

But you should obey the rulers because you know it is the right thing to do, and not just because of God's anger. You must also pay your taxes. The authorities are God's servants, and it is their duty to take care of these matters. Pay all that you owe, whether it is taxes and fees or respect and honor.

ROMANS 13:5–7 CEV

Make the Master proud of you by being good citizens. Respect the authorities, whatever their level; they are God's emissaries for keeping order. It is God's will that by doing good, you might cure the ignorance of the fools who think you're a danger to society. Exercise your freedom by serving God, not by breaking the rules. Treat everyone you meet with dignity. Love your spiritual family. Revere God. Respect the government.

1 PETER 2:13–17 MSG

TAKING CARE OF YOUR EMPLOYEES

For the Scripture says, "Do not muzzle the ox while it is treading out the grain," and "The worker deserves his wages."

1 TIMOTHY 5:18 NIV

Masters, treat your slaves justly and fairly, knowing that you also have a Master in heaven.

COLOSSIANS 4:1 ESV

If you hire poor people to work for you, don't hold back their pay, whether they are Israelites or foreigners who live in your town.

DEUTERONOMY 24:14 CEV

"Don't exploit your friend or rob him. Don't hold back the wages of a hired hand overnight."

LEVITICUS 19:13 MSG

Now to the one who works, his wages are not counted as a gift but as his due.

ROMANS 4:4 ESV

RIDDING YOURSELF OF FRAUD

Moses said to Israel: Don't try to cheat people by having two sets of weights or measures, one to get more when you are buying, and the other to give less when you are selling. If you weigh and measure things honestly, the LORD your God will let you enjoy a long life in the land he is giving you. But the LORD is disgusted with anyone who cheats or is dishonest.

DEUTERONOMY 25:13–16 CEV

Use honest scales and don't cheat when you weigh or measure anything. I am the LORD your God. I rescued you from Egypt.

LEVITICUS 19:35 CEV

ONE MOMENT AT A TIME
GIVING WHEN IT HURTS

1. **Create a plan.** Refuse to live under the thumb of your credit card company. Work hard at paying off your balances and create plans to avoid falling into a debt trap.

2. **Get a tax accountant.** There's no shame in getting help with your taxes. The tax code is thousands of pages long, and keeping on top of the yearly changes is a tall order. Even if you want to do your own taxes, it might be wise to have a professional check your work every few years. You don't want to miss something you could benefit from.

3. **Renew your attitude.** Most people resent paying their taxes. If that describes you, then try this exercise: For the next twenty-four hours, add up the things you benefit from that are financed by your local, state, or federal government. Include everything—from roads to police to fire protection. How might your life be different if these benefits didn't exist?

4. **Get organized.** Don't let your tax bill surprise you. If you typically have to write a check to the government, then diligently save enough each month so that the actual check-writing event is less painful.

CHAPTER 7

BUDGETING: GETTING AHEAD

The best change I ever made in my life has been creating a monthly budget. I've set down how much I plan to spend each month for rent, food, eating out–everything. For unpredictable items (like car repairs and dentist bills), I put away some money each month so I have enough when the bills arrive. Yes, living within my budget is difficult. I often have to say no to something I'd like to do but haven't budgeted for. But while those moments can be disappointing, they are far less agonizing than the hours I used to spend worrying about rent money.

■ *Chelsea, age 27, Washington* ■

LIVING WITHIN YOUR MEANS

It's stupid to try to get something for nothing, or run up huge bills you can never pay.
PROVERBS 17:18 MSG

The poor are always ruled over by the rich, so don't borrow and put yourself under their power.
PROVERBS 22:7 MSG

Know the state of your flocks, and put your heart into caring for your herds, for riches don't last forever, and the crown might not be passed on to the next generation. And you will have enough goats' milk for yourself, your family, and your servant girls.
PROVERBS 27:23–24, 27 NLT

"Is there anyone here who, planning to build a new house, doesn't first sit down and figure the cost so you'll know if you can complete it?"
LUKE 14:28 MSG

"Better to have one handful with quietness than two handfuls with hard work and chasing the wind."
ECCLESIASTES 4:6 NLT

PLANNING AHEAD

Good planning and hard work lead to prosperity, but hasty shortcuts lead to poverty.
PROVERBS 21:5 NLT

A house is built by wisdom and becomes strong through good sense. Through knowledge its rooms are filled with all sorts of precious riches and valuables.
PROVERBS 24:3–4 NLT

Be sensible and store up precious treasures—don't waste them like a fool.

PROVERBS 21:20 CEV

In his heart a man plans his course, but the LORD determines his steps.

PROVERBS 16:9 NIV

A prudent person foresees danger and takes precautions. The simpleton goes blindly on and suffers the consequences.

PROVERBS 22:3 NLT

First plant your fields; then build your barn.

PROVERBS 24:27 MSG

"And now let Pharaoh look for a discerning and wise man and put him in charge of the land of Egypt. Let Pharaoh appoint commissioners over the land to take a fifth of the harvest of Egypt during the seven years of abundance. They should collect all the food of these good years that are coming and store up the grain under the authority of Pharaoh, to be kept in the cities for food. This food should be held in reserve for the country, to be used during the seven years of famine that will come upon Egypt, so that the country may not be ruined by the famine."

GENESIS 41:33–36 NIV

Whoever watches the wind will not plant; whoever looks at the clouds will not reap.

ECCLESIASTES 11:4 NIV

PUTTING MONEY AWAY FOR A RAINY DAY

Go to the ant, you sluggard; consider its ways and be wise! It has no commander, no overseer or ruler, yet it stores its provisions in summer and gathers its food at harvest.

PROVERBS 6:6–8 NIV

The wise have wealth and luxury, but fools spend whatever they get.

PROVERBS 21:20 NLT

Wealth gained hastily will dwindle, but whoever gathers little by little will increase it.

PROVERBS 13:11 ESV

Ants are creatures of little strength, yet they store up their food in the summer.

PROVERBS 30:25 NIV

An inheritance quickly gained at the beginning will not be blessed at the end.

PROVERBS 20:21 NIV

HONORING YOUR PARENTS

But if a widow has children or grandchildren, they should learn to serve God by taking care of her, as she once took care of them. This is what God wants them to do.

1 TIMOTHY 5:4 CEV

If anyone does not provide for his relatives, and especially for his

227

immediate family, he has denied the faith and is worse than an unbeliever.

1 TIMOTHY 5:8 NIV

"Honor your father and your mother, so that you may live long in the land the LORD your God is giving you."

EXODUS 20:12 NIV

"For instance, Moses gave you this law from God: 'Honor your father and mother,' and 'Anyone who speaks disrespectfully of father or mother must be put to death.' But you say it is all right for people to say to their parents, 'Sorry, I can't help you. For I have vowed to give to God what I would have given to you.' In this way, you let them disregard their needy parents. And so you cancel the word of God in order to hand down your own tradition. And this is only one example among many others."

MARK 7:10−13 NLT

CARING FOR YOUR CHILDREN

Children should not have to save up for their parents, but parents for their children.

2 CORINTHIANS 12:14 NIV

There was not a woman in that country as beautiful as Job's daughters. Their father treated them as equals with their brothers, providing the same inheritance.

JOB 42:15 MSG

House and wealth are inherited from fathers, but a prudent wife is from the LORD.

PROVERBS 19:14 ESV

Good people leave an inheritance to their grandchildren, but the sinner's wealth passes to the godly.

PROVERBS 13:22 NLT

ONE MOMENT AT A TIME
BUDGETING YOUR MONEY

1. **Sharpen your pencil.** If you don't already have one, create a monthly budget. If you get stuck on where to begin, do an Internet search or find a basic computer program that will provide sample budgets that will help get you started.

2. **Get everyone on board.** It does no good to create a budget if other people in the household don't stick to it. If others are affected by your budget (a spouse or kids or housemates), make sure they all see the value in the limits you want to set. Consider getting everyone's involvement in setting targets so that each person will buy into the changes that are required.

3. **Stick to it.** Review your spending weekly and monthly to ensure you are still within your limits. Creating a budget you never follow up with is like filling a lifesaving medical prescription that you never take.

CHAPTER 8

TRUE RICHES: MORE VALUABLE THAN MONEY

Money has often consumed my waking hours. How will I make more? Will I have enough to retire? Could I save money on my insurance payment? Can I really afford to send the kids to the dentist again? As I read my Bible recently, I was convicted by how much I think about these little green pieces of paper. As I read, I found a long list of traits that God cares about much more than the balance in my bank account.

■ *Natasha, age 48, North Carolina* ■

KNOWING GOD

When you enter the land the LORD your God is giving you and have taken possession of it and settled in it, and you say, "Let us set a king over us like all the nations around us," be sure to appoint over you the king the LORD your God chooses. He must be from among your own brothers. Do not place a foreigner over you, one who is not a brother Israelite. The king, moreover, must not acquire great numbers of horses for himself or make the people return to Egypt to get more of them, for the LORD has told you, "You are not to go back that way again." He must not take many wives, or his heart will be led astray. He must not accumulate large amounts of silver and gold.

DEUTERONOMY 17:14–17 NIV

"Don't store up treasures here on earth, where moths eat them and rust destroys them, and where thieves break in and steal. Store your treasures in heaven, where moths and rust cannot destroy, and thieves do not break in and steal. Wherever your treasure is, there the desires of your heart will also be."

MATTHEW 6:19–21 NLT

GAINING WISDOM

My child, you must follow and treasure my teachings and my instructions. Keep in tune with wisdom and think what it means to have common sense. Beg as loud as you can for good common sense. Search for wisdom as you would search for silver or hidden treasure. Then you will understand what it means to respect and to know the LORD God.

PROVERBS 2:1–5 CEV

Wisdom is more valuable than precious jewels; nothing you want compares with her.

PROVERBS 3:15 CEV

"Choose my instruction rather than silver, and knowledge rather than pure gold. For wisdom is far more valuable than rubies. Nothing you desire can compare with it."

PROVERBS 8:10–11 NLT

"I have riches and honor, as well as enduring wealth and justice. My gifts are better than gold, even the purest gold, my wages better than sterling silver!"

PROVERBS 8:18–19 NLT

It's much better to be wise and sensible than to be rich.

PROVERBS 16:16 CEV

Buy truth, and do not sell it; buy wisdom, instruction, and understanding.

PROVERBS 23:23 ESV

OBEYING GOD

When God is angry, money won't help you. Obeying God is the only way to be saved from death.

PROVERBS 11:4 CEV

Better a little with the fear of the LORD than great wealth with turmoil.

PROVERBS 15:16 NIV

"What good will it be for a man if he gains the whole world, yet forfeits his soul? Or what can a man give in exchange for his soul?"

MATTHEW 16:26 NIV

HAVING INTEGRITY

Better a little with righteousness than much gain with injustice.

PROVERBS 16:8 NIV

Better is a poor person who walks in his integrity than one who is crooked in speech and is a fool.

PROVERBS 19:1 ESV

A good name is to be chosen rather than great riches, and favor is better than silver or gold.

PROVERBS 22:1 ESV

Better a poor man whose walk is blameless than a rich man whose ways are perverse.

PROVERBS 28:6 NIV

"I know, my God, that you test the heart and are pleased with integrity. All these things have I given willingly and with honest intent. And now I have seen with joy how willingly your people who are here have given to you."

1 CHRONICLES 29:17 NIV

"Whoever can be trusted with very little can also be trusted with much, and whoever is dishonest with very little will also be dishonest with much."

LUKE 16:10 NIV

Ill-gotten treasures are of no value, but righteousness delivers from death. The LORD does not let the righteous go hungry but he thwarts the craving of the wicked.

PROVERBS 10:2–3 NIV

The integrity of the honest keeps them on track; the deviousness of crooks brings them to ruin.

PROVERBS 11:3 MSG

The wicked take bribes under the table; they show nothing but contempt for justice.

PROVERBS 17:23 MSG

God gives helpful advice to everyone who obeys him and protects all of those who live as they should. God sees that justice is done, and he watches over everyone who is faithful to him.

PROVERBS 2:7–8 CEV

Getting treasures by a lying tongue is the fleeting fantasy of those who seek death.

PROVERBS 21:6 NKJV

The man of integrity walks securely, but he who takes crooked paths will be found out.

PROVERBS 10:9 NIV

In everything set them an example by doing what is good. In your teaching show integrity, seriousness and soundness of speech that cannot be condemned, so that those who oppose you may be ashamed because they have nothing bad to say about us.

TITUS 2:7–8 NIV

MARRYING THE RIGHT PERSON

Who can find a virtuous and capable wife? She is worth more than precious rubies.

PROVERBS 31:10 NLT

It's better to live alone in the corner of an attic than with a quarrelsome wife in a lovely home.

PROVERBS 21:9 NLT

POSSESSING HUMILITY

Better to live humbly with the poor than to share plunder with the proud.

PROVERBS 16:19 NLT

A rich man may be wise in his own eyes, but a poor man who has discernment sees through him.

PROVERBS 28:11 NIV

FINDING ETERNAL RICHES

Praise be to the God and Father of our Lord Jesus Christ! In his great mercy he has given us new birth into a living hope through the resurrection of Jesus Christ from the dead, and into an inheritance that can never perish, spoil or fade—kept in heaven for you, who through faith are shielded by God's power until the coming of the salvation that is ready to be revealed in the last time.

1 PETER 1:3–5 NIV

But in keeping with his promise we are looking forward to a new heaven and a new earth, the home of righteousness.

2 PETER 3:13 NIV

You were kind to people in jail. And you gladly let your possessions be taken away, because you knew you had something better, something that would last forever.

HEBREWS 10:34 CEV

Abraham was confidently looking forward to a city with eternal foundations, a city designed and built by God.

HEBREWS 11:10 NLT

"Naked I came from my mother's womb, and naked I will depart. The LORD gave and the LORD has taken away; may the name of the LORD be praised."

JOB 1:21 NIV

I saw a new heaven and a new earth. The first heaven and the first earth had disappeared, and so had the sea. Then I saw New Jerusalem, that holy city, coming down from God in heaven. It was like a bride dressed in her wedding gown and ready to meet her husband. I heard a loud voice shout from the throne: God's home is now with his people. He will live with them, and they will be his own. Yes, God will make his home among his people. He will wipe all tears from their eyes, and there will be no more death, suffering, crying, or pain. These things of the past are gone forever. Then the one sitting on the throne said: I am making everything new. Write down what I have said. My words are true and can be trusted.

REVELATION 21:1–5 CEV

The LORD said. . ."I am your share and your inheritance among the Israelites."

NUMBERS 18:20 NIV

But we are citizens of heaven and are eagerly waiting for our Savior to come from there. Our Lord Jesus Christ has power over everything, and he will make these poor bodies of ours like his own glorious body.

PHILIPPIANS 3:20–21 CEV

ONE MOMENT AT A TIME
SETTING TRUE PRIORITIES

1. **Rate these traits.** Review the list below and rank them in the order you think about them:

___ Having enough money
___ Thinking about things you'd like to buy
___ Fantasizing about places to travel to or things to do
___ Developing your character
___ Deepening your relationship with God
___ Focusing on eternal rewards

2. **Spend time in prayer.** Tell God about your financial concerns, but also tell Him about the other areas you'd like to grow in. Ask for His help in growing in these areas, too.

3. **Make a plan.** Most people have financial goals. While those goals aren't always written down, they are often foremost in our minds. Don't let your planning focus on money only. Take a morning to create a specific plan for your own character and spiritual life development.

WHAT THE BIBLE SAYS ABOUT DIVORCE

INTRODUCTION

WHY IS THIS HAPPENING TO ME?

Many counselors believe that divorce is one of the most painful events that can happen to a person. Because of the prolonged fights, hurts, and feelings of rejection, some divorced individuals can take longer to heal than other people whose spouses die unexpectedly. If the logistics of divorce weren't hard enough, the feelings that accompany them can make life feel unbearable. But even in the worst of times, you're not alone. God has not abandoned you during this difficult time. And while His presence is near, His comforting words can provide much of the healing and direction you need.

Enclosed in this book are carefully chosen words of God for you during this difficult time. They're accompanied by the words of men and women who have experienced many of the same things you're experiencing. You'll also find some practical thoughts to help you take some healthy next steps.

While today may not be easy, you don't have to take the steps alone. Find hope as you enjoy taking God's hand through the days ahead.

CHAPTER 1

CAN THESE HURTS BE HEALED?

The tears come so quickly. When I got married, I never imagined that all our dreams could shatter into pieces like this. I feel like a complete failure–rejected and alone. I'm so hurt and depressed, and I don't see myself ever getting past this. To be honest, it's hard to find much reason to get out of bed in the morning. It just hurts too badly to face the future.

■ *Alissa, age 27, Rhode Island* ■

FEELING LIKE A FAILURE

My flesh and my heart fail; but God is the strength of my heart and my portion forever.

PSALM 73:26 NKJV

To him who is able to keep you from stumbling and to present you blameless before the presence of his glory with great joy, to the only God, our Savior, through Jesus Christ our Lord, be glory, majesty, dominion, and authority, before all time and now and forever. Amen.

JUDE 24–25 ESV

"The LORD will fight for you; you need only to be still."

EXODUS 14:14 NIV

I will be glad and rejoice in your unfailing love, for you have seen my troubles, and you care about the anguish of my soul.

PSALM 31:7 NLT

We are afflicted in every way, but not crushed; perplexed, but not driven to despair; persecuted, but not forsaken; struck down, but not destroyed; always carrying in the body the death of Jesus, so that the life of Jesus may also be manifested in our bodies.

2 CORINTHIANS 4:8–10 ESV

FEELING CRUSHED

The LORD is close to the broken-hearted; he rescues those whose spirits are crushed.

PSALM 34:18 NLT

Trust in him at all times, O people; pour out your hearts to him, for God is our refuge.

PSALM 62:8 NIV

God cares for you, so turn all your worries over to him.

1 PETER 5:7 CEV

"Don't be afraid, I've redeemed you. I've called your name. You're mine. When you're in over your head, I'll be there with you. When you're in rough waters, you will not go down. When you're between a rock and a hard place, it won't be a dead end—because I am GOD, your personal God, the Holy of Israel, your Savior. I paid a huge price for you: all of Egypt, with rich Cush and Seba thrown in! That's how much you mean to me! That's how much I love you! I'd sell off the whole world to get you back, trade the creation just for you."

ISAIAH 43:1–4 MSG

Praise the LORD, O my soul; all my inmost being, praise his holy name. Praise the LORD, O my soul, and forget not all his benefits—who forgives all your sins and heals all your diseases, who redeems your life from the pit and crowns you with love and compassion.

PSALM 103:1–4 NIV

The LORD God is waiting to show how kind he is and to have pity on you. The LORD always does right; he blesses those who trust him.

ISAIAH 30:18 CEV

What, then, shall we say in response to this? If God is for us, who can be against us? He who did not spare his own Son, but gave him up for us all—how will he not also, along with him, graciously give us all things? Who will bring any charge against those whom God has chosen? It is God who justifies. Who is he that

condemns? Christ Jesus, who died—more than that, who was raised to life—is at the right hand of God and is also interceding for us. Who shall separate us from the love of Christ? Shall trouble or hardship or persecution or famine or nakedness or danger or sword? As it is written: "For your sake we face death all day long; we are considered as sheep to be slaughtered." No, in all these things we are more than conquerors through him who loved us.

ROMANS 8:31–37 NIV

FEELING REJECTED

Since God assured us, "I'll never let you down, never walk off and leave you," we can boldly quote, God is there, ready to help; I'm fearless no matter what. Who or what can get to me?

HEBREWS 13:5 MSG

For this is what the LORD says: ". . .As a mother comforts her child, so will I comfort you. . . ." When you see this, your heart will rejoice and you will flourish like grass; the hand of the LORD will be made known to his servants, but his fury will be shown to his foes.

ISAIAH 66:12–14 NIV

The LORD is my shepherd, I shall not be in want. He makes me lie down in green pastures, he leads me beside quiet waters, he restores my soul. He guides me in paths of righteousness for his name's sake.

PSALM 23:1–3 NIV

"Do not let your hearts be troubled. Trust in God; trust also in me. In my Father's house are many rooms; if it were not so, I would have told you. I am going there to prepare a place for you. And if I go and prepare a place for you, I will come back and take you to be with me that you also may be where I am. You know the way to the place where I am going."

JOHN 14:1–4 NIV

But Zion said, "I don't get it. God has left me. My Master has forgotten I even exist."[And God replied,] "Can a mother forget the infant at her breast, walk away from the baby she bore? But even if mothers forget, I'd never forget you—never. Look, I've written your names on the backs of my hands. The walls you're rebuilding are never out of my sight. Your builders are faster than your wreckers. The demolition crews are gone for good. Look up, look around, look well! See them all gathering, coming to you?"

ISAIAH 49:14–16 MSG

FINDING HEALING

"I will give you back your health and heal your wounds," says the LORD.

JEREMIAH 30:17 NLT

Therefore we do not lose heart. Though outwardly we are wasting away, yet inwardly we are being renewed day by day.

2 CORINTHIANS 4:16 NIV

"Blessed are you who are poor, for yours is the kingdom of God. Blessed are you who are hungry now, for you shall be satisfied. Blessed are you who weep now, for you shall laugh."

LUKE 6:20–21 ESV

Beloved, do not be surprised at the fiery trial when it comes upon you to test you, as though something strange were happening to you. But rejoice insofar as you share Christ's sufferings, that you may also rejoice and be glad when his glory is revealed.

1 PETER 4:12–13 ESV

Heal me, O LORD, and I shall be healed; save me, and I shall be saved, for You are my praise.

JEREMIAH 17:14 NKJV

O LORD my God, I cried to you for help, and you have healed me.

PSALM 30:2 NRSV

"I will heal my people and will let them enjoy abundant peace and security."

JEREMIAH 33:6 NIV

RESTORING THE BROKEN

He heals the brokenhearted and binds up their wounds.

PSALM 147:3 NIV

May our Lord Jesus Christ himself and God our Father, who loved us and by his grace gave us eternal encouragement and good hope, encourage your hearts and strengthen you in every good deed and word.

2 THESSALONIANS 2:16–17 NIV

So if Christ keeps giving me his power, I will gladly brag about how weak I am. Yes, I am glad to be weak or insulted or mistreated or to have troubles and sufferings, if it is for Christ. Because when I am weak, I am strong.

2 CORINTHIANS 12:9–10 CEV

Be strong and take heart, all you who hope in the LORD.

PSALM 31:24 NIV

He personally carried our sins in his body on the cross so that we can be dead to sin and live for what is right. By his wounds you are healed.

1 PETER 2:24 NLT

"The thief comes only to steal and kill and destroy; I have come that they may have life, and have it to the full."

JOHN 10:10 NIV

The Spirit of God, who raised Jesus from the dead, lives in you. And just as God raised Christ Jesus from the dead, he will give life to your mortal bodies by this same Spirit living within you.

ROMANS 8:11 NLT

OVERCOMING AN ABUSIVE PAST

"You're blessed when you feel you've lost what is most dear to you. Only then can you be embraced by the One most dear to you."

MATTHEW 5:4 MSG

Yet what we suffer now is nothing compared to the glory he will reveal to us later.

ROMANS 8:18 NLT

On that day you will be glad, even if you have to go through many hard trials for a while. Your faith will be like gold that has been tested in a fire. And these trials will prove that your faith is worth much more than gold that can be destroyed. They will show that you will be given praise and honor and glory when Jesus Christ returns. You have never seen Jesus, and you don't see him now. But still you love him and have faith in him, and no words can tell how glad and happy you are to be saved. That's why you have faith.

1 PETER 1:6–9 CEV

As he passed by, he saw a man blind from birth. And his disciples asked him, "Rabbi, who sinned, this man or his parents, that he was born blind?" Jesus answered, "It was not that this man sinned, or his parents, but that the works of God might be displayed in him."

JOHN 9:1–3 ESV

The prudent sees danger and hides himself, but the simple go on and suffer for it.

PROVERBS 22:3 ESV

For God gave us a spirit not of fear but of power and love and self-control.

2 TIMOTHY 1:7 ESV

ONE MOMENT AT A TIME
HEALING THE HURTS

1. **Grieve the loss.** Divorce is always a loss. While every situation is unique, feelings of anger, guilt, insecurity, and sadness are normal. It's important to work through each emotion and understand what you're feeling so that you can find the closure you need.

2. **Accept the change.** While divorce may not be your first choice, it's likely to be a defining moment in your life. While there are surely lessons to learn from the past, there is no benefit in dwelling on past hurts or failures. Yes, life is different now. No, don't wallow over what's happened. Though life will never be the same as it was, your future still holds hope.

3. **Get supportive help.** Don't walk through these days alone. Connect with a counselor, a pastor, or a mature friend. Supportive help during this time can help you implement life changes, keep a positive outlook, and maintain personal growth.

4. **Work at moving on.** Choose to make this change good for you. Find ways to embrace your new life. Each day, make it a point to find at least one thing for which to praise and thank God.

CHAPTER 2

WHAT DOES GOD THINK OF ME NOW?

When I'm at church, I look around at the other people sitting comfortably in their pews. They've got their acts together and are successful in their lives and marriages. Me? I'm the newly divorced guy—apparently inept at marriage. It's hard not to sit there and feel like a complete failure. But then I remember God's love and I realize that He did not save me from my sins so that I'd feel this way. Not at all. The fact is, I'm forgiven. And no one in this building has experienced His love more than I have.

■ *Jonathan, age 34, Pennsylvania* ■

KNOWING YOUR IDENTITY IN CHRIST

But to all who did receive him, who believed in his name, he gave the right to become children of God.
JOHN 1:12 ESV

For you are all children of God through faith in Christ Jesus.
GALATIANS 3:26 NLT

For all who are led by the Spirit of God are children of God. So you have not received a spirit that makes you fearful slaves. Instead, you received God's Spirit when he adopted you as his own children. Now we call him, "Abba, Father."
ROMANS 8:14–15 NLT

"I no longer call you servants, because a servant does not know his master's business. Instead, I have called you friends, for everything that I learned from my Father I have made known to you."
JOHN 15:15 NIV

All this is from God, who reconciled us to himself through Christ and gave us the ministry of reconciliation: that God was reconciling the world to himself in Christ, not counting men's sins against them. And he has committed to us the message of reconciliation. We are therefore Christ's ambassadors, as though God were making his appeal through us. We implore you on Christ's behalf: Be reconciled to God. God made him who had no sin to be sin for us, so that in him we might become the righteousness of God.
2 CORINTHIANS 5:18–21 NIV

Praise the God and Father of our Lord Jesus Christ for the spiritual blessings that Christ has brought us from heaven! Before the world was created, God had Christ choose us to live with him and to be his holy and innocent and loving people. God was kind and decided that Christ would choose us to be God's own adopted children. God was very kind to us because of the Son he dearly loves, and so we should praise God.

EPHESIANS 1:3–6 CEV

Therefore, since we have been made right in God's sight by faith, we have peace with God because of what Jesus Christ our Lord has done for us.

ROMANS 5:1 NLT

"For the LORD will not forsake His people, for His great name's sake, because it has pleased the LORD to make you His people."

1 SAMUEL 12:22 NKJV

Know that the LORD, He is God; it is He who has made us, and not we ourselves; we are His people and the sheep of His pasture.

PSALM 100:3 NKJV

BELIEVING IN GOD'S FORGIVENESS

My dear children, I am writing this to you so that you will not sin. But if anyone does sin, we have an advocate who pleads our case before the Father. He is Jesus Christ, the one who is truly righteous.

1 JOHN 2:1 NLT

If we confess our sins, he is faithful and just and will forgive us our sins and purify us from all unrighteousness.

1 JOHN 1:9 NIV

So whenever we are in need, we should come bravely before the throne of our merciful God. There we will be treated with undeserved kindness, and we will find help.

HEBREWS 4:16 CEV

God rescued us from dead-end alleys and dark dungeons. He's set us up in the kingdom of the Son he loves so much, the Son who got us out of the pit we were in, got rid of the sins we were doomed to keep repeating.

COLOSSIANS 1:13–14 MSG

But you, O Lord, are a compassionate and gracious God, slow to anger, abounding in love and faithfulness.

PSALM 86:15 NIV

Help us, O God of our salvation. Help us for the glory of your name. Save us and forgive our sins for the honor of your name.

PSALM 79:9 NLT

In him we have redemption through his blood, the forgiveness of sins, in accordance with the riches of God's grace that he lavished on us with all wisdom and understanding.

EPHESIANS 1:7–8 NIV

"Come now, let's settle this," says the LORD. "Though your sins are like scarlet, I will make them as white as snow. Though they are red like crimson, I will make them as white as wool."

ISAIAH 1:18 NLT

"I—yes, I alone—will blot out your sins for my own sake and will never think of them again."

ISAIAH 43:25 NLT

SENSING GOD'S LOVE

But the LORD watches over those who fear him, those who rely on his unfailing love.

PSALM 33:18 NLT

"For God so loved the world, that he gave his only Son, that whoever believes in him should not perish but have eternal life."

JOHN 3:16 ESV

But God demonstrates his own love for us in this: While we were still sinners, Christ died for us.

ROMANS 5:8 NIV

Great is his faithfulness; his mercies begin afresh each morning. I say to myself, "The LORD is my inheritance; therefore, I will hope in him!"

LAMENTATIONS 3:23–24 NLT

We know what real love is because Jesus gave up his life for us.

1 JOHN 3:16 NLT

The LORD isn't slow about keeping his promises, as some people think he is. In fact, God is patient, because he wants everyone to turn from sin and no one to be lost.

2 PETER 3:9 CEV

The LORD is good, a refuge in times of trouble. He cares for those who trust in him.

NAHUM 1:7 NIV

But God put his love on the line for us by offering his Son in sacrificial death while we were of no use whatever to him.

ROMANS 5:8 MSG

He found them in a desert land, in an empty, howling wasteland. He surrounded them and watched over them; he guarded them as he would guard his own eyes.

DEUTERONOMY 32:10 NLT

For I am convinced that neither death nor life, neither angels nor demons, neither the present nor the future, nor any powers, neither height nor depth, nor anything else in all creation, will be able to separate us from the love of God that is in Christ Jesus our Lord.

ROMANS 8:38–39 NIV

AVOIDING SELF-PITY AND SHAME

As the Scripture says, "Anyone who trusts in him will never be put to shame."

ROMANS 10:11 NIV

He has never let you down, never looked the other way when you were being kicked around. He has never wandered off to do his own thing; he has been right there, listening.

PSALM 22:24 MSG

From the ends of the earth I call to you, I call as my heart grows faint; lead me to the rock that is higher than I. For you have been my refuge, a strong tower against the foe.

PSALM 61:2–3 NIV

"Do not be afraid; you will not suffer shame. Do not fear disgrace; you will not be humiliated. You will forget the shame of your youth and remember no more the reproach of your widowhood."

ISAIAH 54:4 NIV

In you, O LORD, do I take refuge; let me never be put to shame!

PSALM 71:1 ESV

That is why I am suffering as I am. Yet I am not ashamed, because I know whom I have believed, and am convinced that he is able to guard what I have entrusted to him for that day.

2 TIMOTHY 1:12 NIV

Humble yourselves, therefore, under God's mighty hand, that he may lift you up in due time.

1 PETER 5:6 NIV

He will wipe all tears from their eyes, and there will be no more death, suffering, crying, or pain. These things of the past are gone forever.

REVELATION 21:4 CEV

So now there is no condemnation for those who belong to Christ Jesus.

ROMANS 8:1 NLT

A happy heart makes the face cheerful, but heartache crushes the spirit.

PROVERBS 15:13 NIV

But as for me, it is good to be near God. I have made the Sovereign LORD my refuge; I will tell of all your deeds.

PSALM 73:28 NIV

Don't be like the people of this world, but let God change the way you think. Then you will know how to do everything that is good and pleasing to him.

ROMANS 12:2 CEV

For our light and momentary troubles are achieving for us an eternal glory that far outweighs them all.

2 CORINTHIANS 4:17 NIV

This then is how we know that we belong to the truth, and how we set our hearts at rest in his presence whenever our hearts condemn us. For God is greater than our hearts, and he knows everything.

1 JOHN 3:19–20 NIV

Let us fix our eyes on Jesus, the author and perfecter of our faith, who for the joy set before him endured the cross, scorning its shame, and sat down at the right hand of the throne of God. Consider him who endured such opposition from sinful men, so that you will not grow weary and lose heart.

HEBREWS 12:2–3 NIV

ONE MOMENT AT A TIME
REINFORCING GOD'S TRUTH

1. **Reflect on God's forgiveness.** Reread the section that tells about God's forgiveness and bolster your belief that God's forgiveness is not conditional.

2. **Identify where you find your worth.** Some people find their value in being a spouse or a parent. Others find it in their career or in their role at church. God wants you to find your identity as His child.

3. **Remember that Jesus can never love you more or less than He loves you right now.** As His child, you have God's constant love. No trouble, divorce, or sin can ever diminish His love for you.

4. **God does not grow angry or ashamed of His children.** Self-pity and shame are natural human emotions, but they're not ones you should dwell on. God forgives and empowers. And when He moves on, so should you.

CHAPTER 3

AM I WRONG TO FEEL THIS WAY?

*Sometimes I hang up the phone after talking with my ex and
I just want to scream. Nothing makes my blood pressure soar
as much as when someone merely mentions his name.
I know I need to get past this, but the anger won't go away.*

■ *LaDawn, age 44, Oregon* ■

FACING YOUR ANGER

"In your anger do not sin: Do not let the sun go down while you are still angry."

EPHESIANS 4:26 NIV

Be patient and trust the LORD. Don't let it bother you when all goes well for those who do sinful things. Don't be angry or furious. Anger can lead to sin.

PSALM 37:7–8 CEV

Human anger does not produce the righteousness God desires.

JAMES 1:20 NLT

But now you must stop doing such things. You must quit being angry, hateful, and evil. You must no longer say insulting or cruel things about others.

COLOSSIANS 3:8 CEV

Don't be quick to fly off the handle. Anger boomerangs. You can spot a fool by the lumps on his head.

ECCLESIASTES 7:9 MSG

Don't befriend angry people or associate with hot-tempered people, or you will learn to be like them and endanger your soul.

PROVERBS 22:24–25 NLT

Beloved, never avenge yourselves, but leave it to the wrath of God, for it is written, "Vengeance is mine, I will repay, says the Lord." To the contrary, "if your enemy is hungry, feed him; if he is thirsty, give him something to drink; for by so doing you will heap burning coals on his head." Do not be overcome by evil, but overcome evil with good.

ROMANS 12:19–21 ESV

"I'm telling you that anyone who is so much as angry with a brother or sister is guilty of murder. Carelessly call a brother 'idiot!' and you just might find yourself hauled into court. Thoughtlessly yell 'stupid!' at a sister and you are on the brink of hellfire. The simple moral fact is that words kill."

MATTHEW 5:22 MSG

If you see your enemy hungry, go buy him lunch; if he's thirsty, bring him a drink. Your generosity will surprise him with goodness, and GOD will look after you.

PROVERBS 25:21–22 MSG

FINDING GOD'S GRACE

"But in your great mercy you did not put an end to them or abandon them, for you are a gracious and merciful God."

NEHEMIAH 9:31 NIV

You surely don't think much of God's wonderful goodness or of his patience and willingness to put up with you. Don't you know that the reason God is good to you is because he wants you to turn to him?

ROMANS 2:4 CEV

For it is by grace you have been saved, through faith—and this not from yourselves, it is the gift of God—not by works, so that no one can boast.

EPHESIANS 2:8–9 NIV

"You have granted me life and steadfast love, and your care has preserved my spirit."

JOB 10:12 ESV

I always thank God for you because of his grace given you in Christ Jesus. For in him you have been enriched in every way—in all your speaking and in all your knowledge—because our testimony about Christ was confirmed in you. Therefore you do not lack any spiritual gift as you eagerly wait for our Lord Jesus Christ to be revealed. He will keep you strong to the end, so that you will be blameless on the day of our Lord Jesus Christ.

1 CORINTHIANS 1:4–8 NIV

For you are a people holy to the LORD your God. The LORD your God has chosen you out of all the peoples on the face of the earth to be his people, his treasured possession.

DEUTERONOMY 7:6 NIV

And God is able to make all grace abound to you, so that in all things at all times, having all that you need, you will abound in every good work.

2 CORINTHIANS 9:8 NIV

"Repent, then, and turn to God, so that your sins may be wiped out, that times of refreshing may come from the Lord."

ACTS 3:19 NIV

Each of you has been blessed with one of God's many wonderful gifts to be used in the service of others. So use your gift well.

1 PETER 4:10 CEV

RESISTING BITTERNESS

Above all else, guard your heart, for it is the wellspring of life.

PROVERBS 4:23 NIV

Anyone who claims to be in the light but hates his brother is still in the darkness. Whoever loves his brother lives in the light, and there is nothing in him to make him stumble. But whoever hates his brother is in the darkness and walks around in the darkness; he does not know where he is going, because the darkness has blinded him.

1 JOHN 2:9–11 NIV

Don't grumble against each other, brothers, or you will be judged. The Judge is standing at the door!

JAMES 5:9 NIV

Hatred stirs up strife, but love covers all offenses.

PROVERBS 10:12 ESV

People may cover their hatred with pleasant words, but they're deceiving you. They pretend to be kind, but don't believe them. Their hearts are full of many evils. While their hatred may be concealed by trickery, their wrongdoing will be exposed in public.

PROVERBS 26:24–26 NLT

Imitate God, therefore, in everything you do, because you are his dear children. Live a life filled with love, following the example of Christ. He loved us and offered himself as a sacrifice for us, a pleasing aroma to God.

EPHESIANS 5:1–2 NLT

Keep a sharp eye out for weeds of bitter discontent. A thistle or two gone to seed can ruin a whole garden in no time.

HEBREWS 12:15 MSG

My friends, you were chosen to be free. So don't use your freedom as an excuse to do anything you want. Use it as an opportunity to serve each other with love. All that the Law says can be summed up in the command to love others as much as you love yourself. But if you keep attacking each other like wild animals, you had better watch out or you will destroy yourselves.

GALATIANS 5:13–15 CEV

Brothers, if someone is caught in a sin, you who are spiritual should restore him gently. But watch yourself, or you also may be tempted.

GALATIANS 6:1 NIV

DEALING WITH DEPRESSION

See how very much our Father loves us, for he calls us his children, and that is what we are!

1 JOHN 3:1 NLT

"The LORD your God is in your midst, a mighty one who will save; he will rejoice over you with gladness; he will quiet you by his love, he will exult over you with loud singing."

ZEPHANIAH 3:17 ESV

Give thanks in all circumstances, for this is God's will for you in Christ Jesus.

1 THESSALONIANS 5:18 NIV

I waited patiently for the LORD to help me, and he turned to me and heard my cry. He lifted me out of the pit of despair, out of the mud and the mire. He set my feet on solid ground and steadied me as I walked along.

PSALM 40:1–2 NLT

Don't worry about anything; instead, pray about everything. Tell God what you need, and thank him for all he has done. Then you will experience God's peace, which exceeds anything we can understand. His peace will guard your hearts and minds as you live in Christ Jesus.

PHILIPPIANS 4:6–7 NLT

I have received such wonderful revelations from God. So to keep me from becoming proud, I was given a thorn in my flesh, a messenger from Satan to torment me and keep me from becoming proud. Three different times I begged the Lord to take it away. Each time he said, "My grace is all you need. My power works best in weakness." So now I am glad to boast about my weaknesses, so that the power of Christ can work through me.

2 CORINTHIANS 12:7–9 NLT

"He cuts off every branch in me that bears no fruit, while every branch that does bear fruit he prunes so that it will be even more fruitful."

JOHN 15:2 NIV

"I have told you these things, so that in me you may have peace. In this world you will have trouble. But take heart! I have overcome the world."

JOHN 16:33 NIV

Yet you brought me out of the womb; you made me trust in you even at my mother's breast. From birth I was cast upon you; from my mother's womb you have been my God. Do not be far from me, for trouble is near and there is no one to help.

PSALM 22:9–11 NIV

For the creation was subjected to frustration, not by its own choice, but by the will of the one who subjected it, in hope that the creation itself will be liberated from its bondage to decay and brought into the glorious freedom of the children of God.

ROMANS 8:20–21 NIV

Yet you are enthroned as the Holy One; you are the praise of Israel. In you our fathers put their trust; they trusted and you delivered them. They cried to you and were saved; in you they trusted and were not disappointed.

PSALM 22:3–5 NIV

"Ask and it will be given to you; seek and you will find; knock and the door will be opened to you. For everyone who asks receives; he who seeks finds; and to him who knocks, the door will be opened."

MATTHEW 7:7–8 NIV

LETTING GO

"Come to me, all you who are weary and burdened, and I will give you rest."

MATTHEW 11:28 NIV

Don't stay far away, LORD! My strength comes from you, so hurry and help. Rescue me from enemy swords and save me from those dogs. Don't let lions eat me. You rescued me from the horns of wild bulls.

PSALM 22:19–21 CEV

Not that I have already obtained all this, or have already been made perfect, but I press on to take hold of that for which Christ Jesus took hold of me.

PHILIPPIANS 3:12 NIV

Do not be deceived: God cannot be mocked. A man reaps what he sows. The one who sows to please his sinful nature, from that nature will reap destruction; the one who sows to please the Spirit, from the Spirit will reap eternal life.

GALATIANS 6:7–8 NIV

But I tell you to love your enemies and pray for anyone who mistreats you.

MATTHEW 5:44 CEV

"Be still, and know that I am God; I will be exalted among the nations, I will be exalted in the earth."

PSALM 46:10 NIV

"Therefore do not worry about tomorrow, for tomorrow will worry about itself. Each day has enough trouble of its own."

MATTHEW 6:34 NIV

ONE MOMENT AT A TIME
HANDLING TURBULENT EMOTIONS

1. **Expect anger.** Even an amicable divorce is going to leave you feeling angry at some moments. Divorce can often bring out the worst of each party.

2. **Remember there are two sides.** While you may be growing angry at your former spouse, don't forget that you have your own weaknesses. The other party needs grace extended just as you do.

3. **Choose to forgive.** Despite the profound pain and offense received, resist the temptation to hold on to bitterness. While it may take time to dismiss angry feelings, you can ensure those feelings don't affect the way you act or speak to your former spouse.

4. **Get supportive help.** There is no shame in getting help during this difficult time. Find a supportive friend, pastor, or counselor who can help you work through these natural feelings. Don't let anger or depression become all-consuming without seeking support.

CHAPTER 4

AM I ALONE?

After initial news of our separation got around the gossip mill, people generally stopped checking up on me. I find myself home alone most nights. The phone never rings. The e-mail box is empty. Sometimes I'm tempted to go out and meet someone else—but I know this can't be the right time and that rebound relationships usually end in a second disaster. But I can't stand to be alone. I need to reach out and get connected with supportive people. I need to get into their lives and I'll need to allow them to get into mine, too.

■ *Steve, age 26, Nevada* ■

FINDING HEAVENLY COMFORT

The LORD is near to all who call on him, to all who call on him in truth.

PSALM 145:18 NIV

Come near to God and he will come near to you.

JAMES 4:8 NIV

I'm still in your presence, but you've taken my hand. You wisely and tenderly lead me, and then you bless me.

PSALM 73:23–24 MSG

You notice everything I do and everywhere I go.

PSALM 139:3 CEV

For this is what the high and lofty One says—he who lives forever, whose name is holy: "I live in a high and holy place, but also with him who is contrite and lowly in spirit, to revive the spirit of the lowly and to revive the heart of the contrite."

ISAIAH 57:15 NIV

For in this hope we were saved. But hope that is seen is no hope at all. Who hopes for what he already has? But if we hope for what we do not yet have, we wait for it patiently. In the same way, the Spirit helps us in our weakness. We do not know what we ought to pray for, but the Spirit himself intercedes for us with groans that words cannot express.

ROMANS 8:24–26 NIV

The beloved of the LORD rests in safety—the High God surrounds him all day long—the beloved rests between his shoulders.

DEUTERONOMY 33:12 NRSV

"The young women will dance for joy, and the men—old and young—will join in the celebration. I will turn their mourning into joy. I will comfort them and exchange their sorrow for rejoicing."

JEREMIAH 31:13 NLT

"And God will wipe away every tear from their eyes."

REVELATION 7:17 NIV

Know therefore that the LORD your God is God; he is the faithful God, keeping his covenant of love to a thousand generations of those who love him and keep his commands.

DEUTERONOMY 7:9 NIV

Love the LORD your God with all your heart and with all your soul and with all your strength.

DEUTERONOMY 6:5 NIV

The LORD your God will be watching to find out whether or not you love him with all your heart and soul.

DEUTERONOMY 13:3 CEV

Do not love the world or anything in the world. If anyone loves the world, the love of the Father is not in him.

1 JOHN 2:15 NIV

Whom have I in heaven but you? And earth has nothing I desire besides you.

PSALM 73:25 NIV

Delight yourself in the LORD and he will give you the desires of your heart.

PSALM 37:4 NIV

FINDING EARTHLY SUPPORT

Share each other's burdens, and in this way obey the law of Christ.

GALATIANS 6:2 NLT

If one part of our body hurts, we hurt all over. If one part of our body is honored, the whole body will be happy.

1 CORINTHIANS 12:26 CEV

Be devoted to one another in brotherly love. Honor one another above yourselves.

ROMANS 12:10 NIV

Jesus replied: " 'Love the Lord your God with all your heart and with all your soul and with all your mind.' This is the first and greatest commandment. And the second is like it: 'Love your neighbor as yourself.' All the Law and the Prophets hang on these two commandments."

MATTHEW 22:37–40 NIV

Let's see how inventive we can be in encouraging love and helping out.

HEBREWS 10:24 MSG

There is no fear in love. But perfect love drives out fear, because fear has to do with punishment. The one who fears is not made perfect in love.

1 JOHN 4:18 NIV

It's better to have a partner than go it alone. Share the work, share the wealth. And if one falls down, the other helps, but if there's no one to help, tough! Two in a bed warm each other. Alone, you shiver all night. By yourself you're unprotected. With a friend you can face the worst. Can you round up a third? A three-stranded rope isn't easily snapped.

ECCLESIASTES 4:9–12 MSG

LEARNING TO TRUST GOD

Though my father and mother forsake me, the LORD will receive me.

PSALM 27:10 NIV

"I will be a Father to you, and you will be my sons and daughters, says the Lord Almighty."

2 CORINTHIANS 6:18 NIV

God makes homes for the homeless, leads prisoners to freedom, but leaves rebels to rot in hell.

PSALM 68:6 MSG

"Surely I am with you always, to the very end of the age."

MATTHEW 28:20 NIV

"I am with you and will watch over you wherever you go, and I will bring you back to this land. I will not leave you until I have done what I have promised you."

GENESIS 28:15 NIV

Those who know your name will trust in you, for you, LORD, have never forsaken those who seek you.

PSALM 9:10 NIV

You, LORD, are the light that keeps me safe. I am not afraid of anyone. You protect me, and I have no fears.

PSALM 27:1 CEV

Yet I am poor and needy; may the Lord think of me. You are my help and my deliverer; O my God, do not delay.

PSALM 40:17 NIV

The steps of a good man are ordered by the LORD, and He delights in his way.

PSALM 37:23 NKJV

Where can I go from your Spirit? Where can I flee from your presence? If I go up to the heavens, you are there; if I make my bed in the depths, you are there. If I rise on the wings of the dawn, if I settle on the far side of the sea, even there your hand will guide me, your right hand will hold me fast.

PSALM 139:7–10 NIV

PLUGGING INTO A GOOD CHURCH

But God has combined the members of the body and has given greater honor to the parts that lacked it, so that there should be no division in the body, but that its parts should have equal concern for each other.

1 CORINTHIANS 12:24–25 NIV

Now these are the gifts Christ gave to the church: the apostles, the prophets, the evangelists, and the pastors and teachers. Their responsibility is to equip God's people to do his work and build up the church, the body of Christ. This will continue until we all come to such unity in our faith and knowledge of God's Son that we will be mature in the Lord, measuring up to the full and complete standard of Christ.

EPHESIANS 4:11–13 NLT

Just as each of us has one body with many members, and these members do not all have the same function, so in Christ we who are many form one body, and each member belongs to all the others.

ROMANS 12:4–5 NIV

Let the peace of Christ rule in your hearts, since as members of one body you were called to peace. And be thankful.

COLOSSIANS 3:15 NIV

Consequently, you are no longer foreigners and aliens, but fellow citizens with God's people and members of God's household. . . . And in him you too are being built together to become a dwelling in which God lives by his Spirit.

EPHESIANS 2:19, 22 NIV

And you are living stones that God is building into his spiritual temple. What's more, you are his holy priests. Through the mediation of Jesus Christ, you offer spiritual sacrifices that please God.

1 PETER 2:5 NLT

Your kingdom is an everlasting kingdom, and your dominion endures through all generations. The LORD is faithful to all his promises and loving toward all he has made.

PSALM 145:13 NIV

For a day in your courts is better than a thousand elsewhere. I would rather be a doorkeeper in the house of my God than dwell in the tents of wickedness.

PSALM 84:10 ESV

AVOIDING THE REBOUND

A righteous man is cautious in friendship, but the way of the wicked leads them astray.

PROVERBS 12:26 NIV

Let us behave decently, as in the daytime, not in orgies and drunkenness, not in sexual immorality and debauchery, not in dissension and jealousy.

ROMANS 13:13 NIV

Those who trust their own insight are foolish, but anyone who walks in wisdom is safe.

PROVERBS 28:26 NLT

Friends come and friends go, but a true friend sticks by you like family.

PROVERBS 18:24 MSG

ONE MOMENT AT A TIME
REFUSING TO BE ALONE

1. **Let others love you.** Sometimes it can be difficult to let others help you. Accept their love as a mark of friendship and as an example of Christ's love. Don't try to keep track of the good deeds so that you can repay them later.

2. **Get involved in a Christ-centered community.** God created the church as a place where God's love can be given, received, and shared in practical ways. Churches are made up of struggling people, and they exist to provide help as you continue to further your walk with Christ.

3. **Avoid the rebound.** Rebound relationships can be tempting but almost always deliver additional heartbreak. Have a friend keep you accountable in your relationships with the opposite sex. Now may not be the best time to get involved again.

CHAPTER 5

WHERE WILL THE MONEY COME FROM?

I used to be a mom who flagged down the ice-cream truck and let the kids each grab a candy from the grocery checkout line. Now each time I hear the bells of that truck or see a display of bubble gum, I'm reminded that I don't even have the money to pay the rent. I've whittled and whittled the budget, but there's still not enough to get through the month.

■ *Amanda, age 40, California* ■

ASKING GOD FOR HELP

"For I know the plans I have for you," declares the LORD, "plans to prosper you and not to harm you, plans to give you hope and a future."
JEREMIAH 29:11 NIV

"Which of you, if his son asks for bread, will give him a stone? Or if he asks for a fish, will give him a snake? If you, then, though you are evil, know how to give good gifts to your children, how much more will your Father in heaven give good gifts to those who ask him!"
MATTHEW 7:9–11 NIV

All silver and gold belong to me [says the LORD].
HAGGAI 2:8 CEV

The earth is the LORD's, and everything in it, the world, and all who live in it.
PSALM 24:1 NIV

Tell them to have faith in God, who is rich and blesses us with everything we need to enjoy life.
1 TIMOTHY 6:17 CEV

"Until now you have not asked for anything in my name. Ask and you will receive, and your joy will be complete."
JOHN 16:24 NIV

And we are confident that he hears us whenever we ask him for anything that pleases him. And since we know he hears us when we make our requests, we also know that he will give us what we ask for.
1 JOHN 5:14–15 NLT

You want what you don't have, so you scheme and kill to get it. You are jealous of what others have, but you can't get it, so you fight and wage war to take it away from them. Yet you don't have what you want because you don't ask God for it.
JAMES 4:2 NLT

257

Every good and perfect gift is from above, coming down from the Father of the heavenly lights, who does not change like shifting shadows.

JAMES 1:17 NIV

FINDING GOD'S PROVISION

"Don't store up treasures here on earth, where moths eat them and rust destroys them, and where thieves break in and steal. Store your treasures in heaven, where moths and rust cannot destroy, and thieves do not break in and steal. Wherever your treasure is, there the desires of your heart will also be.

"Your eye is a lamp that provides light for your body. When your eye is good, your whole body is filled with light. But when your eye is bad, your whole body is filled with darkness. And if the light you think you have is actually darkness, how deep that darkness is!

"No one can serve two masters. For you will hate one and love the other; you will be devoted to one and despise the other. You cannot serve both God and money.

"That is why I tell you not to worry about everyday life—whether you have enough food and drink, or enough clothes to wear. Isn't life more than food, and your body more than clothing? Look at the birds. They don't plant or harvest or store food in barns, for your heavenly Father feeds them. And aren't you far more valuable to him than they are? Can all your worries add a single moment to your life?

"And why worry about your clothing? Look at the lilies of the field and how they grow. They don't work or make their clothing, yet Solomon in all his glory was not dressed as beautifully as they are. And if God cares so wonderfully for wildflowers that are here today and thrown into the fire tomorrow, he will certainly care for you. Why do you have so little faith?

"So don't worry about these things, saying, 'What will we eat? What will we drink? What will we wear?' These things dominate the thoughts of unbelievers, but your heavenly Father already knows all your needs. Seek the Kingdom of God above all else, and live righteously, and he will give you everything you need."

MATTHEW 6:19–33 NLT

The Maker of heaven and earth, the sea, and everything in them—the LORD, who remains faithful forever. He upholds the cause of the oppressed and gives food to the hungry. The LORD sets prisoners free, the LORD gives sight to the blind, the LORD lifts up those who are bowed down, the LORD loves the righteous. The LORD watches over the alien and sustains the fatherless and the widow, but he frustrates the ways of the wicked.

PSALM 146:6–9 NIV

Do not wear yourself out to get rich; have the wisdom to show restraint. Cast but a glance at riches, and they are gone, for they will surely sprout wings and fly off to the sky like an eagle.

PROVERBS 23:4–5 NIV

Not that I was ever in need, for I have learned how to be content with whatever I have. I know how to live on almost nothing or with everything. I have learned the secret of living in every situation, whether it is with a full stomach or empty, with plenty or little. For I can do everything through Christ, who gives me strength.

PHILIPPIANS 4:11–13 NLT

BECOMING A GOOD STEWARD

"For all the animals of the forest are mine, and I own the cattle on a thousand hills. I know every bird on the mountains, and all the animals of the field are mine. If I were hungry, I would not tell you, for all the world is mine and everything in it."

PSALM 50:10–12 NLT

Everything comes from the Lord. All things were made because of him and will return to him. Praise the Lord forever! Amen.

ROMANS 11:36 CEV

God's blessing makes life rich; nothing we do can improve on God.

PROVERBS 10:22 MSG

But remember the LORD your God, for it is he who gives you the ability to produce wealth, and so confirms his covenant, which he swore to your forefathers, as it is today.

DEUTERONOMY 8:18 NIV

Moreover, it is required of stewards that they be found trustworthy.

1 CORINTHIANS 4:2 ESV

"From everyone who has been given much, much will be demanded; and from the one who has been entrusted with much, much more will be asked."

LUKE 12:48 NIV

259

ONE MOMENT AT A TIME
LOOKING TO GOD

1. **Define your needs.** Make a list of the things you need to live. Try to separate things that you'd like to have from things you need to have.

2. **Spend regular time in prayer.** God loves you very much. Tell Him about the needs you have.

3. **Make necessary changes.** Divorce often changes immediate living or buying habits. Consider big changes such as moving to a smaller, more affordable home. Be strong in little changes such as resisting impulse items at the store.

4. **Allow others to help.** It can be difficult to let others know about your needs, but by doing so you may find that there are friends, family members, or people at church who want to help you with no expectation of anything in return.

CHAPTER 6

HOW WILL THIS AFFECT MY KIDS?

Many nights I lie awake and wonder how I'm going to make it through this. More than that, I worry about how my kids are handling the divorce. I worry that they might feel like it's their fault or that I've totally messed up their lives. While I had some choice in this, they're being unfairly pulled along. I can't help but want to vent at the kids, but I know it's not fair to put them in the middle like that. I just don't know how to help them through this.

■ *Beth, age 40, South Carolina* ■

MINIMIZING THEIR GUILT

But Jesus said, "Let the little children come to me and do not hinder them, for to such belongs the kingdom of heaven."

MATTHEW 19:14 ESV

He comforts us in all our troubles so that we can comfort others. When they are troubled, we will be able to give them the same comfort God has given us.

2 CORINTHIANS 1:4 NLT

God is our refuge and strength, always ready to help in times of trouble.

PSALM 46:1 NLT

"Take my yoke upon you and learn from me, for I am gentle and humble in heart, and you will find rest for your souls. For my yoke is easy and my burden is light."

MATTHEW 11:29–30 NIV

LORD, if you kept a record of our sins, who, O Lord, could ever survive? But you offer forgiveness, that we might learn to fear you.

PSALM 130:3–4 NLT

Have mercy on me, O God, have mercy on me, for in you my soul takes refuge. I will take refuge in the shadow of your wings until the disaster has passed.

PSALM 57:1 NIV

God is love. . . . The thought of being punished is what makes us afraid. It shows that we have not really learned to love.

1 JOHN 4:16, 18 CEV

261

I am surrounded by trouble, but you protect me against my angry enemies. With your own powerful arm you keep me safe.

PSALM 138:7 CEV

HELPING THEM HEAL

Stoop down and reach out to those who are oppressed. Share their burdens, and so complete Christ's law.

GALATIANS 6:2 MSG

Be brave and strong! Don't be afraid. . . The LORD your God will always be at your side, and he will never abandon you.

DEUTERONOMY 31:6 CEV

"Have I not commanded you? Be strong and courageous. Do not be terrified; do not be discouraged, for the LORD your God will be with you wherever you go."

JOSHUA 1:9 NIV

"Peace I leave with you; my peace I give to you. Not as the world gives do I give to you. Let not your hearts be troubled, neither let them be afraid."

JOHN 14:27 ESV

CARRYING YOUR OWN BURDENS

Fathers, do not embitter your children, or they will become discouraged.

COLOSSIANS 3:21 NIV

I look up to the mountains; does my strength come from mountains? No, my strength comes from God, who made heaven, and earth, and mountains.

PSALM 121:1–2 MSG

Don't be afraid. I am with you. Don't tremble with fear. I am your God. I will make you strong, as I protect you with my arm and give you victories.

ISAIAH 41:10 CEV

"I, your GOD, have a firm grip on you and I'm not letting go. I'm telling you, 'Don't panic. I'm right here to help you.' "

ISAIAH 41:13 MSG

"Be fair to the poor and to orphans. Defend the helpless and everyone in need."

PSALM 82:3–4 CEV

AVOIDING A TOXIC RELATIONSHIP WITH YOUR EX

My dear friends, we must love each other. Love comes from God, and when we love each other, it shows that we have been given new life. We are now God's children, and we know him.

1 JOHN 4:7 CEV

If you churn milk you get butter; if you pound on your nose, you get blood—and if you stay angry, you get in trouble.

PROVERBS 30:33 CEV

A hot-tempered person starts fights; a cool-tempered person stops them.
PROVERBS 15:18 NLT

Fools show their anger at once, but the prudent ignore an insult.
PROVERBS 12:16 NRSV

Greed causes fighting; trusting the LORD leads to prosperity.
PROVERBS 28:25 NLT

Do not gloat when your enemy falls; when he stumbles, do not let your heart rejoice, or the LORD will see and disapprove.
PROVERBS 24:17–18 NIV

Work at living in peace with everyone, and work at living a holy life, for those who are not holy will not see the Lord.
HEBREWS 12:14 NLT

Therefore let us pursue the things which make for peace and the things by which one may edify another.
ROMANS 14:19 NKJV

ONE MOMENT AT A TIME
HELPING YOUR KIDS ENDURE DIVORCE

1. **Keep the peace.** No matter the differences you face and the injustices you feel, your kids need you to handle this situation civilly. While you may not feel like offering Christian love and kindness to your ex, your kids need you to.

2. **Don't put them in the middle.** Don't let your children become pawns in the disagreements. The differences you face with your ex are yours, not theirs. It's almost never appropriate to vent to them about the frustrations you feel about your ex. Don't force your kids to take sides.

3. **Work it out.** Parents need to be at ball games, recitals, and concerts. Don't let bickering with a spouse keep you away from supporting your kids and showing the love they need.

4. **Find some support.** You're not the only person in this who needs a friend and listening ear. Let your kids visit with friends and their families and travel to see Grandma, and consider a professional counselor to help them work through their own issues.

CHAPTER 7

WILL I ALWAYS BE THIS EXHAUSTED?

Every afternoon it's the same: I drive from ballet to baseball to scouts and finally find my way home. I put the kids to bed and get caught up on the office work that I bring home. Usually after midnight, I'm able to haul myself to bed. The morning begins again with the relentless routine of getting the kids off to school and myself to work. Once the workday ends, the afternoon merry-go-round begins again. I've been working on five hours of sleep for too long. I'm not sure how much longer I'll be able to make it.

■ *Ben, age 34, Illinois* ■

FINDING PHYSICAL REST

Do you not know? Have you not heard? The LORD is the everlasting God, the Creator of the ends of the earth. He will not grow tired or weary, and his understanding no one can fathom. He gives strength to the weary and increases the power of the weak. Even youths grow tired and weary, and young men stumble and fall; but those who hope in the LORD will renew their strength. They will soar on wings like eagles; they will run and not grow weary, they will walk and not be faint.

ISAIAH 40:28–31 NIV

But he replied, "My kindness is all you need. My power is strongest when you are weak."

2 CORINTHIANS 12:9 CEV

Though an army besiege me, my heart will not fear; though war break out against me, even then will I be confident.

PSALM 27:3 NIV

"The eternal God is your refuge, and underneath are the everlasting arms."

DEUTERONOMY 33:27 NIV

When I felt my feet slipping, you came with your love and kept me steady. And when I was burdened with worries, you comforted me and made me feel secure.

PSALM 94:18–19 CEV

BEING STILL FOR A MOMENT

"Be still, and know that I am God; I will be exalted among the nations, I will be exalted in the earth."

PSALM 46:10 NIV

The LORD replied, "My Presence will go with you, and I will give you rest."

EXODUS 33:14 NIV

Cast all your anxiety on him because he cares for you.

I PETER 5:7 NIV

Showing respect to the LORD brings true life—if you do it, you can relax without fear of danger.

PROVERBS 19:23 CEV

"You keep him in perfect peace whose mind is stayed on you, because he trusts in you. Trust in the LORD forever, for the LORD GOD is an everlasting rock."

ISAIAH 26:3–4 ESV

"Can all your worries add a single moment to your life? And if worry can't accomplish a little thing like that, what's the use of worrying over bigger things?"

LUKE 12:25–26 NLT

I sought the LORD, and he answered me; he delivered me from all my fears.

PSALM 34:4 NIV

Think about the things of heaven, not the things of earth. For you died to this life, and your real life is hidden with Christ in God. And when Christ, who is your life, is revealed to the whole world, you will share in all his glory.

COLOSSIANS 3:2–4 NLT

REFRESHING YOUR HEART

The LORD is near to all who call on him, to all who call on him in truth. He fulfills the desires of those who fear him; he hears their cry and saves them.

PSALM 145:18–19 NIV

When I called, you answered me; you made me bold and stouthearted.

PSALM 138:3 NIV

Search me, O God, and know my heart; test me and know my anxious thoughts.

PSALM 139:23 NLT

Let me abide in your tent forever, find refuge under the shelter of your wings.

PSALM 61:4 NRSV

Let all bitterness and wrath and anger and clamor and slander be put away from you, along with all malice.

EPHESIANS 4:31 ESV

Wait for the LORD; be strong and take heart and wait for the LORD.

PSALM 27:14 NIV

ONE MOMENT AT A TIME
FEELING MAXED OUT?

1. **Look for changes.** Make a list of the activities that exhaust you. While you may prefer to leave your routine alone, are you able to make some changes—even temporarily—to help ease the stress?

2. **Be realistic.** You can't work ninety hours a week, be a full-time parent, coach your kid's team, and find time to sing in the church choir. Prioritize what you can do and choose to feel good about the things God has allowed you to do.

3. **Don't forget God.** As you grow busy and tired, it may become easy for you to reduce your regular time spent with God. Don't do it. Your dependency on God is more vital now than ever.

4. **Do something for yourself.** Find some time each week to take a genuine break. It can be some quiet moments in the car or a few extra minutes in the shower. Do your best to push the busy and exhausting thoughts from your mind and just enjoy the quiet.

CHAPTER 8

WHAT ABOUT SEX?

I miss sex. I know that sounds crazy to some women, but I really miss the physical and emotional intimacy. Sometimes the tempting thoughts come while I'm with a coworker or even sometimes when I'm at church. There are a couple of men at each place who flirt with me and I think they may be interested. Sometimes I'm tempted to think, What would be the harm?

■ *Jocelyn, age 39 Washington DC* ■

PRESERVING PURITY

Instead, clothe yourself with the presence of the Lord Jesus Christ. And don't let yourself think about ways to indulge your evil desires.
ROMANS 13:14 NLT

Run from anything that stimulates youthful lusts. Instead, pursue righteous living, faithfulness, love, and peace. Enjoy the companionship of those who call on the Lord with pure hearts.
2 TIMOTHY 2:22 NLT

The acts of the sinful nature are obvious: sexual immorality, impurity and debauchery.
GALATIANS 5:19 NIV

Put to death, therefore, whatever belongs to your earthly nature: sexual immorality, impurity, lust, evil desires and greed, which is idolatry.
COLOSSIANS 3:5 NIV

Or do you not know that your body is the temple of the Holy Spirit who is in you, whom you have from God, and you are not your own? For you were bought at a price; therefore glorify God in your body and in your spirit, which are God's.
1 CORINTHIANS 6:19–20 NKJV

But now you must be holy in everything you do, just as God who chose you is holy. For the Scriptures say, "You must be holy because I am holy."
1 PETER 1:15–16 NLT

God's will is for you to be holy, so stay away from all sexual sin.
1 THESSALONIANS 4:3 NLT

"But I tell you that anyone who looks at a woman lustfully has already committed adultery with her in his heart."
MATTHEW 5:28 NIV

But each person is tempted when he is lured and enticed by his own desire.
JAMES 1:14 ESV

Honor marriage, and guard the sacredness of sexual intimacy between wife and husband. God draws a firm line against casual and illicit sex.

HEBREWS 13:4 MSG

AVOIDING TEMPTATION

Be self-controlled and alert. Your enemy the devil prowls around like a roaring lion looking for someone to devour. Resist him, standing firm in the faith, because you know that your brothers throughout the world are undergoing the same kind of sufferings. And the God of all grace, who called you to his eternal glory in Christ, after you have suffered a little while, will himself restore you and make you strong, firm and steadfast.

1 PETER 5:8–10 NIV

So humble yourselves before God. Resist the devil, and he will flee from you.

JAMES 4:7 NLT

The temptations in your life are no different from what others experience. And God is faithful. He will not allow the temptation to be more than you can stand. When you are tempted, he will show you a way out so that you can endure.

1 CORINTHIANS 10:13 NLT

God blesses those who patiently endure testing and temptation. Afterward they will receive the crown of life that God has promised to those who love him. And remember, when you are being tempted, do not say, "God is tempting me." God is never tempted to do wrong, and he never tempts anyone else.

JAMES 1:12–13 NLT

For we do not have a high priest who is unable to sympathize with our weaknesses, but we have one who has been tempted in every way, just as we are—yet was without sin. Let us then approach the throne of grace with confidence, so that we may receive mercy and find grace to help us in our time of need.

HEBREWS 4:15–16 NIV

How can a young person stay pure? By obeying your word. I have tried hard to find you—don't let me wander from your commands. I have hidden your word in my heart, that I might not sin against you.

PSALM 119:9–11 NLT

KNOWING YOUR LIMITATIONS

Finally, brothers, whatever is true, whatever is noble, whatever is right, whatever is pure, whatever is lovely, whatever is admirable—if anything is excellent or praiseworthy—think about such things.

PHILIPPIANS 4:8 NIV

But among you there must not be even a hint of sexual immorality, or of any kind of impurity, or of greed, because these are improper for God's holy people.

EPHESIANS 5:3 NIV

So let us not grow weary in doing what is right, for we will reap at harvest time, if we do not give up.

GALATIANS 6:9 NRSV

Those who live according to the sinful nature have their minds set on what that nature desires; but those who live in accordance with the Spirit have their minds set on what the Spirit desires.

ROMANS 8:5 NIV

With all your heart you must trust the LORD and not your own judgment. Always let him lead you, and he will clear the road for you to follow.

PROVERBS 3:5–6 CEV

For the grace of God that brings salvation has appeared to all men. It teaches us to say "No" to ungodliness and worldly passions, and to live self-controlled, upright and godly lives in this present age.

TITUS 2:11–12 NIV

As obedient children, do not conform to the evil desires you had when you lived in ignorance.

1 PETER 1:14 NIV

Don't be selfish; don't try to impress others. Be humble, thinking of others as better than yourselves. Don't look out only for your own interests, but take an interest in others, too.

PHILIPPIANS 2:3–4 NLT

Train me in good common sense; I'm thoroughly committed to living your way.

PSALM 119:66 MSG

I will instruct you and teach you in the way you should go; I will counsel you and watch over you.

PSALM 32:8 NIV

Put on all the armor that God gives, so you can defend yourself against the devil's tricks.

EPHESIANS 6:11 CEV

For this reason, since the day we heard about you, we have not stopped praying for you and asking God to fill you with the knowledge of his will through all spiritual wisdom and understanding. And we pray this in order that you may live a life worthy of the Lord and may please him in every way: bearing fruit in every good work, growing in the knowledge of God, being strengthened with all power according to his glorious might so that you may have great endurance and patience, and joyfully giving thanks to the Father, who has qualified you to share in the inheritance of the saints in the kingdom of light.

COLOSSIANS 1:9–12 NIV

ACKNOWLEDGING YOUR NEED FOR INTIMACY

The LORD God said, "It is not good for the man to be alone. I will make a helper suitable for him." . . .So the LORD God caused the man to fall into a deep sleep; and while he was sleeping, he took one of the man's ribs and closed up the place with flesh. Then the LORD God made a woman from the rib he had taken out of the man, and he brought her to the man. The man said, "This is now bone of my bones and flesh of my flesh; she shall be called 'woman,' for she was taken out of man." For this reason a man will leave his father and mother and be united to his wife, and they will become one flesh.

GENESIS 2:18, 21–24 NIV

Wise friends make you wise, but you hurt yourself by going around with fools.

PROVERBS 13:20 CEV

Don't fool yourselves. Bad friends will destroy you.

1 CORINTHIANS 15:33 CEV

Stay away from fools, for you won't find knowledge on their lips.

PROVERBS 14:7 NLT

You can trust a friend who corrects you, but kisses from an enemy are nothing but lies.

PROVERBS 27:6 CEV

ONE MOMENT AT A TIME
ESTABLISHING BOUNDARIES?

1. **Remember God's standards.** While our society has redefined and accepted casual sex, God's standards haven't changed. Keep your heart focused on Christ.

2. **Acknowledge your need for intimacy.** God created you with a desire for intimacy. Realize that need is natural; then spend your efforts deepening your relationship with Him and with friends of the same sex.

3. **Know your limitations.** If certain magazines, books, or movies feed your sexual desires, then put them aside. If you find that certain people in your life invite temptation, then change the way you interact with them. Have a friend of the same sex hold you accountable to God's standards.

4. **Be honest with yourself.** Sexual temptation is easy to enjoy. Recognize when you find yourself lingering on thoughts or images you should dismiss and then move quickly to do so.

CHAPTER 9

DO I HAVE TO FORGIVE?

*I'm so hurt and angry that I find myself lashing out in ways
I didn't think were possible for me. My ex-husband and I can't be
in the same room without one or both of us screaming at the other.
We've tried to discuss our differences over the phone, but we can't last
more than two minutes without one of us hanging up on the other.
Now we do all of our talking through lawyers.*

■ *Becca, age 52, Colorado* ■

FORGIVING YOUR EX

Be kind and compassionate to one another, forgiving each other, just as in Christ God forgave you.
EPHESIANS 4:32 NIV

The LORD passed before him, and proclaimed, "The LORD, the LORD, a God merciful and gracious, slow to anger, and abounding in steadfast love and faithfulness."
EXODUS 34:6 NRSV

Dear friends, let us continue to love one another, for love comes from God. Anyone who loves is a child of God and knows God. But anyone who does not love does not know God—for God is love.
1 JOHN 4:7–8 NLT

"But love your enemies, do good to them, and lend to them without expecting to get anything back. Then your reward will be great, and you will be sons of the Most High, because he is kind to the ungrateful and wicked. Be merciful, just as your Father is merciful. Do not judge, and you will not be judged. Do not condemn, and you will not be condemned. Forgive, and you will be forgiven. Give, and it will be given to you. A good measure, pressed down, shaken together and running over, will be poured into your lap. For with the measure you use, it will be measured to you."
LUKE 6:35–38 NIV

He who covers a transgression seeks love, but he who repeats a matter separates friends.
PROVERBS 17:9 NKJV

Then Peter came to Jesus and asked, "Lord, how many times shall I forgive my brother when he sins against me? Up to seven times?" Jesus answered, "I tell you, not seven times, but seventy-seven times."
MATTHEW 18:21–22 NIV

"So watch yourselves! If another believer sins, rebuke that person; then if there is repentance, forgive. Even if that person wrongs you seven times a day and each time turns again and asks forgiveness, you must forgive."

LUKE 17:3–4 NLT

"But when you are praying, first forgive anyone you are holding a grudge against, so that your Father in heaven will forgive your sins, too."

MARK 11:25 NLT

DEALING WITH ADVERSARIAL PEOPLE

Only fools get angry quickly and hold a grudge.

ECCLESIASTES 7:9 CEV

Do not let any unwholesome talk come out of your mouths, but only what is helpful for building others up according to their needs, that it may benefit those who listen.

EPHESIANS 4:29 NIV

Never pay back evil with more evil. Do things in such a way that everyone can see you are honorable. Do all that you can to live in peace with everyone.

ROMANS 12:17–18 NLT

Short-tempered people do foolish things, and schemers are hated.

PROVERBS 14:17 NLT

"You shall not hate your brother in your heart, but you shall reason frankly with your neighbor, lest you incur sin because of him. You shall not take vengeance or bear a grudge against the sons of your own people, but you shall love your neighbor as yourself: I am the LORD."

LEVITICUS 19:17–18 ESV

Quick, GOD, I need your helping hand! The last decent person just went down, all the friends I depended on gone.

PSALM 12:1 MSG

One who is slow to anger is better than the mighty, and one whose temper is controlled than one who captures a city.

PROVERBS 16:32 NRSV

HANDLING WELL-MEANING BUT INSENSITIVE PEOPLE

A gentle answer turns away wrath, but a harsh word stirs up anger.

PROVERBS 15:1 NIV

My dear friends, you should be quick to listen and slow to speak or to get angry.

JAMES 1:19 CEV

"Do not judge others, and you will not be judged. For you will be treated as you treat others. The standard you use in judging is the standard by which you will be judged. And why worry about a speck in your friend's eye when you have a log in your own? How can you think of saying to your friend, 'Let me help you get rid of that speck in your eye,' when you can't see past the log in your own eye? Hypocrite! First get rid of the log in your own eye; then you will see well enough to deal with the speck in your friend's eye."

MATTHEW 7:1–5 NLT

Blessed are those who are persecuted because of righteousness, for theirs is the kingdom of heaven. Blessed are you when people insult you, persecute you and falsely say all kinds of evil against you because of me. Rejoice and be glad, because great is your reward in heaven, for in the same way they persecuted the prophets who were before you."

MATTHEW 5:10–12 NIV

"For if you forgive others their trespasses, your heavenly Father will also forgive you."

MATTHEW 6:14 ESV

Sensible people control their temper; they earn respect by overlooking wrongs.

PROVERBS 19:11 NLT

ONE MOMENT AT A TIME
EXTENDING FORGIVENESS

1. **Focus on the true victim.** If you refuse to forgive someone, the person who suffers is you. You're the one who lives with the regular reminders of the pain.

2. **Make a list.** It's important to realize why you are angry so you can fully forgive and move past the situation. Make a list of things that have bothered you. Then burn the paper or throw the list away. Ask God to help you move past the hurts, too.

3. **Understand forgiveness.** Forgiveness is choosing to act toward someone as if the offense did not occur. While hurt feelings may take time to dissipate, your words and actions toward that individual can change today.

4. **Seek God's help.** True forgiveness may be bigger than what you can accomplish on your own. Spend time with God, asking Him to show you the depth of His forgiveness. Ask for His help in forgiving the people to whom you need to extend similar grace.

CHAPTER 10

IS RECONCILIATION POSSIBLE?

The ink was hardly dry on our divorce documents when my ex-husband started saying that he wanted to reconcile. I don't know if his motivation is guilt, money, sex, or power. Whatever it is, the thought of getting back together scares me. I know God hates divorce, but I can't take my kids and go back into a bad situation. While divorce hasn't been a good option, it's better than living with the verbal abuse he often heaped on us. And while he's promised to change, I don't see enough evidence yet that he really has.

■ *Joanna, age 37, New Hampshire* ■

BEING OPEN TO RECONCILIATION

Love is patient, love is kind. It does not envy, it does not boast, it is not proud. It is not rude, it is not self-seeking, it is not easily angered, it keeps no record of wrongs. Love does not delight in evil but rejoices with the truth. It always protects, always trusts, always hopes, always perseveres. Love never fails.

1 CORINTHIANS 13:4–8 NIV

Always be humble and gentle. Patiently put up with each other and love each other.

EPHESIANS 4:2 CEV

Therefore, as God's chosen people, holy and dearly loved, clothe yourselves with compassion, kindness, humility, gentleness and patience. Bear with each other and forgive whatever grievances you may have against one another. Forgive as the Lord forgave you. And over all these virtues put on love, which binds them all together in perfect unity.

COLOSSIANS 3:12–14 NIV

So husbands ought to love their own wives as their own bodies; he who loves his wife loves himself. For no one ever hated his own flesh, but nourishes and cherishes it, just as the Lord does the church. For we are members of His body, of His flesh and of His bones. "For this reason a man shall leave his father and mother and be joined to his wife, and the two shall become one flesh."

EPHESIANS 5:28–31 NJKV

PURSUING RECONCILIATION

Most important of all, you must sincerely love each other, because love wipes away many sins.

1 PETER 4:8 CEV

Therefore, as we have opportunity, let us do good to all people, especially to those who belong to the family of believers.

GALATIANS 6:10 NIV

Reckless words pierce like a sword, but the tongue of the wise brings healing.

PROVERBS 12:18 NIV

"Now that I, your Lord and Teacher, have washed your feet, you also should wash one another's feet. I have set you an example that you should do as I have done for you."

JOHN 13:14–15 NIV

"A new command I give you: Love one another. As I have loved you, so you must love one another."

JOHN 13:34 NIV

Don't just pretend to love others. Really love them. Hate what is wrong. Hold tightly to what is good. Love each other with genuine affection, and take delight in honoring each other.

ROMANS 12:9–10 NLT

Husbands, love your wives and do not be harsh with them.

COLOSSIANS 3:19 NIV

Do two people walk hand in hand if they aren't going to the same place?

AMOS 3:3 MSG

Finishing is better than starting. Patience is better than pride.

ECCLESIASTES 7:8 NLT

SEEKING WISDOM

Search for wisdom as you would search for silver or hidden treasure.

PROVERBS 2:4 CEV

It's much better to be wise and sensible than to be rich.

PROVERBS 16:16 CEV

"First seek the counsel of the LORD."

1 KINGS 22:5 NIV

Fools think their own way is right, but the wise listen to others.

PROVERBS 12:15 NLT

Listen to advice and accept instruction, and in the end you will be wise.

PROVERBS 19:20 NIV

ONE MOMENT AT A TIME
CONSIDERING RECONCILIATION

1. **Get good counsel.** It's easy to find a friend who will tell you what you want to hear or who will push an agenda (either reconciling or staying apart). Find a friend, counselor, or pastor who can be objective and help you evaluate your unique situation.

2. **Don't rush.** While you may feel pressure to make a quick decision, don't act impulsively. Time apart can help determine true motivations as well as provide you the chance to see if the problems that caused the divorce in the first place are still present.

3. **Be objective.** Don't let wishful thinking or swinging emotions drive you to make a decision you'll regret.

4. **Work together.** If both parties want reconciliation, then work together in that process. Undergo counseling together before taking big steps to ensure you will be able to live together again under one roof.

CHAPTER 11

CAN I REBUILD MY LIFE?

It's been two years since I first heard the words "I want a divorce." My now ex-husband has already remarried and has taken a job in another city. As for me, I struggle to keep the kids (and our lives) together. While it's been difficult, I've sensed God's presence during this time. He's helped me get through the pain and given me perspective on myself and the future.

■ *Cyndi, age 28, Texas* ■

DEALING WITH LINGERING HURTS

I'll never forget the trouble, the utter lostness, the taste of ashes, the poison I've swallowed. I remember it all—oh, how well I remember—the feeling of hitting the bottom. But there's one other thing I remember, and remembering, I keep a grip on hope: God's loyal love couldn't have run out, his merciful love couldn't have dried up.

LAMENTATIONS 3:19–22 MSG

Bring joy to your servant, for to you, O Lord, I lift up my soul.

PSALM 86:4 NIV

Pray that our LORD will make us strong and give us peace.

PSALM 29:11 CEV

Praise be to the God and Father of our Lord Jesus Christ, the Father of compassion and the God of all comfort.

2 CORINTHIANS 1:3 NIV

For he has not ignored or belittled the suffering of the needy. He has not turned his back on them, but has listened to their cries for help.

PSALM 22:24 NLT

I learned God-worship when my pride was shattered. Heart-shattered lives ready for love don't for a moment escape God's notice.

PSALM 51:17 MSG

FINDING NEW HOPE

Being confident of this, that he who began a good work in you will carry it on to completion until the day of Christ Jesus.

PHILIPPIANS 1:6 NIV

But you, O Sovereign LORD, deal well with me for your name's sake; out of the goodness of your love, deliver me. For I am poor and needy, and my heart is wounded within me.

PSALM 109:21–22 NIV

277

For you have been my hope, O Sovereign LORD, my confidence since my youth.

PSALM 71:5 NIV

To all who mourn in Israel, he will give a crown of beauty for ashes, a joyous blessing instead of mourning, festive praise instead of despair. In their righteousness, they will be like great oaks that the LORD has planted for his own glory.

ISAIAH 61:3 NLT

I am still confident of this: I will see the goodness of the LORD in the land of the living. Wait for the LORD; be strong and take heart and wait for the LORD.

PSALM 27:13–14 NIV

Why am I discouraged? Why am I restless? I trust you! And I will praise you again because you help me.

PSALM 42:5 CEV

And this same God who takes care of me will supply all your needs from his glorious riches, which have been given to us in Christ Jesus.

PHILIPPIANS 4:19 NLT

Trust in the LORD and do good. Then you will live safely in the land and prosper.

PSALM 37:3 NLT

Praise the LORD! Oh give thanks to the LORD, for he is good, for his steadfast love endures forever!

PSALM 106:1 ESV

Consider it pure joy, my brothers, whenever you face trials of many kinds, because you know that the testing of your faith develops perseverance. Perseverance must finish its work so that you may be mature and complete, not lacking anything.

JAMES 1:2–4 NIV

BELIEVING YOUR SELF-WORTH

I praise you because I am fearfully and wonderfully made; your works are wonderful, I know that full well.

PSALM 139:14 NIV

"Before I shaped you in the womb, I knew all about you. Before you saw the light of day, I had holy plans for you."

JEREMIAH 1:5 MSG

How far has the LORD taken our sins from us? Farther than the distance from east to west!

PSALM 103:12 CEV

How great is the love the Father has lavished on us, that we should be called children of God! And that is what we are! The reason the world does not know us is that it did not know him.

1 JOHN 3:1 NIV

But thanks be to God! He gives us the victory through our Lord Jesus Christ.

1 CORINTHIANS 15:57 NIV

How precious are your thoughts about me, O God. They cannot be numbered! I can't even count them; they outnumber the grains of sand! And when I wake up, you are still with me!

PSALM 139:17–18 NLT

Therefore, if anyone is in Christ, he is a new creation; the old has gone, the new has come!

2 CORINTHIANS 5:17 NIV

He gave his life to free us from every kind of sin, to cleanse us, and to make us his very own people, totally committed to doing good deeds.

TITUS 2:14 NLT

HEALING THE HEARTBREAK

So we can say with confidence, "The LORD is my helper, so I will have no fear. What can mere people do to me?"

HEBREWS 13:6 NLT

The LORD will lead you into the land. He will always be with you and help you, so don't ever be afraid of your enemies.

DEUTERONOMY 31:8 CEV

The LORD is my rock, my fortress and my deliverer; my God is my rock, in whom I take refuge. He is my shield and the horn of my salvation, my stronghold.

PSALM 18:2 NIV

For he will command his angels concerning you to guard you in all your ways.

PSALM 91:11 NIV

You are my hiding place; you will protect me from trouble and surround me with songs of deliverance.

PSALM 32:7 NIV

"When you pass through the waters, I will be with you; and through the rivers, they shall not overflow you. When you walk through the fire, you shall not be burned, nor shall the flame scorch you."

ISAIAH 43:2 NKJV

Though you have made me see troubles, many and bitter, you will restore my life again; from the depths of the earth you will again bring me up.

PSALM 71:20 NIV

These hard times are small potatoes compared to the coming good times, the lavish celebration prepared for us.

2 CORINTHIANS 4:17 MSG

Therefore we will not fear, though the earth give way and the mountains fall into the heart of the sea, though its waters roar and foam and the mountains quake with their surging.

PSALM 46:2–3 NIV

You don't need to cry anymore. The Lord is kind, and as soon as he hears your cries for help, he will come.

ISAIAH 30:19 CEV

279

ONE MOMENT AT A TIME
PUTTING THE PIECES BACK TOGETHER

1. **Recall God's purpose for your life.** Remember that God created you intentionally. Part of that purpose is to praise Him; part of that purpose may be to raise the children He's given you. What else has God empowered you to do?

2. **Have patience.** Divorce takes a lot out of you physically, emotionally, socially, and financially. Don't expect to walk out of divorce court with a sense of closure. It takes most people a couple of years to get past the hurt and get back on their feet. Be patient with yourself and allow yourself the time you need.

3. **Refuse to remain discouraged.** Lingering in a state of discouragement is a choice. When those thoughts arise, put them aside and thank God for the blessings He's brought you. In place of feeling defeated, get involved with Christian friends who can direct you closer to Christ. Let good friends help you cultivate your dreams and take next steps in meeting them.

4. **Consider your children.** While it may be tempting to jump back into a dating relationship or to venture off in a new career, remember that if you have children, you can't make these decisions without consequences. Children need stability and safety. Be sure to consider them in your decision-making process.

WHAT THE BIBLE SAYS ABOUT PRAYING

INTRODUCTION

DRAWING NEAR

Some people pray while they kneel. Others pray as they walk. Some people get up early to spend lengthy times in prayer, whereas others lie in bed and whisper a few words of prayer before drifting off to sleep.

Though people pray in many different ways, there are few who feel their prayer lives need no improvement. Most of us want to experience genuine intimacy in our relationship with God, yet this often seems elusive or difficult to achieve. We either struggle with understanding what it means to draw near to God or wrestle with practicing it.

It probably comes as no surprise that the Bible has much to say on the topic of prayer. Explore the following pages to discover the Bible's instructions for prayer—and to see how the men and women of the Bible drew near to God.

CHAPTER 1

THE VALUE OF PRAYER

*One of the best practices I've employed in my prayer life is to take it
slow. By nature, I simply want to get my prayers done, check the task
off my list, and get on with parts of my day that feel more productive.
A number of years ago, though, I found the value of taking my time in
prayer. Now I often linger until I can fully clear my mind of distraction
and truly connect with God. I can't always afford to take that time
every day, but I try to do so at least once or twice a week.*

◼ *Claire, age 27, Ireland* ◼

REMAINING IN GOD'S PRESENCE

Better is one day in your courts
than a thousand elsewhere; I would
rather be a doorkeeper in the house
of my God than dwell in the tents
of the wicked.

PSALM 84:10 NIV

You know me inside and out, you
hold me together, you never fail to
stand me tall in your presence so I
can look you in the eye.

PSALM 41:12 MSG

Seek the LORD while He may be
found; call upon Him while He is
near.

ISAIAH 55:6 NASB

May the grace of the Lord Jesus
Christ, and the love of God, and
the fellowship of the Holy Spirit be
with you all.

2 CORINTHIANS 13:14 NIV

Each day the LORD pours his unfailing love upon me, and through
each night I sing his songs, praying
to God who gives me life.

PSALM 42:8 NLT

When we trust in him, we're free to
say whatever needs to be said, bold
to go wherever we need to go.

EPHESIANS 3:12 MSG

He found them in a desert land, in
an empty, howling wasteland. He
surrounded them and watched over
them; he guarded them as he would
guard his own eyes.

DEUTERONOMY 32:10 NLT

REMINDING YOURSELF OF GOD'S CARE

The LORD is near to all who call on
him, to all who call on him in truth.

PSALM 145:18 NIV

GOD keeps an eye on his friends, his ears pick up every moan and groan.

PSALM 34:15 MSG

You don't need to cry anymore. The Lord is kind, and as soon as he hears your cries for help, he will come.

ISAIAH 30:19 CEV

I pray that you, being rooted and established in love, may have power, together with all the saints, to grasp how wide and long and high and deep is the love of Christ, and to know this love that surpasses knowledge—that you may be filled to the measure of all the fullness of God.

EPHESIANS 3:17–19 NIV

STRENGTHENING YOUR SPIRITUAL LIFE

But you, dear friends, carefully build yourselves up in this most holy faith by praying in the Holy Spirit.

JUDE 20 MSG

"Call to me and I will answer you and tell you great and unsearchable things you do not know."

JEREMIAH 33:3 NIV

Therefore, I urge you, brothers, in view of God's mercy, to offer your bodies as living sacrifices, holy and pleasing to God—this is your spiritual act of worship. Do not conform any longer to the pattern of this world, but be transformed by the renewing of your mind. Then you will be able to test and approve what God's will is—his good,

pleasing and perfect will.

ROMANS 12:1–2 NIV

Immediately the boy's father exclaimed, "I do believe; help me overcome my unbelief!"

MARK 9:24 NIV

Moses said to the LORD, "You have been telling me, 'Lead these people,' but you have not let me know whom you will send with me. You have said, 'I know you by name and you have found favor with me.' If you are pleased with me, teach me your ways so I may know you and continue to find favor with you. Remember that this nation is your people."

EXODUS 33:12–13 NIV

EXPERIENCING THE BLESSING

"If you sinful people know how to give good gifts to your children, how much more will your heavenly Father give good gifts to those who ask him."

MATTHEW 7:11 NLT

"Until now you have not asked for anything in my name. Ask and you will receive, and your joy will be complete."

JOHN 16:24 NIV

For there is no difference between Jew and Gentile—the same Lord is Lord of all and richly blesses all who call on him.

ROMANS 10:12 NIV

ONE MOMENT AT A TIME
TAKE SOME TIME

1. **Move prayer up the priority list.** For many of us, prayer is the first thing to go when the schedule gets chaotic. When something has to be cut from your day, choose something else. Prayer is too valuable to cut it regularly from your schedule.

2. **Commit to a prayer experiment.** Carve out time to pray for the next fourteen days no matter how you feel or how busy your schedule becomes. At the end of the two weeks, write down the ways you saw prayer make a difference in your life and attitude.

3. **Realize it's okay to ask God for help.** Some people are hesitant to ask God to bless them, but God wants to help and bless His children. Make sure your prayers include specific requests for the help you need.

CHAPTER 2

MEETING THE GOD OF OUR PRAYER

I grew up in a stuffy church where the only prayers I ever said were the memorized ones we prayed on Sunday mornings. When I went to college, I met some other Christians who surprised me by their constant encouragement to pray. I took their advice—partly because I wanted to humor them, and partly because I was hoping they were right about God. I was hoping to find a God who really did care about me and my life. I was so happy to learn that they were right! God is much bigger and more personal than I had ever understood.

■ *Jaimie, age 24, Iowa* ■

FINDING HIM APPROACHABLE

One thing I ask of the LORD, this is what I seek: that I may dwell in the house of the LORD all the days of my life, to gaze upon the beauty of the LORD and to seek him in his temple.

PSALM 27:4 NIV

But now in Christ Jesus you who once were far off have been brought near by the blood of Christ.

EPHESIANS 2:13 NKJV

And he came and preached peace to you who were far off and peace to those who were near. For through him we both have access in one Spirit to the Father.

EPHESIANS 2:17–18 ESV

Blessed are those you choose and bring near to live in your courts! We are filled with the good things of your house, of your holy temple.

PSALM 65:4 NIV

Come near to God, and he will come near to you. Clean up your lives, you sinners. Purify your hearts, you people who can't make up your mind.

JAMES 4:8 CEV

The Spirit and the bride say, "Come!" And let him who hears say, "Come!" Whoever is thirsty, let him come; and whoever wishes, let him take the free gift of the water of life.

REVELATION 22:17 NIV

285

"The God who made the world and everything in it is the Lord of heaven and earth and does not live in temples built by hands. And he is not served by human hands, as if he needed anything, because he himself gives all men life and breath and everything else. From one man he made every nation of men, that they should inhabit the whole earth; and he determined the times set for them and the exact places where they should live. God did this so that men would seek him and perhaps reach out for him and find him, though he is not far from each one of us."

ACTS 17:24–27 NIV

LEARNING HE IS PERSONAL

GOD, high above, sees far below; no matter the distance, he knows everything about us.

PSALM 138:6 MSG

Taste and see that the LORD is good; blessed is the man who takes refuge in him.

PSALM 34:8 NIV

"And Solomon, my son, learn to know the God of your ancestors intimately. Worship and serve him with your whole heart and a willing mind. For the LORD sees every heart and knows every plan and thought. If you seek him, you will find him. But if you forsake him, he will reject you forever."

1 CHRONICLES 28:9 NLT

Therefore, since we have been justified through faith, we have peace with God through our Lord Jesus Christ.

ROMANS 5:1 NIV

"Let us acknowledge the LORD; let us press on to acknowledge him. As surely as the sun rises, he will appear; he will come to us like the winter rains, like the spring rains that water the earth."

HOSEA 6:3 NIV

But the foundation that God has laid is solid. On it is written, "The Lord knows who his people are. So everyone who worships the Lord must turn away from evil."

2 TIMOTHY 2:19 CEV

"Two sparrows cost only a penny, but not even one of them can die without your Father's knowing it. God even knows how many hairs are on your head. So don't be afraid. You are worth much more than many sparrows."

MATTHEW 10:29–31 NCV

KNOWING THAT HE HEARS

LORD, you hear the desire of the afflicted; you will strengthen their heart; you will incline your ear.

PSALM 10:17 ESV

He who planted the ear, does he not hear? He who formed the eye, does he not see?

PSALM 94:9 ESV

Listen! The LORD's arm is not too weak to save you, nor is his ear too deaf to hear you call.

ISAIAH 59:1 NLT

In my alarm I said, "I am cut off from your sight!" Yet you heard my cry for mercy when I called to you for help.

PSALM 31:22 NIV

Listen to my cry for help, my King and my God, for I pray to no one but you.

PSALM 5:2 NLT

I call on you, O God, for you will answer me; give ear to me and hear my prayer.

PSALM 17:6 NIV

For the eyes of the Lord are on the righteous and his ears are attentive to their prayer, but the face of the Lord is against those who do evil.

1 PETER 3:12 NIV

He grants the desires of those who fear him; he hears their cries for help and rescues them.

PSALM 145:19 NLT

For the LORD hears the cries of the needy; he does not despise his imprisoned people.

PSALM 69:33 NLT

The LORD has heard my plea; the LORD will answer my prayer.

PSALM 6:9 NLT

"Then you will call upon me and come and pray to me, and I will listen to you."

JEREMIAH 29:12 NIV

The LORD said: I have seen how my people are suffering as slaves in Egypt, and I have heard them beg for my help because of the way they are being mistreated. I feel sorry for them, and I have come down to rescue them from the Egyptians.

EXODUS 3:7–8 CEV

But certainly God has heard me; He has attended to the voice of my prayer. Blessed be God, who has not turned away my prayer, nor His mercy from me!

PSALM 66:19–20 NKJV

But you, O God, do see trouble and grief; you consider it to take it in hand. The victim commits himself to you; you are the helper of the fatherless.

PSALM 10:14 NIV

This is the confidence which we have before Him, that, if we ask anything according to His will, He hears us.

1 JOHN 5:14 NASB

I called on your name, O LORD, from the depths of the pit. You heard my plea: "Do not close your ears to my cry for relief." You came near when I called you, and you said, "Do not fear." O Lord, you took up my case; you redeemed my life.

LAMENTATIONS 3:55–58 NIV

Praise be to the LORD, for he has heard my cry for mercy.

PSALM 28:6 NIV

TRUSTING HIM TO ANSWER

Everyone will come to you because you answer prayer.

PSALM 65:2 CEV

"So I say to you: Ask and it will be given to you; seek and you will find; knock and the door will be opened to you. For everyone who asks receives; he who seeks finds; and to him who knocks, the door will be opened."

LUKE 11:9–10 NIV

"Whatever you ask in my name, this I will do, that the Father may be glorified in the Son. If you ask me anything in my name, I will do it."

JOHN 14:13–14 ESV

"You didn't choose me. I chose you. I appointed you to go and produce lasting fruit, so that the Father will give you whatever you ask for, using my name."

JOHN 15:16 NLT

"They caused the cry of the poor to come to him, and he heard the cry of the afflicted."

JOB 34:28 ESV

Then my enemies will turn back when I call for help. By this I will know that God is for me.

PSALM 56:9 NIV

And if we know that he hears us—whatever we ask—we know that we have what we asked of him.

1 JOHN 5:15 NIV

The LORD says, "I will rescue those who love me. I will protect those who trust in my name."

PSALM 91:14 NLT

"Therefore I tell you, whatever you ask for in prayer, believe that you have received it, and it will be yours."

MARK 11:24 NIV

He will respond to the prayer of the destitute; he will not despise their plea.

PSALM 102:17 NIV

Elijah was just as human as we are, and for three and a half years his prayers kept the rain from falling. But when he did pray for rain, it fell from the skies and made the crops grow.

JAMES 5:17–18 CEV

About that time Hezekiah became deathly ill. He prayed to the LORD, who healed him and gave him a miraculous sign.

2 CHRONICLES 32:24 NLT

"And whatever things you ask in prayer, believing, you will receive."

MATTHEW 21:22 NKJV

Then you will call, and the LORD will answer; you will cry for help, and he will say: Here am I.

ISAIAH 58:9 NIV

"Tears of joy will stream down their faces, and I will lead them home with great care. They will walk beside quiet streams and on smooth paths where they will not stumble. For I am Israel's father, and Ephraim is my oldest child."

JEREMIAH 31:9 NLT

"For truly, I say to you, if you have faith like a grain of mustard seed, you will say to this mountain, 'Move from here to there,' and it will move, and nothing will be impossible for you."

MATTHEW 17:20 ESV

"As soon as you began to pray, an answer was given, which I have come to tell you, for you are highly esteemed. Therefore, consider the message and understand the vision."

DANIEL 9:23 NIV

ONE MOMENT AT A TIME
GETTING COMFORTABLE

1. **Explore a new routine.** If you've always prayed kneeling, try standing up or going for a walk. If you've always prayed in the evening, try getting up and making prayer a part of your morning. By doing so, you may be able to make prayer less rote and more personal.

2. **Focus on God.** People are often surprised to learn that God is personal and cares for them and their needs. God knows everything about you, and He went to great lengths to make it possible for you to know Him also. Before you pray next, read a psalm or two from the Bible and find an attribute or name of God that strikes you afresh. As you pray, reflect on how that attribute can affect the praise and requests you bring before Him.

3. **Bring a blank "to do" list.** As much as possible, try to pray in an environment that is conducive to uninterrupted thought. If you become distracted and begin thinking about tasks you need to complete, then have a paper and pen nearby so you can write down the items on your mind and get back to the business of prayer.

CHAPTER 3

THE PRAYER OF ADORATION

The longer I spend praising God, the more I'm reminded that life is much bigger than me and the concerns I have for my family. As I praise Him, I'm reminded of how wide, deep, and tall He is, and then the problems of the day seem to get put into better perspective. And while I still worry about my daughter and her kids, praising God reminds me that the almighty God of the universe is still in charge, still sees the big picture, and still cares about me (and them) very much!

■ *Millie, age 66, Vermont* ■

UNDERSTANDING OUR DUTY TO PRAISE

But you are a chosen people, a royal priesthood, a holy nation, a people belonging to God, that you may declare the praises of him who called you out of darkness into his wonderful light.

1 PETER 2:9 NIV

Then a voice came from the throne, saying: "Praise our God, all you his servants, you who fear him, both small and great!"

REVELATION 19:5 NIV

Blessed be the LORD, the God of Israel, from everlasting even to everlasting. And let all the people say, "Amen." Praise the LORD!

PSALM 106:48 NASB

Sing to the LORD, you saints of his; praise his holy name.

PSALM 30:4 NIV

The LORD will bring about justice and praise in every nation on earth, like flowers blooming in a garden.

ISAIAH 61:11 CEV

Praise God, all you people of Israel; praise the LORD, the source of Israel's life.

PSALM 68:26 NLT

"Do you hear what these children are saying?" they asked him. "Yes," replied Jesus, "have you never read, 'From the lips of children and infants you have ordained praise'?"

MATTHEW 21:16 NIV

Sing to God, O kingdoms of the earth; sing praises to the Lord.

PSALM 68:32 NASB

"For as a belt is bound around a man's waist, so I bound the whole house of Israel and the whole house of Judah to me," declares the LORD, "to be my people for my renown and praise and honor. But they have not listened."

JEREMIAH 13:11 NIV

And you also were included in Christ when you heard the word of truth, the gospel of your salvation. Having believed, you were marked in him with a seal, the promised Holy Spirit, who is a deposit guaranteeing our inheritance until the redemption of those who are God's possession—to the praise of his glory.

EPHESIANS 1:13–15 NIV

The wild animals honor me, the jackals and the owls, because I provide water in the desert and streams in the wasteland, to give drink to my people, my chosen.

ISAIAH 43:20 NIV

STANDING IN AWE OF GOD

LORD All-Powerful, you are greater than all others. No one is like you, and you alone are God. Everything we have heard about you is true.

2 SAMUEL 7:22 CEV

Join with me in praising the wonderful name of the LORD our God.

DEUTERONOMY 32:3 CEV

Fear the LORD your God and serve him. Hold fast to him and take your oaths in his name. He is your praise; he is your God, who performed for you those great and awesome wonders you saw with your own eyes.

DEUTERONOMY 10:20–21 NIV

For great is the LORD and most worthy of praise; he is to be feared above all gods. For all the gods of the nations are idols, but the LORD made the heavens. Splendor and majesty are before him; strength and glory are in his sanctuary. Ascribe to the LORD, O families of nations, ascribe to the LORD glory and strength. Ascribe to the LORD the glory due his name; bring an offering and come into his courts. Worship the LORD in the splendor of his holiness; tremble before him, all the earth.

PSALM 96:4–9 NIV

LORD, our Lord, how majestic is Your name in all the earth, who have displayed Your splendor above the heavens!

PSALM 8:1 NASB

"There is no one like·you, O LORD, and there is no God but you, as we have heard with our own ears."

1 CHRONICLES 17:20 NIV

Oh, the depth of the riches of the wisdom and knowledge of God! How unsearchable his judgments, and his paths beyond tracing out! "Who has known the mind of the Lord? Or who has been his counselor?" "Who has ever given to God, that God should repay him?" For from him and through him and to him are all things. To him be the glory forever! Amen.

ROMANS 11:33–36 NIV

In the council of the holy ones God is greatly feared; he is more awesome than all who surround him.

PSALM 89:7 NIV

Lord, you have been our dwelling place in all generations. Before the mountains were brought forth, or ever you had formed the earth and the world, from everlasting to everlasting you are God.

PSALM 90:1–2 ESV

"Praise be to you, O LORD, God of our father Israel, from everlasting to everlasting. Yours, O LORD, is the greatness and the power and the glory and the majesty and the splendor, for everything in heaven and earth is yours. Yours, O LORD, is the kingdom; you are exalted as head over all. Wealth and honor come from you; you are the ruler of all things. In your hands are strength and power to exalt and give strength to all. Now, our God, we give you thanks, and praise your glorious name."

1 CHRONICLES 29:10–13 NIV

You turn man back into dust and say, "Return, O children of men." For a thousand years in Your sight are like yesterday when it passes by, or as a watch in the night.

PSALM 90:3–4 NASB

Come and see what God has done, how awesome his works in man's behalf!

PSALM 66:5 NIV

LORD, you have examined my heart and know everything about me. You know when I sit down or stand up. You know my thoughts even when I'm far away. You see me when I travel and when I rest at home. You know everything I do. You know what I am going to say even before I say it, LORD. You go before me and follow me. You place your hand of blessing on my head. Such knowledge is too wonderful for me, too great for me to understand!

PSALM 139:1–6 NLT

LORD, I have heard of your fame; I stand in awe of your deeds, O LORD. Renew them in our day, in our time make them known; in wrath remember mercy.

HABAKKUK 3:2 NIV

Let them know that you, whose name is the LORD—that you alone are the Most High over all the earth.

PSALM 83:18 NIV

"Who among the gods is like you, O LORD? Who is like you—majestic in holiness, awesome in glory, working wonders?"

EXODUS 15:11 NIV

"Declare and set forth your case; indeed, let them consult together. Who has announced this from of old? Who has long since declared it? Is it not I, the LORD? And there is no other God besides Me, a righteous God and a Savior; there is none except Me. Turn to Me and be saved, all the ends of the earth; for I am God, and there is no other."

ISAIAH 45:21–22 NASB

REVERING GOD

Great is the LORD! He is most worthy of praise! He is to be feared above all gods.

1 CHRONICLES 16:25 NLT

Therefore, since we are receiving a kingdom that cannot be shaken, let us be thankful, and so worship God acceptably with reverence and awe, for our "God is a consuming fire."

HEBREWS 12:28–29 NIV

"Great and marvelous are your deeds, Lord God Almighty. Just and true are your ways, King of the ages. Who will not fear you, O Lord, and bring glory to your name? For you alone are holy. All nations will come and worship before you, for your righteous acts have been revealed."

REVELATION 15:3–4 NIV

"Stand up and bless the LORD your God from everlasting to everlasting. Blessed be your glorious name, which is exalted above all blessing and praise. You are the LORD, you alone. You have made heaven, the heaven of heavens, with all their host, the earth and all that is on it, the seas and all that is in them; and you preserve all of them; and the host of heaven worships you."

NEHEMIAH 9:5–6 ESV

How great are your works, O LORD, how profound your thoughts! The senseless man does not know, fools do not understand, that though the wicked spring up like grass and all evildoers flourish, they will be forever destroyed. But you, O LORD, are exalted forever.

PSALM 92:5–8 NIV

It was in the year King Uzziah died that I saw the Lord. He was sitting on a lofty throne, and the train of his robe filled the Temple. Attending him were mighty seraphim, each having six wings. With two wings they covered their faces, with two they covered their feet, and with two they flew. They were calling out to each other, "Holy, holy, holy is the LORD of Heaven's Armies! The whole earth is filled with his glory!"

ISAIAH 6:1–3 NLT

For the LORD, the Most High, is to be feared, a great king over all the earth.

PSALM 47:2 ESV

"No one is holy like the LORD! There is no one besides you; there is no Rock like our God."

1 SAMUEL 2:2 NLT

Then Moses said to Aaron, "This is what the LORD meant when he said, 'I will display my holiness through those who come near me. I will display my glory before all the people.'" And Aaron was silent.

LEVITICUS 10:3 NLT

"See now that I myself am He! There is no god besides me. I put to death and I bring to life, I have wounded and I will heal, and no one can deliver out of my hand."

DEUTERONOMY 32:39 NIV

But I, by your great mercy, will come into your house; in reverence will I bow down toward your holy temple.

PSALM 5:7 NIV

PRAISING GOD

I will exalt you, my God and King, and praise your name forever and ever. I will praise you every day; yes, I will praise you forever. Great is the LORD! He is most worthy of praise! No one can measure his greatness. Let each generation tell its children of your mighty acts; let them proclaim your power. I will meditate on your majestic, glorious splendor and your wonderful miracles. Your awe-inspiring deeds will be on every tongue; I will proclaim your greatness. Everyone will share the story of your wonderful goodness; they will sing with joy about your righteousness. The LORD is merciful and compassionate, slow to get angry and filled with unfailing love. The LORD is good to everyone. He showers compassion on all his creation.

PSALM 145:1–9 NLT

Each of the four living creatures had six wings and was covered with eyes all around, even under his wings. Day and night they never stop saying: "Holy, holy, holy is the Lord God Almighty, who was, and is, and is to come."

REVELATION 4:8 NIV

Praise the LORD! Praise God in his sanctuary; praise him in his mighty heavens! Praise him for his mighty deeds; praise him according to his excellent greatness! Praise him with trumpet sound; praise him with lute and harp! Praise him with tambourine and dance; praise him with strings and pipe! Praise him with sounding cymbals; praise him with loud clashing cymbals! Let everything that has breath praise the LORD! Praise the LORD!

PSALM 150:1–6 ESV

But I will hope continually and will praise you yet more and more.

PSALM 71:14 ESV

Praise the LORD. Praise, O servants of the LORD, praise the name of the LORD. Let the name of the LORD be praised, both now and forevermore. From the rising of the sun to the place where it sets, the name of the LORD is to be praised. The LORD is exalted over all the nations, his glory above the heavens. Who is like the LORD our God, the One who sits enthroned on high, who stoops down to look on the heavens and the earth?

PSALM 113:1–6 NIV

ONE MOMENT AT A TIME
GETTING YOUR EYES ON GOD

1. **Get outdoors.** One of the best ways to glimpse the majesty of God is to get outdoors and see His great creation. Spend an hour outside praying in a place where you can enjoy the sky, the trees, the ocean, or a river. As you pray, remind yourself of the God who made it all and is worthy of your deepest praise.

2. **Make music.** While we enjoy reading the psalms of praise from the Bible, we tend to forget these words were originally written as lyrics to music. Find a hymn or song of worship you can sing to God, or sing along to a praise tape as a way of prompting your time of praise.

3. **Begin a prayer journal.** Many people are easily distracted during prayer. One practical way to beat those distractions is to write out what you want to say to God. Try taking a simple sheet of paper with you and using it to write down your prayer of praise. You may be surprised at how this helps you to remain focused. If the exercise works, consider creating a prayer journal and making this activity a regular part of your prayer time.

CHAPTER 4

THE PRAYER OF CONFESSION

*I fail God so often that confessing my sins comes pretty easy. And when
I finally think I'm through confessing them, He brings something else
to mind. While I could become quite discouraged by this, it really never
turns into the pity party it may sound like. In fact, it's quite the opposite.
The more I confess, the more I realize He's holy and I'm driven to praise
Him yet again. And as I confess, I realize how great His forgiveness and
His love for me are. Nothing feels so good as coming clean with God.*

■ *Cody, age 36, Florida* ■

ACKNOWLEDGING YOUR SIN

"When anyone is guilty in any of
these ways, he must confess in what
way he has sinned."

LEVITICUS 5:5 NIV

Lord, open my lips, and my mouth
will declare your praise. You do
not delight in sacrifice, or I would
bring it; you do not take pleasure
in burnt offerings. The sacrifices of
God are a broken spirit; a broken
and contrite heart, O God, you will
not despise.

PSALM 51:15–17 NIV

Saul said to Samuel, "I have
sinned, for I have transgressed the
commandment of the LORD and
your words, because I feared the
people and obeyed their voice. Now
therefore, please pardon my sin and
return with me that I may worship
the LORD."

1 SAMUEL 15:24–25 ESV

We have sinned, even as our fathers
did; we have done wrong and acted
wickedly.

PSALM 106:6 NIV

Search me, O God, and know
my heart; test me and know my
anxious thoughts. See if there is any
offensive way in me, and lead me in
the way everlasting.

PSALM 139:23–24 NIV

"How many wrongs and sins have
I committed? Show me my offense
and my sin."

JOB 13:23 NIV

For our offenses are many in your
sight, and our sins testify against
us. Our offenses are ever with us,
and we acknowledge our iniquities:
rebellion and treachery against the
LORD, turning our backs on our
God, fomenting oppression and
revolt, uttering lies our hearts have
conceived.

ISAIAH 59:12–13 NIV

We know our wickedness, O LORD, the iniquity of our fathers, for we have sinned against You.

JEREMIAH 14:20 NASB

If we claim to be without sin, we deceive ourselves and the truth is not in us.

1 JOHN 1:8 NIV

As for me, I said, "O LORD, be gracious to me; heal my soul, for I have sinned against You."

PSALM 41:4 NASB

"Listen to my prayer! Look down and see me praying night and day for your people Israel. I confess that we have sinned against you. Yes, even my own family and I have sinned! We have sinned terribly by not obeying the commands, decrees, and regulations that you gave us through your servant Moses."

NEHEMIAH 1:6–7 NLT

REQUESTING FORGIVENESS

Listen from your home in heaven, forgive the sins of your servants, your people Israel. Then start over with them; train them to live right and well; send rain on the land you gave as inheritance to your people.

2 CHRONICLES 6:27 MSG

"Listen to the supplications of Your servant and of Your people Israel when they pray toward this place; hear from Your dwelling place, from heaven; hear and forgive. . . .

Then hear from heaven and forgive the sin of Your people Israel, and bring them back to the land which You have given to them and to their fathers."

2 CHRONICLES 6:21, 25 NASB

Then David said to God, "I have sinned greatly by doing this. Now, I beg you, take away the guilt of your servant. I have done a very foolish thing."

1 CHRONICLES 21:8 NIV

Return, O Israel, to the LORD your God, for your sins have brought you down. Bring your confessions, and return to the LORD. Say to him, "Forgive all our sins and graciously receive us, so that we may offer you our praises."

HOSEA 14:1–2 NLT

Listen from your home in heaven to their prayers desperate and devout; Do what is best for them. Forgive your people who have sinned against you.

2 CHRONICLES 6:39 MSG

"I admit I once lived by rumors of you; now I have it all firsthand— from my own eyes and ears! I'm sorry—forgive me. I'll never do that again, I promise! I'll never again live on crusts of hearsay, crumbs of rumor."

JOB 42:5–6 MSG

"Forgive us our debts, as we also have forgiven our debtors."

MATTHEW 6:12 NIV

Then I acknowledged my sin to you and did not cover up my iniquity. I said, "I will confess my transgressions to the LORD"—and you forgave the guilt of my sin.

PSALM 32:5 NIV

EMBRACING FORGIVENESS

He will not always accuse, nor will he harbor his anger forever; he does not treat us as our sins deserve or repay us according to our iniquities. For as high as the heavens are above the earth, so great is his love for those who fear him; as far as the east is from the west, so far has he removed our transgressions from us. As a father has compassion on his children, so the LORD has compassion on those who fear him.

PSALM 103:9–13 NIV

"My sins will be stuffed in a sack and thrown into the sea—sunk in deep ocean."

JOB 14:17 MSG

If you, O LORD, kept a record of sins, O Lord, who could stand? But with you there is forgiveness; therefore you are feared.

PSALM 130:3–4 NIV

Who may ascend into the hill of the LORD? And who may stand in His holy place? He who has clean hands and a pure heart, who has not lifted up his soul to falsehood, and has not sworn deceitfully. He shall receive a blessing from the LORD and righteousness from the God of his salvation.

PSALM 24:3–5 NASB

"Come now, let's settle this," says the LORD. "Though your sins are like scarlet, I will make them as white as snow. Though they are red like crimson, I will make them as white as wool."

ISAIAH 1:18 NLT

I have swept away your offenses like a cloud, your sins like the morning mist. Return to me, for I have redeemed you.

ISAIAH 44:22 NIV

"No longer will a man teach his neighbor, or a man his brother, saying, 'Know the LORD,' because they will all know me, from the least of them to the greatest," declares the LORD. "For I will forgive their wickedness and will remember their sins no more."

JEREMIAH 31:34 NIV

CONFESSING SIN

Remember not the sins of my youth or my transgressions; according to your steadfast love remember me, for the sake of your goodness, O LORD! Good and upright is the LORD; therefore he instructs sinners in the way. He leads the humble in what is right, and teaches the humble his way. All the paths of the LORD are steadfast love and faithfulness, for those who keep his covenant and his testimonies. For your name's sake, O LORD, pardon my guilt, for it is great. Who is the man who fears the LORD? Him will he instruct in the way that he should choose. His soul shall abide in well-being, and his offspring shall inherit the land. The friendship of the LORD is for those who fear him, and he makes known to them his covenant. My eyes are ever toward the LORD, for he will pluck my feet out of the net. Turn to me and be gracious to me, for I am lonely and afflicted. The troubles of my heart are enlarged; bring me out of my distresses. Consider my affliction and my trouble, and forgive all my sins.

PSALM 25:7–18 ESV

Wash away all my iniquity and cleanse me from my sin. For I know my transgressions, and my sin is always before me. Against you, you only, have I sinned and done what is evil in your sight, so that you are proved right when you speak and justified when you judge. Surely I was sinful at birth, sinful from the time my mother conceived me. Surely you desire truth in the inner parts; you teach me wisdom in the inmost place. Cleanse me with hyssop, and I will be clean; wash me, and I will be whiter than snow.

PSALM 51:2–7 NIV

For I know that nothing good dwells in me, that is, in my flesh. For I have the desire to do what is right, but not the ability to carry it out. For I do not do the good I want, but the evil I do not want is what I keep on doing. Now if I do what I do not want, it is no longer I who do it, but sin that dwells within me. So I find it to be a law that when I want to do right, evil lies close at hand. For I delight in the law of God, in my inner being, but I see in my members another law waging war against the law of my mind and making me captive to the law of sin that dwells in my members. Wretched man that I am! Who will deliver me from this body of death? Thanks be to God through Jesus Christ our Lord!

ROMANS 7:18–25 ESV

If we confess our sins, he is faithful and just and will forgive us our sins and purify us from all unrighteousness.

1 JOHN 1:9 NIV

ONE MOMENT AT A TIME
COMING CLEAN

1. **Destroy the list.** Give yourself a visual picture of what God's forgiveness means. As you pray, write down a list of sins you need to confess. When you've finished, take the list and destroy it—perhaps shred it or safely burn it. Let that image illustrate the way God has removed your sins from His record.

2. **Review the day.** While guilt and confession come easily for some people, others move so quickly through their day that they can't come up with much to confess. Review the last twenty-four hours and remember the places you went, conversations you had, and attitudes you felt. If Jesus were physically standing next to you, what interactions or thoughts would make you blush? Those may be good indications of areas needing confession.

3. **Find accountability.** If you find yourself quick to gossip, grow angry, or succumb to another sin regularly, ask a close friend to help keep you accountable for changing in this area. With a little help from a friend, maybe you will be able to confess this sin a little less often.

CHAPTER 5

THE PRAYER OF THANKSGIVING

A few weeks ago I was in church and heard the pastor speak about being thankful. As I listened, it struck me that I hadn't said "thank you" to God in a really, really long time. I'm fairly quick to ask for His help, but I'm not so fast when it comes to being grateful. Since then, I've been very purposeful about being thankful. I've been thanking God for the big things as well as the little things. When I got my latest sales bonus, I thanked God. When my car started this morning, I thanked God. I've realized that every blessing comes from God and I've been doing much better at acknowledging that.

■ *Pamela, age 48, Missouri* ■

BEING INTENTIONAL IN THANKS

This is the day the LORD has made; let us rejoice and be glad in it.
PSALM 118:24 NIV

Devote yourselves to prayer with an alert mind and a thankful heart.
COLOSSIANS 4:2 NLT

Then David assigned some of the Levites to the Chest of GOD to lead worship—to intercede, give thanks, and praise the GOD of Israel.
1 CHRONICLES 16:4 MSG

O give thanks to the LORD, for He is good; for His lovingkindness is everlasting.
1 CHRONICLES 16:34 NASB

I will give you thanks in the great assembly; among throngs of people I will praise you.
PSALM 35:18 NIV

"Now, our God, we give you thanks, and praise your glorious name."
1 CHRONICLES 29:13 NIV

After consulting the people, Jehoshaphat appointed men to sing to the LORD and to praise him for the splendor of his holiness as they went out at the head of the army, saying: "Give thanks to the LORD, for his love endures forever."
2 CHRONICLES 20:21 NIV

Give thanks to the LORD, for he is good. . . . Let them give thanks to the LORD for his unfailing love and his wonderful deeds for men.
PSALM 107:1, 8 NIV

301

Rejoice always.

1 THESSALONIANS 5:16 NASB

THANKING GOD FOR SALVATION

Open to me the gates of righteousness; I shall enter through them, I shall give thanks to the LORD.

PSALM 118:19 NASB

I delight greatly in the LORD; my soul rejoices in my God. For he has clothed me with garments of salvation and arrayed me in a robe of righteousness, as a bridegroom adorns his head like a priest, and as a bride adorns herself with her jewels.

ISAIAH 61:10 NIV

Save us, O God of our salvation, and gather and deliver us from among the nations, that we may give thanks to your holy name, and glory in your praise.

1 CHRONICLES 16:35 ESV

I am grateful that God always makes it possible for Christ to lead us to victory. God also helps us spread the knowledge about Christ everywhere, and this knowledge is like the smell of perfume.

2 CORINTHIANS 2:14 CEV

I pray that you will be grateful to God for letting you have part in what he has promised his people in the kingdom of light.

COLOSSIANS 1:12 CEV

All the angels were standing around the throne and around the elders and the four living creatures. They fell down on their faces before the throne and worshiped God, saying: "Amen! Praise and glory and wisdom and thanks and honor and power and strength be to our God for ever and ever. Amen!"

REVELATION 7:11–12 NIV

APPRECIATING HIS KINDNESS

We give thanks to you, O God, we give thanks, for your Name is near; men tell of your wonderful deeds.

PSALM 75:1 NIV

So thank GOD for his marvelous love, for his miracle mercy to the children he loves.

PSALM 107:31 MSG

I will tell of the kindnesses of the LORD, the deeds for which he is to be praised, according to all the LORD has done for us—yes, the many good things he has done for the house of Israel, according to his compassion and many kindnesses.

ISAIAH 63:7 NIV

Sing to the LORD! Praise the LORD! For though I was poor and needy, he rescued me from my oppressors.

JEREMIAH 20:13 NLT

Shout for joy, O heavens; rejoice, O earth; burst into song, O mountains! For the LORD comforts his people and will have compassion on his afflicted ones.

ISAIAH 49:13 NIV

I will praise you, LORD! You always do right. I will sing about you, the LORD Most High.

PSALM 7:17 CEV

BEING GRATEFUL IN EVERYTHING

And whatever you do, whether in word or deed, do it all in the name of the Lord Jesus, giving thanks to God the Father through him.

COLOSSIANS 3:17 NIV

Give thanks in all circumstances; for this is the will of God in Christ Jesus for you.

1 THESSALONIANS 5:18 ESV

I will sing to the LORD, for he has been good to me.

PSALM 13:6 NIV

More joy in one ordinary day than they get in all their shopping sprees. At day's end I'm ready for sound sleep, for you, God, have put my life back together.

PSALM 4:7–8 MSG

Speak to one another with psalms, hymns and spiritual songs. Sing and make music in your heart to the Lord, always giving thanks to God the Father for everything, in the name of our Lord Jesus Christ.

EPHESIANS 5:19–20 NIV

ENJOYING ANSWERED PRAYERS

And you will say in that day: "Give thanks to the LORD, call upon his name, make known his deeds among the peoples, proclaim that his name is exalted. Sing praises to the LORD, for he has done gloriously; let this be made known in all the earth."

ISAIAH 12:4–5 ESV

"I thank and praise you, O God of my fathers: You have given me wisdom and power, you have made known to me what we asked of you, you have made known to us the dream of the king."

DANIEL 2:23 NIV

"Praise be to the LORD, who has given rest to his people Israel just as he promised. Not one word has failed of all the good promises he gave through his servant Moses."

1 KINGS 8:56 NIV

"We cried out to the LORD, the God of our fathers, and the LORD heard our voice and saw our misery, toil and oppression. So the LORD brought us out of Egypt with a mighty hand and an outstretched arm, with great terror and with miraculous signs and wonders."

DEUTERONOMY 26:7–8 NIV

I will praise you, LORD, with all my heart; I will tell of all the marvelous things you have done. I will be filled with joy because of you. I will sing praises to your name, O Most High.

PSALM 9:1–2 NLT

303

I love you, O LORD, my strength.
The LORD is my rock, my fortress
and my deliverer; my God is my
rock, in whom I take refuge. He is
my shield and the horn of my salvation, my stronghold.

PSALM 18:1–2 NIV

VALUING THE PEOPLE IN YOUR LIFE

We always thank God, the Father
of our Lord Jesus Christ, when we
pray for you, because we have heard
of your faith in Christ Jesus and of
the love you have for all the saints.

COLOSSIANS 1:3–4 NIV

Every time I think of you, I give
thanks to my God. Whenever I
pray, I make my requests for all of
you with joy, for you have been
my partners in spreading the Good
News about Christ from the time
you first heard it until now.

PHILIPPIANS 1:3–5 NLT

I always thank my God as I remember you in my prayers.

PHILEMON 1:4 NIV

I thank my God always concerning
you for the grace of God which was
given to you by Christ Jesus.

1 CORINTHIANS 1:4 NKJV

Ever since I first heard of your
strong faith in the Lord Jesus and
your love for God's people everywhere, I have not stopped thanking God for you. I pray for you
constantly.

EPHESIANS 1:15–16 NLT

We always thank God for all of you,
mentioning you in our prayers.

1 THESSALONIANS 1:2 NIV

ONE MOMENT AT A TIME
COUNT YOUR BLESSINGS

1. **Learn to be thankful.** Put a three-by-five-inch card in your wallet or in
your pocket. As good things happen to you throughout the day, take a moment to write them down. At your next time of prayer, pull out the list and
thank God for all He's done for you in the last day.

2. **Keep a running tally.** Consider creating a prayer journal that records
both prayer requests and answers to prayer. Be sure to take time to thank
God for every prayer He answers.

3. **Give T-H-A-N-K-S.** Use an acronym like the word *thanks* to organize
and prompt your prayer. Think of an area of your life (such as your job or
your family) and thank God for different things that begin with each letter
of the word you've chosen.

CHAPTER 6

THE PRAYER OF SUPPLICATION

I used to think that asking God to meet my needs was selfish. My logic was that I should spend time praising God for who He is and thanking Him for the blessings in my life. The more I read the Bible, however, the more I realized that the Bible is filled with instructions to ask God for help. Finally it hit me that not asking God for help was pretty prideful of me. I can't control my health, my family, or my job status. What I can control is my faithfulness to God and my effort to humbly bring my requests before the One who holds today's outcomes in His hands.

■ *Kenneth, age 51, Arizona* ■

REQUESTING HEALING

Heal me, O LORD, and I will be healed; save me and I will be saved, for You are my praise.
JEREMIAH 17:14 NASB

LORD my God, I cried to You for help, and You healed me.
PSALM 30:2 NASB

Dear friend, I pray that you may enjoy good health and that all may go well with you, even as your soul is getting along well.
3 JOHN 2 NIV

Have compassion on me, LORD, for I am weak. Heal me, LORD, for my bones are in agony.
PSALM 6:2 NLT

Bless the LORD, O my soul, and forget not all his benefits, who forgives all your iniquity, who heals all your diseases, who redeems your life from the pit, who crowns you with steadfast love and mercy, who satisfies you with good so that your youth is renewed like the eagle's.
PSALM 103:2–5 ESV

ASKING FOR PROTECTION

"Hear, O LORD, the cry of Judah; bring him to his people. With his own hands he defends his cause. Oh, be his help against his foes!"
DEUTERONOMY 33:7 NIV

Asa called to the LORD his God and said, "LORD, there is no one like you to help the powerless against the mighty. Help us, O LORD our God, for we rely on you, and in your name we have come against this vast army. O LORD, you are our

God; do not let man prevail against you."

2 CHRONICLES 14:11 NIV

I call upon the LORD, who is worthy to be praised, and I am saved from my enemies.

PSALM 18:3 ESV

Don't let those proud and merciless people kick me around or chase me away.

PSALM 36:11 CEV

In times of trouble, may the LORD answer your cry. May the name of the God of Jacob keep you safe from all harm.

PSALM 20:1 NLT

LORD my God, in you do I take refuge; save me from all my pursuers and deliver me.

PSALM 7:1 ESV

Deliver me from my enemies, O God; protect me from those who rise up against me. Deliver me from evildoers and save me from bloodthirsty men.

PSALM 59:1–2 NIV

Deliver me, O LORD, from evil men; preserve me from violent men, who plan evil things in their heart and stir up wars continually. They make their tongue sharp as a serpent's, and under their lips is the venom of asps. Guard me, O LORD, from the hands of the wicked; preserve me from violent men, who have planned to trip up my feet.

PSALM 140:1–4 ESV

Please rescue me from my enemies, LORD! I come to you for safety.

PSALM 143:9 CEV

My times are in your hands; deliver me from my enemies and from those who pursue me.

PSALM 31:15 NIV

SEEKING DELIVERANCE DURING ADVERSITY

Vindicate me, O God, and plead my cause against an ungodly nation; rescue me from deceitful and wicked men. You are God my stronghold. Why have you rejected me? Why must I go about mourning, oppressed by the enemy? Send forth your light and your truth, let them guide me; let them bring me to your holy mountain, to the place where you dwell.

PSALM 43:1–3 NIV

Vindicate me in your righteousness, O LORD my God; do not let them gloat over me.

PSALM 35:24 NIV

In you, O LORD, I have taken refuge; let me never be put to shame. Rescue me and deliver me in your righteousness; turn your ear to me and save me. Be my rock of refuge, to which I can always go; give the command to save me, for you are my rock and my fortress. Deliver me, O my God, from the hand of the wicked, from the grasp of evil and cruel men.

PSALM 71:1–4 NIV

Come with great power, O God, and rescue me! Defend me with your might. Listen to my prayer, O God. Pay attention to my plea. For strangers are attacking me; violent people are trying to kill me. They care nothing for God. But God is my helper. The Lord keeps me alive!

PSALM 54:1–4 NLT

FINDING HELP

This poor man called, and the LORD heard him; he saved him out of all his troubles. The angel of the LORD encamps around those who fear him, and he delivers them.

PSALM 34:6–7 NIV

Israel, no other god is like ours— the clouds are his chariot as he rides across the skies to come and help us. The eternal God is our hiding place; he carries us in his arms. When God tells you to destroy your enemies, he will make them run.

DEUTERONOMY 33:26–27 CEV

You are my hiding place; you will protect me from trouble and surround me with songs of deliverance.

PSALM 32:7 NIV

We wait in hope for the LORD; he is our help and our shield.

PSALM 33:20 NIV

You, LORD, never fail to have pity on me; your love and faithfulness always keep me secure.

PSALM 40:11 CEV

But you, O LORD, be not far off; O my Strength, come quickly to help me.

PSALM 22:19 NIV

In my distress I called upon the LORD, and cried to my God for help; He heard my voice out of His temple, and my cry for help before Him came into His ears.

PSALM 18:6 NASB

PRAYING DURING TROUBLED TIMES

Hear my prayer, O LORD; let my cry come to you! Do not hide your face from me in the day of my distress! Incline your ear to me; answer me speedily in the day when I call!

PSALM 102:1–2 ESV

Cast your cares on the LORD and he will sustain you; he will never let the righteous fall.

PSALM 55:22 NIV

Be not far from me, for trouble is near; for there is none to help.

PSALM 22:11 NASB

As for God, his way is perfect; the word of the LORD is flawless. He is a shield for all who take refuge in him.

PSALM 18:30 NIV

In my distress I called to the LORD, and he answered me.

PSALM 120:1 ESV

In my anguish I cried to the LORD, and he answered by setting me free.

PSALM 118:5 NIV

You were in serious trouble, but you prayed to the LORD, and he rescued you.

PSALM 107:6 CEV

Call upon me in the day of trouble; I will deliver you, and you will honor me.

PSALM 50:15 NIV

Make haste, O God, to deliver me! O LORD, make haste to help me!

PSALM 70:1 ESV

Answer me when I call to you, O my righteous God. Give me relief from my distress; be merciful to me and hear my prayer.

PSALM 4:1 NIV

The troubles of my heart have multiplied; free me from my anguish.

PSALM 25:17 NIV

I cry aloud to God, aloud to God, and he will hear me. In the day of my trouble I seek the Lord; in the night my hand is stretched out without wearying; my soul refuses to be comforted. When I remember God, I moan; when I meditate, my spirit faints. You hold my eyelids open; I am so troubled that I cannot speak.

PSALM 77:1–4 ESV

Don't hide from your servant; answer me quickly, for I am in deep trouble!

PSALM 69:17 NLT

The righteous cry out, and the LORD hears them; he delivers them from all their troubles.

PSALM 34:17 NIV

The thought of my suffering and homelessness is bitter beyond words. I will never forget this awful time, as I grieve over my loss. Yet I still dare to hope when I remember this: The faithful love of the LORD never ends! His mercies never cease. Great is his faithfulness; his mercies begin afresh each morning. I say to myself, "The LORD is my inheritance; therefore, I will hope in him!"

LAMENTATIONS 3:19–24 NLT

Because of the extravagance of those revelations, and so I wouldn't get a big head, I was given the gift of a handicap to keep me in constant touch with my limitations. Satan's angel did his best to get me down; what he in fact did was push me to my knees. No danger then of walking around high and mighty! At first I didn't think of it as a gift, and begged God to remove it. Three times I did that, and then he told me, My grace is enough; it's all you need. My strength comes into its own in your weakness. Once I heard that, I was glad to let it happen. I quit focusing on the handicap and began appreciating the gift. It was a case of Christ's strength moving in on my weakness. Now I take limitations in stride, and with good cheer, these limitations that cut me down to size—abuse, accidents, opposition, bad breaks. I just let Christ take over! And so the weaker I get, the stronger I become.

2 CORINTHIANS 12:7–10 MSG

I wait for your salvation, O LORD,
and I follow your commands.

PSALM 119:166 NIV

Wait for the LORD; be strong and
take heart and wait for the LORD.

PSALM 27:14 NIV

REQUESTING PROVISION

For he delivers the needy when he
calls, the poor and him who has no
helper.

PSALM 72:12 ESV

Which one of you fathers would
give your hungry child a snake if
the child asked for a fish?

LUKE 11:11 CEV

"This, then, is how you should
pray: Our Father in heaven, hallowed be your name. . . . Give us
today our daily bread."

MATTHEW 6:9, 11 NIV

Then, turning to his disciples, Jesus
said, "That is why I tell you not to
worry about everyday life—whether
you have enough food to eat or
enough clothes to wear. For life is
more than food, and your body
more than clothing. Look at the
ravens. They don't plant or harvest
or store food in barns, for God
feeds them. And you are far more
valuable to him than any birds!
Can all your worries add a single
moment to your life? And if worry
can't accomplish a little thing like
that, what's the use of worrying
over bigger things?

"Look at the lilies and how they
grow. They don't work or make their
clothing, yet Solomon in all his glory
was not dressed as beautifully as they
are. And if God cares so wonderfully
for flowers that are here today and
thrown into the fire tomorrow, he
will certainly care for you. Why do
you have so little faith?

"And don't be concerned about
what to eat and what to drink.
Don't worry about such things.
These things dominate the thoughts
of unbelievers all over the world,
but your Father already knows your
needs. Seek the Kingdom of God
above all else, and he will give you
everything you need."

LUKE 12:22–31 NLT

SEEKING SUCCESS

Please, LORD, please save us. Please,
LORD, please give us success.

PSALM 118:25 NLT

Jabez cried out to the God of Israel,
"Oh, that you would bless me and
enlarge my territory! Let your hand
be with me, and keep me from
harm so that I will be free from
pain." And God granted his request.

1 CHRONICLES 4:10 NIV

"O Lord, let your ear be attentive
to the prayer of this your servant
and to the prayer of your servants
who delight in revering your name.
Give your servant success today by
granting him favor in the presence
of this man."

NEHEMIAH 1:11 NIV

REMEMBERING THE ELDERLY

Do not cast me off in the time of old age; forsake me not when my strength is spent.

PSALM 71:9 ESV

Be merciful to me, O LORD, for I am in distress; my eyes grow weak with sorrow, my soul and my body with grief. My life is consumed by anguish and my years by groaning; my strength fails because of my affliction, and my bones grow weak.

PSALM 31:9–10 NIV

For you, O Lord, are my hope, my trust, O LORD, from my youth.

PSALM 71:5 ESV

And I'll keep on carrying you when you're old. I'll be there, bearing you when you're old and gray. I've done it and will keep on doing it, carrying you on my back, saving you.

ISAIAH 46:4 MSG

ONE MOMENT AT A TIME
BRINGING YOUR REQUESTS TO GOD

1. **Make one-sentence prayers a habit.** Prayer time doesn't always need to be long. Get comfortable offering God short, one-sentence prayers during the day when you need His help. No matter the setting, take a moment to pray when you face your next challenge.

2. **Turn off the electronics.** Radios, cell phones, and MP3 players offer constant distraction. During an upcoming drive in your car, turn everything off and pray in silence while you make your trip. Or if you're at home, leave the cell phone off and in the other room as you spend time bringing your requests to your heavenly Father.

3. **Set a timer.** Try to find a block of time where you can pray without encountering great distraction. Pray without keeping an eye on the clock and without worrying about what you might need to do next. If you have some place to be, then set a timer nearby to indicate when your time needs to be done. Until it goes off, spend undistracted one-on-one time with God.

CHAPTER 7

PRAYERS OF THE HEART

I take a lot of comfort in Romans 8 [:26 NIV], which reads, "We do not know what we ought to pray for, but the Spirit himself intercedes for us with groans that words cannot express." Sometimes I'm so confused or broken up over a situation that I don't know how to pray. I'm not sure how to deal with the pain or what the right answer is to the problem I'm facing. During those difficult moments, I sometimes just spend time crying in God's presence. And while I can leave those prayers without feeling like I actually prayed many specific words, it's enough for me to know that God sees my heart and hears my groans.

■ *Jackie, age 41, California* ■

AVOIDING TEMPTATION

"Keep watching and praying that you may not enter into temptation; the spirit is willing, but the flesh is weak."

MATTHEW 26:41 NASB

There he told them, "Pray that you will not give in to temptation."

LUKE 22:40 NLT

Create in me a clean heart, O God, and renew a steadfast spirit within me.

PSALM 51:10 NASB

Submit yourselves, then, to God. Resist the devil, and he will flee from you.

JAMES 4:7 NIV

LORD, be gracious to us; we long for you. Be our strength every morning, our salvation in time of distress.

ISAIAH 33:2 NIV

EXPERIENCING JOY

The LORD is my strength and my shield; my heart trusts in him, and I am helped. My heart leaps for joy and I will give thanks to him in song.

PSALM 28:7 NIV

Sing the glory of his name; give to him glorious praise! Say to God, "How awesome are your deeds! So great is your power that your enemies come cringing to you."

PSALM 66:2–3 ESV

311

Let the righteous rejoice in the LORD and take refuge in him; let all the upright in heart praise him!

PSALM 64:10 NIV

"Until now you have asked nothing in my name. Ask, and you will receive, that your joy may be full."

JOHN 16:24 ESV

Why are you cast down, O my soul? And why are you disquieted within me? Hope in God; for I shall yet praise Him, the help of my countenance and my God.

PSALM 42:11 NKJV

Though the fig tree should not blossom, nor fruit be on the vines, the produce of the olive fail and the fields yield no food, the flock be cut off from the fold and there be no herd in the stalls, yet I will rejoice in the LORD; I will take joy in the God of my salvation. GOD, the Lord, is my strength; he makes my feet like the deer's; he makes me tread on my high places.

HABAKKUK 3:17–19 ESV

HOPING FOR GRACE AND MERCY

Therefore let us draw near with confidence to the throne of grace, so that we may receive mercy and find grace to help in time of need.

HEBREWS 4:16 NASB

Hear my prayer, O LORD; listen to my cry for mercy.

PSALM 86:6 NIV

I love God because he listened to me, listened as I begged for mercy.

PSALM 116:1 MSG

And God is able to make all grace abound to you, so that in all things at all times, having all that you need, you will abound in every good work.

2 CORINTHIANS 9:8 NIV

Hear my prayer, O LORD; give ear to my pleas for mercy! In your faithfulness answer me, in your righteousness!

PSALM 143:1 ESV

But grow in the grace and knowledge of our Lord and Savior Jesus Christ. To him be glory both now and forever! Amen.

2 PETER 3:18 NIV

I say to the LORD, You are my God; give ear to the voice of my pleas for mercy, O LORD!

PSALM 140:6 ESV

Grace, mercy and peace from God the Father and from Jesus Christ, the Father's Son, will be with us in truth and love.

2 JOHN 3 NIV

SEARCHING FOR PEACE

I pray that God will be kind to you and will let you live in perfect peace! May you keep learning more and more about God and our Lord Jesus.

2 PETER 1:2 CEV

"The LORD bless you and keep you; the LORD make his face to shine upon you and be gracious to you; the LORD lift up his countenance upon you and give you peace."

NUMBERS 6:24–26 ESV

"Come to Me, all who are weary and heavy-laden, and I will give you rest."

MATTHEW 11:28 NASB

Be my rock of safety where I can always hide. Give the order to save me, for you are my rock and my fortress.

PSALM 71:3 NLT

In peace I will lie down and sleep, for you alone, O LORD, will keep me safe.

PSALM 4:8 NLT

But now, O Jacob, listen to the LORD who created you. O Israel, the one who formed you says, "Do not be afraid, for I have ransomed you. I have called you by name; you are mine. When you go through deep waters, I will be with you. When you go through rivers of difficulty, you will not drown. When you walk through the fire of oppression, you will not be burned up; the flames will not consume you. For I am the LORD, your God, the Holy One of Israel, your Savior. I gave Egypt as a ransom for your freedom; I gave Ethiopia and Seba in your place."

ISAIAH 43:1–3 NLT

Do not be anxious about anything, but in everything, by prayer and petition, with thanksgiving, present your requests to God. And the peace of God, which transcends all understanding, will guard your hearts and your minds in Christ Jesus.

PHILIPPIANS 4:6–7 NIV

LONGING FOR SPIRITUAL GROWTH

Praise be to you, O LORD; teach me your decrees.

PSALM 119:12 NIV

May the words of my mouth and the meditation of my heart be pleasing to you, O LORD, my rock and my redeemer.

PSALM 19:14 NLT

And we pray. . .that you may live a life worthy of the Lord and may please him in every way: bearing fruit in every good work, growing in the knowledge of God, being strengthened with all power according to his glorious might so that you may have great endurance and patience.

COLOSSIANS 1:10–11 NIV

Teach me to do Your will, for You are my God; Your Spirit is good. Lead me in the land of uprightness.

PSALM 143:10 NKJV

I recounted my ways and you answered me; teach me your decrees. Let me understand the teaching of your precepts; then I will meditate on your wonders.

PSALM 119:26–27 NIV

Teach me your decrees, O Lord; I will keep them to the end. Give me understanding and I will obey your instructions; I will put them into practice with all my heart.

PSALM 119:33–34 NLT

I believe in your commands; now teach me good judgment and knowledge. I used to wander off until you disciplined me; but now I closely follow your word. You are good and do only good; teach me your decrees.

PSALM 119:66–68 NLT

Like newborn babies, you must crave pure spiritual milk so that you will grow into a full experience of salvation. Cry out for this nourishment, now that you have had a taste of the Lord's kindness.

1 PETER 2:2–3 NLT

Teach me how to live, O Lord. Lead me along the right path, for my enemies are waiting for me.

PSALM 27:11 NLT

Show me your ways, O Lord, teach me your paths.

PSALM 25:4 NIV

God, listen to me shout, bend an ear to my prayer. When I'm far from anywhere, down to my last gasp, I call out, "Guide me up High Rock Mountain!"

PSALM 61:1–2 MSG

Guard my life and rescue me; let me not be put to shame, for I take refuge in you. May integrity and uprightness protect me, because my hope is in you.

PSALM 25:20–21 NIV

NEEDING COMFORT

My soul is weary with sorrow; strengthen me according to your word.

PSALM 119:28 NIV

Even though I walk through the valley of the shadow of death, I will fear no evil, for you are with me; your rod and your staff, they comfort me.

PSALM 23:4 NIV

All praise to God, the Father of our Lord Jesus Christ. God is our merciful Father and the source of all comfort. He comforts us in all our troubles so that we can comfort others. When they are troubled, we will be able to give them the same comfort God has given us.

2 CORINTHIANS 1:3–4 NLT

"I will comfort you there in Jerusalem as a mother comforts her child."

ISAIAH 66:13 NLT

As the deer pants for the water brooks, so my soul pants for You, O God. My soul thirsts for God, for the living God; when shall I come and appear before God?

PSALM 42:1–2 NASB

My groaning has worn me out. At night my bed and pillow are soaked with tears. Sorrow has made my eyes dim, and my sight has failed because of my enemies. You, Lord, heard my crying.

PSALM 6:6–8 CEV

FEELING LONELY

Turn to me and be gracious to me, for I am lonely and afflicted.

PSALM 25:16 NIV

"Do not fear, for I am with you; do not anxiously look about you, for I am your God. I will strengthen you, surely I will help you, surely I will uphold you with My righteous right hand."

ISAIAH 41:10 NASB

Our LORD, you bless those who join in the festival and walk in the brightness of your presence.

PSALM 89:15 CEV

For I hold you by your right hand—I, the LORD your God. And I say to you, "Don't be afraid. I am here to help you."

ISAIAH 41:13 NLT

The LORD is with me; I will not be afraid. What can man do to me? The LORD is with me; he is my helper. I will look in triumph on my enemies. It is better to take refuge in the LORD than to trust in man.

PSALM 118:6–8 NIV

Where can I go from your Spirit? Where can I flee from your presence?

PSALM 139:7 NIV

FINDING HOPE

May your unfailing love rest upon us, O LORD, even as we put our hope in you.

PSALM 33:22 NIV

"And now, Lord, for what do I wait? My hope is in You."

PSALM 39:7 NASB

No one whose hope is in you will ever be put to shame, but they will be put to shame who are treacherous without excuse.

PSALM 25:3 NIV

Hear my cry for mercy as I call to you for help, as I lift up my hands toward your Most Holy Place.

PSALM 28:2 NIV

Why am I discouraged? Why is my heart so sad? I will put my hope in God! I will praise him again—my Savior and my God!

PSALM 42:5–6 NLT

I waited patiently for the LORD; he turned to me and heard my cry. He lifted me out of the slimy pit, out of the mud and mire; he set my feet on a rock and gave me a firm place to stand. He put a new song in my mouth, a hymn of praise to our God. Many will see and fear and put their trust in the LORD.

PSALM 40:1–3 NIV

You are my refuge and my shield; I have put my hope in your word.

PSALM 119:114 NIV

From early on your Sanctuary was set high, a throne of glory, exalted! O God, you're the hope of Israel. All who leave you end up as fools.

JEREMIAH 17:12–13 MSG

315

It is good to wait quietly for the salvation of the LORD.

LAMENTATIONS 3:26 NIV

May the God of hope fill you with all joy and peace in believing, so that by the power of the Holy Spirit you may abound in hope.

ROMANS 15:13 ESV

Let all that I am wait quietly before God, for my hope is in him.

PSALM 62:5 NLT

OBTAINING WISDOM

If any of you lacks wisdom, he should ask God, who gives generously to all without finding fault, and it will be given to him.

JAMES 1:5 NIV

Surely you desire truth in the inner parts; you teach me wisdom in the inmost place.

PSALM 51:6 NIV

"Praise be to the name of God for ever and ever; wisdom and power are his. He changes times and seasons; he sets up kings and deposes them. He gives wisdom to the wise and knowledge to the discerning."

DANIEL 2:20–21 NIV

That night God appeared to Solomon and said, "What do you want? Ask, and I will give it to you!" Solomon replied to God, "You showed faithful love to David, my father, and now you have made me king in his place. O LORD God, please continue to keep your promise to David my father, for you have made me king over a people as numerous as the dust of the earth! Give me the wisdom and knowledge to lead them properly, for who could possibly govern this great people of yours?" God said to Solomon, "Because your greatest desire is to help your people, and you did not ask for wealth, riches, fame, or even the death of your enemies or a long life, but rather you asked for wisdom and knowledge to properly govern my people—I will certainly give you the wisdom and knowledge you requested. But I will also give you wealth, riches, and fame such as no other king has had before you or will ever have in the future!"

2 CHRONICLES 1:7–12 NLT

"Call to me and I will answer you and tell you great and unsearchable things you do not know."

JEREMIAH 33:3 NIV

Guide me in your truth and teach me, for you are God my Savior, and my hope is in you all day long.

PSALM 25:5 NIV

LOOKING FOR GUIDANCE

For this God is our God for ever and ever; he will be our guide even to the end.

PSALM 48:14 NIV

Trust in the LORD with all your heart and lean not on your own understanding; in all your ways acknowledge him, and he will make your paths straight.

PROVERBS 3:5–6 NIV

Since you are my rock and my fortress, for the sake of your name lead and guide me.

PSALM 31:3 NIV

Lead me in the right path, O LORD, or my enemies will conquer me. Make your way plain for me to follow.

PSALM 5:8 NLT

If I rise on the wings of the dawn, if I settle on the far side of the sea,

even there your hand will guide me, your right hand will hold me fast.

PSALM 139:9–10 NIV

May the peoples praise you, O God; may all the peoples praise you. May the nations be glad and sing for joy, for you rule the peoples justly and guide the nations of the earth.

PSALM 67:3–4 NIV

Direct my footsteps according to your word; let no sin rule over me.

PSALM 119:133 NIV

ONE MOMENT AT A TIME
HAVING A TENDER HEART

1. **Pray scripture.** Praying scripture is an extremely helpful way to prime your own prayers, and it gives you words to pray when you don't know what to say. Pull out some of the scriptures from this chapter and pray them back to God.

2. **Pray the Lord's Prayer.** The prayer Jesus taught His disciples is found in Matthew 6:9–13. Use it as a model for your own prayer today. As you pray each line, concentrate on its meaning and augment each phrase with your own prayer.

3. **Light a candle.** While many church traditions use candles as symbols in their prayers, others never use them. If you have a specific need you're praying for, pray as you light the candle. As the flame goes upward, remember that your prayer is also heard by God. While there's nothing magical about a candle, it can be a useful tool in helping you focus.

CHAPTER 8

PRAYERS FOR OTHERS

I never knew how much my dad prayed for me until I went home be-
tween semesters of college. As I moved my bags back into my old room, I
noticed some footprints on my floor. When I say footprints, it was really
a well-worn path in the carpet between the door of my room and the
head of my bed. I pointed to them and asked my mom what caused the
spots on the carpet. She told me that my dad would come into my room
at least twice a day to pray for me while I was away.

■ *Kelly, age 20, Kentucky* ■

HEEDING THE CALL

"As for me, far be it from me that
I should sin against the LORD by
failing to pray for you. And I will
teach you the way that is good and
right."

1 SAMUEL 12:23 NIV

If you see a Christian brother or
sister sinning in a way that does not
lead to death, you should pray, and
God will give that person life. But
there is a sin that leads to death,
and I am not saying you should
pray for those who commit it.

1 JOHN 5:16 NLT

Pray for us, for our conscience is
clear and we want to live honorably
in everything we do.

HEBREWS 13:18 NLT

I thank God, whom I serve, as
my forefathers did, with a clear
conscience, as night and day I
constantly remember you in my
prayers.

2 TIMOTHY 1:3 NIV

LIFTING UP YOUR CHILDREN

May the LORD make you increase,
both you and your children. May
you be blessed by the LORD, the
Maker of heaven and earth.

PSALM 115:14–15 NIV

When a period of feasting had run
its course, Job would send and have
them purified. Early in the morning
he would sacrifice a burnt offering
for each of them, thinking, "Perhaps my children have sinned and
cursed God in their hearts." This
was Job's regular custom.

JOB 1:5 NIV

David pleaded with God for the child. He fasted and went into his house and spent the nights lying on the ground.

2 SAMUEL 12:16 NIV

BLESSING YOUR ENEMIES

"But I tell you who hear me: Love your enemies, do good to those who hate you, bless those who curse you, pray for those who mistreat you."

LUKE 6:27–28 NIV

"But I say to you, love your enemies and pray for those who persecute you."

MATTHEW 5:44 NASB

[Stephen] fell to his knees, shouting, "Lord, don't charge them with this sin!" And with that, he died.

ACTS 7:60 NLT

Jesus said, "Father, forgive them, for they do not know what they are doing." And they divided up his clothes by casting lots.

LUKE 23:34 NIV

INTERCEDING FOR OTHERS

So we have not stopped praying for you since we first heard about you. We ask God to give you complete knowledge of his will and to give you spiritual wisdom and understanding.

COLOSSIANS 1:9 NLT

And this I pray, that your love may abound still more and more in real knowledge and all discernment, so that you may approve the things that are excellent, in order to be sincere and blameless until the day of Christ; having been filled with the fruit of righteousness which comes through Jesus Christ, to the glory and praise of God.

PHILIPPIANS 1:9–11 NASB

And I am praying that you will put into action the generosity that comes from your faith as you understand and experience all the good things we have in Christ.

PHILEMON 6 NLT

So we keep on praying for you, asking our God to enable you to live a life worthy of his call. May he give you the power to accomplish all the good things your faith prompts you to do. Then the name of our Lord Jesus will be honored because of the way you live, and you will be honored along with him. This is all made possible because of the grace of our God and Lord, Jesus Christ.

2 THESSALONIANS 1:11–12 NLT

And may the Lord make your love for one another and for all people grow and overflow, just as our love for you overflows. May he, as a result, make your hearts strong, blameless, and holy as you stand before God our Father when our Lord Jesus comes again with all his holy people. Amen.

1 THESSALONIANS 3:12–13 NLT

319

Therefore, confess your sins to one another, and pray for one another so that you may be healed. The effective prayer of a righteous man can accomplish much.

JAMES 5:16 NASB

LOOKING FOR EVANGELISTIC OPPORTUNITIES

He said to his disciples, "The harvest is great, but the workers are few. So pray to the Lord who is in charge of the harvest; ask him to send more workers into his fields."

MATTHEW 9:37–38 NLT

Pray also for me, that whenever I open my mouth, words may be given me so that I will fearlessly make known the mystery of the gospel, for which I am an ambassador in chains. Pray that I may declare it fearlessly, as I should.

EPHESIANS 6:19–20 NIV

For this I will praise you, O LORD, among the nations, and sing to your name.

PSALM 18:49 ESV

Sing a new song to the LORD! Let the whole earth sing to the LORD! Sing to the LORD; praise his name. Each day proclaim the good news that he saves. Publish his glorious deeds among the nations. Tell everyone about the amazing things he does.

PSALM 96:1–3 NLT

Then Jesus came to them and said, "All authority in heaven and on earth has been given to me. Therefore go and make disciples of all nations, baptizing them in the name of the Father and of the Son and of the Holy Spirit, and teaching them to obey everything I have commanded you. And surely I am with you always, to the very end of the age."

MATTHEW 28:18–20 NIV

ONE MOMENT AT A TIME
HAVING A TENDER HEART

1. **Don't let "out of sight, out of mind" happen to you.** Hang a small bulletin board or build a small photo album of pictures of people you want to pray for regularly. Use these images as a reminder to keep those you love in prayer.

2. **Don't become overwhelmed.** When you add in relatives, friends, coworkers, and even enemies, you may generate a long list of people you hope to pray for. Rather than get overwhelmed because the list is so long, try dividing them up for days of the week. For example, on Monday pray for people from church; Tuesday pray for extended family; Wednesday pray for coworkers; and so forth.

3. **Post prompters.** Tape a note or two to different places you traffic each day as prompters to pray for the people listed on each one. Good places to tape notes may include your computer, bathroom mirror, and refrigerator.

CHAPTER 9

QUALITIES OF EFFECTIVE PRAYER

I was at the store last week and saw a perfect illustration of myself. I watched this young child being disruptive. He was both loud and out of control. When his mother tried to call him over to get his attention, the youngster defiantly looked at her, yelled, "No," and kept acting out. I admit, my first thought was judgmental toward the mother. How could she let that child act that way? As I left the store and starting walking to my car, I realized, Oh my goodness, that's me. How many times does God beckon me and I defiantly go my own way? How many times do I forget to treat Him with respect? More times than I can even remember.

■ Juanita, age 41, New York ■

PRIORITIZING PURITY

The eyes of the LORD are on the righteous and his ears are attentive to their cry.

PSALM 34:15 NIV

"God blesses those whose hearts are pure, for they will see God."

MATTHEW 5:8 NLT

The LORD is far from the wicked, but he hears the prayer of the righteous.

PROVERBS 15:29 ESV

The end of all things is near. Therefore be clear minded and self-controlled so that you can pray.

1 PETER 4:7 NIV

I want everyone everywhere to lift innocent hands toward heaven and pray, without being angry or arguing with each other.

1 TIMOTHY 2:8 CEV

Truly God is good to Israel, to those who are pure in heart. But as for me, my feet had almost stumbled, my steps had nearly slipped. For I was envious of the arrogant when I saw the prosperity of the wicked. . . . And they say, "How can God know? Is there knowledge in the Most High?" . . . If I had said, "I will speak thus," I would have betrayed the generation of your children. . . . Nevertheless, I am continually with you; you hold my right hand. . . . Whom have I in heaven but you? And there is nothing on earth that I desire besides you. My flesh and my heart may fail, but God is the strength of my heart and my portion forever.

PSALM 73:1–3, 11, 15, 23, 25–26 ESV

But know that the LORD has set apart the godly man for Himself; The LORD hears when I call to Him.

PSALM 4:3 NASB

LORD, I call to you; come quickly to me. Hear my voice when I call to you. . . . Set a guard over my mouth, O LORD; keep watch over the door of my lips.

PSALM 141:1, 3 NIV

KEEPING THE FAITH

"You can pray for anything, and if you have faith, you will receive it."

MATTHEW 21:22 NLT

"If you abide in me, and my words abide in you, ask whatever you wish, and it will be done for you."

JOHN 15:7 ESV

I lift up my eyes to the hills—where does my help come from? My help comes from the LORD, the Maker of heaven and earth.

PSALM 121:1–2 NIV

And without faith it is impossible to please Him, for he who comes to God must believe that He is and that He is a rewarder of those who seek Him.

HEBREWS 11:6 NASB

O my people, trust in him at all times. Pour out your heart to him, for God is our refuge.

PSALM 62:8 NLT

Let us draw near to God with a sincere heart in full assurance of faith, having our hearts sprinkled to cleanse us from a guilty conscience and having our bodies washed with pure water.

HEBREWS 10:22 NIV

In him and through faith in him we may approach God with freedom and confidence.

EPHESIANS 3:12 NIV

DEPENDING ON THE HOLY SPIRIT

And pray in the Spirit on all occasions with all kinds of prayers and requests. With this in mind, be alert and always keep on praying for all the saints.

EPHESIANS 6:18 NIV

In the same way, the Spirit helps us in our weakness. We do not know what we ought to pray for, but the Spirit himself intercedes for us with groans that words cannot express. And he who searches our hearts knows the mind of the Spirit, because the Spirit intercedes for the saints in accordance with God's will.

ROMANS 8:26–27 NIV

And because you are sons, God has sent the Spirit of his Son into our hearts, crying, "Abba! Father!"

GALATIANS 4:6 ESV

QUIETING YOURSELF

"Be still, and know that I am God!
I will be honored by every nation.
I will be honored throughout the
world."

PSALM 46:10 NLT

Be still before the LORD and wait
patiently for him; fret not yourself
over the one who prospers in his
way, over the man who carries out
evil devices!

PSALM 37:7 ESV

He makes me lie down in green
pastures, he leads me beside quiet
waters, he restores my soul. He
guides me in paths of righteousness
for his name's sake.

PSALM 23:2–3 NIV

I remember the days of old; I meditate on all Your doings; I muse on
the work of Your hands.

PSALM 143:5 NASB

So what shall I do? I will pray with
my spirit, but I will also pray with
my mind; I will sing with my spirit,
but I will also sing with my mind.

1 CORINTHIANS 14:15 NIV

They will speak of the glorious
splendor of your majesty, and I will
meditate on your wonderful works.

PSALM 145:5 NIV

Instead, I have calmed and quieted
myself, like a weaned child who no
longer cries for its mother's milk.
Yes, like a weaned child is my soul
within me.

PSALM 131:2 NLT

BEING PERSISTENT

Seek the LORD and His strength;
seek His face continually.

1 CHRONICLES 16:11 NASB

Let us hold tightly without waver-
ing to the hope we affirm, for God
can be trusted to keep his promise.

HEBREWS 10:23 NLT

I praise you seven times a day because your laws are fair.

PSALM 119:164 CEV

You paid attention to me, and so I
will pray to you as long as I live.

PSALM 116:2 CEV

Then, teaching them more about
prayer, he used this story: "Suppose you went to a friend's house at
midnight, wanting to borrow three
loaves of bread. You say to him, 'A
friend of mine has just arrived for a
visit, and I have nothing for him to
eat.' And suppose he calls out from
his bedroom, 'Don't bother me.
The door is locked for the night,
and my family and I are all in bed.
I can't help you.' But I tell you
this—though he won't do it for
friendship's sake, if you keep knocking long enough, he will get up and
give you whatever you need because
of your shameless persistence. And
so I tell you, keep on asking, and
you will receive what you ask for.
Keep on seeking, and you will find.
Keep on knocking, and the door
will be opened to you."

LUKE 11:5–9 NLT

Then Jesus told his disciples a parable to show them that they should always pray and not give up. He said: "In a certain town there was a judge who neither feared God nor cared about men. And there was a widow in that town who kept coming to him with the plea, 'Grant me justice against my adversary.'

"For some time he refused. But finally he said to himself, 'Even though I don't fear God or care about men, yet because this widow keeps bothering me, I will see that she gets justice, so that she won't eventually wear me out with her coming!' "

And the Lord said, "Listen to what the unjust judge says. And will not God bring about justice for his chosen ones, who cry out to him day and night? Will he keep putting them off? I tell you, he will see that they get justice, and quickly. However, when the Son of Man comes, will he find faith on the earth?"

LUKE 18:1–8 NIV

Be joyful in hope, patient in affliction, faithful in prayer.

ROMANS 12:12 NIV

Pray without ceasing.

1 THESSALONIANS 5:17 KJV

FINDING TIME IN THE MORNING AND EVENING

By day the LORD commands his steadfast love, and at night his song is with me, a prayer to the God of my life.

PSALM 42:8 ESV

But I call to God, and the LORD saves me. Evening, morning and noon I cry out in distress, and he hears my voice.

PSALM 55:16–17 NIV

LORD, the God who saves me, day and night I cry out before you. . . . But I cry to you for help, O LORD; in the morning my prayer comes before you.

PSALM 88:1, 13 NIV

Accept my prayer as incense offered to you, and my upraised hands as an evening offering.

PSALM 141:2 NLT

Give ear to my words, O LORD; consider my groaning. . . . LORD, in the morning you hear my voice; in the morning I prepare a sacrifice for you and watch.

PSALM 5:1, 3 ESV

Before daybreak the next morning, Jesus got up and went out to an isolated place to pray.

MARK 1:35 NLT

I rise early, before the sun is up; I cry out for help and put my hope in your words. I stay awake through the night, thinking about your promise.

PSALM 119:147–148 NLT

HUMBLING YOUR HEART

"If my people, who are called by my name, will humble themselves and pray and seek my face and turn from their wicked ways, then will I hear from heaven and will forgive their sin and will heal their land."

2 CHRONICLES 7:14 NIV

Good and upright is the LORD; therefore he instructs sinners in the way. He leads the humble in what is right, and teaches the humble his way.

PSALM 25:8–9 ESV

Since God chose you to be the holy people he loves, you must clothe yourselves with tenderhearted mercy, kindness, humility, gentleness, and patience.

COLOSSIANS 3:12 NLT

Humble yourselves, therefore, under God's mighty hand, that he may lift you up in due time. Cast all your anxiety on him because he cares for you.

1 PETER 5:6–7 NIV

ONE MOMENT AT A TIME
STAYING FOCUSED

1. **Try praying with ACTS.** Demonstrated in the organization of this book, the ACTS model of prayer can help organize your prayer time. Divide your prayer time into four sections, taking appropriate amounts of time for prayers of Adoration (or praise), prayers of Confession, prayers of Thanksgiving, and prayers of Supplication (or asking for God's help).

2. **Go for a walk.** Go outside and enjoy nature. Look for objects along the way that can remind you of God's character. For example, a small rock might remind you of God's strength. A leaf might remind you of the life He provides. Pick up one or two of them and carry them along as reminders of God's character while you pray.

3. **Create a bookmark.** Choose a verse from this chapter that has been the best reminder to you about offering effective prayer. Create a bookmark you place in your Bible or prayer journal and begin to memorize the verse as you pray this next week.

CHAPTER 10

HINDRANCES TO PRAYER

As a pastor, one of the biggest complaints I hear from my congregation is that they feel like their prayers are "bouncing off the ceiling." To many, God often seems distant and their prayers seem to go unheard. Sometimes we go through natural seasons where our emotions cause us to feel that way. Other times, though, there's a specific reason we feel distant: It's because we are distant. We have put up our own ceiling of pride, doubts, fears, anxiety, or sin. When those things happen, we become the cause of our own problem.

■ *Melvin, age 63, Illinois* ■

HAVING ANXIETY AND DOUBT

Don't worry about anything; instead, pray about everything. Tell God what you need, and thank him for all he has done.
PHILIPPIANS 4:6 NLT

If any of you lacks wisdom, he should ask God, who gives generously to all without finding fault, and it will be given to him. But when he asks, he must believe and not doubt, because he who doubts is like a wave of the sea, blown and tossed by the wind. That man should not think he will receive anything from the Lord.
JAMES 1:5–7 NIV

"If God gives such attention to the appearance of wildflowers—most of which are never even seen—don't you think he'll attend to you, take pride in you, do his best for you? What I'm trying to do here is to get you to relax, to not be so preoccupied with getting, so you can respond to God's giving. People who don't know God and the way he works fuss over these things, but you know both God and how he works. Steep your life in God-reality, God-initiative, God-provisions. Don't worry about missing out. You'll find all your everyday human concerns will be met. Give your entire attention to what God is doing right now, and don't get worked up about what may or may not happen tomorrow. God will help you deal with whatever hard things come up when the time comes."
MATTHEW 6:30–34 MSG

327

BEING FILLED WITH HYPOCRISY OR PRIDE

"And when you pray, do not be like the hypocrites, for they love to pray standing in the synagogues and on the street corners to be seen by men. I tell you the truth, they have received their reward in full."

MATTHEW 6:5 NIV

There are six or seven kinds of people the LORD doesn't like: Those who are too proud or tell lies or murder, those who make evil plans or are quick to do wrong, those who tell lies in court or stir up trouble in a family.

PROVERBS 6:16–19 CEV

The LORD is more pleased when we do what is right and just than when we offer him sacrifices. Haughty eyes, a proud heart, and evil actions are all sin.

PROVERBS 21:3–4 NLT

He also told this parable to some who trusted in themselves that they were righteous, and treated others with contempt: "Two men went up into the temple to pray, one a Pharisee and the other a tax collector. The Pharisee, standing by himself, prayed thus: 'God, I thank you that I am not like other men, extortioners, unjust, adulterers, or even like this tax collector. I fast twice a week; I give tithes of all that I get.' But the tax collector, standing far off, would not even lift up his eyes to heaven, but beat his breast, saying, 'God, be merciful to me, a sinner!' I tell you, this man went down to his house justified, rather than the other. For everyone who exalts himself will be humbled, but the one who humbles himself will be exalted."

LUKE 18:9–14 ESV

HOLDING ON TO SELFISHNESS AND SIN

The LORD detests the sacrifice of the wicked, but he delights in the prayers of the upright.

PROVERBS 15:8 NLT

If I had not confessed the sin in my heart, the Lord would not have listened.

PSALM 66:18 NLT

"We know that God does not hear sinners; but if anyone is God-fearing and does His will, He hears him."

JOHN 9:31 NASB

My God will reject them because they have not obeyed him; they will be wanderers among the nations.

HOSEA 9:17 NIV

You ask and do not receive, because you ask with wrong motives, so that you may spend it on your pleasures.

JAMES 4:3 NASB

If you won't help the poor, don't expect to be heard when you cry out for help.

PROVERBS 21:13 CEV

"And when you stand praying, if
you hold anything against anyone,
forgive him, so that your Father in
heaven may forgive you your sins."

MARK 11:25 NIV

ONE MOMENT AT A TIME
BREAKING THROUGH

1. **Pray out loud.** If you normally pray silently, try going to a private place and speaking your prayer out loud. Talk to God as you would talk to a friend. Whether you pray silently or with your lips, God will hear you.

2. **Pray a psalm.** The psalms are some of the most powerful prayers in the Bible and a helpful way to stimulate your own prayer. If you need a psalm of praise, try reading Psalm 19, 47, 66, 100, 103, or 104. If you need a psalm of confession, try Psalm 51. For thanksgiving, turn to Psalm 136. Dealing with doubts? Read Psalms 13 and 73. And if anxiety weighs you down, read Psalms 1, 23, 46, and 139.

3. **Read a book on prayer.** A book on the subject of prayer can be a great way to deepen your prayer life. Books worth considering: *Prayer* by Richard Foster; *Too Busy Not to Pray* by Bill Hybels; *Becoming a Woman of Prayer* by Cynthia Heald; *Letters to Malcom Chiefly on Prayer* by C. S. Lewis; *The Practice of the Presence of God* by Brother Lawrence; and *Prayer* by Ole Hallesby.

CONCLUSION

*Three things have helped me improve my intimacy with God. First, I set
aside daily time to pray. Sometimes I can afford a full hour, sometimes
it's a lot shorter—but I try never to miss my appointment with God.
Second, I don't let my morning "Amen" cut off my conversation with
God. Since God is always with me, I talk to Him believing that He is
alongside me every day. I thank Him for good things, pray for people as
we encounter them, and ask for His help when challenges arrive. Third,
I read my Bible. The Bible helps me understand God better and
lets me hear from Him. While in prayer I do most of the talking,
by reading the Bible I get to do most of the listening.*

■ *Walter, age 30, British Columbia* ■

FINDING INTIMACY WITH GOD

Yes. What other great nation has gods that are intimate with them the way GOD, our God, is with us, always ready to listen to us?

DEUTERONOMY 4:7 MSG

"Here I am! I stand at the door and knock. If you hear my voice and open the door, I will come in and eat with you, and you will eat with me."

REVELATION 3:20 NCV

The LORD your God will always be at your side, and he will never abandon you.

DEUTERONOMY 31:6 CEV

We saw it, we heard it, and now we're telling you so you can experience it along with us, this experience of communion with the Father and his Son, Jesus Christ.

1 JOHN 1:3 MSG

Then Jesus declared, "I am the bread of life. He who comes to me will never go hungry, and he who believes in me will never be thirsty."

JOHN 6:35 NIV

"Live in me. Make your home in me just as I do in you. In the same way that a branch can't bear grapes by itself but only by being joined to the vine, you can't bear fruit unless you are joined with me."

JOHN 15:4 MSG

God is faithful, by whom you were called into the fellowship of his Son, Jesus Christ our Lord.

1 CORINTHIANS 1:9 ESV

ONE MOMENT AT A TIME
GOING DEEPER

1. **Build a memorial.** Often in Old Testament stories, the people of Israel set up a memorial to remind themselves what God had done. Consider building one of your own. Put a jar on your dresser and place a small rock inside the jar every time you see God answer a prayer. (You might even consider writing the answer on the rock.) Over time, as the jar fills up, you'll be encouraged to see how God interacts with your life.

2. **Plant something.** Plant a tree or shrub in your yard (or a flower indoors) that reminds you of God's beauty and care in your life. Tend to the plant regularly just as you tend to your prayer life. And while you do your part in nurturing it, you'll enjoy seeing God make it grow.

3. **Encourage someone else along the way.** Having a prayer partner can be a practical way for you (and that person) to grow in faith. E-mail and text each other requests and praise and then meet periodically to pray together.

WHAT THE BIBLE SAYS ABOUT WORSHIP

INTRODUCTION

GETTING EVERYTHING STRAIGHT

In recent years, many have come to view worship as synonymous with "praise and worship" songs. This misconception leads some people to the conclusion that their worship each week exists solely within the realm of the songs they sing in church or certain music they listen to on their MP3 players.

God's Word, however, points us to an infinitely broader view of worship—one that encompasses everything we do. Our thoughts, prayers, words, actions, relationships, work—even our play—can become vehicles for worship if our hearts are tuned to worship God. Read the pages that follow to have your view of worship challenged and expanded.

CHAPTER 1

WHY WE WORSHIP

Right after a tragedy occurred in our community, I participated in what was probably the most impactful worship service of my life. In response to the tragedy, our church organized an impromptu service where we spent time praying and praising God. While I attended in an effort to support other community members who were directly affected by the tragedy, the service was surprisingly touching for me personally. As I worshipped God in prayer and song, He impressed upon me that He has the answers to the big "why" questions we all were asking. The reminder that God is still on the throne and that He knows what He's doing—even when I can't see it—proved to be a great comfort to me and gave me the hope I needed to be an encouragement to those around me.

■ *Ellie, age 37, West Virginia* ■

WORSHIP HIM BECAUSE HE IS WORTHY

The LORD is great and deserves our greatest praise! He is the only God worthy of our worship.
1 CHRONICLES 16:25 CEV

All the nations you have made shall come and worship before you, O Lord, and shall glorify your name.
PSALM 86:9 ESV

For great is the LORD and most worthy of praise; he is to be feared above all gods.
PSALM 96:4 NIV

"You must fear the LORD your God and worship him and cling to him. Your oaths must be in his name alone. He alone is your God, the only one who is worthy of your praise, the one who has done these mighty miracles that you have seen with your own eyes."
DEUTERONOMY 10:20–21 NLT

We praise you, LORD God, and we worship you at your sacred mountain. Only you are God!
PSALM 99:9 CEV

Offer praise to God our Savior because of our Lord Jesus Christ! Only God can keep you from falling and make you pure and joyful in his glorious presence. Before

333

time began and now and forevermore, God is worthy of glory, honor, power, and authority. Amen.

JUDE 24–25 CEV

O nations of the world, recognize the LORD, recognize that the LORD is glorious and strong. Give to the LORD the glory he deserves! Bring your offering and come into his presence. Worship the LORD in all his holy splendor.

1 CHRONICLES 16:28–29 NLT

Praise be to the LORD God, the God of Israel, who alone does marvelous deeds. Praise be to his glorious name forever; may the whole earth be filled with his glory. Amen and Amen.

PSALM 72:18–19 NIV

"Dominion and awe belong to God; he establishes order in the heights of heaven."

JOB 25:2 NIV

In a loud voice they sang: "Worthy is the Lamb, who was slain, to receive power and wealth and wisdom and strength and honor and glory and praise!"

REVELATION 5:12 NIV

WORSHIP IS COMMANDED

Then a voice came from the throne, saying: "Praise our God, all you his servants, you who fear him, both small and great!"

REVELATION 19:5 NIV

"Be still, and know that I am God; I will be exalted among the nations, I will be exalted in the earth."

PSALM 46:10 NIV

It is the LORD your God you must follow, and him you must revere. Keep his commands and obey him; serve him and hold fast to him.

DEUTERONOMY 13:4 NIV

Give to the LORD the glory he deserves! Bring your offering and come into his courts.

PSALM 96:8 NLT

Praise be to the LORD, the God of Israel, from everlasting to everlasting. Let all the people say, "Amen!" Praise the LORD.

PSALM 106:48 NIV

Declare his glory among the nations, his marvelous deeds among all peoples.

1 CHRONICLES 16:24 NIV

Honor the LORD, you heavenly beings; honor the LORD for his glory and strength.

PSALM 29:1 NLT

Declare his glory among the nations, his marvelous works among all the peoples!

PSALM 96:3 ESV

The Sovereign LORD will show his justice to the nations of the world. Everyone will praise him! His righteousness will be like a garden in early spring, with plants springing up everywhere.

ISAIAH 61:11 NLT

So thank GOD for his marvelous love, for his miracle mercy to the children he loves.

PSALM 107:31 MSG

But you are a chosen people, a royal priesthood, a holy nation, a people belonging to God, that you may declare the praises of him who called you out of darkness into his wonderful light.

1 PETER 2:9 NIV

WORSHIP BLESSES US

Praise the LORD. Blessed is the man who fears the LORD, who finds great delight in his commands.

PSALM 112:1 NIV

Blessed are all who fear the LORD, who walk in his ways. You will eat the fruit of your labor; blessings and prosperity will be yours. Your wife will be like a fruitful vine within your house; your sons will be like olive shoots around your table. Thus is the man blessed who fears the LORD.

PSALM 128:1–4 NIV

What a stack of blessing you have piled up for those who worship you, ready and waiting for all who run to you to escape an unkind world.

PSALM 31:19 MSG

Better is one day in your courts than a thousand elsewhere; I would rather be a doorkeeper in the house of my God than dwell in the tents of the wicked.

PSALM 84:10 NIV

Praise the LORD! How good to sing praises to our God! How delightful and how fitting!

PSALM 147:1 NLT

Blessed are those you choose and bring near to live in your courts! We are filled with the good things of your house, of your holy temple.

PSALM 65:4 NIV

He will bless those who fear the LORD, the small together with the great.

PSALM 115:13 NASB

GOD's angel sets up a circle of protection around us while we pray. . . .Worship GOD if you want the best; worship opens doors to all his goodness.

PSALM 34:7, 9 MSG

"The LORD commanded us to obey all these decrees and to fear the LORD our God, so that we might always prosper and be kept alive, as is the case today."

DEUTERONOMY 6:24 NIV

You have made known to me the path of life; you will fill me with joy in your presence, with eternal pleasures at your right hand.

PSALM 16:11 NIV

Watch this: God's eye is on those who respect him, the ones who are looking for his love.

PSALM 33:18 MSG

No, the LORD's delight is in those who fear him, those who put their hope in his unfailing love.

PSALM 147:11 NLT

What a beautiful thing, GOD, to give thanks, to sing an anthem to you, the High God!

PSALM 92:1 MSG

WORSHIP ENCOURAGES OTHERS

When you meet together, sing psalms, hymns, and spiritual songs, as you praise the Lord with all your heart. Always use the name of our Lord Jesus Christ to thank God the Father for everything.

EPHESIANS 5:19–20 CEV

Oh come, let us sing to the LORD; let us make a joyful noise to the rock of our salvation! Let us come into his presence with thanksgiving; let us make a joyful noise to him with songs of praise! For the LORD is a great God, and a great King above all gods.

PSALM 95:1–3 ESV

Listen! Your watchmen lift up their voices; together they shout for joy. When the LORD returns to Zion, they will see it with their own eyes. Burst into songs of joy together, you ruins of Jerusalem, for the LORD has comforted his people, he has redeemed Jerusalem.

ISAIAH 52:8–9 NIV

Let the message about Christ, in all its richness, fill your lives. Teach and counsel each other with all the wisdom he gives. Sing psalms and hymns and spiritual songs to God with thankful hearts.

COLOSSIANS 3:16 NLT

Glorify the LORD with me; let us exalt his name together.

PSALM 34:3 NIV

We should keep on encouraging each other to be thoughtful and to do helpful things. Some people have gotten out of the habit of meeting for worship, but we must not do that. We should keep on encouraging each other, especially since you know that the day of the Lord's coming is getting closer.

HEBREWS 10:24–25 CEV

ONE MOMENT AT A TIME
WORSHIPPING THE KING

1. **Remember God's place.** When community and world events affect us in painful ways, it is helpful to remember that God is still king of the universe. He still sits on the throne and is in control—even when we don't understand what is happening.

2. **Write a note.** Write a note to a missionary or friend encouraging them to remember and worship God in their work. As you think through how to encourage someone else, you'll find your own heart contemplating all the ways that God is worthy of your worship.

3. **Memorize a psalm.** Consider memorizing a psalm (or part of one) that can serve as a reminder to worship. Psalms like these can help create your own framework for worshipping God: Psalms 19, 47, 66, 100, 103, 104, and 145. To help you memorize, print a portable copy of these psalms from a Bible study Web site such as BibleGateway.com.

CHAPTER 2

THE FOCUS OF OUR WORSHIP

God gets a lot of competition for my worship. I wish that weren't the case, but it's true. Rather than keeping my thoughts focused on Him, I find myself worshipping my possessions, money, and my job. And as a single guy, there are times when I'm busy worshipping my latest love interest. No, I don't sing praise songs or lift my hands toward them like I do at church, but they do consume my thoughts and receive the bulk of my time and energy. It doesn't take much for these things to take first priority in my life–instead of God.

■ *Terry, age 32, Florida* ■

WORSHIP THE ONE AND ONLY GOD

Jesus answered, "It is written: 'Worship the Lord your God and serve him only.' "

LUKE 4:8 NIV

"I am the LORD; that is my name! I will not give my glory to another or my praise to idols."

ISAIAH 42:8 NIV

All creation, come praise the name of the LORD. Praise his name alone. The glory of God is greater than heaven and earth.

PSALM 148:13 CEV

At the time when the LORD had made his solemn agreement with the people of Israel, he told them: Do not worship any other gods!

Do not bow down to them or offer them a sacrifice. Worship only me! I am the one who rescued you from Egypt with my mighty power. Bow down to me and offer sacrifices. Never worship any other god, always obey my laws and teachings, and remember the solemn agreement between us. I will say it again: Do not worship any god except me. I am the LORD your God, and I will rescue you from all your enemies.

2 KINGS 17:35–39 CEV

The idols of the nations are silver and gold, made by the hands of men. They have mouths, but cannot speak, eyes, but they cannot see; they have ears, but cannot hear, nor is there breath in their mouths. Those who make them will be like them, and so will all who trust in them. . . . Praise be to the LORD from Zion, to him who dwells in

Jerusalem. Praise the LORD.
PSALM 135:15–18, 21 NIV

"For who is God besides the LORD? And who is the Rock except our God?"
2 SAMUEL 22:32 NIV

Is there any god like GOD? Are we not at bedrock?
PSALM 18:31 MSG

"Who among the gods is like you, O LORD? Who is like you—majestic in holiness, awesome in glory, working wonders?"
EXODUS 15:11 NIV

With every bone in my body I will praise him: "LORD, who can compare with you? Who else rescues the helpless from the strong? Who else protects the helpless and poor from those who rob them?"
PSALM 35:10 NLT

"O LORD, God of Israel, there is no God like you in heaven above or on earth below—you who keep your covenant of love with your servants who continue wholeheartedly in your way."
1 KINGS 8:23 NIV

"Then people all over the earth will know that the LORD alone is God and there is no other."
1 KINGS 8:60 NLT

No pagan god is like you, O Lord. None can do what you do!
PSALM 86:8 NLT

He then went back to the Holy Man, he and his entourage, stood before him, and said, "I now know beyond a shadow of a doubt that there is no God anywhere on earth other than the God of Israel. In gratitude let me give you a gift."
2 KINGS 5:15 MSG

"You shall have no other gods before Me."
EXODUS 20:3 NASB

"You must worship no other gods, for the LORD, whose very name is Jealous, is a God who is jealous about his relationship with you."
EXODUS 34:14 NLT

Hezekiah prayed before the LORD and said, "O LORD, the God of Israel, who are enthroned above the cherubim, You are the God, You alone, of all the kingdoms of the earth. You have made heaven and earth."
2 KINGS 19:15 NASB

"This is what the LORD says— Israel's King and Redeemer, the LORD Almighty: I am the first and I am the last; apart from me there is no God."
ISAIAH 44:6 NIV

WORSHIP THE GREAT ONE

"How great you are, O Sovereign LORD! There is no one like you, and there is no God but you, as we have

heard with our own ears."
2 SAMUEL 7:22 NIV

"Great and marvelous are your works, O Lord God, the Almighty. Just and true are your ways, O King of the nations. Who will not fear you, Lord, and glorify your name? For you alone are holy. All nations will come and worship before you, for your righteous deeds have been revealed."
REVELATION 15:3–4 NLT

I will exalt you, my God the King; I will praise your name for ever and ever. Every day I will praise you and extol your name for ever and ever. Great is the LORD and most worthy of praise; his greatness no one can fathom.
PSALM 145:1–3 NIV

I will remember the deeds of the LORD; yes, I will remember your wonders of old. I will ponder all your work, and meditate on your mighty deeds. . . . You are the God who works wonders; you have made known your might among the peoples. You with your arm redeemed your people, the children of Jacob and Joseph.
PSALM 77:11–12, 14–15 ESV

LORD, there is no one like you! For you are great, and your name is full of power.
JEREMIAH 10:6 NLT

For the LORD your God is God of gods and Lord of lords, the great God, mighty and awesome, who shows no partiality and accepts no bribes.
DEUTERONOMY 10:17 NIV

How awesome is the LORD Most High, the great King over all the earth!
PSALM 47:2 NIV

"Yours, O LORD, is the greatness and the power and the glory and the victory and the majesty, indeed everything that is in the heavens and the earth; Yours is the dominion, O LORD, and You exalt Yourself as head over all."
1 CHRONICLES 29:11 NASB

Oh, the depth of the riches of the wisdom and knowledge of God! How unsearchable his judgments, and his paths beyond tracing out! "Who has known the mind of the Lord? Or who has been his counselor?"
ROMANS 11:33–34 NIV

"Who has ever given to God, that God should repay him?" For from him and through him and to him are all things. To him be the glory forever! Amen.
ROMANS 11:35–36 NIV

Splendor and majesty are before him; strength and joy in his dwelling place.
1 CHRONICLES 16:27 NIV

WORSHIP THE HOLY ONE

"Do not come any closer," God said. "Take off your sandals, for the place where you are standing is holy ground."

EXODUS 3:5 NIV

Moses then said to Aaron, "This is what the LORD spoke of when he said: 'Among those who approach me I will show myself holy; in the sight of all the people I will be honored.' "

LEVITICUS 10:3 NIV

Our LORD and our God, we praise you and kneel down to worship you, the God of holiness!

PSALM 99:5 CEV

To the LORD I cry aloud, and he answers me from his holy hill.

PSALM 3:4 NIV

O God! Your way is holy! No god is great like God!

PSALM 77:13 MSG

Ascribe to the LORD the glory due to His name; worship the LORD in holy array.

PSALM 29:2 NASB

Yet you are enthroned as the Holy One; you are the praise of Israel.

PSALM 22:3 NIV

WORSHIP THE CREATOR OF EVERYTHING

"Ah Lord GOD! Behold, You have made the heavens and the earth by Your great power and by Your outstretched arm! Nothing is too difficult for You."

JEREMIAH 32:17 NASB

"Fear God," he shouted. "Give glory to him. For the time has come when he will sit as judge. Worship him who made the heavens, the earth, the sea, and all the springs of water."

REVELATION 14:7 NLT

Know that the LORD is God. It is he who made us, and we are his; we are his people, the sheep of his pasture.

PSALM 100:3 NIV

Blessed be the LORD God of Israel, that made heaven and earth, who hath given to David the king a wise son, endued with prudence and understanding, that might build an house for the LORD, and an house for his kingdom.

2 CHRONICLES 2:12 KJV

For every house is built by some-one, but God is the builder of everything.

HEBREWS 3:4 NIV

"Stand up and praise the LORD your God, who is from everlasting to everlasting. Blessed be your glorious name, and may it be exalted above all blessing and praise. You alone are the LORD. You made the heavens, even the highest heavens, and all their starry host, the earth and all that is on it, the seas and all that is in them. You give life to everything, and the multitudes of heaven wor-ship you."

NEHEMIAH 9:5–6 NIV

The LORD merely spoke, and the heavens were created. He breathed the word, and all the stars were born. He assigned the sea its boundaries and locked the oceans in vast reservoirs. Let the whole world fear the LORD, and let everyone stand in awe of him. For when he spoke, the world began! It appeared at his command.

PSALM 33:6–9 NLT

God alone stretched out the sky, stepped on the sea, and set the stars in place—the Big Dipper and Orion, the Pleiades and the stars in the southern sky. Of all the miracles God works, we cannot understand a one.

JOB 9:8–10 CEV

Let all that I am praise the LORD. O LORD my God, how great you are! You are robed with honor and majesty. You are dressed in a robe of light. You stretch out the starry curtain of the heavens; you lay out the rafters of your home in the rain clouds. You make the clouds your chariot; you ride upon the wings of the wind. The winds are your messengers; flames of fire are your servants. . . . O LORD, what a variety of things you have made! In wisdom you have made them all.

PSALM 104:1–4, 24 NLT

Lord, through all the generations you have been our home! Before the mountains were born, before you gave birth to the earth and the world, from beginning to end, you are God.

PSALM 90:1–2 NLT

When I consider your heavens, the work of your fingers, the moon and the stars, which you have set in place, what is man that you are mindful of him, the son of man that you care for him? You made him a little lower than the heavenly beings and crowned him with glory and honor.

PSALM 8:3–5 NIV

For by Him all things were created, both in the heavens and on earth, visible and invisible, whether thrones or dominions or rulers or authorities—all things have been created through Him and for Him. He is before all things, and in Him all things hold together.

COLOSSIANS 1:16–17 NASB

How many are your works, O LORD! In wisdom you made them all; the earth is full of your creatures.

PSALM 104:24 NIV

WORSHIP THE RULER OF ALL

For God is the King of all the earth; sing to him a psalm of praise.

PSALM 47:7 NIV

The LORD reigns, he is robed in majesty; the LORD is robed in majesty and is armed with strength. The world is firmly established; it cannot be moved. Your throne was established long ago; you are from all eternity.

PSALM 93:1–2 NIV

Make them realize that you are the LORD Most High, the only ruler of earth!

PSALM 83:18 CEV

I know that the LORD is great, that our Lord is greater than all gods. The LORD does whatever pleases him, in the heavens and on the earth, in the seas and all their depths. He makes clouds rise from the ends of the earth; he sends lightning with the rain and brings out the wind from his storehouses.

PSALM 135:5–7 NIV

The earth is the LORD's and the fullness thereof, the world and those who dwell therein.

PSALM 24:1 ESV

To the LORD your God belong the heavens, even the highest heavens, the earth and everything in it.

DEUTERONOMY 10:14 NIV

"He is the God who made the world and everything in it. Since he is Lord of heaven and earth, he doesn't live in man-made temples, and human hands can't serve his needs—for he has no needs. He himself gives life and breath to everything, and he satisfies every need. From one man he created all the nations throughout the whole earth. He decided beforehand when they should rise and fall, and he determined their boundaries. His purpose was for the nations to seek after God and perhaps feel their way toward him and find him—though he is not far from any one of us. For

in him we live and move and exist. As some of your own poets have said, 'We are his offspring.' "

ACTS 17:24–28 NLT

"Yours, O LORD, is the greatness and the power and the glory and the majesty and the splendor, for everything in heaven and earth is yours. Yours, O LORD, is the kingdom; you are exalted as head over all. Wealth and honor come from you; you are the ruler of all things. In your hands are strength and power to exalt and give strength to all."

1 CHRONICLES 29:11–12 NIV

God will be king over all the earth, one God and only one. What a Day that will be!

ZECHARIAH 14:9 MSG

WORSHIP THE LIVING GOD

But God is the real thing—the living God, the eternal King. When he's angry, Earth shakes. Yes, and the godless nations quake.

JEREMIAH 10:10 MSG

My soul longs, yes, faints for the courts of the LORD; my heart and flesh sing for joy to the living God.

PSALM 84:2 ESV

"For he is the living God, and he will endure forever. His kingdom will never be destroyed, and his rule will never end."

DANIEL 6:26 NLT

343

My soul thirsts for God, for the living God. When can I go and meet with God?

PSALM 42:2 NIV

"We have come to bring you the Good News that you should turn from these worthless things and turn to the living God, who made heaven and earth, the sea, and everything in them."

ACTS 14:15 NLT

But Christ was sinless, and he offered himself as an eternal and spiritual sacrifice to God. That's why his blood is much more powerful and makes our consciences clear. Now we can serve the living God and no longer do things that lead to death.

HEBREWS 9:14 CEV

WORSHIP THE APPROACHABLE FATHER

The Spirit and the bride say, "Come!" And let him who hears say, "Come!" Whoever is thirsty, let him come; and whoever wishes, let him take the free gift of the water of life.

REVELATION 22:17 NIV

Let us then approach the throne of grace with confidence, so that we may receive mercy and find grace to help us in our time of need.

HEBREWS 4:16 NIV

For there is only one God and one Mediator who can reconcile God and humanity—the man Christ Jesus.

I TIMOTHY 2:5 NLT

GOD, high above, sees far below; no matter the distance, he knows everything about us.

PSALM 138:6 MSG

Pay close attention! Come to me and live. I will promise you the eternal love and loyalty that I promised David.

ISAIAH 55:3 CEV

"And you, my son Solomon, acknowledge the God of your father, and serve him with wholehearted devotion and with a willing mind, for the LORD searches every heart and understands every motive behind the thoughts. If you seek him, he will be found by you; but if you forsake him, he will reject you forever."

I CHRONICLES 28:9 NIV

Come near to God and he will come near to you. Wash your hands, you sinners, and purify your hearts, you double-minded.

JAMES 4:8 NIV

But now in Christ Jesus you who once were far off have been brought near by the blood of Christ.

EPHESIANS 2:13 NKJV

And he came and preached peace to you who were far off and peace to those who were near. For through him we both have access in one Spirit to the Father.

EPHESIANS 2:17–18 ESV

ONE MOMENT AT A TIME
GOD FIRST

1. **Identify your idols.** Few people reading this book are likely to erect and worship statues in their home. Still, idols come in all shapes and forms. Anything that you make sacrifices for, anything that commands your time and attention, or anything that takes center stage in your heart could be considered an idol. Take a few moments and contemplate which things in your life divert your attention from God. For many, these might include jobs, possessions, 401(k) accounts, hobbies, or relationships. What are these for you?

2. **Create worship prompters.** Keep your eyes focused on Christ by reminding yourself to worship God. Create a reminder you'll see or hear throughout the day to prompt you to take a few moments to worship God. Ideas include a note taped to your computer monitor or bathroom mirror, a daily reminder on your PDA, or an alarm set on your watch.

3. **Make room in your schedule.** Adding worship to your already crowded day can be difficult, especially if it is a new exercise. Try treating it like an exercise program and begin with small steps. Begin with five minutes of worship. As you become more comfortable, expand it to ten minutes, then fifteen.

CHAPTER 3

WHO SHOULD WORSHIP GOD

The book of Psalms ranked as my least favorite Bible book for a long time. Since I'm just not a very emotional person, I've always had trouble relating to the unrestrained prayers found in the book. Usually, when choosing a part of the Bible to read, I'd just skip over this one. Our pastor recently preached through some psalms, and I realized that as I've neglected this portion of God's Word, I've neglected to worship. The Bible makes it clear that everyone is to worship—even private, and often stoic, people like me. The way I worship might look different than it would for someone with a different personality, but God deserves my worship, and I know I need to grow in this area. It hasn't gotten magically easy, but I'm trying.

■ *Buck, age 50, Colorado* ■

WORSHIP IS DUE FROM EVERYONE

Shout to the LORD, all the earth; break out in praise and sing for joy!
PSALM 98:4 NLT

May the peoples praise you, O God; may all the peoples praise you.
PSALM 67:5 NIV

Sing to God, you kingdoms of the earth. Sing praises to the Lord.
PSALM 68:32 NLT

I will perpetuate your memory through all generations; therefore the nations will praise you for ever and ever.
PSALM 45:17 NIV

The LORD sits in majesty in Jerusalem, exalted above all the nations. Let them praise your great and awesome name. Your name is holy!
PSALM 99:2–3 NLT

Sing to the LORD a new song, and His praise from the ends of the earth, you who go down to the sea, and all that is in it, you coastlands and you inhabitants of them! Let the wilderness and its cities lift up their voice, the villages that Kedar inhabits. Let the inhabitants of Sela sing, let them shout from the top of the mountains.
ISAIAH 42:10–11 NKJV

"All the earth bows down to you; they sing praise to you, they sing praise to your name."
PSALM 66:4 NIV

May all the kings of the earth praise you, O LORD, when they hear the words of your mouth. May they sing of the ways of the LORD, for the glory of the LORD is great.

PSALM 138:4–5 NIV

Then I heard every creature in heaven and on earth and under the earth and on the sea, and all that is in them, singing: "To him who sits on the throne and to the Lamb be praise and honor and glory and power, for ever and ever!"

REVELATION 5:13 NIV

Praise the LORD, all nations! Extol him, all peoples!

PSALM 117:1 ESV

Therefore God has highly exalted him and bestowed on him the name that is above every name, so that at the name of Jesus every knee should bow, in heaven and on earth and under the earth, and every tongue confess that Jesus Christ is Lord, to the glory of God the Father.

PHILIPPIANS 2:9–11 ESV

WORSHIP IS OFFERED BY CREATION

The heavens declare the glory of God; the skies proclaim the work of his hands.

PSALM 19:1 NIV

Praise the LORD, everything he has created, everything in all his kingdom. Let all that I am praise the LORD.

PSALM 103:22 NLT

Sing, O heavens, for the LORD has done this wondrous thing. Shout for joy, O depths of the earth! Break into song, O mountains and forests and every tree! For the LORD has redeemed Jacob and is glorified in Israel.

ISAIAH 44:23 NLT

"You will go out in joy and be led forth in peace; the mountains and hills will burst into song before you, and all the trees of the field will clap their hands."

ISAIAH 55:12 NIV

Let the heavens be glad, and the earth rejoice! Let the sea and everything in it shout his praise! Let the fields and their crops burst out with joy! Let the trees of the forest rustle with praise before the LORD, for he is coming! He is coming to judge the earth. He will judge the world with justice, and the nations with his truth.

PSALM 96:11–13 NLT

Praise him, sun and moon! Praise him, all you twinkling stars! Praise him, skies above! Praise him, vapors high above the clouds! Let every created thing give praise to the LORD, for he issued his command, and they came into being. He set them in place forever and ever. His decree will never be revoked. Praise the LORD from the earth, you creatures of the ocean

347

depths, fire and hail, snow and clouds, wind and weather that obey him, mountains and all hills, fruit trees and all cedars, wild animals and all livestock, small scurrying animals and birds.

PSALM 148:3–10 NLT

Let the sea and everything in it shout his praise! Let the earth and all living things join in. Let the rivers clap their hands in glee! Let the hills sing out their songs of joy.

PSALM 98:7–8 NLT

WORSHIP IS GIVEN BY ANGELS

Praise the LORD, you his angels, you mighty ones who do his bidding, who obey his word. Praise the LORD, all his heavenly hosts, you his servants who do his will.

PSALM 103:20–21 NIV

Praise the LORD! Praise the LORD from the heavens; praise him in the heights! Praise him, all his angels; praise him, all his hosts!

PSALM 148:1–2 ESV

And suddenly there was with the angel a multitude of the heavenly host praising God and saying, "Glory to God in the highest!"

LUKE 2:13–14 ESV

"Where were you when I laid the earth's foundation? Tell me, if you understand. . . . while the morning stars sang together and all the angels shouted for joy?"

JOB 38:4, 7 NIV

I looked again. I heard a company of Angels around the Throne, the Animals, and the Elders—ten thousand times ten thousand their number, thousand after thousand after thousand in full song: The slain Lamb is worthy! Take the power, the wealth, the wisdom, the strength! Take the honor, the glory, the blessing!

REVELATION 5:11–12 MSG

When he presents his honored Son to the world, he says, "All angels must worship him."

HEBREWS 1:6 MSG

All the angels were standing around the throne and around the elders and the four living creatures. They fell down on their faces before the throne and worshiped God.

REVELATION 7:11 NIV

WORSHIP IS ENCOURAGED FROM CHILDREN

"Do you hear what these children are saying?" they asked him. "Yes," replied Jesus, "have you never read, " 'From the lips of children and infants you have ordained praise'?"

MATTHEW 21:16 NIV

Young men and maidens, old men and children. Let them praise the name of the LORD, for his name alone is exalted; his splendor is above the earth and the heavens.

PSALM 148:12–13 NIV

LORD, our Lord, how majestic is your name in all the earth! You have set your glory above the heavens. From the lips of children and infants you have ordained praise because of your enemies, to silence the foe and the avenger.

PSALM 8:1–2 NIV

WORSHIP IS PRESENTED BY HIS PEOPLE

Praise the Lord. Praise the name of the LORD; praise him, you servants of the LORD, you who minister in the house of the LORD, in the courts of the house of our God.

PSALM 135:1–2 NIV

Sing to the LORD, you saints of his; praise his holy name.

PSALM 30:4 NIV

Sing joyfully to the LORD, you righteous; it is fitting for the upright to praise him.

PSALM 33:1 NIV

All you have made will praise you, O LORD; your saints will extol you.

PSALM 145:10 NIV

Surely the righteous will praise your name and the upright will live before you.

PSALM 140:13 NIV

Rejoice in the LORD, you who are righteous, and praise his holy name.

PSALM 97:12 NIV

Praise the LORD, all you servants of the LORD who minister by night in the house of the LORD. Lift up your hands in the sanctuary and praise the LORD.

PSALM 134:1–2 NIV

"Blessed be GOD who has delivered you from the power of Egypt and Pharaoh, who has delivered his people from the oppression of Egypt."

EXODUS 18:10 MSG

"And blessed be GOD, your God, who took such a liking to you and made you king. Clearly, GOD's love for Israel is behind this, making you king to keep a just order and nurture a God-pleasing people."

1 KINGS 10:9 MSG

Join with me in praising the wonderful name of the LORD our God. The LORD is a mighty rock, and he never does wrong. God can always be trusted to bring justice.

DEUTERONOMY 32:3–4 CEV

Sing to him, sing praise to him; tell of all his wonderful acts. . . . For great is the LORD and most worthy of praise; he is to be feared above all gods.

1 CHRONICLES 16:9, 25 NIV

ONE MOMENT AT A TIME
CHOOSING TO WORSHIP

1. **Worship without singing.** While many people equate worship with singing, the two are not exclusively linked. Praise God with a reverent spirit, the words you speak, and the attitudes you carry with you throughout the day. You can find a way to worship God in every activity throughout your day—without singing a single note.

2. **Disregard your feelings.** The Bible encourages us to worship at all times—whether we feel like it or not. Make it a priority to spend time worshipping God regularly, no matter what emotions you're feeling.

3. **Read a story from the Gospels.** Read an episode from the life of Christ in Matthew, Mark, Luke, or John. As you read the story, look for attributes of God you find in Christ. Pause and worship God as you encounter each one.

CHAPTER 4

HOW WE SHOULD WORSHIP

While no one has ever told me this, I think I've figured out that worship is an acquired skill. Yes, certain aspects of worship come pretty easily, but others require work. I've realized that I need to constantly pursue improving in those areas, and even then, I'll probably never perfect them. Learning to keep an attitude of reverence in all things is especially difficult for me because I'm pretty self-absorbed. Maintaining a grateful spirit never comes easily for me because I'm a "glass half empty" person. I have noticed, though, that as I think about it and work on it, God slowly changes me.

■ *Tanya, age 32, Oklahoma* ■

WORSHIP WITH CONSTANT PRAISE

Look to the LORD and his strength; seek his face always.
1 CHRONICLES 16:11 NIV

What joy for those who can live in your house, always singing your praises.
PSALM 84:4 NLT

Rejoice in hope, be patient in tribulation, be constant in prayer.
ROMANS 12:12 ESV

I will sing to the LORD as long as I live. I will praise my God to my last breath!
PSALM 104:33 NLT

My mouth is filled with your praise, declaring your splendor all day long.
PSALM 71:8 NIV

But as for me, I will always proclaim what God has done; I will sing praises to the God of Jacob.
PSALM 75:9 NLT

The LORD will save me, and we will sing with stringed instruments all the days of our lives in the temple of the LORD.
ISAIAH 38:20 NIV

Then my tongue shall tell of your righteousness and of your praise all the day long.
PSALM 35:28 ESV

Because he turned his ear to me, I will call on him as long as I live.
PSALM 116:2 NIV

I will praise the LORD all my life; I will sing praise to my God as long as I live.
PSALM 146:2 NIV

351

In God we boast all day long, and praise Your name forever.

PSALM 44:8 NKJV

WORSHIP WITH GREAT JOY

Shout for joy, O heavens! And rejoice, O earth! Break forth into joyful shouting, O mountains! For the LORD has comforted His people and will have compassion on His afflicted.

ISAIAH 49:13 NASB

This is the day the LORD has made; let us rejoice and be glad in it.

PSALM 118:24 NIV

I will shout for joy and sing your praises, for you have ransomed me.

PSALM 71:23 NLT

Sing praises to God and to his name! Sing loud praises to him who rides the clouds. His name is the LORD—rejoice in his presence!

PSALM 68:4 NLT

Then will I go to the altar of God, to God, my joy and my delight. I will praise you with the harp, O God, my God.

PSALM 43:4 NIV

You have filled my heart with greater joy than when their grain and new wine abound. I will lie down and sleep in peace, for you alone, O LORD, make me dwell in safety.

PSALM 4:7–8 NIV

I will be glad and rejoice in you; I will sing praise to your name, O Most High.

PSALM 9:2 NIV

WORSHIP WITH REVERENT FEAR

You are the most fearsome of all who live in heaven; all the others fear and greatly honor you.

PSALM 89:7 CEV

You alone are to be feared. Who can stand before you when you are angry?

PSALM 76:7 NIV

"Look now; I myself am he! There is no other god but me! I am the one who kills and gives life; I am the one who wounds and heals; no one can be rescued from my powerful hand!"

DEUTERONOMY 32:39 NLT

"Have you no respect for me? Why don't you tremble in my presence? I, the LORD, define the ocean's sandy shoreline as an everlasting boundary that the waters cannot cross. The waves may toss and roar, but they can never pass the boundaries I set."

JEREMIAH 5:22 NLT

Who should not revere you, O King of the nations? This is your due. Among all the wise men of the nations and in all their kingdoms, there is no one like you.

JEREMIAH 10:7 NIV

For all the gods of the nations are idols, but the LORD made the heavens. Splendor and majesty are before him; strength and glory are in his sanctuary. Ascribe to the LORD, O families of nations, ascribe to the LORD glory and strength. . . . Worship the LORD in the splendor of his holiness; tremble before him, all the earth.

PSALM 96:5–7, 9 NIV

WORSHIP WITH GRATEFUL HEARTS

So, God's people, shout praise to God, give thanks to our Holy God!

PSALM 97:12 MSG

We give thanks to you, O God, we give thanks, for your Name is near; men tell of your wonderful deeds.

PSALM 75:1 NIV

Give thanks to the LORD, for he is good; his love endures forever.

1 CHRONICLES 16:34 NIV

So thank GOD for his marvelous love, for his miracle mercy to the children he loves.

PSALM 107:8 MSG

Devote yourselves to prayer, keeping alert in it with an attitude of thanksgiving.

COLOSSIANS 4:2 NASB

David appointed the following Levites to lead the people in worship before the Ark of the LORD—to invoke his blessings, to give thanks, and to praise the LORD, the God of Israel.

1 CHRONICLES 16:4 NLT

"Now, our God, we give you thanks, and praise your glorious name."

1 CHRONICLES 29:13 NIV

Enter his gates with thanksgiving and his courts with praise; give thanks to him and praise his name.

PSALM 100:4 NIV

WORSHIP WITH THE SPIRIT'S HELP

"Yet a time is coming and has now come when the true worshipers will worship the Father in spirit and truth, for they are the kind of worshipers the Father seeks. God is spirit, and his worshipers must worship in spirit and in truth."

JOHN 4:23–24 NIV

But you, dear friends, carefully build yourselves up in this most holy faith by praying in the Holy Spirit.

JUDE 20 MSG

Pray in the Spirit on all occasions with all kinds of prayers and requests. With this in mind, be alert and always keep on praying for all the saints.

EPHESIANS 6:18 NIV

In the same way, the Spirit helps us in our weakness. We do not know what we ought to pray for, but the Spirit himself intercedes for us with groans that words cannot express. And he who searches our hearts knows the mind of the Spirit, because the Spirit intercedes for the saints in accordance with God's will.

ROMANS 8:26–27 NIV

Don't you know that you yourselves are God's temple and that God's Spirit lives in you?

1 CORINTHIANS 3:16 NIV

ONE MOMENT AT A TIME
LEARNING TO WORSHIP

1. **Understand reverence.** Look up the word *reverence* in a dictionary. Then see how the word is used in Nehemiah 5:15; Psalm 5:7; Daniel 6:26; Ephesians 5:21; and Hebrews 12:28. What do you learn about reverence? If you went about your next day's required activities with a spirit of reverence, what would look different?

2. **Create a poster.** Get a big poster board like a child might use in grade school. Write two or three things on the board that remind you that God is worthy of your praise. Add one or two items each day until your board is full.

3. **Ask for help.** The Holy Spirit is your greatest ally in learning to praise God. Ask for His help as you seek to praise God throughout this next week.

CHAPTER 5

WORSHIPPING GOD WITH OUR ACTIONS

As an athlete growing up, I had a lot of coaches. Once, I had a Christian coach who took me under her wing and really impressed on me that every action can be an act of worship—even those done on the court. Developing my God-given gifts is an act of worship. Competing hard and for God's glory is an act of worship. My interaction with teammates and opponents can be an act of worship. I had never thought of it that way before, but it caused me to realize that if athletics can be a form of worship, then anything can.

■ *Trinity, age 26, Michigan* ■

WORSHIP BY DEVELOPING YOUR GIFTS

It was he who gave some to be apostles, some to be prophets, some to be evangelists, and some to be pastors and teachers, to prepare God's people for works of service, so that the body of Christ may be built up.

EPHESIANS 4:11–12 NIV

There are different kinds of gifts, but the same Spirit. There are different kinds of service, but the same Lord. There are different kinds of working, but the same God works all of them in all men. Now to each one the manifestation of the Spirit is given for the common good.

1 CORINTHIANS 12:4–7 NIV

Each of you has been blessed with one of God's many wonderful gifts to be used in the service of others. So use your gift well. If you have the gift of speaking, preach God's message. If you have the gift of helping others, do it with the strength that God supplies. Everything should be done in a way that will bring honor to God because of Jesus Christ, who is glorious and powerful forever. Amen.

1 PETER 4:10–11 CEV

Whether, then, you eat or drink or whatever you do, do all to the glory of God.

1 CORINTHIANS 10:31 NASB

Whatever you do, work at it with all your heart, as working for the Lord, not for men.

COLOSSIANS 3:23 NIV

Never give up. Eagerly follow the Holy Spirit and serve the Lord.

ROMANS 12:11 CEV

"This is to my Father's glory, that you bear much fruit, showing yourselves to be my disciples."

JOHN 15:8 NIV

WORSHIP BY LIVING RIGHTEOUSLY

Do not offer the parts of your body to sin, as instruments of wickedness, but rather offer yourselves to God, as those who have been brought from death to life; and offer the parts of your body to him as instruments of righteousness.

ROMANS 6:13 NIV

Therefore, I urge you, brothers, in view of God's mercy, to offer your bodies as living sacrifices, holy and pleasing to God—this is your spiritual act of worship. Do not conform any longer to the pattern of this world, but be transformed by the renewing of your mind. Then you will be able to test and approve what God's will is—his good, pleasing and perfect will.

ROMANS 12:1–2 NIV

And this is my prayer: that your love may abound more and more in knowledge and depth of insight, so that you may be able to discern what is best and may be pure and blameless until the day of Christ, filled with the fruit of righteousness that comes through Jesus Christ—

to the glory and praise of God.

PHILIPPIANS 1:9–11 NIV

To this end we always pray for you, that our God may make you worthy of his calling and may fulfill every resolve for good and every work of faith by his power, so that the name of our Lord Jesus may be glorified in you, and you in him, according to the grace of our God and the Lord Jesus Christ.

2 THESSALONIANS 1:11–12 ESV

Do you not know that your body is a temple of the Holy Spirit, who is in you, whom you have received from God? You are not your own; you were bought at a price. Therefore honor God with your body.

1 CORINTHIANS 6:19–20 NIV

Who may worship in your sanctuary, LORD? Who may enter your presence on your holy hill? Those who lead blameless lives and do what is right, speaking the truth from sincere hearts.

PSALM 15:1–2 NLT

God "will give to each person according to what he has done." To those who by persistence in doing good seek glory, honor and immortality, he will give eternal life.

ROMANS 2:6–7 NIV

We exhorted each one of you and encouraged you and charged you to walk in a manner worthy of God, who calls you into his own kingdom and glory.

1 THESSALONIANS 2:12 ESV

WORSHIP BY GIVING

Honor the LORD with your wealth, with the firstfruits of all your crops; then your barns will be filled to overflowing, and your vats will brim over with new wine.

PROVERBS 3:9–10 NIV

And now I have it all—and keep getting more! The gifts you sent with Epaphroditus were more than enough, like a sweet-smelling sacrifice roasting on the altar, filling the air with fragrance, pleasing God no end.

PHILIPPIANS 4:18 MSG

"Bring your full tithe to the Temple treasury so there will be ample provisions in my Temple. Test me in this and see if I don't open up heaven itself to you and pour out blessings beyond your wildest dreams."

MALACHI 3:10 MSG

WORSHIP BY CARING FOR THE NEEDY

But don't forget to help others and to share your possessions with them. This too is like offering a sacrifice that pleases God.

HEBREWS 13:16 CEV

"Then the King will say to those on his right, 'Come, you who are blessed by my Father; take your inheritance, the kingdom prepared for you since the creation of the world. For I was hungry and you gave me something to eat, I was thirsty and you gave me something to drink, I was a stranger and you invited me in, I needed clothes and you clothed me, I was sick and you looked after me, I was in prison and you came to visit me.' . . . "The King will reply, 'I tell you the truth, whatever you did for one of the least of these brothers of mine, you did for me.' "

MATTHEW 25:34–36, 40 NIV

If anyone considers himself religious and yet does not keep a tight rein on his tongue, he deceives himself and his religion is worthless. Religion that God our Father accepts as pure and faultless is this: to look after orphans and widows in their distress and to keep oneself from being polluted by the world.

JAMES 1:26–27 NIV

ONE MOMENT AT A TIME
REACHING OUT

1. **Make a list.** Create a list of the gifts, talents, and opportunities God has given you. How could verses like Romans 12:1–2 affect how you develop each of those?

2. **Write your own psalm.** While the Bible has 150 psalms that can serve as model prayers, they are not all-inclusive. Write your own prayer and psalm and offer it as a gift of worship to God.

3. **Expand your vision.** While it's easy to see that attending church or singing worship choruses can be acts of worship, you may have to work at looking for new ways you can worship God. Seek out new ways to express your worship to God—like reaching out to someone in need, giving of your money, or using your talents to benefit someone else—and you'll find the possibilities are endless.

CHAPTER 6

FORMS OF WORSHIP

We often have visitors at our church who are used to more reserved worship styles. I enjoy watching their wide-eyed responses when some of our young people dance during the service. Sometimes our students will dance alongside someone else who is kneeling or even step over someone who is lying down as they pray before God. We don't hold anything back, so I can understand why they're surprised to see us be so free. We express our worship differently than many do. That doesn't make our worship any better or any worse than someone else's. It just means that we understand that there is more than one appropriate way to worship and give God the glory He deserves.

■ *Mariano, age 41, Dominican Republic* ■

WORSHIP WITH OTHERS

I will sacrifice a thank offering to you and call on the name of the Lord. I will fulfill my vows to the Lord in the presence of all his people, in the courts of the house of the Lord—in your midst, O Jerusalem. Praise the Lord.
PSALM 116:17–19 NIV

Glorify the Lord with me; let us exalt his name together.
PSALM 34:3 NIV

Praise our God, O peoples, let the sound of his praise be heard.
PSALM 66:8 NIV

Come, let us sing for joy to the Lord; let us shout aloud to the Rock of our salvation. . . . For he is our God and we are the people of his pasture, the flock under his care.
PSALM 95:1, 7 NIV

I'll tell my good friends, my brothers and sisters, all I know about you; I'll join them in worship and praise to you.
HEBREWS 2:12 MSG

I will declare your name to my brothers; in the congregation I will praise you.
PSALM 22:22 NIV

Praise God in the great congregation; praise the Lord in the assembly of Israel.
PSALM 68:26 NIV

I will give you thanks in the great assembly; among throngs of people I will praise you.

PSALM 35:18 NIV

From you comes the theme of my praise in the great assembly; before those who fear you will I fulfill my vows.

PSALM 22:25 NIV

"Again, I tell you that if two of you on earth agree about anything you ask for, it will be done for you by my Father in heaven."

MATTHEW 18:19 NIV

WORSHIP WITH SONG

He has given me a new song to sing, a hymn of praise to our God. Many will see what he has done and be amazed. They will put their trust in the LORD.

PSALM 40:3 NLT

Serve the LORD with gladness! Come into his presence with singing!

PSALM 100:2 ESV

Shout praises to the LORD! Sing him a new song of praise when his loyal people meet.

PSALM 149:1 CEV

Sing to the LORD a new song; sing to the LORD, all the earth.

PSALM 96:1 NIV

Sing praises to God, sing praises! Sing praises to our King, sing praises!

PSALM 47:6 ESV

Is any one of you in trouble? He should pray. Is anyone happy? Let him sing songs of praise.

JAMES 5:13 NIV

I will give thanks to you, O Lord, among the peoples; I will sing praises to you among the nations.

PSALM 57:9 ESV

I will sing to the LORD, for he has been good to me.

PSALM 13:6 NIV

Therefore I will praise you among the nations, O LORD; I will sing praises to your name.

PSALM 18:49 NIV

"Listen, you kings! Pay attention, you mighty rulers! For I will sing to the LORD. I will make music to the LORD, the God of Israel."

JUDGES 5:3 NLT

"Therefore I will give thanks to You, O LORD, among the nations, And I will sing praises to Your name."

2 SAMUEL 22:50 NASB

Then Moses and the Israelites sang this song to the LORD: "I will sing to the LORD, for he is highly exalted. The horse and its rider he has hurled into the sea."

EXODUS 15:1 NIV

WORSHIP WITH MUSICAL INSTRUMENTS

Tell everyone on this earth to sing happy songs in praise of the LORD.

Make music for him on harps. Play beautiful melodies!

> PSALM 98:4–5 CEV

Praise the LORD, for the LORD is good; celebrate his lovely name with music.

> PSALM 135:3 NLT

My heart is steadfast, O God, my heart is steadfast; I will sing and make music.

> PSALM 57:7 NIV

Then my head will be exalted above the enemies who surround me; at his tabernacle will I sacrifice with shouts of joy; I will sing and make music to the LORD.

> PSALM 27:6 NIV

Shout praises to the LORD! Praise God in his temple. Praise him in heaven, his mighty fortress. Praise our God! His deeds are wonderful, too marvelous to describe. Praise God with trumpets and all kinds of harps. Praise him with tambourines and dancing, with stringed instruments and woodwinds. Praise God with cymbals, with clashing cymbals. Let every living creature praise the LORD. Shout praises to the LORD!

> PSALM 150:1–6 CEV

David and the whole house of Israel were celebrating with all their might before the LORD, with songs and with harps, lyres, tambourines, sistrums and cymbals.

> 2 SAMUEL 6:5 NIV

Praise the LORD with the harp; make music to him on the ten-stringed lyre. Sing to him a new song; play skillfully, and shout for joy.

> PSALM 33:2–3 NIV

WORSHIP WITH WHAT YOU SAY

May the words of my mouth and the meditation of my heart be pleasing in your sight, O LORD, my Rock and my Redeemer.

> PSALM 19:14 NIV

I will praise the LORD at all times. I will constantly speak his praises.

> PSALM 34:1 NLT

With my mouth I will greatly extol the LORD; in the great throng I will praise him. For he stands at the right hand of the needy one, to save his life from those who condemn him.

> PSALM 109:30–31 NIV

O Lord, open my lips, and my mouth will declare your praise.

> PSALM 51:15 NIV

My soul will be satisfied as with fat and rich food, and my mouth will praise you with joyful lips.

> PSALM 63:5 ESV

Don't repay evil for evil. Don't retaliate with insults when people insult you. Instead, pay them back with a blessing. That is what God has called you to do, and he will bless you for it. For the Scriptures say, "If you want to enjoy life and see many happy days, keep your tongue from speaking evil and your lips from telling lies. Turn away from evil and do good. Search for peace, and work to maintain it."

1 PETER 3:9–11 NLT

Do not let any unwholesome talk come out of your mouths, but only what is helpful for building others up according to their needs, that it may benefit those who listen.

EPHESIANS 4:29 NIV

All of us do many wrong things. But if you can control your tongue, you are mature and able to control your whole body. . . . My dear friends, with our tongues we speak both praises and curses. We praise our Lord and Father, and we curse people who were created to be like God, and this isn't right.

JAMES 3:2, 9–10 CEV

WORSHIP WITH REVERENT POSTURE

Then David said to the whole assembly, "Praise the LORD your God." So they all praised the LORD, the God of their fathers; they bowed low and fell prostrate before the LORD and the king.

1 CHRONICLES 29:20 NIV

Come, let us worship and bow down. Let us kneel before the LORD our maker.

PSALM 95:6 NLT

My response is to get down on my knees before the Father, this magnificent Father who parcels out all heaven and earth.

EPHESIANS 3:14–15 MSG

And Hezekiah the king and the officials commanded the Levites to sing praises to the LORD with the words of David and of Asaph the seer. And they sang praises with gladness, and they bowed down and worshiped.

2 CHRONICLES 29:30 ESV

I will praise you as long as I live, and in your name I will lift up my hands.

PSALM 63:4 NIV

I lift up my hands to your commands, which I love, and I meditate on your decrees.

PSALM 119:48 NIV

Lift up your hands in the sanctuary and praise the LORD.

PSALM 134:2 NIV

WORSHIP WITH DANCE

Praise his name with dancing, accompanied by tambourine and harp.

PSALM 149:3 NLT

"Hear, O LORD, and be merciful to me; O LORD, be my help." You turned my wailing into dancing; you removed my sackcloth and clothed me with joy.

PSALM 30:10–11 NIV

Then Miriam the prophet, Aaron's sister, took a tambourine and led all the women as they played their tambourines and danced. And Miriam sang this song: "Sing to the LORD, for he has triumphed gloriously; he has hurled both horse and rider into the sea."

EXODUS 15:20–21 NLT

When those who were carrying the ark of the LORD had taken six steps, he sacrificed a bull and a fattened calf. David, wearing a linen ephod, danced before the LORD with all his might, while he and the entire house of Israel brought up the ark of the LORD with shouts and the sound of trumpets.

2 SAMUEL 6:13–15 NIV

WORSHIP WITH PRAYER

The one thing I ask of the LORD—the thing I seek most—is to live in the house of the LORD all the days of my life, delighting in the LORD's perfections and meditating in his Temple.

PSALM 27:4 NLT

To God only wise, be glory through Jesus Christ for ever. Amen.

ROMANS 16:27 KJV

Grace to you and peace from God our Father and the Lord Jesus Christ, who gave Himself for our sins so that He might rescue us from this present evil age, according to the will of our God and Father, to whom be the glory forevermore. Amen.

GALATIANS 1:3–5 NASB

Now unto him that is able to do exceeding abundantly above all that we ask or think, according to the power that worketh in us, unto him be glory in the church by Christ Jesus throughout all ages, world without end. Amen.

EPHESIANS 3:20–21 KJV

May the God of peace, who through the blood of the eternal covenant brought back from the dead our Lord Jesus, that great Shepherd of the sheep, equip you with everything good for doing his will, and may he work in us what is pleasing to him, through Jesus Christ, to whom be glory for ever and ever. Amen.

HEBREWS 13:20–21 NIV

But grow in the grace and knowledge of our Lord and Savior Jesus Christ. To him be glory both now and forever! Amen.

2 PETER 3:18 NIV

"Amen! Blessing and glory and wisdom and thanksgiving and honor and power and might be to our God forever and ever! Amen."

REVELATION 7:12 ESV

"The Lamb who was killed is worthy to receive power, riches, wisdom, strength, honor, glory, and praise. . . . Praise, honor, glory, and strength forever and ever to the one who sits on the throne and to the Lamb!"

REVELATION 5:12–13 CEV

ONE MOMENT AT A TIME
EXPANDING HORIZONS

1. **Attend a new service.** When the opportunity presents itself, visit a church that has a different worship style than the one you're used to. The differences found in a liturgical, charismatic, or other unfamiliar style can expand your view of God and worship.

2. **Try a prayer book.** Many liturgical prayer books can help you worship God using words or prayers that you haven't considered before. Add such a book to your devotional routine for a few weeks and allow it to broaden your perspective of praise.

3. **Learn a new skill.** Teach yourself to play basic chords on the guitar (or pick up another instrument). Once you have some basics down, consider adding the instrument to your worship routine.

CHAPTER 7

PERSONAL REASONS TO WORSHIP GOD

As a recent seminary graduate, I found that I approached worship very academically. I knew the history of church services, the benefits of worship, and our obligations in this area. What I had forgotten, and am learning to reclaim, is the personal nature of worship. God is worthy of worship because of what He's done for me. He loves me. He's forgiven me. With all the billions of people in the world to keep track of, He remembers and cares for me. God is certainly worthy of praise!

■ *Toby, age 29, Washington DC* ■

WORSHIP BECAUSE OF HIS LOVE

Because your love is better than life, my lips will glorify you.
PSALM 63:3 NIV

Give thanks to the LORD, for he is good; his love endures forever.
1 CHRONICLES 16:34 NIV

The LORD's lovingkindnesses indeed never cease, for His compassions never fail. They are new every morning; great is Your faithfulness.
LAMENTATIONS 3:22–23 NASB

Your love, O LORD, reaches to the heavens, your faithfulness to the skies. Your righteousness is like the mighty mountains, your justice like the great deep. O LORD, you preserve both man and beast.
PSALM 36:5–6 NIV

For GOD is sheer beauty, all-generous in love, loyal always and ever.
PSALM 100:5 MSG

How priceless is your unfailing love! Both high and low among men find refuge in the shadow of your wings.
PSALM 36:7 NIV

The LORD appeared to us in the past, saying: "I have loved you with an everlasting love; I have drawn you with loving-kindness."
JEREMIAH 31:3 NIV

Know therefore that the LORD your God is God; he is the faithful God, keeping his covenant of love to a thousand generations of those who

365

love him and keep his commands.
DEUTERONOMY 7:9 NIV

WORSHIP BECAUSE OF HIS ANSWERS TO PRAYER

But God did listen! He paid attention to my prayer. Praise God, who did not ignore my prayer or withdraw his unfailing love from me.
PSALM 66:19–20 NLT

I call on you, O God, for you will answer me; give ear to me and hear my prayer.
PSALM 17:6 NIV

"I thank and praise you, O God of my fathers: You have given me wisdom and power, you have made known to me what we asked of you, you have made known to us the dream of the king."
DANIEL 2:23 NIV

The LORD has heard my plea; the LORD will answer my prayer.
PSALM 6:9 NLT

I called on your name, O LORD, from the depths of the pit. You heard my plea: "Do not close your ears to my cry for relief." You came near when I called you, and you said, "Do not fear." O Lord, you took up my case; you redeemed my life.
LAMENTATIONS 3:55–58 NIV

"Praise be to the LORD, who has given rest to his people Israel just as he promised. Not one word has failed of all the good promises he gave through his servant Moses."
1 KINGS 8:56 NIV

My soul makes its boast in the LORD; let the humble hear and be glad. . . . I sought the LORD, and he answered me and delivered me from all my fears.
PSALM 34:2, 4 ESV

Then we cried out to the LORD, the God of our fathers, and the LORD heard our voice and saw our misery, toil and oppression. So the LORD brought us out of Egypt with a mighty hand and an outstretched arm, with great terror and with miraculous signs and wonders.
DEUTERONOMY 26:7–8 NIV

WORSHIP BECAUSE OF HIS FORGIVENESS

He has paid a full ransom for his people. He has guaranteed his covenant with them forever. What a holy, awe-inspiring name he has!
PSALM 111:9 NLT

"Our Redeemer—the LORD Almighty is his name—is the Holy One of Israel."
ISAIAH 47:4 NIV

"He redeemed my soul from going down to the pit, and I will live to enjoy the light."
JOB 33:28 NIV

Who is a God like you, pardoning iniquity and passing over transgression for the remnant of his inheritance? He does not retain his anger forever, because he delights in steadfast love. He will again have compassion on us; he will tread our iniquities underfoot. You will cast all our sins into the depths of the sea.

MICAH 7:18–19 ESV

Give thanks to the LORD, for he is good! His faithful love endures forever. Has the LORD redeemed you? Then speak out! Tell others he has redeemed you from your enemies.

PSALM 107:1–2 NLT

Praise the LORD. . .who forgives all your sins and heals all your diseases.

PSALM 103:1, 3 NIV

He will not constantly accuse us, nor remain angry forever. He does not punish us for all our sins; he does not deal harshly with us, as we deserve. For his unfailing love toward those who fear him is as great as the height of the heavens above the earth. He has removed our sins as far from us as the east is from the west. The LORD is like a father to his children, tender and compassionate to those who fear him.

PSALM 103:9–13 NLT

Who may ascend the hill of the LORD? Who may stand in his holy place? He who has clean hands and a pure heart, who does not lift up his soul to an idol or swear by what is false. He will receive blessing from the LORD and vindication from God his Savior.

PSALM 24:3–5 NIV

WORSHIP BECAUSE OF HIS MERCY AND GRACE

Praise be to the God and Father of our Lord Jesus Christ! In his great mercy he has given us new birth into a living hope through the resurrection of Jesus Christ from the dead.

1 PETER 1:3 NIV

"If you return to the LORD, then your brothers and your children will be shown compassion by their captors and will come back to this land, for the LORD your God is gracious and compassionate. He will not turn his face from you if you return to him."

2 CHRONICLES 30:9 NIV

Therefore the LORD waits to be gracious to you, and therefore he exalts himself to show mercy to you. For the LORD is a God of justice; blessed are all those who wait for him.

ISAIAH 30:18 ESV

But you, O Lord, are a God merciful and gracious, slow to anger and abounding in steadfast love and faithfulness.

PSALM 86:15 ESV

Have mercy on me, O God, because of your unfailing love. Because of your great compassion, blot out the stain of my sins.

PSALM 51:1 NLT

I love the LORD, because he has heard my voice and my pleas for mercy.

PSALM 116:1 ESV

367

God is sheer mercy and grace; not easily angered, he's rich in love.

PSALM 103:8 MSG

WORSHIP BECAUSE OF HIS SALVATION

Sing to the LORD, all the earth; proclaim his salvation day after day.

1 CHRONICLES 16:23 NIV

I will praise You, for You have answered me, and have become my salvation.

PSALM 118:21 NKJV

"The LORD is my strength and my song; he has become my salvation. He is my God, and I will praise him, my father's God, and I will exalt him."

EXODUS 15:2 NIV

Praise be to the God and Father of our Lord Jesus Christ, who has blessed us in the heavenly realms with every spiritual blessing in Christ. For he chose us in him before the creation of the world to be holy and blameless in his sight. In love he predestined us to be adopted as his sons through Jesus Christ, in accordance with his pleasure and will—to the praise of his glorious grace, which he has freely given us in the One he loves. In him we have redemption through his blood, the forgiveness of sins, in accordance with the riches of God's grace.

EPHESIANS 1:3–7 NIV

"The ransomed of the LORD will return. They will enter Zion with singing; everlasting joy will crown their heads. Gladness and joy will overtake them, and sorrow and sighing will flee away."

ISAIAH 51:11 NIV

Our LORD, let your worshipers rejoice and be glad. They love you for saving them, so let them always say, "The LORD is wonderful!"

PSALM 40:16 CEV

My soul finds rest in God alone; my salvation comes from him. He alone is my rock and my salvation; he is my fortress, I will never be shaken.

PSALM 62:1–2 NIV

And it will be said in that day, "Behold, this is our God for whom we have waited that He might save us. This is the LORD for whom we have waited; let us rejoice and be glad in His salvation."

ISAIAH 25:9 NASB

I pray that you will be grateful to God for letting you have part in what he has promised his people in the kingdom of light.

COLOSSIANS 1:12 CEV

But thanks be to God, who always leads us in triumphal procession in Christ and through us spreads everywhere the fragrance of the knowledge of him.

2 CORINTHIANS 2:14 NIV

WORSHIP BECAUSE OF HIS HELP

Praise be to the Lord, to God our Savior, who daily bears our burdens.

PSALM 68:19 NIV

Sing to the LORD! Give praise to the LORD! He rescues the life of the needy from the hands of the wicked.

JEREMIAH 20:13 NIV

Praise the LORD, all you who fear him! Honor him, all you descendants of Jacob! Show him reverence, all you descendants of Israel! For he has not ignored or belittled the suffering of the needy. He has not turned his back on them, but has listened to their cries for help.

PSALM 22:23–24 NLT

I will give thanks to the LORD with all my heart; I will tell of all Your wonders. . . . When my enemies turn back, they stumble and perish before You.

PSALM 9:1, 3 NASB

The LORD lives, and blessed be my rock; and exalted be the God of my salvation, the God who executes vengeance for me, and subdues peoples under me. He delivers me from my enemies; surely You lift me above those who rise up against me; You rescue me from the violent man.

PSALM 18:46–48 NASB

Blessed be the LORD! For he has heard the voice of my pleas for mercy. The LORD is my strength and my shield; in him my heart trusts,

and I am helped; my heart exults, and with my song I give thanks to him.

PSALM 28:6–7 ESV

WORSHIP BECAUSE OF HIS COMFORT

How kind the LORD is! How good he is! So merciful, this God of ours!

PSALM 116:5 NLT

God blesses those people who grieve. They will find comfort!

MATTHEW 5:4 CEV

All praise to God, the Father of our Lord Jesus Christ. God is our merciful Father and the source of all comfort. He comforts us in all our troubles so that we can comfort others. When they are troubled, we will be able to give them the same comfort God has given us. For the more we suffer for Christ, the more God will shower us with his comfort through Christ.

2 CORINTHIANS 1:3–5 NLT

In that day you will sing: "I will praise you, O LORD! You were angry with me, but not any more. Now you comfort me."

ISAIAH 12:1 NLT

God our Father loves us. He is kind and has given us eternal comfort and a wonderful hope.

2 THESSALONIANS 2:16 CEV

The LORD is good to all; he has compassion on all he has made. All you have made will praise you, O

Lord; your saints will extol you.
PSALM 145:9–10 NIV

Let the ruins of Jerusalem break into joyful song, for the Lord has comforted his people. He has redeemed Jerusalem.
ISAIAH 52:9 NLT

The Lord cares for his nation, just as shepherds care for their flocks. He carries the lambs in his arms, while gently leading the mother sheep.
ISAIAH 40:11 CEV

WORSHIP BECAUSE OF HIS PROVISION

When you have eaten and are satisfied, praise the Lord your God for the good land he has given you.
DEUTERONOMY 8:10 NIV

"Then this city will bring me renown, joy, praise and honor before all nations on earth that hear of all the good things I do for it; and they will be in awe and will tremble at the abundant prosperity and peace I provide for it."
JEREMIAH 33:9 NIV

You care for the land and water it; you enrich it abundantly. The streams of God are filled with water to provide the people with grain, for so you have ordained it.
PSALM 65:9 NIV

Great are the works of the Lord; they are pondered by all who delight in them. . . . He provides food for those who fear him; he remembers his covenant forever.
PSALM 111:2, 5 NIV

But remember the Lord your God, for it is he who gives you the ability to produce wealth, and so confirms his covenant, which he swore to your forefathers, as it is today.
DEUTERONOMY 8:18 NIV

Every good and perfect gift is from above, coming down from the Father of the heavenly lights, who does not change like shifting shadows.
JAMES 1:17 NIV

By his divine power, God has given us everything we need for living a godly life. We have received all of this by coming to know him, the one who called us to himself by means of his marvelous glory and excellence.
2 PETER 1:3 NLT

God will lavish you with good things: children from your womb, offspring from your animals, and crops from your land, the land that God promised your ancestors that he would give you. God will throw open the doors of his sky vaults and pour rain on your land on schedule and bless the work you take in hand. You will lend to many nations but you yourself won't have to take out a loan.
DEUTERONOMY 28:11–12 MSG

WORSHIP BECAUSE OF HIS GOOD WORKS

You did it: You changed wild lament into whirling dance; you ripped off my black mourning band and decked me with wildflowers. I'm about to burst with song; I can't keep quiet about you. GOD, my God, I can't thank you enough.

PSALM 30:11–12 MSG

From the end of the earth I call to you when my heart is faint. Lead me to the rock that is higher than I, for you have been my refuge, a strong tower against the enemy. . . . For you, O God, have heard my vows; you have given me the heritage of those who fear your name.

PSALM 61:2–3, 5 ESV

O LORD, You are my God; I will exalt You, I will give thanks to Your name; for You have worked wonders, plans formed long ago, with perfect faithfulness.

ISAIAH 25:1 NASB

Praise the LORD God, the God of Israel, who alone does such wonderful things.

PSALM 72:18 NLT

Sing to him, sing praise to him; tell of all his wonderful acts.

PSALM 105:2 NIV

Sing praises to the LORD, enthroned in Zion; proclaim among the nations what he has done.

PSALM 9:11 NIV

You made me so happy, GOD. I saw your work and I shouted for joy.

PSALM 92:4 MSG

I wash my hands in innocence, and go about your altar, O LORD, proclaiming aloud your praise and telling of all your wonderful deeds.

PSALM 26:6–7 NIV

I will praise you forever for what you have done; in your name I will hope, for your name is good. I will praise you in the presence of your saints.

PSALM 52:9 NIV

Bless the LORD, O my soul. . .who crowns you with steadfast love and mercy, who satisfies you with good so that your youth is renewed like the eagle's.

PSALM 103:2, 4–5 ESV

May the peoples praise you, O God; may all the peoples praise you. May the nations be glad and sing for joy, for you rule the peoples justly and guide the nations of the earth.

PSALM 67:3–4 NIV

One generation will commend your works to another; they will tell of your mighty acts. They will speak of the glorious splendor of your majesty, and I will meditate on your wonderful works. They will tell of the power of your awesome works, and I will proclaim your great deeds. They will celebrate your abundant goodness and joyfully sing of your righteousness.

PSALM 145:4–7 NIV

WORSHIP BECAUSE OF HIS WORD

Seven times a day I praise you for your righteous laws.

PSALM 119:164 NIV

I praise God for what he has promised. I trust in God, so why should I be afraid? What can mere mortals do to me? . . . I praise God for what he has promised; yes, I praise the LORD for what he has promised.

PSALM 56:4, 10 NLT

I will praise you with an upright heart as I learn your righteous laws. I will obey your decrees; do not utterly forsake me.

PSALM 119:7–8 NIV

All Scripture is inspired by God and is useful to teach us what is true and to make us realize what is wrong in our lives. It corrects us when we are wrong and teaches us to do what is right. God uses it to prepare and equip his people to do every good work.

2 TIMOTHY 3:16–17 NLT

I have hidden your word in my heart that I might not sin against you. Praise be to you, O LORD; teach me your decrees.

PSALM 119:11–12 NIV

Accept, O LORD, the willing praise of my mouth, and teach me your laws. Though I constantly take my life in my hands, I will not forget your law.

PSALM 119:108–109 NIV

What God has said isn't only alive and active! It is sharper than any double-edged sword. His word can cut through our spirits and souls and through our joints and marrow, until it discovers the desires and thoughts of our hearts.

HEBREWS 4:12 CEV

WORSHIP BECAUSE OF HIS PROTECTION AND STRENGTH

You who fear the LORD, trust in the LORD; He is their help and their shield.

PSALM 115:11 NASB

O my Strength, I sing praise to you; you, O God, are my fortress, my loving God.

PSALM 59:17 NIV

May he be enthroned in God's presence forever; appoint your love and faithfulness to protect him. Then will I ever sing praise to your name and fulfill my vows day after day.

PSALM 61:7–8 NIV

I am in pain and distress; may your salvation, O God, protect me. I will praise God's name in song and glorify him with thanksgiving.

PSALM 69:29–30 NIV

Whom have I in heaven but you? And earth has nothing I desire besides you. My flesh and my heart may fail, but God is the strength of my heart and my portion forever.

Those who are far from you will perish; you destroy all who are unfaithful to you. But as for me, it is good to be near God. I have made the Sovereign LORD my refuge; I will tell of all your deeds.

PSALM 73:25–28 NIV

"The LORD is my rock, my fortress, and my savior; my God is my rock, in whom I find protection. He is my shield, the power that saves me, and my place of safety. He is my refuge, my savior, the one who saves me from violence. I called on the LORD, who is worthy of praise, and he saved me from my enemies."

2 SAMUEL 22:2–4 NLT

The LORD reigns forever; he has established his throne for judgment. He will judge the world in righteousness; he will govern the peoples with justice. The LORD is a refuge for the oppressed, a stronghold in times of trouble. Those who know your name will trust in you, for you, LORD, have never forsaken those who seek you.

PSALM 9:7–10 NIV

You are awesome, O God, in your sanctuary; the God of Israel gives power and strength to his people. Praise be to God!

PSALM 68:35 NIV

I praise you, LORD, for answering my prayers. You are my strong shield, and I trust you completely. You have helped me, and I will celebrate and thank you in song.

PSALM 28:6–7 CEV

O LORD my God, in You I have taken refuge; save me from all those who pursue me, and deliver me.

PSALM 7:1 NASB

I have been young, and now am old, yet I have not seen the righteous forsaken or his children begging for bread.

PSALM 37:25 ESV

Five sparrows are sold for just two pennies, but God doesn't forget a one of them. Even the hairs on your head are counted. So don't be afraid! You are worth much more than many sparrows.

LUKE 12:6–7 CEV

ONE MOMENT AT A TIME
PERSONAL REFLECTIONS

1. **Create a cross.** Get a pad of sticky notes and write one personal reason to praise God on each one. Arrange the notes in the shape of a cross and thank God for the reasons He's given you to praise Him.

2. **Encourage your family.** If you don't do so already, take regular time as a family to praise God together. Share prayer requests, answers, and lessons He's teaching you that encourage you to praise.

3. **Create a mix.** Create a CD or playlist on your MP3 player that reminds you of attributes of God and His work in your life. Use these reminders to drive you to worship Him.

CHAPTER 8

EXAMPLES OF WORSHIP

Since I had never thought much about it, I used to think that worship was limited to what I did at church. I'd sit reverently, sing on cue, and listen attentively—at least, I'd try to. But I'm learning that worship is much more than what happens on Sunday mornings. The Bible talks about people who worshipped God outside of church in some unusual ways. Some danced before God, others wept in front of others, and still others sang hymns while chained to a jail floor. The more I learn, the more I realize my views of worship have been too limited.

■ *Mika, age 23, Illinois* ■

WORSHIP WITHOUT NEEDING SOCIAL APPROVAL

The Ark of the LORD remained there in Obed-edom's house for three months, and the LORD blessed Obed-edom and his entire household. Then King David was told, "The LORD has blessed Obed-edom's household and everything he has because of the Ark of God." So David went there and brought the Ark. . . to the City of David with a great celebration. After the men who were carrying [it] had gone six steps, David sacrificed a bull and a fattened calf. And David danced before the LORD with all his might, wearing a priestly garment. So David and all . . .Israel brought up the Ark of the LORD with shouts of joy and the blowing of rams' horns.

2 SAMUEL 6:11–15 NLT

Now one of the Pharisees was requesting [Jesus] to dine with him, and He entered the Pharisee's house and reclined at the table. And there was a woman in the city who was a sinner; and when she learned that He was reclining at the table in the Pharisee's house, she brought an alabaster vial of perfume, and standing behind Him at His feet, weeping, she began to wet His feet with her tears, and kept wiping them with the hair of her head, and kissing His feet and anointing them with the perfume. . . . Then He said to her, "Your sins have been forgiven. . . . Your faith has saved you; go in peace."

LUKE 7:36–38, 48, 50 NASB

WORSHIP DURING DIFFICULT TIMES

They seized Paul and Silas and . . .commanded them to be beaten with rods. And when they had laid many stripes on them, they threw them into prison, commanding the jailer to keep them securely. Having received such a charge, he put them into the inner prison and fastened their feet in the stocks. But at midnight Paul and Silas were praying and singing hymns to God, and the prisoners were listening to them. Suddenly there was a great earthquake, so that the foundations of the prison were shaken; and immediately all the doors were opened and everyone's chains were loosed. And the keeper of the prison, awaking from sleep and seeing the prison doors open, supposing the prisoners had fled, drew his sword and was about to kill himself. But Paul called with a loud voice, saying, "Do yourself no harm, for we are all here." Then he called for a light, ran in, and fell down trembling before Paul and Silas. And he brought them out and said, "Sirs, what must I do to be saved?" So they said, "Believe on the Lord Jesus Christ, and you will be saved, you and your household."

ACTS 16:19, 22–31 NKJV

WORSHIP THROUGH GRIEF

There was a man in the land of Uz whose name was Job, and that man was blameless and upright, one who feared God and turned away from evil. There were born to him seven sons and three daughters. He possessed 7,000 sheep, 3,000 camels, 500 yoke of oxen, and 500 female donkeys, and very many servants, so that this man was the greatest of all the people of the east. . . . Now there was a day when. . .there came a messenger to Job and said, "The oxen were plowing and the donkeys feeding beside them, and the Sabeans fell upon them and took them and struck down the servants with the edge of the sword, and I alone have escaped to tell you." While he was yet speaking, there came another and said, "The fire of God fell from heaven and burned up the sheep and the servants and consumed them, and I alone have escaped to tell you." While he was yet speaking, there came another and said, "The Chaldeans formed three groups and made a raid on the camels and took them and struck down the servants with the edge of the sword, and I alone have escaped to tell you." While he was yet speaking, there came another and said, "Your sons and daughters were eating and drinking wine in their oldest brother's house, and behold, a great wind came across the wilderness and struck the four corners of the house, and it fell upon the young people, and they are dead, and I alone have escaped to tell you." Then Job arose and tore his robe and shaved his head and fell on the ground and worshiped. And he said, "Naked I came from my mother's womb, and naked shall I return. The LORD gave, and the LORD has taken away; blessed be the name of the LORD."

JOB 1:1–3, 13–21 ESV

WORSHIP ON THE BATTLEFIELD

When Gideon [was spying on his enemy's camp], behold, a man was telling a dream to his comrade. And he said, "Behold, I dreamed a dream, and behold, a cake of barley bread tumbled into the camp of Midian and came to the tent and struck it so that it fell and turned it upside down, so that the tent lay flat." And his comrade answered, "This is no other than the sword of Gideon the son of Joash, a man of Israel; God has given into his hand Midian and all the camp." As soon as Gideon heard the telling of the dream and its interpretation, he worshiped. And he returned to the camp of Israel and said, "Arise, for the LORD has given the host of Midian into your hand."

JUDGES 7:13–15 ESV

WORSHIP BEFORE A GREAT UNDERTAKING

When the builders laid the foundation of the temple of the LORD, the priests in their vestments and with trumpets, and the Levites (the sons of Asaph) with cymbals, took their places to praise the LORD, as prescribed by David king of Israel. With praise and thanksgiving they sang to the LORD: "He is good; his love to Israel endures forever." And all the people gave a great shout of praise to the LORD, because the foundation of the house of the LORD was laid.

EZRA 3:10–11 NIV

ONE MOMENT AT A TIME
EXPRESSING YOURSELF

1. **Look beyond the hymnbook.** Worship at church and through songs is very valuable. But what unexpected—even routine—events do you have coming up that can provide a place for you to worship God?

2. **Concern yourself with God.** Our concern for what others will think can affect what we wear to church or how we act while we're there. Worship passionately and without fear of what others might think.

3. **Bring worship with you in difficult times.** Stress, grief, and pain may not seem like traditional times to worship, but focusing on God during these times can be life changing. Follow the examples of Jonah, David, and Job, who worshipped during their most troubling circumstances.

Notes

NOTES

NOTES

_____

_____

_____

_____

_____

_____

_____

_____

_____

_____

_____

_____

_____

_____

_____

_____

_____

NOTES

NOTES

Other popular Bible reference books
from Barbour Publishing

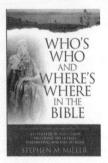

Who's Who and Where's Where in the Bible
6" x 9" / Paperback / 400 pages
ISBN 978-1-59310-111-4

Here's a Bible dictionary that's actually fun to read! Dig deeply into the stories of 500 people and places that make the Bible such a fascinating book.

500 Questions & Answers from the Bible
6" x 9" / Paperback / 256 pages
ISBN 978-1-59789-473-9

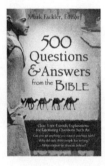

For inquisitive readers of any age—adults and students alike—here's a book to shed light on the Bible's great questions. And it's fully illustrated in color!

The Complete Guide to the Bible
7" x 9½" / Paperback / 528 pages
ISBN 978-1-59789-374-9

A reliable, jargon-free handbook for average people who want to better understand the entire Bible. Beautifully illustrated in full color, with photos, paintings, and maps.

Available wherever Christian books are sold.